Computer-Assisted Reporting

LEA'S COMMUNICATION SERIES
Jennings Bryant/Dolf Zillmann, General Editors

Selected titles in Journalism (Maxwell McCombs, Advisory Editor) include:

Fensch • The Sports Writing Handbook, Second Edition

Garrison • Advanced Reporting: Skills for the Professional

Garrison • Computer-Assisted Reporting

Garrison • Professional Feature Writing, Second Edition

Merritt • Public Journalism and Public Life: Why Telling the News Is Not Enough

For a complete list of other titles in LEA's Communication Series, please contact Lawrence Erlbaum Associates, Publishers.

Computer-Assisted Reporting

Bruce Garrison
University of Miami

 Lawrence Erlbaum Associates, Publishers
1995   Hillsdale, New Jersey   Hove, UK

Lawrence Erlbaum Associates
365 Broadway
Hillsdale, New Jersey 07642

Cover design by Randy Stano
Cover illustration by Martin Rinco

Library of Congress Cataloging-in-Publication Data

Garrison, Bruce, 1950–
    Computer-assisted reporting / Bruce Garrison.
        p. cm.
    Includes bibliographical references and index.
    ISBN 0-8058-1632-1 (cloth). — ISBN 0-8058-1633-X
(pbk.)
        1. Journalism—Data processing. 2. Reporters and
    reporting. I. Title.
    PN4784.E5G37 1995
    070.4'3'0285—dc20   95-2554
                                                        CIP

Books published by Lawrence Erlbaum Associates are
printed on acid-free paper, and their bindings are chosen for
strength and durability.

Printed in the United States of America
10 9 8 7 6 5 4 3 2

Contents

Preface

Steven Segal and I met at a conference in Raleigh, NC, in Fall 1993. We have continued to keep in touch, sending electronic mail messages back and forth between his office near Pittsburgh and mine near Miami. Segal is an information graphics and database specialist for the Greensburg, PA, *Tribune-Review*. Although it is not a large or prominent newspaper, his news organization is typical of those beginning to integrate the tools for computer-assisted reporting (CAR) into their daily reporting effort. Segal is one of the individuals leading his newspaper into the CAR era:

"When I was in college in 1984, somebody told me there was a word I should learn that would change newspapers forever. The word was 'pagination.' I didn't know what it meant. For those in college in 1994, they all should know what 'computer-assisted reporting' means," Segal (personal communication, 1994) says. But he also believes CAR is not the sole means of success in analytical reporting. "Computers don't make great reporters. A computer is a tool that is only as good as the person using it. It is curiosity that makes great reporters."

Not long after I met Segal, I met Brant Houston, managing director of the National Institute for Computer-Assisted Reporting (NICAR) at the University of Missouri. A former reporter in Hartford and Kansas City, he is also one of the new breed of computer-oriented journalists. He chose to leave reporting in 1994 because he takes the computerization of reporting seriously. He believes computers are the future of reporting. He preaches this message every chance he gets—at press association meetings, NICAR "boot camps," national journalism conventions, and other gatherings of journalists interested enough to listen to him.

Houston (1994) stated:

One of the reasons I took the job at Missouri is that I really believe this is journalism's future. I think that if we don't pay attention to how to get to information electronically, how to access it, how to analyze it, and how to disseminate it, we're going to be in a situation of going on the information superhighway in a horse and buggy. Two things are going to happen: One is that we're never going to get there on time and we won't have the news. The other is that we are just going to get run over. So I think we are really going to have start taking this a lot more seriously and integrating it into a routine of our newsrooms.

When I go to audiences now—newspaper people and broadcasters—often the percentage of people who have the ability to use the computer and go online is much, much less than the percentage of people in the general audiences I talked to when I was at the *Hartford Courant*. A higher percentage of them are more comfortable with computers than we are. That's what I mean by getting outrun. Our readers are outrunning us. It's time to to catch up and get ahead.

As personal computing grows, so do its uses and applications in the newsroom. Significant new hardware technology is introduced almost monthly. Improved versions of existing software and entirely new products are introduced on an annual basis. DOS, the traditional disk operating system on which PCs work, is on the way out. Other operating systems for improved hardware are being introduced. Desktop systems may be on the way out, too, with more powerful portable systems that can do everything a desktop system can do. As more individuals in the newsroom become involved in CAR for uses including online news research, the use of these tools grows exponentially.

This book can only be a beginning. Its purpose is to introduce readers to computer-assisted reporting and to describe how leading journalists are using personal computers for news gathering in the modern newsroom. It was not that long ago, if time is taken to think about it, that computers were introduced into newsrooms as fancy electronic typewriters, and that was just about all they did as far as journalists were concerned. These dedicated systems could not do anything else, not even send messages across the newsroom. It was only the far-sighted individuals in accounting or marketing who used the company's mainframe computer for anything quantitative or qualitative beyond writing and editing.

But all that has changed.

A recent national survey conducted by the Roper Center for Public Opinion Research and sponsored by the Freedom Forum Media Studies Center revealed that professional development is one of the main concerns of working journalists in the mid-1990s. Almost half of the 2,000 journalists at 400 newspapers found, as the Freedom Forum reported, that they "often or sometimes felt poorly prepared to cover a story well." The Freedom Forum's study also found that journalists said they "don't get enough professional training" ("No train, no gain," 1993, p. 4). Evidence of this in the area of computer applications in the newsroom was the 500-plus individuals who attended the Investigative Reporters and Editors (IRE) conference on computer-assisted reporting in Raleigh in October 1993 and the even larger number at the San Jose conference a year later. News managers want their reporters and editors to be computer literate, but literacy expectations have gone beyond operation of a dedicated word processing system. The mid-1990s reporter and editor need to know numerous other applications of computers to enhance news gathering and presentation.

One of the key areas that concerns journalists and their continuing professional development is technology. Philip S. Balboni (1993), a special assistant to the president of Hearst Corporation and former vice president and news director of WCVB-TV in Boston, concluded there are three main steps needed for journalists to survive in the information age:

- Overcome naiveté about technology. Too many journalists hate it, ignore it, or love it blindly.
- Become more knowledgeable about the economics of the new information age.
- Pay close attention to federal communications policy.

This book focuses on one area of Balboni's concerns by providing a thorough discussion of technology and its applications to news reporting, perhaps a step in the right direction. As the Freedom Forum study shows, journalists and students want to learn about the changing nature of their work. They want to attend seminars and workshops, but they also want books and other materials that lay out concerns and issues in more permanent fashion.

American society has been inundated by a flood of computerized public and private records. Databases are being compiled on all aspects of life. Many records formerly kept on paper are now stored in computers. And many records that were never before kept are now retained in databases. This development has made news reporting increasingly computer oriented during the past decade. Much, if not most, news reporting depends on knowledge and use of computers. Knowledge of how to access and use computer databases is essential for the journalists of the future.

This book, therefore, focuses on the *computerization of news reporting*. Not only does the personal computer of the mid-1990s assist journalists by making writing easier, it makes reporting more efficient. As it begins, this book demonstrates methods for reporters to get more from their computers, such as data retrieval, data analysis, information storage, and dissemination of that information in both processed and unprocessed forms. The book concludes with a proposal of five stages for development of computer literacy in the newsroom.

This book does not assume that computers are the answer to everything. They are superior starting points for many stories, however. Perhaps there will come a day, as a lot of people who think about this topic maintain, that we will not have to discuss "computer-assisted" reporting any more than we discuss "telephone-assisted" or "interview-assisted" reporting. Any strong reporting, investigative or otherwise, that uses computers as information gathering or information analyzing tools, must be supplemented with other forms of more traditional reporting such as interviewing and case studies.

This book discusses current and future developments in the use of computers in information gathering for the news media. This is done in a manner that reduces the chance the material will be dated quickly by technological advancement and innovations. Generally, the book is limited to personal computing technology and innovation, but it also discusses mainframe computers where appropriate. Because they are the most widely used computers in the United States, in general, and because they are the most widely used in the news business as well, much of the discussion in this book focuses on IBM-compatible desktop and notebook systems that run DOS, Windows, and OS/2.

The single most important focus is on the changing nature of news reporting in the wake of the fast-changing power of business-type desktop and portable computers. Numerous new approaches to reporting and research have developed in the past decade in parallel with the evolution of personal computers. With these new techniques coming to the field of reporting in the mid-1990s, there is need for a book that covers both the merger of traditional information gathering methods and the newly developing ones. This book introduces readers to new information gathering and analytical techniques evolving with new computer-based technology.

Any errors are the responsibility of the author alone. I would deeply appreciate any suggestions or comments from readers at any time. I may be reached on the Internet at BGARRISO@UMIAMIVM.IR.MIAMI.EDU or on CompuServe at 73507,160.

ACKNOWLEDGMENTS

Writing this book was a true learning experience for me. As with my other books, though, it was not a solitary effort. There are numerous individuals who contributed assistance, knowingly or not, and made this stronger.

First of all, I would like to thank the dean of the School of Communication at the University of Miami, Edward J. Pfister, for his complete support for this project. He provided research time, travel funding, and various other institutional resources that were used in this project. Without these tools, writing this book would have probably remained only an idea.

My good friend, Professor Alan Prince, a consummate editor and journalist for more than 40 years, continues in a dual role as my leading supporter and occasional critic. Now an instructor at the University of Miami, he read and edited the manuscript. His comments have made this manuscript more understandable.

I also express thanks to another good friend, Ms. Raymonde Bilger, director of budget and personnel for the Division of Student Affairs at the University of Miami. Her interest and support, as well as her love for desktop computing, encouraged me. She was a godsend in helping review some of the technical information in several chapters. Furthermore, her ability to provide certain computer resources assisted me in preparing this manuscript.

I also offer sincerest gratitude to Jim Hyatt, an editor at the *Wall Street Journal* who regularly works with computers, for his timely comments about the book. He read the manuscript and offered numerous good suggestions.

A wide range of individuals in the computer industry should be thanked also. My gratitude goes to Lisa Jacobson at MapInfo® Corporation, Tracy Van Hoof at Microsoft® Corporation, Rob Linsky at Borland® International Corporation, Bea McKinney at askSam® Systems, and Sandy Meadows at the Software Publishers Association in Washington, DC.

Thanks are also offered to a large number of working journalists who offered their suggestions, agreed to be interviewed, or contributed in other ways. Among them are some of my best friends in the profession. Thanks especially go to: Nora Paul, faculty member and library director, The Poynter Institute, St. Petersburg; Jim Leusner, investigative reporter, and John Huff, computer-assisted reporting editor, both at the *Orlando Sentinel*; Tim Kelly, executive editor, and several of his staff members involved in CAR and online newsroom research at the *Lexington Herald-Leader*; Steve Doig and Rich Gordon, CAR editors at *The Miami Herald*; Scott Anderson, CAR editor at the Fort Lauderdale *Sun-Sentinel*; Larry K. Sanders, special projects editor, and Trish Wells, news researcher, at *USA Today;* William Casey, CAR director, and Rich Morin, director of polling, at *The Washington Post;* Lisa Van Asch, news researcher at the Raleigh *News & Observer;* Steven Segal, information graphics specialist at the Greensburg, PA, *Tribune-Review*; Chris Feola, news systems editor in charge of CAR for the *Waterbury Republican-American*; Bob Port, CAR editor, the Associated Press; Debbie Wolfe, news researcher, the *St. Petersburg Times*; John Mollwitz, senior national editor, *The Milwaukee Journal Sentinel*; and Dolores Jenkins, journalism professor and librarian at the University of Florida.

There are others, also. I thank my colleagues at the University of Miami, including Mitchell Shapiro, Sigman Splichal, Paul Steinle, Michael Salwen, and Don Stacks.

I thank Troy Scott, a staff member in the public information office of the Bureau of the Census in Washington, DC, for his advice and for providing materials about census data products on CD-ROM discs.

The contributions of Randy Stano, News-Editorial Art Department Director at *The Miami Herald,* are also noted. Stano and *Herald* artist Martin Rinco developed this book's cover. Thanks go to both of them.

My gratitude, of course, also goes to my research assistant, Beth Glenday, an undergraduate student in the School of Communication at the University of Miami, for completing a variety of support duties with skill and speed, and to Alletta Bowers, a journalism major at UM, who also made useful contributions to this manuscript while studying computer-assisted reporting.

I have written seven books, but I have not offered a dedication in any of those books until now. I am dedicating this book to the memory of Mishi The Cat, my best friend for almost 8 years, who died while this project was underway. She was my companion who quietly urged me forward, especially during the many hours I spent in front of a computer keyboard trying to conduct research, trying to make sense of something, or attempting to write. She will always be deeply missed. This one's for you, Mish!

Bruce Garrison

I Introduction

1 Microchip Journalism: The Evolving World of Computer-Based Reporting

Journalists have been swept into the computer age. It might be called digital journalism, cyberjournalism, or microchip journalism. Computers have become the foundation of most of the most critical functions of the news media—from writing, photography, and news research to production and distribution. Computers are the tools used to get work done in newsrooms of the mid-1990s. Perhaps one of the most seriously affected journalistic processes is news *reporting*. In the past decade, dozens of major changes have forever redefined how news gathering takes place.

As the middle of this decade passes, reporters are becoming part of this new digital reporting age. Sophisticated new tools are in the hands of journalists who once depended only on their senses and a pen and paper to gather news. It could be argued that the typewriter, the telephone, or television was as significant in its impact on journalism. But journalists are only now beginning to understand how significant the computer has become in the daily lives of journalists and, it follows, those who use the products of journalists.

Reporters in the mid-1990s are using highly sophisticated means to gather and process information. It might not be what some people think is real "in-the-streets" journalism. Using a computer to do something besides writing or editing is an alien concept to some "traditionalists," but a growing number of journalists feel it makes sense. A group of faculty members of the National Institute for Advanced Reporting (NIAR) at Indiana University in Indianapolis believes computers have already made a difference: "Journalism in the mid-1990s demands a level of sophistication which permits and encourages reporters to penetrate, interpret and present complex issues," they wrote (Brown, Ricchiardi, Fischer, & Schneider, 1990, p. 2). "Computers are fast becoming the tools enterprising journalists require to gain access to vital information."

University of North Carolina Journalism Professor Philip Meyer saw it coming—almost 30 years ago. Although Meyer might have been far

3

ahead of his peers, he certainly got the attention of a few people. What Meyer called *precision journalism* in the early 1970s became the label often applied to social science-oriented reporting, using the tools of sociologists, psychologists, and others who study human behavior. For many years, Meyer's precision journalism was a less-used term for survey research and polling applied to a news context. To Meyer's credit, he discussed numerous other social science tools in his benchmark book, *Precision Journalism* (Meyer, 1973), but these more precise approaches were rarely used by reporters on news assignments in the 1970s and 1980s.

Slowly, some of these computer-based techniques crossed into news gathering. After all, as numerous communication scholars pointed out, reporters and social scientists are not all that different. Both study group and individual human behavior. Both gather information. Both analyze what they collect. Both disseminate information. For a decade after Meyer's first edition of *Precision Journalism*, most reporters shied away from the approach because it meant using mysterious and expensive mainframe computer systems for some stories. But a decade ago, affordable personal computers for office and home use arrived on the scene and the stage was set for one of the most significant technological shifts in the history of U.S. news reporting: the desktop computerization of newsrooms.

It did not take long for the approaches advocated by Meyer and his small following to catch fire. The blaze grew slowly, but steadily. By the end of the 1980s, a variation on Meyer's original precision journalism theme, computer-assisted journalism, had evolved (Miller, 1988). Reporters are now more frequently using computer-based techniques such as those advocated by Meyer and studied by researchers at NIAR or several other specialized programs. The tools are now more often called *computer-assisted journalism* or *computer-assisted reporting* and *online research*. These are tools that simply did not exist or were much more difficult to access by earlier generations of journalists and by most of the current generation of journalists as well.

Computer-assisted reporting, the term used here, is the use of computers to gather information for a news presentation. To elaborate, it involves use of computers of all sizes, from mainframes to PCs to personal digital assistants (PDAs). CAR, as used here, refers to use of computers on two levels to enhance reporting.

First, it includes use of computers to search for information and retrieve it from other computers and their databases. This is referred to as *online research*. Second, the term includes use of computers to analyze original databases and databases from other sources for information for news stories. This is sometimes referred to as *database journalism*. The term computer-assisted reporting is also often used interchangeably with the term computer-assisted journalism. In this book, use of the terms refers to the same reporting process.

In more practical terms, what is CAR? Brant Houston (1994), managing director for the National Institute for Computer-Assisted Reporting (NICAR) in Missouri, explained his approach:

> Computer-assisted reporting is a big tool, an application. It should be used on a daily basis, on a deadline basis, in addition to those great tree-eating projects we do and get prizes for. I think for a while, this appeared to be magic. There weren't that many people who knew how to do this. Elliot Jaspin, my predecessor, who was a pioneer in this field, would just blow people's minds by showing a computer tape and how data can be downloaded, how you can look at 100,000 records in a few seconds, and so forth. It's a little less magical now. The software is much easier to deal with, the equipment is much more accessible. We're not dealing with a lot of equipment now that's hard to buy or too expensive to buy. The software is much, much friendlier. It's not the technical hurdle it was a few years ago.

San Francisco State University journalism professor Tom Johnson (1993) says it is "managing data to turn it into information and communicating that information" (p. 6). CAR is *not* something separate from traditional journalism, Johnson adds; it is information management skills. Computer-assisted reporting includes the following examples:

- Veteran reporters Marjie Lundstrom and Rochelle Sharpe of Gannett News Service (GNS) using computers to search thousands of child-abuse-related death case records. Their original analysis revealed that the real cause of hundreds of abuse-related deaths goes undetected because of medical examiner errors. Lundstrom, who later became a senior reporter for the *Sacramento Bee*, and Sharpe, a national correspondent for GNS in Washington, DC, won the 1991 Pulitzer Prize for national reporting for their articles. "The focus of the story was the database, which was analyzed. The data was [sic] from 1987 because that was the last year available. What we found was a lot of children who had died under suspicious circumstances had no autopsy performed on them. We found out that more than 500 deaths had no autopsy," (Gersh & Case, 1991, p. 32) they explained. The reporters found that most deaths were the result of sudden infant death syndrome.
- *The Miami Herald's* director of computer-assisted reporting, Stephen K. Doig, helping his newspaper win the 1993 Pulitzer Prize gold medal for public service for its coverage following Hurricane Andrew. Doig contributed a highly sophisticated analysis of property damaged by the hurricane in 1992. While the metropolitan area was still reeling from the storm, Doig and his colleagues in the newsroom gathered public records data about the thousands of damaged and destroyed homes. They produced in-depth reports for a 16-page special section of news articles entitled "What Went Wrong." The project concluded that con-

struction quality and building design "largely determined the degree of hurricane damage" (Doig, 1992, p. 1). Doig, Jeff Leen, Lisa Getter, and the rest of the team of *Herald* reporters merged large databases to lead to their conclusions. They obtained 45 computer tapes containing county government property damage inspections, property tax rolls, building master files, and building and zoning permits databases. These millions of database records individually told the reporters about the property, but the unique combination of the aggregate data by Doig and the subsequent analysis by the team of reporters and editors led them to determine the major housing weaknesses that led to the damage caused by the storm.

EDITOR: 'I KNOW THIS MUCH: I CAN LEARN THIS OR GET OUT OF NEWSPAPERING IN A DECADE'

Dewey English, Assistant Managing Editor of the Jackson, MS *Clarion-Ledger* stated:

> Computer-assisted reporting came to *The Clarion-Ledger* last year after a long labor. I believe the child to be healthy, although I cannot tell if we will always be close. I am a former reporter/city editor who got into CAR by insisting for years that our paper needed to be doing it. So when we decided to do it, I was put in charge. Think of it as mounting the steering wheel on the car horn, rather than the other way around.
>
> The way has been rough. Three problems are foremost:
>
> • Our technical experts from the computer department have hundreds of responsibilities building-wide. They cannot spend time parsing our tables or unzipping our files.
> • We have to develop rank-and-file leaders.
> • We don't have any real idea what data is out there or what stories we might want to do.
>
> We sort of lurch from thing to thing, thang to thang, as some in Mississippi would say. Still, I know this much: I can learn this or get out of newspapering in a decade. Used to be a good editor knew by instinct where big stories might have flaws. Years of hard reporting and trench-line editing give you that. He could say, "show me the report you based this on" or "let me read the transcript," and right away he had a piece of paper.
>
> One day, reporters are going to give that editor a big story but not a piece of paper he can hold. They'll claim the jumble of numbers spinning on the nine-track tape reel came out just so. What of instinct then? And what of his guts if his instinct is all gone?
>
> I'm not going to be that editor. (English, personal communication, February 14, 1994)

• A medium-size western Pennsylvania daily, the *Tribune-Review* in Greensburg, demonstrating that a news organization can jump into computer-assisted reporting with some success in a relatively short period of time. In an effort coordinated by Steven Segal, the newspaper's information graphics specialist, the newspaper used a personal computer to help analyze a large multimillion dollar state tax slush fund of walking around money (called "WAM"). This discretionary spending fund had been questionably spent on parties, private schools, family planning, cultural groups, world travel, and more. Reporters Debra Erdley, Richard Gazarik, and David Josar learned for their two separate series of stories that ran in Spring and Fall 1993. The newspaper also analyzed racial disparity in home loan rejection rates in Pennsylvania. Studying more than 270,000 statewide Federal Reserve Board lending records, Josar found Black applicants much less likely to be given loans for homes. "I was looking for a relatively easy, fast project that could acquaint me with the pitfalls and ecstasy of a computer database," he says (Josar, 1993, p. 5). Segal (personal communication, April 1994) added:

> The *Tribune-Review* is just in the infancy of CAR projects. The WAM series was the first and most ambitious project undertaken. The public response was overwhelming. Currently, there is a lawsuit against the legality of WAMs. WAMs were a major campaign issue in the 1994 gubernatorial race. Most of the candidates are calling for the abolition of the process—or at least a major cutback in the funding. Although WAMs still exist, they are much more open—and the politicians know it.

• *Columbus Dispatch* reporter Mike Berens working on a story about deaths of prostitutes. He believed that the deaths in Ohio were part of a bigger pattern of murders. His investigation for the 265,000-circulation state capitol daily was aided by *Dispatch* librarian Jim Hunter and use of an online database now part of Knowledge Index and CompuServe. Berens and Hunter found 11 similar slayings in nearby states. Berens' first step was to conduct background research using the online computer database. The pair searched newspaper articles from other newspapers to find out names of victims, dates of deaths, details of the circumstances of the deaths, and even the names of the investigating police agencies. No one had previously linked the murders because no police agency had accessed local newspaper articles about similar deaths. "For example, Vu/Text put me on the trail of the New York homicide, and got me past the police misinformation regarding the death. Based on the article I found in Vu/Text, I was able to use forensic evidence to prove that the woman had died in the same fashion as the other victims," Berens said (Kimbrough, 1991, p. 2). As a result of his article, law enforcement investigators reopened the case to try to locate the serial killer.

- The *Eagle-Tribune*, a 56,000-daily circulation newspaper based in Lawrence, MA, has found computer-based reporting and research to be a valuable tool in its coverage of Massachusetts. From 1991 to 1993, the newspaper produced at least four CAR projects covering a wide range of social and political issues. The newspaper has reported news, with the aid of computer analysis, about abuse in the Massachusetts public welfare program, campaign financing, business deals by a candidate for Congress, and problems in the state worker's compensation program. Special projects reporter Brad Goldstein coordinates the newspaper's CAR and online research programs. Database analysis was not the only tool used for these projects. "Several of our campaign finance stories could not have been done without online research," Goldstein (personal communication, December 21, 1993) said.

Think about it:

- Reporters using desktop or larger computers to conduct their own analyses of sophisticated public data.
- Reporters using commercial online computer databases to search for facts about seemingly unrelated murder cases.

These examples represent advanced reporting techniques. "Our society is changing so quickly we've got to be able to understand and use the technology for reporting," said Olive Talley, who reports for *The Dallas Morning News* (T. Wilson, 1993, p. 1B). "If we don't, we won't be able to get the information we need to do our jobs."

Computer-savvy reporters can achieve much more than their computer-fearing counterparts. Databases available through telephone connections can reveal much about the communities and the individuals reporters cover. Reporters no longer have to go to city hall to look at property tax records, visit the city clerk's office for election registration data, fax or call the department of motor vehicles to find out who owns a vehicle, or go to the police department for crime statistics. These things can be done with a computer and a modem.

Similarly, reporters no longer have to be dependent on nameless and hard-to-find bureaucrats to analyze and disseminate public data at their own speed or discretion. With computer-assisted reporting tools, reporters can take public records and analyze them on their own for new understanding of the political, social, and economic trends in their communities. "Flashy projects are great—and we certainly do our share," said *Columbus Dispatch* Metro Editor Gerald Tebben (personal communication, December 28, 1993). "But the real future of CAR is in the day-to-day reporting—using computers to get better information faster, to contact people we can't reach by phone."

SHOULD SMALL PUBLICATIONS USE CAR?

Walt Wooton (1994), former operations manager for *The Independent Florida Alligator,* a student-oriented newspaper serving the University of Florida and Gainesville, argues that small newspapers can also benefit from computer-assisted reporting. Here's what he says:

A recent *Alligator* alumnus, a reporter at a small Florida daily newspaper, was telling me about the fierce competition his paper faces from another small daily and a large metro paper for the loyalty of a fast-growing suburban market. It's a familiar story in Florida: Several papers fight for dominance in a rapidly growing market, knowing that only one will survive.

I suggested to my friend that the aggressive use of microcomputers could provide his paper a competitive edge in the struggle for market share. A computer-assisted reporting program could generate investigative series as well as improve the quality of the paper's day-to-day reporting. Access to online databases could enrich news stories with secondary sources and provide reporters with better and more efficient backgrounding. Putting the paper's own articles online rather than tossing them in the bit bucket at the end of the night would give his paper an institutional memory despite the frequent staff changes that are to be expected at a small paper.

My young friend listened, eagerly at first, but finally he shook his head. "My editor's not going to go for any of this," he said. "There isn't any money."

My response to him was simple: If his old college newspaper, the *Alligator,* was doing these things, why couldn't a few thousand dollars be found to help distinguish the reporting of a newspaper battling for the possession of a multimillion dollar market?

The truth is that small media outlets can't afford not to have computer-assisted reporting programs. Computers provide the leverage that small staffs must have if they are to compete with larger newspapers.

Computers have changed the way we report news about our communities. As with any new technology, it will take time, perhaps an entire generation, before these changes have worked their way into all levels of journalism. After all, journalists are, for the most part, wordsmiths, not computer "nerds." Journalists have spent most of their time writing and not crunching numbers or worrying about the electronic "handshakes" of modems. Journalists are definitely not computer technicians. But they still need to learn a little about PCMCIA cards, motherboards, RAM, or active color matrix notebook displays.

With computerization of public records and most everything else, it is only natural that journalists would find their way around the new environment. As they did for generations before them, many reporters still must go to offices and flip through hundreds or thousands of pages to find information for stories. With paper records and paper database files, reporters sorted, read, and extracted meaning. They developed tools for that means of reporting as well. Now, as U.S. society moves toward a paperless record of its existence, reporters are finding computers to be the best means for keeping up and for managing the volumes of available information.

The major benefit is that these new tools often go beyond just organizing and finding information. These new tools are allowing computer-assisted reporters to extract *meaning* as well. Where other official analyses have been done, or where no analyses have been done at all, reporters can find not only data, they can find new ways of looking at old things, new aggregate views, and even specific examples to support intuition or other generalizations.

Major investigative news stories are being produced by using computers. So are ordinary, day-to-day stories. Some fun-to-read feature articles are being generated as well. For 6 consecutive years, as described in Fig. 1.1, computer-assisted stories have won Pulitzer Prizes. In 1994, reporters at the *Akron Beacon Journal* won the public service prize for a project it developed entitled "A Question of Color." That project used a number of databases in analyzing local racial attitudes. In 1993, *The Miami Herald's* coverage of Hurricane Andrew included computer-based stories. Jeff Taylor and Mike McGraw, reporters for the *Kansas City Star*, won the award a year earlier for their analysis of the U.S. Department of Agriculture's (USDA) problems involving fraud, waste, and favoritism shown to the food lobbies. *The Indianapolis Star* won recognition in 1991 for its analysis of medical malpractice problems in Indiana. In 1990, *The Star Tribune* of Minneapolis used CAR tools to report about an arson scheme involving firefighters. Perhaps the current generation of CAR was inaugurated by the Associated Press' CAR Editor, Bill Dedman, who was then a reporter for the *Atlanta Journal and Constitution,* and his series, "The Color of Money," which revealed racist policies behind redlining lending practices of Atlanta-area financial institutions. The project won a 1989 Pulitzer Prize for Dedman.

The *Kansas City Star* is representative of the success stories. The investigation into the USDA would not have been completed, however, without support from upper level newsroom management. "We have excellent support. Managing Editor Mark Zieman is a long-time supporter of computer-assisted reporting," stated *Star* Special Assignment/Database Reporter Gregory S. Reeves (personal communication, December 28, 1993). "He headed the investigative reporting team that pushed for and received the USDA computer tapes detailing the $10 billion-a-year farm subsidy program. I processed those tapes as part of the package that won Mark McGraw and Jeff Taylor the 1992 Pulitzer

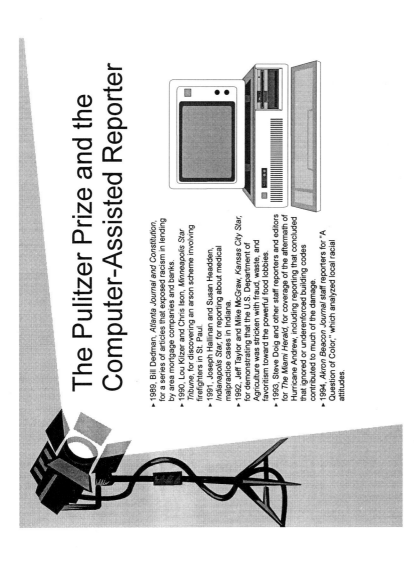

The Pulitzer Prize and the Computer-Assisted Reporter

▶ 1989, Bill Dedman, *Atlanta Journal and Constitution*, for a series of articles that exposed racism in lending by area mortgage companies and banks.

▶ 1990, Lou Kilzer and Chris Ison, *Minneapolis Star Tribune*, for discovering an arson scheme involving firefighters in St. Paul.

▶ 1991, Joseph Hallinan and Susan Headden, *Indianapolis Star*, for reporting about medical malpractice cases in Indiana.

▶ 1992, Jeff Taylor and Mike McGraw, *Kansas City Star*, for demonstrating that the U.S. Department of Agriculture was stricken with fraud, waste, and favoritism toward the powerful food lobbies.

▶ 1993, Steve Doig and other staff reporters and editors for *The Miami Herald*, for coverage of the aftermath of Hurricane Andrew, including reporting that concluded that ignored or underenforced building codes contributed to much of the damage.

▶ 1994, *Akron Beacon Journal* staff reporters for "A Question of Color," which analyzed local racial attitudes.

FIG. 1.1. The Pulitzer Prize and the computer-assisted reporter.

Prize. Mark has supported the expansion of my hardware and software needs for several years."

More and more daily assignments are utilizing online and computer analysis reporting tools. Many newspapers now use online research to begin investigative projects simply to find out what else has been written about the subject. They routinely use online research to check facts and find expert sources for stories in progress. This is becoming the standard reporting procedure for many of the new breed of computer-oriented reporters.

Occasionally, some purely fun and simply entertaining feature stories can be generated by computer databases. *The Miami Herald*, behind CAR editor Doig's direction, once purchased an animal license database from Metro-Dade County government and a reporter wrote a widely read package of articles about where dogs and cats are most populous in the county—complete with a pet population density map. But what many people talked about when the stories were published was not the density data, but the most popular names of dogs and cats.

INNOVATIVE NEWSROOM USES
OF PERSONAL COMPUTERS

Throughout this century, journalists have been slow to adapt to new technology in their reporting. Communication scholars, as well as beat reporters, realize that new technology changes the way things get done. Marshall McLuhan (1964) established that such technological innovation as the invention of the typewriter changed the way people thought during the writing process. The typewriter, McLuhan wrote, caused "an entirely different attitude to the written and printed word" (p. 228). Researchers Melvin DeFleur and Sandra Ball-Rokeach (1975) accurately predicted two decades ago that the computer would forever alter the communication process and the communicator.

Reporters, especially, have always seemed content with things the way they are. But gradually, those things change, and news sections have been greatly affected by technology over the past two centuries (Lacy & Simon, 1993). The patterns were established with the telegraph and typewriter in the late 19th century, the telephone at the turn of this century, and, in the late 1970s, computers as word processing tools. Early refusals by some journalists to try something new, or the general apprehension and fear of the new technology, usually abate after a period of adjustment and trial (Garrison, 1979). Some new technologies are easier to learn than others, some intimidate, and some require new skills (Lacy & Simon, 1993).

As reporters and their project editors begin to see the benefits of computer-assisted reporting and online research, they have begun to come up with creative approaches to stories and community issues and problems. Simple use of commercial online services such as CompuServe, Dialog, Dow Jones, DataTimes, Lexis/Nexis, Information America, and other services has led to major projects, breaking stories, and beat stories about such subjects as the personal histories of convicted murderers or accused mass killers, the persons involved in a major traffic accident, background on a mysterious company involved in a major scandal, research about area contractors and their work for the local government, research about campaign contributors in elections at all levels, child abuse cases, and more.

Computer database analysis has led to stories about black talon bullets, toxic pollution, population shifts, city and county budgets, locations of car thefts, slush funds, child labor and injuries on the job, concealed weapons, bad bridges, auto emissions, agricultural tax breaks used by developers and nonfarmers, teachers and misconduct, crime statistics, and even local weather trends.

Some of these became major news stories for their communities and regions. Some were just another story in the news budget, but the computer analysis added a new dimension to that story. These are but a few examples of computer use representing only the beginning of uses of these tools.

A REVOLUTION IN DIGITALIZATION OF INFORMATION

For the past two decades, the world has been experiencing a digital revolution. U.S. society is changing rapidly in that regard. Some experts logically argue this is what is driving the rise in computer-based news reporting: The effects are certainly felt in the news business of the 1990s (Aumente, 1989). Simply, more information is now computerized than ever before. "What's happened over the last 10 years is that the government has increasingly used computers to manage its operations, so there's been an enormous transfer of data to electronic form. . . . You need a computer to get at it," observed Elliot Jaspin, the CAR pioneer who won the Pulitzer Prize for special local reporting in 1979 while at the *Pottsville, PA, Republican* (Morokuma, 1993, p. 4). Jaspin founded the University of Missouri's National Institute for Computer-Assisted Reporting (NICAR) in 1989, which has grown rapidly in stature and importance since it opened, before he returned to journalism with Cox Newspapers in Washington, DC.

In the early 1970s, newspapers began to think about computers as more than devices to be used for business-side purposes, such as accounting, payroll, billing, and subscription list management. The first computer-based writing and editing systems began to appear and by the end of that decade many major newspapers had made the conversion from electric typewriters to dedicated word processing systems. These "front-end" systems, perhaps in their second or third generations, can still be found in some newsrooms across the country, but these systems did little more than permit a user to type text and automatically set type. The early versions of the systems did not even have electronic messaging, or E-mail, potential.

As personal computing emerged in the early 1980s, mainframe and minicomputers became less important and costs began to drop for computing at newspapers. Hardware and software improved. The tools became more powerful and capable. The first PC spreadsheets were developed in the early 1980s and the first database software was introduced at about the same time. Personal computers could be connected to each other or to mainframes using acoustic couplers or modems using telephone lines.

By the beginning of the 1990s, personal computing had become the means of publishing newspapers and magazines for many companies. The dedicated word processing systems are being gradually phased out and PCs are replacing them (Aumente, 1989). This has meant several significant things to newspapers and their reporters and editors. Most important, it has meant that reporters suddenly have much more powerful tools in their hands. Their once-limited terminals can do more. In addition to writing stories, they can be used to check databases in house or elsewhere. They can be used for database creation or analysis using spreadsheets, database packages, and other programs. They can be used for such routine things as scheduling appointments, maintaining address and telephone lists, and planning projects. It seems we are only beginning to see the potential for these tools for reporting and for news gathering in general.

This is the digital revolution era in the newsroom. It extends far beyond reporting. It has completely changed how newspapers are produced. With pagination systems, newspaper, magazine, and newsletter pages are completed on a computer screen. With electronic darkrooms, photographs are "processed" at a terminal. With computer-aided informational graphics, artwork is often produced with a mouse and keyboard as easily as with pen and ink. The entire package comes together, very often without paper involved until the newspaper rolls off the presses. Many of the same types of changes are occurring in television and radio station newsrooms as well. Systems capable of not only preparing scripts, generating on-screen graphics, scheduling, and managing production resources, but also accessing databases for research are becoming more and more common.

Distribution of publications is changing also. There is the technical capacity to distribute a publication electronically. Although the general public might not be ready for it yet, the merging technologies of this decade indicate this is not far away, either. Perhaps the PC as we know it, the television set, the telephone, sound systems, and other electronic media will all be available in a single unit that can do everything we currently depend on individual systems to do—and be as portable as a copy of a favorite magazine or newspaper.

IMPLICATIONS FOR JOURNALISTS

These new tools and ways of gathering and disseminating information have wide and deep implications for reporters and their editors. The newsroom is undergoing a radical metamorphosis, but it is occurring rather slowly and, perhaps, imperceptibly, at present. But as technological breakthroughs occur—ones as significant as the introduction of the PC a little more than a decade ago—the changes accelerate geometrically. That next major computing advance could be tomorrow, or next week.

These new tools have meant new workstyles. Reporters do not have to work in the office. If they do work in remote locations, they do not sacrifice any technological tools. These new tools have meant greater reporting potential, as well as power, in bureaus and other remote locations. Working alone is a desired characteristic of the job for some reporters, and a necessary one for others, who can do the same job or an even better one from their home offices or from a hotel room near the site of a breaking story.

The portability and global linkages of computing systems mean much to computer-wise news reporters. Being able to do anything from just about anywhere has immediate journalistic rewards. First, there can be much more complete work from remote locations. Second, stories can be filed instantly and much closer to deadlines. Third, the work tends to be more accurate.

The changes also mean new forms of information dissemination. The new world of digital reporting also brings greater accessibility and affordability for small publications, such as weeklies, newsletters, and the smallest dailies and magazines. It helps the dailies, too, even though the major dailies usually have all the new tools, complete with the accessorized bells and whistles. The era of reporting haves and have-nots is waning and the gap between the two groups is already closing in terms of advanced reporting techniques.

"The technology offers the promise of more timely, more accurate and more complete stories than were previously possible," one assessment says in *The Forum*, published by The Freedom Forum (Morokuma, 1993, p. 4). "PC-powered journalism is a fact in a small but growing number of news operations. Journalists armed with computers can fish out megabytes of raw information upstream of spin doctors and press releases, sort it, study it and come to their own conclusions. Computers also enable reporters to tackle stories that once were impractical—even impossible—to do."

MOTIVATIONS FOR COMPUTERIZATION

Typically, newspaper companies adopt new technology when it reduces costs, increases revenue, or offers a combination of both advantages (Lacy & Simon, 1993). This is often true in news departments, too. Many editors and reporters who have thought about using computers to aid their reporting have rejected the notion because they think computers are expensive, require a computer programmer, are designed for only large newspapers or magazines with staff resources to handle it, that CAR can be used only for long-term projects, that it will always turn out award-winning articles, and that it requires advanced computer skills.

On each of those counts, the doers say these criticisms just cannot hold up.

A newspaper can use an existing PC and outfit it with the proper software for just a few hundred dollars. Online searching can also be controlled through a central location in the newsroom or library using free or low-cost services. Most of the CAR work being done in the mid-1990s does not require computer *programming* skills, although a familiarity with computer software users' guides and a willingness to learn will help. Because of the decreasing cost of hardware and increasing power of desktop PCs and software, more and more small and medium-sized newspapers, magazines, and newsletters are using CAR tools. Furthermore, these publications are using CAR skills for day-to-day news stories on beats and on general assignments. All this leads to the conclusion that there are no high barriers to doing this sort of work. As with any tool, there is some learning involved, but the skills are no more difficult to learn than those required to learn word processing, graphics, or pagination tools widely in use in those same newsrooms.

There are a number of compelling reasons for considering bringing CAR into the newsroom:

- Increased productivity of reporters and special projects editors.
- Cost savings in information gathering at all levels and on all news beats.
- Increased quality of local reporting.
- Increased meaning in analysis of information and less dependence on sources for interpretation of that information.
- Keeping up with the competition.
- Increased access to information.
- Technical reliability and greater accuracy of information.
- Better storage and retrieval for follow-up uses and other needs.

And all this means:

1. *Increased productivity of reporters.* The PC assists in organizing and presenting information. This alone saves time. Reporters and editors using the tools of PCs and CAR in an efficient manner will be much more productive with their time allocated to stories and projects. They will be able to get bigger stories, broader-based stories, and deeper stories.

2. *Cost savings in information gathering.* To physically go to a location to find the same information that could be obtained online or to go through paper records at the site where they are kept, especially those in electronic form that could be sorted and reviewed by a PC, is far more costly. Transportation, housing, food, and other expenses mount quickly, even on short trips to get necessary information. As the base of a story broadens from local to regional or national, the costs escalate. Then there is also the cost of the information itself. Photocopies, clerical time, and other costs on site add more expense. There is also the cost of the reporter's time. Online and database costs seem high in a vacuum, but compared to the bigger picture, CAR is a bargain.

3. *Increased quality of local reporting.* Typically, editors and reporters who use CAR feel the quality of news stories, both the big ones and the ordinary ones, is increased. Information is more thorough, more accurate, and more appropriate. Instead of generalizations supported by one or two examples or another generalization, reporters are able to cite specific cases and how many of those specific examples exist. Sources are more diverse and better qualified. Reporting in general is enhanced and the stories are improved.

4. *Increased meaning in analysis of information and less dependence on sources for interpretation of that information.* Typically, reporters are at the mercy of their sources to explain and interpret volumes of data and other information that has gone through bureaucratic filters and spins. With the tools of CAR, reporters are less dependent on sources for sole analysis of the data. Furthermore, reporters can add layers of new meaning to existing or conventional wisdom about a given data set. The more voices, the better. The more interpreters of data, the better, too.

5. *Keeping up with the competition.* In this world of constant competition across and within news media, CAR permits news organizations of all sizes and markets to handle stories that someone else will be doing or thinking about doing. At the individual level, it also means reporters can offer something that other reporters might not be doing. And in the mid-1990s, any edge can translate into a job opportunity or an extra step toward a promotion.

6. *Increased access to information.* There is no doubt that computers give reporters, news researchers, and their editors much greater access to information. There is not only more information available, it is

available in more depth and is obtained faster than going after it in person. The accessibility factor will only grow as more and more public information becomes computerized and more private information goes onto the market for sale.

7. *Technical reliability and greater accuracy of information.* There is no doubting the capability of a properly used personal computer to add accuracy to the information contained in a story. Although there are errors in databases and users of software can also make mistakes, generally the use of PCs improves accuracy and precision in a news story. CAR and online research can be used to verify information in terms of fundamental fact-checking as well as other functions to make stories stronger. The technical reliability of computers also adds the edge of precision to stories dealing with large numbers of sources or amounts of information.

8. *Better storage and faster retrieval for follow-up uses and other needs.* Use of CAR and online tools permits storage of information that once might have been used one time and discarded. With the organizational power of PCs, finding that stored information is easier and faster than rummaging through file boxes or desk drawers. Storage is also a space bargain, with disks taking far less space than file cabinets, report storage boxes, and file folders. With added ease in access to stored information, more frequent retrieval makes sense and is encouraged. What results, obviously, is more frequent follow-up use of information.

San Francisco's Tom Johnson (personal communication, December 22, 1993) offers three advantages to using computer-assisted reporting:

> First, it allows us to throw a much larger loop to retrieve information without a high price in terms of time and money, as least as much as it might be. Second, in doing so, we get away from the "golden Rolodex" syndrome of using the same sources over and over, and those are mostly White and male. An example might be the CD-ROM yellow pages where you can find people very easily, such as a minority business owner. And third, it allows us to make the invisible visible. We see patterns in cultural, political, and social action we might not otherwise see. An example would be the act of a break to start a game of pool. We can see one ball roll, perhaps two. But we cannot follow three or more balls moving at the same time. A computer, though, can track all of them, their colors, direction, speed, and so forth.

COMPUTERS IN INFORMATION GATHERING AND ANALYSIS

Dwight Morris, an investigative reporter with the *Los Angeles Times,* has spent much of his professional career finding information, and he has developed the knack for finding it buried in computer databases. Morris, a political science and computer science major in college and a former editor in Atlanta, has investigated campaign financing among other topics. He preaches the value of computer-based journalism in finding the news needle in haystacks: "It's amazing how much is out there (in Washington), that if you can figure out how to get hold of it and make sense out of it, it makes really fascinating news" (Matlack, 1991, p. 88).

Mary Ann Chick Whiteside (1991), assistant metro editor for the Flint, MI, *Journal,* directs CAR work at her newspaper. She notes that the use of the term computer-assisted journalism might scare off reporters and editors who might otherwise be attracted to the idea of using a new tool for their work. It is, she says, just another reporting tool. Purists argue that it is no different than fax-assisted reporting or telephone-assisted reporting. Whiteside agrees and says, "Whatever the name for the research techniques, it is clear that journalists need to learn to use computers to do a good job today" (p. 20PC).

Tom Johnson (personal communication, December 22, 1993), a former journalist who has spent much of his career as an educator thinking about computers and information gathering, is more philosophical about using computers in information gathering and analysis:

> CAR is the vehicle which we use to explore the information matrix. Growth of this is increasing with phenomenal speed in recent months. If we are going to use this tool, to, one, retrieve information, and, two, to analyze the information, then we must ask: "How and when should it be used?" Any story other than one on the strictest of deadlines should use it if there is time. And even on deadline, it can be used if the user is fast enough. "When shouldn't it be used?" It is hard to say, but perhaps when it cannot [be] or is not used properly. Then reporters should be much like physicians and seek additional expert consultants, for second opinions. We must be sensitive to that. We have to use judgment.

Johnson believes adoption of the computer as a common reporting tool will take time. Adjustment to new technologies is not always fast. There is still much to be thought about and learned in the area of information gathering and analysis using computers. Some news organizations have formed newsroom committees. Some have hired and named newsroom computer "czars" (or more aptly labeled *systems editors,* or an equivalent title indicating that they have their feet in both the heavenly digital and more earthly journalistic worlds) for the newsroom. Some have assigned the job to an editor who knows little about computers. Some have found a computer "nerd" in the information systems department who knows very little about news reporting to do the job. No matter the approach, there is not a single way to decide how to handle this thing called computer-based information gathering and analysis. A common ground may emerge at some point. It will represent a synthesis and distillation of thinking about how to manage CAR. But the news business is not there yet. One idealized view of this world follows.

PCs ARE NOT JUST FOR WORD PROCESSING

What can personal computers do to benefit reporters and editors? In a model mid-1990s newsroom, personal computers—preferably portables—are on the desks of all reporters, copy editors, information graphic specialists, librarians and news researchers, photographers, and their editors.

In this model, it does not matter what type of computer is used. Some news organizations prefer IBM-compatible or DOS networked systems. Some are moving to newer 32-bit operating systems designed for the latest processors. Other news organizations, although fewer than those using DOS, prefer the Macintosh operating system. Many newsrooms in the mid-1990s use both systems—DOS systems for one set of tasks and Macintoshes for a different set. In the end, a newspaper is published.

Reporters and editors will continue to use the computer system for the basics, such as reporting and writing stories and then copy editing them, and then for the layout and design of pages and other elements that make up the total package for a news story. This much is assumed. But it will be enhanced with the new tools. Word processing can be used for organizing stories and a variety of other writing aids (such as style- and grammar-checkers, dictionaries, etc.). They can also be used for searching and editing large blocks of text.

Journalists will not have to give up the writing function in favor of other tools. Instead, the other functions are add-ons that take advantage of the increased functionality and power of the desktop workstation that, at most publications, is a PC consisting of a keyboard, a mouse, a high-resolution color monitor, and some sort of processor with its own storage potential, such as a hard drive and disk drives.

After that, the sky seems the limit. Reporters and projects editors can use the systems at their disposal for some or all of these reporting and editing duties:

1. *Personal information organization and newsroom and department management.* Clearly, computers can assist reporters in keeping track of sources, telephone numbers, and other information. A category of software has even developed toward that purpose. These programs, often called *personal information managers,* allow reporters to develop electronic Rolodexes or card files of sorts. As with an individual, other

---

THE *RALEIGH NEWS & OBSERVER:* **INTEGRATING CAR INTO DAILY REPORTING**

There are many different ways to use computer-assisted reporting. Some news organizations use it only on special projects. Others have tried to integrate CAR approaches into daily newsroom activity, such as beat reporting.

One newspaper that has already built a national reputation for its computer-assisted reporting approach is the *News & Observer,* the 189,000-circulation morning daily located in North Carolina's capital, Raleigh.

The *N&O* has created CARNET, a computer-assisted reporting network that links all reporters in the newsroom with databases and CAR tools. In early 1994, the newspaper had approximately 30 IBM-compatible 486 PCs linked by a Novell network, two 9-track tape readers, and two CD-ROM readers.

Explained reporter Bill Krueger (1993):

> Unlike many newspapers, which have used computer databases almost exclusively on major projects, the *News & Observer* is trying to make computer-assisted reporting part of its daily routine for all reporters.
>
> More than 40 *N&O* reporters have written computer-assisted stories. Since 1991, the newspaper has published more than 160 stories that relied heavily on information from computer databases. Additionally, several *N&O* reporters make frequent use of spreadsheets to analyze data, follow trends, and organize material. The paper also has designed a front-end system to give reporters easy access to the latest census data for North Carolina. Finally, a few reporters and the paper's News Research Department make regular use of the Internet, CompuServe and other online services to supplement daily news stories.
>
> The newspaper has developed numerous databases of its own, some from scratch and some from existing public records, which are frequently updated and regularly used for news and feature stories. One such database is called "The Money Machine"—a growing database of thousands of state and local election campaign contributors dating to 1987. Another less serious but useful database is a restaurants database for the Raleigh-Durham-Chapel Hill areas in which routine restaurant listing-type information used by the newspaper's reporters and feature writers is updated.

software permits reporters and editors to manage departments, beats, or the entire newsroom. These planning and scheduling programs take care of mundane tasks like scheduling, just as spreadsheet programs can help with budgeting resources.

2. *Personal story assignments, beat tracking, and story tracking.* Software permits more efficient tracking of story progress and the

developing issues and events on beats or other reporting specializations. Furthermore, a PC and the right software can allow a reporter or editor to track a story even after initial reports have been published—a form of electronic reminders to do follow-ups and related stories that otherwise might slip through the news gathering cracks.

3. *Computer-based communication.* Computers are used for internal office electronic messaging, or *E-mail,* often in the mid-1990s. Reporters find that these systems, often tied to word processing systems, make it easier to communicate with busy editors. Editors, in turn, find it easier to get messages to reporters who often work schedules different from their own, are out of the office frequently, or are assigned to distant bureaus. This communication convenience is expanding to include more than just local network communication. Wide area networks and massive linkages of computers through commercial services or the Internet have made electronic mail much more than just movement of office memos from terminal to terminal. It is not unusual for computer-literate reporters and editors to communicate at a worldwide level with each other and with their sources.

4. *Online connections for research.* An already-discussed tool is online research. It is not always necessary to go to the library or the morgue with computer links by telephone lines. Reporters and news researchers can check for information thousands of miles away from their desktop and portable PCs.

5. *Data gathering and database building.* Perhaps the fastest growing tool of computing in the mid-1990s is database development and analysis. Reporters are not only using databases from other sources (external), but also building their own (internal). PCs help give these order and new meaning, and they certainly make analysis easier. Here's more:

- *Internal databases.* Some reporters track information on their own. This can include team or individual performance in sports, local stocks, neighborhood crime, weather conditions, and so forth.
- *External databases.* Many databases are generated by public sector agencies, as well as private sector organizations with a public interest. These are often sold to or shared at no cost with reporters, who can then analyze them on their own.
- *Interaction with other databases and software.* On some occasions, reporters will be able to share in development of databases or software on larger projects. They can share with other news organizations or with nonnews organizations.

6. *Data analysis.* With larger numbers of databases, that desktop PC can be used to conduct original analysis of the data by sorting, performing mathematical or statistical computations on quantitative information, or searching qualitative or text-based databases.

7. *Wire capture and supplemental reporting.* Numerous news services that offer public or other access have *capture* capabilities. This means having the computer do the work for you. CompuServe, the commercial online service, for example, offers customers an "Executive News Service," which can be programmed to "read" or search more than a dozen national and international news wires for key words and phrases. When those words are found, the item is stored until requested to be read or downloaded—copied—by the user. This means reporters and news researchers can broaden their reach without even reaching.

8. *Informational graphics and presentation.* Computer programs are much more capable of performing a wider range of tasks than ever before. One class of these tasks is generating graphics for presentation, such as those used with news stories. Often a graph or chart helps to make a story clearer to readers. Even a reporter at a small newspaper without a graphics department can become an informational graphic artist. For example, most top-of-the-line spreadsheet and database packages, as well as many first-rate word processors, offer graphing and drawing tools.

9. *Dissemination and distribution of news.* Many news organizations are venturing into the future by contemplating new ways to get the newspaper, magazine, or newsletter into the hands of readers. Electronic distribution using computers is already in place in some communities. Some systems use a videotex service, simply placing text on television screens. Other systems have become even more innovative with existing technology using electronic bulletin board services (BBSs) for computer-oriented readers. And this is just the beginning of what the industry can do with computers to spread the news, literally.

10. *Data and information storage for later use.* One of the most environmentally sensible uses of computers is to store and retrieve information. The paperless newsroom might become a reality some day.

WHAT DOES IT TAKE TO GET STARTED?

Some news organizations get into CAR using a do-it-yourself method. Some reporters are self-taught. Other news organizations send their employees to training seminars and programs offered by a number of organizations. One of the leading groups in educating professionals about CAR is the Investigative Reporters and Editors (IRE), based at the University of Missouri. Another is NICAR, also at Missouri. NIAR, at Indiana University at Indianapolis, takes a lead role also.

Some universities and colleges are offering special seminars at the graduate level or specialized undergraduate courses. Even so, most schools have been quite slow in offering such courses (Johnson, 1992). Regardless of how education and training are obtained, news organizations can invest tens of thousands of dollars and a handful of full-time positions to become involved in computer-assisted reporting and online news research. Or they can buy a used PC, or take one from another department of the company, spend a few hundred dollars on upgrades, a few hundred dollars more on software, and perhaps give a full-timer with computer interests a part-time assignment to get CAR started. Or they can make their starting point somewhere in between.

The easiest way to get started is to get involved with computers in the newsroom. Assess the capabilities of the organization. If there is no PC that can be used, where can one be found? Does someone have one at home that can be used until institutional support can be budgeted and started? There may be an opportunity in that direction. If there is not, then leased or borrowed equipment is an option that could cost less in the short run and will be good for testing the CAR waters on a first project.

If there is at least one PC available in the newsroom that is not constantly tied up, for example, by pagination or graphics work, then try to gain access to it. Consider sharing. Check out the software and hardware configurations. What is already there? Chances are good that it has some sort of word processor. After that, there may not be much that is immediately useful for CAR projects.

The next step is to decide what CAR goals exist. If the goal is limited, such as starting with online research, then the tools needed are also fewer and less complicated. In this case, there will be a need to add a modem and a communications package, the program that allows the computer to "talk" to another computer. A decision about what sort of online services are needed will also have to be made. Inquiries about the services, what they can do, the costs, and so forth follow. Then accounts should be opened to access those services.

Most news organizations that have committed to CAR beyond basic online research have acquired spreadsheet and database software as a minimum. Some have added compact disc, read-only memory (CD-ROM) drive readers to access large public or private databases distributed on compact discs (CDs). Others have invested in nine-track tape disk drives to access data stored on mainframe systems. A few have added optical scanning capability to reduce long-term data entry labor costs. In almost all cases, some sort of printer will be needed. The printer does not have to be an expensive, high-quality model unless the desire is to produce camera-ready output. Finally, it might be a good idea to invest in a few reference books and periodical subscriptions that focus specifically on computers and computer-assisted reporting tools.

The ability to do more depends on the hardware and the operating system available. The size of the storage of the computer, its processing speed, and other factors will determine what journalists can and cannot do with their computers.

2 Using Personal Computers, Modems, and Software

Across the nation, project editors and reporters at news organizations are thinking more often about using computer-assisted reporting and online news research for stories. Some newsrooms are far along in developing a CAR program, whereas others have virtually no plans for using the tools in coverage of their communities. Most newsrooms are somewhere between these two extremes. The subject comes up in newsroom computer or technology committee meetings. Decisions are made and CAR becomes a reality.

John Huff, editor for New Technology for *The Orlando Sentinel,* is responsible for CAR, editorial research, development of electronic media delivery systems, and other editorial department-based electronic systems. He's a believer, but he feels things are not happening fast enough. "I believe we are fighting a kind of cultural revolution in the newsrooms of America against the failure to recognize the consequences of the inevitability of information in electronic form," Huff (personal communication, December 28, 1993) says. "It's a great time to learn how to click on a computer."

John Ullman (1993b) is another one of the early believers in CAR. He is a consultant based in Minneapolis who is regarded as a national authority. He presents a typical scenario:

> You have just returned from a national conference on computer-assisted journalism (you paid your own way) and are all fired up about using computers to help you report on stories.
>
> Unfortunately, your newspaper's only computer is in the controller's office and the only software on it is the Lotus 1-2-3 spreadsheet program he uses to crunch numbers.
>
> But you've got your act together; you've done the research and crunched some numbers of your own. Armed with your proposal, you march into the editor's office and tell her that for only $20,000 you can win a Pulitzer Prize for the newspaper. (p. 1)

Ullman believes getting management support is not a very realistic expectation for many average-sized newspapers—given the facts that there is seldom cash available for such programs, editors often do not know much about computers, and Pulitzer-winning projects frequently are too big for the average newspaper to consider trying. But, he says, newspapers can still get a CAR or an online news research program started by setting more manageable goals, such as small, routine stories that use CAR and online research. Reporters and their editors just need to know how and where to start, he says. "Because of your almost nonexistent resources, that's where you need to start," he says (p. 2).

For any reporter, news researcher, or editor seeking to use online research or advanced information gathering tools such as computer-assisted reporting, there has to be a place to begin. A few insightful news organizations have been using mainframe and smaller computers for special projects and major investigations for more than two decades. Some have been using computers since PCs debuted a decade ago. Others have been dependent on more traditional interview, observation, and document-searching approaches for their major news investigations and projects. A large number of newspapers and magazines, plus some larger broadcast news organizations, are encouraged by the successes of the major dailies discussed in the opening chapter and have begun to think about making CAR a reality in their own newsrooms.

The *Beaumont Enterprise* is typical of the news organizations beginning to use CAR and online news research and starting to develop an in-house program. This 75,000-daily circulation southeast Texas newspaper is only now learning what it can and cannot do with CAR and online news research. "We are in the infancy of our [CAR and online] efforts," said business editor David Galloway (personal communication, December 14, 1993). "As I write this, we have had the equipment in the building for two weeks."

The 50,000-daily circulation Wilkes Barre, PA, *Times Leader* was in a similar situation at the beginning of 1994. "My position was created four months ago. I expect to make better use of computers in the coming months," observed assistant managing editor Scott Wasser (personal communication, December 17, 1993), who coordinates and advises on all technologies in the newsroom.

The *Peoria Journal Star* is still another newspaper just beginning its use of CAR, but so far the work has been stimulating, says Editorial Systems Manager and Features Editor Dennis Diamond (personal communication, December 28, 1993). The 85,000-circulation Illinois daily recently completed a CAR project about local unwed mothers and it has published several census data stories focusing on the Peoria area. "We are just starting and have a long way to go, but it's very exciting," Diamond observed.

Some larger newspapers also are enjoying early successes, but they, of course, had to start at some point. For Oklahoma City's *Daily Oklahoman,* the program began in early 1993. "The *Daily Oklahoman* is nine months into the development of its CAR program," said Database Editor Griff Palmer (personal communication, December 19, 1993). "I anticipate major strides in the program in the coming twelve months as our training effort hits full stride and database/spreadsheet/online research techniques gain wider acceptance in the newsroom."

Some news organizations would like to get involved in CAR and online news research, but they have had to take a "wait and see" attitude about it. These organizations may be held back by lack of available human resources, tight or even shrinking newsroom budgets, or the lack of individuals in the department who have an interest in and knowledge of personal computing sufficient to lead the program.

The 10,000-plus circulation *Key West Citizen* in south Florida is an example. Managing Editor Tim Aten has barely enough reporters and editors to cover his 5-square-mile island community of 30,000 residents. Furthermore, he says his newspaper does not have the budget to invest in a personal computer powerful enough to use for CAR or online news research tools or to pay for online charges. If the *Citizen* did purchase a new personal computer for news use, it likely would be used for other more pressing news and nonnews tasks. With this situation, the prospects of any meaningful CAR or online research seem dim—unless Aten can find other external sources for such reporting.

"We'd really like to be doing some stories like that," Aten (personal communication, December 4, 1993) said. "We should be thinking about some computer investigations. The stories are there to do. I'd just have to think about it a little. I wish we could do that sort of work, but we just don't have the people or computers." Instead of doing without CAR, Aten elected to begin a small CAR program in 1994 by working with faculty and students at the University of Miami. This enabled *The Citizen* to use CAR resources, such as census databases on CD-ROM discs, software, and computers. The first CAR project was a simple analysis of Monroe County census data.

Paul Baker (personal communication, January 31, 1994), city editor for the 25,000-circulation Lebanon, PA, *Daily News,* says his newspaper is a "strongly local" one in terms of coverage. "Most of these [CAR] tools are more relevant to the kind of specialized reporting one might do for a metro," he stated. "I have five reporters. In addition to daily deadline duties—obits, rewrites, police reporting, etcetera—they are expected to produce five to seven stories a week. Needless to say, research is a delightful, but remote, concept."

The managing editor of the 28,000-circulation *Herald-Whig* in Quincy, IL, Mike Hilfrink (personal communication, December 20, 1993), fully understands Aten's difficult position. "I suspect you will find

---

A STUDY OF COMPUTER-ASSISTED REPORTING

A national survey of the use of computer-assisted reporting and online news research was conducted at the University of Miami in 1993–1994 as part of the research presented in this book. Throughout the book, findings are reported, both in aggregate and anecdotal form.

The survey consisted of an initial mailing of 514 cover letters, questionnaires, and stamped, self-addressed envelopes to the nation's largest Sunday and daily newspapers in December 1993. One follow-up mailing was sent in January 1994. Circulation of minimum 20,000 on Sundays was used as the cutoff point. Editors of the selected newspapers were asked either to complete the questionnaire themselves or to forward it to the person in charge of online news research and computer-assisted reporting. In some cases, as many as two or three persons completed various portions of the questionnaire related to their newsroom specializations. A total of 208 responses were received, a response rate of 40.5%.

The questionnaire was developed from discussions and interviews during the Investigative Reporters and Editors Conference on Computer-Assisted Reporting at Raleigh, NC, in 1993. The instrument consisted of four sets of questions including institutional and personal information (6 variables), computer-assisted reporting (21 variables), online news research (29 variables), and field reporting use of computers (4 variables). Respondents were also encouraged to include any additional comments on the subject.

In some cases, follow-up interviews were conducted by telephone. Additionally, in-person interviews were conducted at the Fort Lauderdale *Sun-Sentinel, Lexington, Ky., Herald-Leader, The Miami Herald, The Orlando Sentinel,* the *St. Petersburg Times, Raleigh News & Observer, The Washington Post,* and *USA Today.*

Data were processed using programs from the Microsoft FoxPro relational database system for Windows, Version 2.6, and the Statistical Package for the Social Sciences (SPSS) for Windows, Version 6.0, and SPSS/PC+ Studentware Version 1.0.

CAR more prevalent at larger papers," he said. "Smaller papers have smaller budgets and less time available for staff training and pursuing such projects."

SETTING UP A PLAN

The strongest approach to setting up a computer-assisted reporting and online news research program is to plan it in detail before trying to use it for any news stories. Rushing into a story using CAR tools may not be the best approach because it could lead to problems, even serious errors in stories. Instead, a long-term plan, with goals or objectives, will make more efficient use of limited resources such as personnel and budgeted funds. Even a short-term list of objectives for a single project prepared in advance will make a difference.

Robert H. Giles (1988), editor and publisher of the 400,000-circulation *Detroit News,* maintains that planning is essential to success in any new project or program. The act of anticipating, looking forward, and working toward goals may be difficult for some news organizations, most likely because of the all-consuming effort to produce the daily newspaper with limited resources. Giles said, "The planning process must be assertive, forward-looking, and creative, yet reflect pragmatic estimates of what is possible. Planning is the first management function because it establishes the foundation for the organizing, staffing, directing, and controlling that follow" (pp. 139–140).

There is no doubt that introduction of new technology to a newsroom can cause staff stress. This has occurred whenever any new technology has been introduced, especially that which is computer-based or involves jobs in the newsroom that are already high-stress or high-risk roles, such as deadline or investigative reporting (Garrison, 1979; Giles, 1988; Sohn, Ogan, & Polich, 1986; Willis, 1988).

Part of the success of a CAR and online news research program must involve planning and long-term involvement by all levels of the newsroom, from the executive editor to part-time clerks and typists. "Editors must understand what is involved in CAR for it to work right," said Mitch Lipka (personal communication, December 20, 1993), Database Reporter for Gannett Suburban Newspapers, based in Westchester, NY. "There must be a plan and commitment."

Newspapers that handle the process properly rarely jump in without thinking through what they want to achieve. What types of online service needs are good for a particular newsroom? What types of CAR or online research will enhance the community coverage the news organization already offers? It is best, it seems, for most news organizations to start slowly and, perhaps, in stages.

Two basic questions have to be answered:

- What can be done with existing newsroom resources?
- What can a news organization afford, in terms of time, the annual budget, and its human resources, for growth into CAR and online news research?

Jack Lail is the metro editor for the 128,000-circulation *Knoxville News-Sentinel,* which serves east Tennessee. Among his duties are assisting reporters in doing online searches for their stories, supervising database projects, and advising on software purchases. He says starting into CAR and online research is not easy for some news organizations and it may have to begin with a personal, not institutional, commitment, such as investing in the tools on a personal level first. "Editorial departments aren't used to spending money for hardware and software research tools, much less for subscriptions and connect charges for online services. It's an uphill battle. Also, CAR can involve long learning curves for some. In other words, these tools are often hard to justify to cash-strapped newsrooms. Much of the better equipment and software we use is owned personally by myself or some reporters," Lail (personal communication, December 20, 1993) said.

Typical of newspapers just looking at CAR and online news research is the Athens, GA, *Daily News and Banner-Herald.* "We are in the midst of analyzing our computer needs," said Blake Giles (personal communication, December 19, 1993), managing editor/sports. Giles, the newspaper's system manager, added, "CAR and online are two areas we know we are deficient in and we would like to come up to speed in those areas."

At the end of the planning process should be a reminder to the staff about how CAR and online research must be used. CAR and online research benefits to the newsroom should be only *part* of the total reporting package. This aspect of planning and overall reporting philosophy may often be overlooked. But the analysis and information collection, aided by computers, should be well integrated into the total reporting effort on any project. Rarely, if ever, will CAR or online news research be the sole basis for a story. Any reporter or editor using CAR or online tools alone for a story will shortchange himself or herself and the story. *Lexington Herald-Leader* Executive Editor Tim Kelly strongly advocates this attitude. "We use a CAR approach on some of our stories, but you can never forget that type of reporting must be supplemented by other, more traditional types of reporting such as interviewing," Kelly (personal communication, September 10, 1993) cautions.

Buffalo News deputy managing editor Edward L. Cuddihy (personal communication, December 20, 1993) agrees. "The No. 1 mistake is that technology will substitute for good reporting," argued Cuddihy, who supervises production and computerization for the 325,000-circulation newspaper. "It [CAR and online research] is an important new tool, but the results of its use are no better than the reporter using the tool."

INTEGRATING TRAINING AND EDUCATION PROGRAMS

University of Georgia Media Management Professor Conrad C. Fink (1988) says proper training in the newsroom "can have great impact on quality performance" (p. 163). Fink says in-house training can work, but the normal crush of duties can limit the productivity of such an approach. "Key staffers should be given outside training," he proposes. He also warns that an unstructured and underfunded training approach cannot be expected to produce quality results.

The Rochester, NY, *Democrat and Chronicle/Times Union* is trying the internal approach, and it seems to be working—within limits. Says

Assistant Metro Editor John Reinan (personal communication, December 19, 1993):

> We've made excellent progress in a very short time at this paper. It's been a challenge for me personally, because I have been learning a lot of this on my own, from scratch, and then I've got to turn around and teach others. Everyone looks at me as the expert, and I don't always feel like one! That may be an issue—many papers are trying to rush into CAR, but how are they handling the training of the trainers? Since I have many duties in addition to CAR work, I do feel like I don't get to immerse myself in CAR as much as I'd like. It's a complicated subject, and I don't spend as much hands-on time with hardware and software as I'd like. I've only been here [seven months], so I'm really only just getting rolling on this stuff. It's still fairly new to me.

At this stage in the development of CAR at daily newspapers, at least, many do not have formal internal or external training programs. Some that do not have the programs are planning to begin them, however. Only 27.1% of 208 newspapers in the University of Miami national CAR study reported using training programs in mid-1994. A total of 58.5% did not have a training program of any type and the remaining 14.5% did not reply to the question at all.

DEFINING BASIC COMPUTING TERMS

A journalist new to the world of computers and reporting might run across many computer-oriented terms that are not familiar to him or her. It takes time to get used to the precise language as it would in learning about any other specialization or technology. For many terms used on these pages, brief definitions have been listed in the glossary and others are discussed in the text and Figs. 2.1 and 2.2.

Two of the most often used terms in the computer world are *hardware* and *software*. Hardware is, simply, the physical parts of the computer system. This includes such things as the computer's central processor, the monitor (or display), the keyboard, and the mouse (or pointing device). Hardware also includes all peripherals, such as printers, CD-ROM drive readers, optical scanners, and modems. *Hardware-dependent* refers to any features of a computer system, as well as software, that are tied to a particular computer configuration or individual system. This may be a factor with certain newsroom front-end systems used for production.

Software, on the other hand, is a computer program. Software is the instructions the computer user gives to the computer's processor or other hardware to execute a task. There are two main types of PC software: system software, such as operating systems (e.g., DOS or OS/2), and application software, such as a word processor, spreadsheet,

HOW TO SPEAK 'COMPUTER'

To the uninitiated, the lingo surrounding personal computers is like a foreign language. Here are some simple definitions of common computer terms. Italic words are defined in list.

■ **Binary number system:** A system using only two digits (0 and 1) to represent all numbers. Used in computers because an electrical circuit has two states: on and off.

■ **Bit:** The smallest unit of information in a computer. It's an abbreviation for **B**inary dig**IT**.

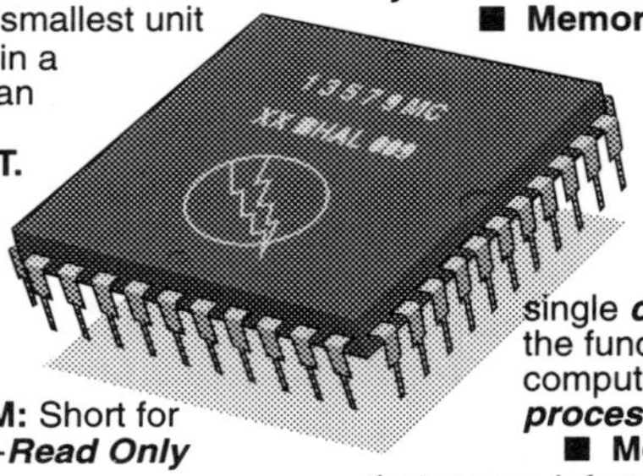

■ **Byte:** A string of **bits**, usually eight, that represent a number or character.

■ **CD-ROM:** Short for Compact Disk-*Read Only Memory*.

■ **Central processing unit:** The part of a computer that executes instructions.

■ **Chip:** An electronic circuit on a tiny piece of semiconductor material, usually silicon.

■ **Clone:** A computer that can run the same *software* as IBM's personal computers.

■ **Floppy disk:** A flexible disk covered in cardboard or plastic; it is used to store data or instructions. Most *programs* are sold on floppy disks.

■ **Gigabyte:** One billion *bytes*.

■ **Hard disk:** A sealed disk used to store data or instructions. It costs more than a *floppy disk* but stores more information and works faster.

■ **Hardware:** The physical parts of a computer system, such as the *keyboard*.

■ **Keyboard:** Typewriter-like device for putting data into a computer or giving it commands.

■ **Kilobyte:** 1,024 *bytes*.

■ **Laser printer:** A *printer* that uses a a laser to print.

■ **Magneto-optical (MO) disk:** A disk, usually removable, that is read and written to by both laser light and magnetic technology. Though slower than magnetic disks, they are considered more durable.

■ **Megabyte:** One million *bytes*.

■ **Memory:** The part of the computer where data or instructions are stored in *binary* form.

■ **Micro-processor:** A single *chip* that has all the functions of a computer's *central processing unit*.

■ **Modem:** A device that moves information between computers, usually over telephone lines.

■ **Monitor:** A television-like screen that displays data.

■ **Mouse:** A hand-held device that moves the cursor on a computer screen.

■ **Operating system:** A *program* that controls all other programs run on a computer system.

■ **Peripherals:** External devices used with a computer, such as *monitors* and *modems*.

■ **Personal computer:** A desktop or portable computer intended for use by an individual.

■ **Printer:** A device that prints numbers, letters or graphic images from a computer.

■ **Program:** Instructions that tell a computer how to do something. For instance, a word processing program tells a computer how to work with text.

■ **ROM:** Read Only *Memory*. Permanent data or instructions that users can't alter.

■ **RAM:** Random Access *Memory*. Temporary memory that users can retrieve and alter.

■ **Software:** Computer *programs*.

BZ:S26 **DAN CLIFFORD** / Miami Herald Staff

FIG. 2.1.   A beginning guide to computer terms.

communications, or database management package. System software literally controls the computer, but is often not noticed or directly addressed by average users. Most users are more concerned with applications.

There are still other categories of software, such as network and language software. Networks link groups of computers together to permit them to communicate and share resources, and this class of software controls the network's functions. Language software is used by programmers who wish to write applications or other programs. *Software-dependent* refers to a device that is tied to a particular program to function properly. Some newsroom word processing systems operate in this manner.

In terms of both hardware and software, computer users often read about or hear other users refer to *support.* This actually refers to two things. First, as a verb, the word reflects the ability to work with another program or peripheral. But as a noun, the term means assistance given by a computer company to users of its product.

There are several other terms related to computers that are widely used and users need to understand them because they describe the capabilities of a particular computer system. Some of the most important ones are included in the following.

For *desktop computers,* key concerns are the basic operating system, the central processor type, RAM size, hard-drive size, central processing unit speed, floppy disk drive size and capacity, and monitor type.

The *basic operating system* refers to the software that controls all the programs and the types of programs the computer can run. Some of the most popular desktop operating systems are MS/DOS, OS/2, and the Macintosh operating system, but there are others not as widely used.

The *environment* is a set of resources available to the system user. Microsoft Windows, which operates in MS/DOS, is a popular graphical environment. The latest version of Windows, Windows 95, combined the operating system and environment into one unit.

The *central processor* is the computational and control unit that drives the computer's processing capabilities. Most often, the unit type is discussed in terms of its microprocessor chip type. For IBM-compatible systems, the most recent microprocessor chip is Intel Corporation's controversial 80586 (called *Pentium),* but the most common to date are the 80486, 80386, and 80286. Some newsrooms may still have PCs using the decade-old 8088 or 8086 chips. Other popular chips are Motorola's 68000, 68020, and 68030. The unit is often called *CPU.*

Central processing unit speed refers to the speed the CPU uses to complete tasks. This is usually reflected in megahertz (MHz), or one million cycles per second. Most PCs run at speeds ranging from 4.77 MHz to as much as 99 MHz, but some recent systems have a capability of more than 99 MHz. Most desktop systems in use in the mid-1990s run at speeds somewhere in the middle of that range, such as 16 to 66 MHz.

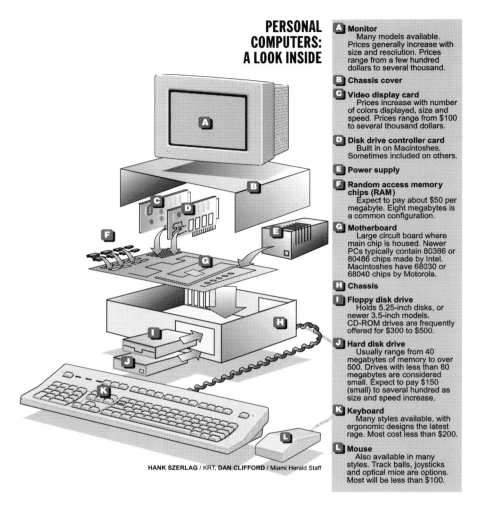

PERSONAL COMPUTERS: A LOOK INSIDE

A Monitor
Many models available. Prices generally increase with size and resolution. Prices range from a few hundred dollars to several thousand.

B Chassis cover

C Video display card
Prices increase with number of colors displayed, size and speed. Prices range from $100 to several thousand dollars.

D Disk drive controller card
Built in on Macintoshes. Sometimes included on others.

E Power supply

F Random access memory chips (RAM)
Expect to pay about $50 per megabyte. Eight megabytes is a common configuration.

G Motherboard
Large circuit board where main chip is housed. Newer PCs typically contain 80386 or 80486 chips made by Intel. Macintoshes have 68030 or 68040 chips by Motorola.

H Chassis

I Floppy disk drive
Holds 5.25-inch disks, or newer 3.5-inch models. CD-ROM drives are frequently offered for $300 to $500.

J Hard disk drive
Usually range from 40 megabytes of memory to over 500. Drives with less than 80 megabytes are considered small. Expect to pay $150 (small) to several hundred as size and speed increase.

K Keyboard
Many styles available, with ergonomic designs the latest rage. Most cost less than $200.

L Mouse
Also available in many styles. Track balls, joysticks and optical mice are options. Most will be less than $100.

HANK SZERLAG / KRT, **DAN CLIFFORD** / Miami Herald Staff

FIG. 2.2   Computer hardware terminology.

RAM size describes the amount of random access memory, or volatile temporary memory, that the computer has available for use. It is volatile because when the system is turned off, or otherwise disrupted, any data in RAM that are not stored elsewhere are lost. Most systems are sold with 4 to 16 MB of RAM—but a few low-end systems were still marketed with as little as 2 MB to 4 MB of RAM in 1995. However, some systems are sold with as much as 16 to 32 MB and are upgradable to 64 MB or more.

Hard drive size simply describes the mass storage capacity of the computer on its fixed, nonremovable internal sealed disk. Hard drive size is referred to in megabytes (MB) or gigabytes (GB). The size range of most drives sold with new computers in 1995 is from about 200 MB to 4 GB, with most around 200 to 500 MB. For some PC-based systems, mass storage can even be larger. One computer company estimated that the typical desktop system will contain a 1.0 GB hard drive in 1996 and a 1.2 GB hard drive by 1997 (Robinson, 1994).

Floppy disk drive size and disk capacity refers to the drive in a computer system that reads data from, and writes data to, floppy disks. The most common IBM-compatible floppy drives are 3.5-inch and 5.25-inch—measured by the size in width of the disks the drive can accommodate. The capacity of the disk refers to the disk's storage size. Common capacities for 3.5-inch are 1.44 MB and 720 KB, and for the 5.25 inch, 1.2 MB and 360 KB.

Monitor type and size refer to the video display capacities of the monitor and the diagonal size of the video screen. Most personal computer monitors will display content in full color, or in single color (monochrome). There are different varieties of color displays that range in quality depending on the detail of the images and number of colors that can be displayed. The diagonal of the monitor is usually reported in inches in U.S.-sold systems. Sharpness of the color is also influenced by the type of video card in the computer.

For *portable computers,* the foregoing terms and definitions apply. Potential portable PC users should be additionally concerned with particular design variations, including screen display type, battery type and strength, electrical system configuration, system expansion slots and ports, keyboard size and configuration, and total unit weight.

Screen display describes the wide range of devices that show images on the typically small and flat screens of portable PCs, Macintoshes, and other systems. Monochrome displays are less expensive and quite functional for basics such as writing and online research, but for certain software used for informational graphics or pagination, color should be considered, perhaps required, despite the additional cost.

Battery type and strength determine the range of independence a portable computer user enjoys. Nickel cadmium (nicad) and nickel hydride are common types, but lithium ion and lithium polymer batteries are also used in some portables. Portable computer batteries are rechargeable, but they do have a limited number of recharges, usually from 200 to 1,000. The real measures are the duration of the charge and the weight. Most nicad batteries provide power for periods ranging from 1 to 4 hours, some even more, depending on the battery type and the power demands made by the computer user. Although some batteries last longer, they may also add considerable weight to the system. Some portable PCs will use alkaline batteries as well for an emergency replacement when rechargeable batteries are dead. Recent developments in battery technology have introduced rechargable alkaline batteries and alkaline-nicad battery rechargers (Booth, 1994).

Expansion slots and ports are important in desktop systems, but are especially important to portable computer users. Expansion includes additional RAM, ability to insert an internal modem or fax/modem, and use of Personal Computer Memory Card International Association (PCMCIA) slot technology. PCMCIA technology offers an expansion capability that was found in about two thirds of all notebook PCs and nearly all subnotebook, palmtop, and personal digital assistant systems at the beginning of 1994 (Magidson, 1994). Generally, the more expansion capability a portable computer offers, the better. Ports permit connection to peripherals such as a printer, scanner, or a pointing device such as a mouse or trackball. Generally, an RS-232 serial port and a parallel port are minimum features on a portable PC.

Keyboards come as a basic part of almost all systems and they are built in, instead of detached, for portables. The design of the keyboard will vary, depending on the portable. Some IBM-types of computers use the smaller 84-key configuration, whereas others use the full 101-key version. Macintosh system keyboards are a little different than IBM-type configurations in terms of their special function keys.

Unit weight simply refers to the total load, in pounds, of the computer. This can become a factor for reporters on the run, perhaps trying to travel with carry-on baggage only. Laptops and notebooks typically weigh less than 10 pounds, most in the 6- to 8-pound range, including the battery.

For *printers,* the main user focus is on selecting one of the five major types; the type of printer determines output quality and speed. The most basic and least expensive is the dot-matrix printer. Ink jet printers are much quieter and increase output quality but cost a little more. For news organizations interested in camera-ready quality output, laser printers, shared laser printers, or color printers may be the answer. These three categories are also the most expensive. Personal laser printers are common in office settings and in some newsrooms. Shared laser printers are fast because they serve a network, but they are expensive and may require tricky installations. Color printers are initially expensive and account for the highest per-page cost. They are also generally slower than other types. Printers are judged not only by the quality of their output, but also by the speed at which a page is printed. Dot-matrix and ink jet printers are frequently rated at characters per second (cps) and laser and color printers are rated at pages per second (pps).

SELECTING THE RIGHT HARDWARE

When the time comes to make critical hardware purchase decisions, there are some additional questions to consider:

- What does this computer need to do? Right now? In 2 years (in 2 years, it is likely to be technologically obsolete)? Can it be upgraded?
- What is the most money, for all hardware components, the budget can afford?
- What is the minimum system configuration needed to get started?
- How many computers are needed for CAR and online research in a newsroom? Can it be done with just one PC or Mac?
- Should separate computers be set aside for separate functions (e.g., online research and communication, database development, spreadsheet analysis)?
- Where can expert technical help be found?
- Has the right "consumer homework" been done?

There will be a varying set of answers for questions like these, and many of these questions are typical of those going through the minds of editors and reporters seeking to start their own CAR and online news research programs. Early in the process, it is important to decide whether the hardware should or should not be portable. Laptop and notebook computers are much more expensive, although they are just as powerful and can do almost everything a sophisticated desktop system can do. But portability and power come with a hefty price tag, often double or more that of an equivalent desktop system. If portability or the capability to do both in-the-newsroom and remote projects with the same system is not important, then a less expensive desktop system may be the best route to take. The chance to spend a little more in the beginning does give a wider range of possibilities for reporters and news researchers working on CAR or online assignments.

There are several strategies for selecting hardware. First, find out what is in the marketplace. What is most common? Then, do some thinking about what can be afforded and do some homework on systems within that range. This might require several steps. Read computer magazines and catalogs. There are a dozen or more of these publications available on a monthly or biweekly basis. Their articles and advertisements give a fast impression of what is available at what price. The next step is to visit local computer retailers and discounters to see the products that are most appealing.

Second, identify in-house computing experts to discuss the market research. These persons may be in the newsroom but could also be in other departments. An obvious place to inquire is the information systems department. Their opinions can be useful in clearing up confusion and giving second opinions.

Third, find out how other newspapers have chosen their systems. Talk to their computer experts, CAR directors, and news researchers.

Fourth, find independent computer experts whose advice can be trusted and who are not financially motivated, such as sales representatives on commission might be, to help with making recommendations.

"Price wars have made powerful computers much more affordable even as the new software made them necessary," wrote *San Jose Mercury News* CAR editor Dan Gillmor (1993, p. 25BM). "But the competitive bloodletting in the marketplace has created a lot of confusion." As each year passes and the personal computer industry improves its products, Gillmor observed, consumers are getting more PC for less money. "The way individual buyers and small businesses buy computers and software, meanwhile, has gone through a complete revolution. Not many years ago, you'd shop for a new machine at a small computer store in a strip mall. But the number of such stores has dwindled in the face of competition from mail-order dealers and superstores."

Gillmor also noted that the big question facing the purchaser of a CAR system, or any other personal computer system, involves how much to spend. "One of the toughest questions is whether to pay a premium for the latest and greatest hardware," Gillmor (1993, p. 25BM) wrote. "In many cases, all you buy for the mega-gear is bragging rights. But if you can . . . [work more efficiently or save a lot of time], it may be well worth it to you. And you'll be better prepared for more advanced and complex software yet to come."

The Miami Herald did not have to look far for its hardware and software experts. CAR editor Steve Doig (personal communication, December 16, 1993) studied computers when he was a student at Dartmouth College, but he also developed his interest in computers as a science reporter and bureau reporter for the newspaper more than a decade ago. He worked with other computer experts in the newspaper's information systems department—those who knew more about hardware—when he needed to do so. Other newspapers are not so lucky and have to go out of the newsroom.

For entry-level CAR and online news research, the basic hardware configuration should include the following:

* *Central processor.* Ideally, a 80486 (or a Pentium 80586) system, or its equivalent in a Macintosh system, will work best. Hard drive size can vary quite a bit, of course, but 500 MB minimum of storage is needed to run DOS, Windows, the larger software packages necessary for CAR, and to store large data files These systems should run at 33 to 66 MHz or faster.
* *RAM.* A minimum of 8 MB, but from 16 to 32 MB of random access memory is advised. To run Windows, a minimum RAM of 4 MB is necessary. Some experienced users recommend 8 MB of RAM if a user plans to run several programs at one time.

• *Floppy disk drives.* For convenience, a system with both 3.5-inch and 5.25-inch high-density disk drives is preferred. As a minimum configuration, one 3.5-inch high-density (1.44 MB) disk drive is necessary. As a rule, avoid double-density disk drives simply because of their storage limitations and the fact that the technology is becoming outdated and unavailable.

• *Internal and external modems.* A modem is required for online research. Ideally, the modem should be an internal 14400 or 28800 baud unit, but a less expensive 2400 or 9600 baud modem will produce affordable results. PCMCIA slot fax/modems are a wise choice for portables.

• *CD-ROM drive.* This is certainly not required, but a CD-ROM drive reader is becoming more and more useful for access to certain databases. The faster the read speed of a CD-ROM reader the better, but speed does increase cost.

• *Printers.* Depending on what is required (e.g., camera-ready), printers that produce rough-draft and notes-type output for writing stories can be quite inexpensive. For a minimum setup, a dot-matrix printer to accompany the system is necessary, but CAR and online research can be done without a printer. Instead of being stored on paper, output can be stored as text files on a hard drive or floppy disk or sent to another computer system—such as the front-end news-editorial system—for use or storage.

Matching writing and news-gathering needs with hardware requires thought and planning. Generally, the best rule is to acquire hardware with growth and expansion in mind. This means a system should have expansion slots for peripherals such as a mouse or trackball, CD-ROM drive readers, optical scanners, and so forth. This means a system also needs expansion space for RAM, as the department's goals and requirements continue to grow. Similarly, the system needs easy replacement capability for the motherboard and CPU, as well as the hard drive. In the beginning, the system should have a large enough hard drive for storage of programs and data files currently needed, but there should be a 50% to 75% buffer of additional hard drive space for growth and expansion over the next year or two, or until the system can be upgraded or replaced. This means that if a user has 60 MB of installed software and data files to start, the hard drive should have a capacity of 120 to 240 MB.

CHOOSING A PRINTER

When a new CAR and online research system is set up, planning to acquire a printer is a smart move. Printers can be very cheap, as little as a few hundred dollars. But there are decisions to make, just as there will be when acquiring other hardware:

- How much money is in the budget to spend?
- What type of output quality is desired? Is camera-ready output needed or will the draft quality be sent to an editorial art department for final preparation?
- What is the per-page cost for printing (e.g., computed by cost of ribbons, toner cartridges, paper, etc.)?
- What is the speed of the printer?

The three major categories of interest to CAR users and online news researchers are laser, ink jet, and dot-matrix. For newsrooms using GUI environments such as Windows or OS/2, a laser printer is the best choice, even though it is most expensive. The quality and speed of output are superior, in most cases, to the alternatives. This is especially valuable and convenient for smaller newspapers seeking camera-ready output for graphics that will accompany stories. But if this is not necessary, then ink jet and dot-matrix printers can also produce draft-quality GUI output that will be satisfactory for writing stories or for graphic artists to use in preparing final graphics for CAR story packages.

USING THE RIGHT OPERATING SYSTEM

There are numerous ways to configure a desktop or portable computer system to perform its functions. The operating system is also often called the *operating platform*. Three of these—DOS, OS/2, and Macintosh— are commonly found in newsrooms. The following is a brief introduction to each of these systems, as well as one other that may be of interest:

1. *DOS*. DOS is an acronym for disk operating system. This refers to the software that controls and uses hardware resources of the computer system such as memory, processor time, disk space, and the peripherals such as a mouse or printer. This term is generic and there are variations such as MS/DOS for Microsoft's version, IBM DOS, and others.

2. *Windows*. This is the trademark name of the graphical user interface software package developed by Microsoft. It offers a standard operating interface for programs with menus and icons, using a mouse or other pointing device. Windows actually operates "on top of" a version of DOS. Use of Windows permits multitasking, or the ability to run several programs at what seems like the same time, and sharing resources, such as type fonts, across programs. The newest version of Windows, Windows 95, integrates DOS into a single package.

3. *OS/2*. OS/2 is IBM and Microsoft's joint effort, called a multimedia presentation manager, used to produce a graphical user interface that permits pre-emptive multitasking and numerous other features. OS/2 has a built in disk operating system.

4. *Macintosh OS*. This is the operating system used by Macintosh systems.

5. *Others*. One of the leading others is Unix. Unix was developed for minicomputers and is often found running on Internet system computers. It is regarded as a powerful system and is available in several varieties. Windows NT is another operating system that is gaining popularity among some high-end users.

Matching the writing and news-gathering needs with platforms is essential when planning to start a CAR desk or project station. There is need for compatibility if there are plans to work with another reporter in another bureau or a reporter at another newspaper. There is also considerable danger that an organization just beginning to work in CAR may underpower or overpower itself in terms of computing. An uninformed person could easily purchase a personal computer that does not have the capability to run certain software. For instance, a new system configured with 4 MB of RAM may not have enough memory to open and run Windows, a word processor, and some of the larger database management systems. These programs may run individually, but one or more may not work well if opened at the same time. System memory resources would be tested to the limits every time the system were used. An upgrade of 4 to 16 MB of RAM would be necessary for efficient operation of that particular system. A too-small hard drive would produce similar unsatisfactory results, forcing the user to constantly remove software and replace programs in time-consuming installation and reinstallation sessions.

A similar risk exists in software purchasing. There is no need to buy a word processor that has pagination capability if this is not needed. Similarly, there is no need to buy an expensive statistical package for analyzing a database when the statistical functions of a spreadsheet or database package may do the job. The bottom line: Users need to know the capabilities and limitations of hardware and software and match them well with specific news-gathering needs.

SELECTING THE RIGHT SOFTWARE

If choosing the best hardware configuration, operating system and platform, or monitor seems challenging, the situation is only made more difficult by the equally large number of tough product choices in the category of software. William Casey (1993c), CAR director at *The Washington Post,* argues for the simpler, the better, when it comes to software. Many major programs of the mid-1990s are more feature rich than they need to be, he thinks, by trying to be everything to every user. At the least, Casey proposes looking carefully at programs to be certain they do what they are needed to do. "All of us don't need every new feature added to word processing, spreadsheet, database or other application programs," Casey wrote (n.p.). "Sadly, few of us know about many features [of software we use] or take the time to learn in an orderly fashion about better ways to do things that we're already doing. Giant strides have been made by virtually all suppliers in ease of use, but ease of use cannot take us all the way."

Associated Press reporter Larry Blasko (1988) recommends serious price comparison research be done before purchasing any software. He likens the pricing strategy of some software companies to that of a carnival. "The business plans for carnival sideshows and certain software houses are roughly the same," he wrote (p. 3B). "Charge as many as you can as much as you can." Blasko recommends searching for software by reading catalogs and looking at features, performance levels, requirements, and prices. Then get demonstrations of the software at local stores, he recommends. Ask questions and look at manuals. "If, after all your research, no serious alarms are raised, this may indeed be the better mousetrap for your particular needs. The Yugo and Mercedes are both automobiles, but the Mercedes is just more so—with a price that reflects it" (p. 3B).

There are some basic decisions to make when setting up software for a personal computer system. What follows is a short list to consider:

- *IBM-compatible or Macintosh?* The two major operating systems are IBM-compatible systems that operate with either DOS or OS/2 or Macintosh. Some newsrooms use both with the IBM types for writing and other computing tasks; the Macs are used primarily for graphics. Obviously, each system can be used for both types of newsroom work. Once the two systems were completely incompatible or, at least, it was very difficult to move files from one to the other. But this is changing and the decision about which to use is not as significant as it once might have been. Clearly, the choice will be impacted by which is most compatible with the existing newsroom systems. Most newsrooms already developing CAR programs have decided to use IBM or IBM-compatible systems. A clear minority of news organizations are working with Macintoshes, although the variety of software has grown and some of the major CAR software packages used in DOS and Windows versions in IBM-compatible systems are now becoming available in Macintosh versions as well.
- *DOS, OS/2, or Windows 95?* This decision is another basic one for any IBM-compatible PC system. With many users opting for IBM-compatible systems, the choice is to use DOS, OS/2, Windows 95, or another environment. Most state-of-the-art CAR software—programs that perform sophisticated qualitative and quantitative data processing tasks—are available in either DOS, Windows, or OS/2 versions. Windows

programs can run in OS/2. Some beginners prefer Windows or another GUI environment, such as OS/2, because of the easy-to-use pull-down menus, ability to share resources, and other interfaces that make working with it easier. It should be noted again that Windows 95, the upgraded 1995 edition of Windows Version 3.x, does not require DOS. Like OS/2, Windows 95 is a complete PC operating system and GUI environment.

• *Word processors.* There is no absolute need for word processing for CAR or online news research, but a versatile word processor is a real convenience for a variety of CAR- and online-related tasks such as cleaning up data files, and basic text searching such as locating names or other key words in large text files. The leading word processors offer several text database management tools in addition to their conventional writing and editing functions.

• *Communications.* These programs are necessary for online news research and for access to some nontext databases for CAR work. Communications programs enable users to operate their modems and fax cards to send and receive data, to access remote databases, and to send and receive faxes.

• *Spreadsheets.* These programs perform the most basic of functions in building and analyzing databases in the standard columns (variables or fields) and rows (cases) format. Spreadsheets are essential tools for CAR work, but they are not needed for online news research.

• *Database management systems.* Database management systems (DBMSs) are essential tools for CAR projects. For news organizations interested only in online news research, a DBMS is not a required software acquisition. Database management programs obviously permit the development and modification of new databases, as well as the import and export of databases from other sources and other formats for analysis. Most CAR desks use relational database systems, which permit two different tables of data to be related, or connected, for analytical purposes by some common link or reference point. Some DBMSs do not have relational analytic power. Many of these programs offer features such as statistical analysis, sorting, database merging and relating, graphing, and formatting output into standard reports.

• *Statistical packages.* These programs perform highly quantitative tasks such as statistical tests and multivariate analyses. These programs are certainly not necessary in most CAR work and are not at all needed in online research. But these programs are extremely helpful in analyzing databases consisting of hundreds or thousands of cases or involving large amounts of numeric variables or fields for each case, such as those generated by public opinion surveys or polls.

• *Graphics.* These are not a necessity for CAR or for online research, but graphics software is an add-on some news organizations will need to convert their data analyses into complete visual packages ready for publication.

- *Other software options.* In addition to the five previous categories, it may be worthwhile to consider personal information managers, financial management, time management, project management, file compression/decompression, and programming development software. Utility programs and antivirus programs are also helpful for file management, safety, and security.
- *Proprietary software.* For some companies and for news departments, there may be certain computer programs that are used for specific purposes and are limited in availability. These programs serve mostly internal purposes, such as for production, budgets, or other database management. As a result, they have limited, if any, use for CAR or online research purposes.

Matching Writing and News-Gathering Needs With Software

No matter what choices are made about software products, it makes sense to match the software to news writing and news-gathering needs. For news organizations on a limited budget and with few editors, reporters, and news researchers for CAR and online research, this makes absolute sense. It goes back to planning and thinking ahead about needs with limited resources. The solution is to link the work plan needs with the capabilities of software. News organizations with limited resources simply cannot go into a computer store or call a mail-order house and ask for "one of everything" from each product category.

The process is reasonably simple: Think about the types of information needed for the story or stories that are being written. Think about the location and form of that information. Think about what needs to be done to make it understandable and most meaningful. After these decisions have been made, take inventory of existing software and its capabilities. If the database analytical needs cannot be satisfied by the software, then some additional shopping may need to be done. Study the descriptions of the programs currently on the market and determine which one or ones can get the job done the easiest and in the least time. It may not be wise to buy expensive programs that offer many features and capabilities that are not needed unless there is the chance these functions may be used at a later date.

Low-Budget Solutions

A number of experts advocate using inexpensive computer software to get started. These programs are readily available and provide many of the most basic features of the more expensive versions. There is a trade-off, though. Because many of the advanced tools may not be included, the program may be slower in executing commands, may not have a polished on-screen appearance, may not have good documentation (if any at all), may have uncorrected errors (or "bugs"), may not be as flexible as the more expensive versions, and probably will not offer any technical support when problems are encountered. For many persons not able to spend hundreds or thousands of dollars solely on software, these options are appealing. This software is often called shareware, freeware, or a handful of other names.

Another option for some news organizations is to work out an arrangement with a software developer to become a test, or "beta," site. Software developers want their products tested in real-life situations before they are introduced for sale in the general marketplace. This may have particular appeal because it places the most current versions of programs in the newsroom at no cost. There are further benefits: The developers are anxious to interact with the users and offer instant technical support and a large amount of training. Furthermore, there is usually a price break offered when the final product is placed into distribution. "The most popular argument for becoming a beta site is that getting new technology ahead of others will offer a competitive

---

USING INEXPENSIVE SOFTWARE

There are numerous low-cost or free programs available via bulletin board systems, distributed through computer clubs, given to customers at computer stores, or through mail-order businesses. Some of these programs are in the public domain. Others are protected by copyright law, but are still distributed at no cost. For a news organization on a very limited budget, free or low-cost software may be one solution to cutting costs. Computer experts Andy Rathbone (1993) and Craig Crossman (1993) compiled these definitions:

Public domain—Free from copyrights or patents, these programs may be used by the public without compensation to the creators.

Freeware—A program to which the author owns the copyright but allows it to be distributed and used free.

Shareware—Copyrighted programs sold on a "try-before-you-buy" honor system. If a user tries and likes a program and continues to use it, the user must pay for the product.

Retail—Traditional copyrighted programs sold through retail or discount outlets.

Bannerware—Freeware that is distributed to promote another product.

Crippleware—A derogatory term used to describe programs that are distributed free or at low cost with certain features disabled. Users are able to get a "feel" for the program but not the full benefits of it. The user, to get the full program, must send in a registration fee.

Donorware—Shareware that requires users to make a donation to the program author's favorite cause.

Postcardware—Shareware that requires users to send the author a postcard instead of a registration fee.

advantage," argued former *Fortune* magazine board of editors member Bro Uttal (1993, p. 112).

But, like anything else that seems too good to be true, there are trade-offs. Beta sites have risks. Testing software can take time and attention away from other activities, such as reporting. New products can have bugs that could result in loss of work or data. Another significant concern involves newsroom ethics. Use of beta copies may conflict with some news organizations' ethics policies involving discounted or free use of products or services provided by businesses they may cover.

Copyright Laws Involving Software

Piracy and software licensing are two major problems users face when acquiring software. It is safest to remain "legal" with software, especially in a commercial environment such as a news company. In fact, many news organizations have strict corporate policies against using any pirated copies or otherwise unauthorized software products in company-owned computers. Software companies and some software organizations, such as the Software Publishers Association (SPA), are becoming aggressive in protecting their copyrights and often seek legal remedies to problems with companies that violate software laws. SPA, founded in 1984 to protect software authors and vendors, offers a free "Self Audit Kit" and software called "SPAudit" that helps newsrooms create an inventory of all commercial software to determine whether software installed on newsroom PCs is authorized. For a copy of SPAudit or if there is any doubt about proper use of software, contact the SPA in Washington, DC. Of course, the original software distributor may be helpful, as well.

Software piracy is a major problem. Some estimates indicate that about half the business software in use is pirated (Business Software Alliance, 1994) and that piracy cost U.S. programmers about $9.7 billion in 1992 and $7.4 billion in 1993 in lost income (Aversa, 1994; Rosenthal & Childs, 1992). Worldwide, the figure was about $12.8 billion in estimated losses to piracy in 1993. There are serious legal penalties on the books for violation of civil and criminal law at state and federal levels. Federal penalties under a 1993 law are wide ranging, including up to 5 years in prison and/or $250,000 in fines for the most severe cases of piracy that involve selling unauthorized copies.

Most software developers consider the *copyright* protection of their products no different from the copyright protection afforded a book. It is easier to think of matters in those terms. Borland International, a California company that develops and distributes Paradox among other products, offers what it calls a "no-nonsense" approach. According to the company's license statement (1993):

This software is protected by copyright law and international copyright treaty. Therefore, you must treat this software just like a book, except that you may copy it onto a computer to be used and you may make archive copies of the software for the sole purpose of backing up our software and protecting your investment from loss. By saying "just like a book," Borland means, for example, that this software may be used by any number of people, and may be freely moved from one computer or location to another, so long as there is *no possibility* of it being used by more than one person at a time. Just as a book can't be read by two different people in two different places at the same time, neither can the software be available for use by two different people in two different places at the same time without Borland's permission. (p. 1)

Of course, pirated copies of software do not come with documentation or technical assistance. For beginners, these may be major barriers that cannot be overcome. Even for experienced users of products, not having documentation and product support may mean not being able to take full advantage of the features offered by a program or loss of work or data due to problems caused by not using documentation.

Finally, a major problem in recent years associated with use of illegal copies of software is *viruses*. Viruses are programs designed by ill-intending individuals to cause problems with computer hardware and destroy or modify software, often resulting in the loss of data. There are numerous viruses circulating at any given time. There is no way of knowing, in some cases, where illegal software copies have been made and what safety measures were taken on those computer systems against software viruses. Even commercial antivirus software is not always able to detect the newest viral "strains." The safest way to avoid viruses is to buy new software that is guaranteed by its distributor.

WHERE TO GET ADVICE AND ASSISTANCE

Having support available and completing formal training programs are probably good ideas for journalists who plan to become involved in CAR or online news research unless there are computer-literate persons already on staff. For most news organizations, there are numerous options for advice and assistance with software applications:

- First, there may be others in the news department who are computer-knowledgeable and willing to assist even if these individuals—such as those in sports, entertainment, the news library, or graphics—may have other reporting, graphics, or editing interests. Helping with computing matters may be part of their newsroom responsibilities, in fact.
- Second, check with other company departments. Often, assistance can be found from computer-oriented persons in the information sys-

tems, business, advertising, or other departments of the news organization.

 • Third, consider available external assistance options. Consultants
and other experts can be brought in to assist over a short-term period
in particular situations. But these options cost money and sometimes
lots of it when time and travel expenses are involved. The major
advantages are the consultant's on-site coaching and hands-on attention
to specific needs.

 • Fourth, many professional organizations and colleges and universities offer noncredit continuing studies seminars and classes about
computers and software. For some individuals already in graduate
study, or perhaps considering it, there may be advanced courses in
journalism and business schools that are available for credit. At the
national level, the Investigative Reporters and Editors (IRE), National
Institute for Computer-Assisted Reporting (NICAR), National Institute
for Advanced Reporting (NIAR), the Poynter Institute for Media Studies, and similar organizations are taking the lead in providing hands-on
training and education involving computers, CAR, and online news
research. But these programs may not be offered frequently enough to
satisfy some of the more pressing needs of some news organizations.

 • Fifth, and finally, some larger retailers, hardware manufacturers,
and software developers and distributors offer seminars and classes
specifically devoted to their products. Schedules and agendas for the
programs are usually announced well in advance and the sites are often
moved to major cities around the country. Some of these programs,
however, can be quite expensive, up to $1,000, for a 1- to 3-day course.

SETTING UP PERSONAL
OR NEWSROOM SYSTEMS

News organizations, particularly newspapers that are using CAR and
online news research, already have a wide range of customized set-ups
which work for them. Figure 2.3 shows how four medium-sized daily
newspapers—the *Beaumont Enterprise* in Texas, the Gannett Suburban
Newspapers in New York, the *Knoxville News-Sentinel* in Tennessee,
and the *Eagle-Tribune* in Lawrence, Massachusetts—set up their CAR
and online research systems in 1994. There are some common elements,
but there is a wide degree of variation in how each decided hardware
needs, software acquisition, and online services.

   In setting up or improving an existing configuration, cost is always a
concern. There are ways to control cash expenses when there are limits
to the budget. Here are a few miscellaneous tips:

 1. *Bargain shop.* Wait for good deals.

Four Successful Startup Stories

▶ **Beaumont, TX, Enterprise**
- 75,000 daily circulation
- One IBM-compatible 486DX/33 MHz, 1.2 GB hard drive, CD-ROM reader
- DOS and Windows, WordPerfect, Procomm Plus, Lotus 1-2-3, FoxPro, SPSS
- Just beginning, but uses Texas state controller's office, Texas Employment Commission, and other government and private databases and BBSs

▶ **Gannett Suburban Newspapers**
- 170,000 daily circulation in Westchester, NY area
- 486/66 MHz, 350 MB; 386, 170 MB, and 286, 40 MB, two CD-ROM readers
- DOS and Windows, Word, Procomm Plus, Lotus 1-2-3, Paradox
- America Online, CompuServe, Dialog, Delphi, Internet, Nexis, Prodigy, credit information services, government BBSs

▶ **Knoxville News-Sentinel**
- 128,000 daily circulation
- Editor's personally owned 386SX, 80 MB
- DOS and Windows, Signature, Qedit, QuattroPro, Paradox, askSam
- CompuServe, PACER (East Tennessee federal civil court records), Internet, government databases, and private BBSs

▶ **Lawrence, MA, Eagle-Tribune**
- 56,000 daily circulation
- one 386, 350 MB; one 486/DX, 454 MB, one CD-ROM reader
- DOS and Windows, Word, Procomm, Lync, Excel, FoxPro, dBase, MapInfo
- Federal Election Commission, PACER, and other government databases and BBSs

Source: School of Communication, University of Miami, 1994.

FIG. 2.3.   Examples of how to start CAR.

2. *Buy products in "bundles."* Many manufacturers sell combined products to increase volume.
3. *Use mail order.* Doing business with an established and proven mail-order computer company can save large sums of money.
4. *Buy "last year's" equipment or software.* Last year's PC model can be just as useful and functional, but these older versions will cost less.
5. *Buy second hand.* Values can be found in the used market.
6. *Accept hand-me-downs.* Computers and software are upgraded. The replaced computers and software (be careful of licensing and copyright concerns, though) may be fine for CAR and online research.
7. *Rent hardware and software.* Test out whether CAR is what the newsroom needs by leasing expensive equipment and software.
8. *Comparison shop.* No matter where equipment and programs are found, there may be competitors to check out.
9. *Share resources.* Certain computer systems and software can serve dual purposes and be useful to more than one master.
10. *Use inexpensive software.* There are numerous low-cost alternatives. One is public domain software, such as shareware.
11. *Take advantage of upgrade deals.* Use product upgrade offers as a means to improve the quality of software used.
12. *Buy "no-name" products.* High-quality systems can be purchased, new, from no-name or "clone" manufacturers.

Getting help in setting up is important for all new computer users and even for many experienced users. Some companies will set up software and configure hardware; some do not. This is important to check before signing the purchase papers and paying the bill. If the help is needed, ask for it in advance.

There is also something called online help; but this does not mean dialing into a distant service for help. When it comes to software, it means on-screen assistance within the program. Many programs include help features available with the press of a key or two or the click of a mouse on an icon.

The third type of help is technical support available by telephone or online. Many vendors offer this for a limited time immediately after purchase. Got trouble getting the new program or modem to work? Check the documentation that accompanied the new product and it should include instructions for getting assistance.

Fourth, read the software manual. The documentation that comes with hardware and software generally is notorious for its inability to communicate with noncomputer-literate readers; but try. Many solutions to problems are found in the manuals.

II Online News and Information

3 Online Information: A 21st-Century News Reporting Tool

News research authority Nora Paul loves to preach the gospel of online information gathering. Paul digs up information about a person with her "people-finding" skills to demonstrate how effective online research can be for reporting. Paul, a faculty member at The Poynter Institute for Media Studies in St. Petersburg, FL, has become one of the nation's leading advocates for use of computers to search for both public and private information for news stories. Since she joined the faculty at the Poynter Institute in 1991, she has worked to convince journalists of the value of using computers to locate background information for breaking stories, as well as features and investigative projects. During her 12 years as a news librarian at *The Miami Herald,* she witnessed the metamorphosis of clipping-riddled musty newspaper "morgues" into state-of-the-art information libraries and research centers linked to other research centers around the world by telephone lines. Paul also witnessed the transition of libraries into database centers responsible for development and maintenance of "electronic clip file" databases.

"Computers have been changing the way journalists do their jobs ever since newsrooms threw out their old Royale typewriters and switched to cold type production systems," Paul says (1994, p. 2). "And just as computer assisted writing has changed the most basic newsroom function, computers are affecting other critical steps in the news-gathering process."

A decade and a half into her career as a news research specialist, Paul continues efforts to convince journalists that online news research is the consummate reporting skill of the 21st century. "Card catalog, printed indices, Rolodex and file clerk, thanks. You did a good job, but you can retire now," Paul (1993a) wrote in *The Quill.* "Libraries without walls, databases, cyber-sources, and government data-streams are replacing the traditional information tools journalists relied upon in the past" (p. 18).

The importance of electronic forms of information accessible from anywhere by just about anyone is not lost on Paul and her disciples.

"Online databases are the dynamite of the information explosion," Paul exhorts (1994, p. 5). "[D]atabases containing information on virtually any subject have been proliferating at a mind-numbing rate." Information, Paul likes to remind listeners by using a banking metaphor, is the currency of journalism and journalists need to learn how to operate this new form of automated teller machine. Why? Because reporters and editors often have to be their own bank tellers these days.

More and more, readers of news stories are finding tiny references to online research, such as credit lines and in-story attributions, and even source location and quotations gathered online. *USA Today* Reporter Lori Sharn (1993) demonstrated this in her 15-column-inch feature story about the television viewing popularity of the Hubble telescope repairs completed by shuttle astronauts. Her story was part of a 1-day spot news package of four stories produced by the newspaper on Hubble repairs. In the middle of her story were these two paragraphs:

> Computer networks are also abuzz with talk of the mission.

> On one CompuServe bulletin board, a Florida man claimed he saw Hubble's discarded solar panel wing glittering in the predawn sky as it orbited Earth Monday morning. (p. 11A)

"She had trouble finding some science-oriented sources, people who would be watching the repairs," said *USA Today* Special Projects Editor Larry K. Sanders (personal communication, January 9, 1994), who directs the newspaper's computer-assisted reporting efforts. "But once she started looking into the online forums such as those on CompuServe, she found what she needed. She was really excited about the success she had."

Many news organizations use online research dozens of times a day as part of their news-gathering routine. Gregory Lippert (personal communication, March 20, 1994), associate managing editor for *The Chicago Tribune,* estimates his newspaper accesses its own in-house database system about 300 times a day and accesses outside database systems about 45 times a day. Lippert, who supervises the *Tribune's* editorial systems support areas, sees clear advantages with online research: "First, it gives reporters information they need to (a) ask appropriate questions and (b) make a story more complete by putting it into context. Second, it adds authority to the information we publish. And third, it helps reporters avoid mistakes," Lippert (personal communication, March 20, 1994) stated.

Efforts are underway to teach reporters how to integrate online news research into every reporting assignment. Many daily newspapers, news magazines, and major broadcast news stations, such as the *Sarasota Herald-Tribune* in Florida, use online research for backgrounding on stories. Assistant Managing Editor Richard Estrin (personal communication, December 28, 1993) says, "Our effort is in its infancy, but we hope to involve everyone. We use online research for background to many stories."

Online news research is an everyday part of reporting and editing at the *Seattle Times,* where Information Systems Manager Steve Wainwright (personal communication, December 28, 1993) says his newspaper spends over $20,000 annually to use online tools to track down information about businesses and missing persons, for example.

At *The Dallas Morning News,* online news research has become a moment-by-moment part of the reporting process. "We use it nearly each hour of every day," said Assistant Projects Editor Allen Pusey (personal communication, December 29, 1993), who serves as liaison for use of computers by reporters and editors for his newsroom. "Online research has become a vital resource. Online research has given us a broader-based view of previous work on a subject *before* we begin stories. It has also given us a higher quality of context to our stories—be they economic, scientific, or legal/social."

For other news organizations, use of online research is the first step in starting a major news project after an idea has been generated. "We begin most projects by checking online to see what other publications have done on the subject," says *Houston Chronicle* Special Projects Editor Don Mason (personal communication, December 28, 1993). "Some of our best successes so far have been early reports on the Michaelangelo virus and issues involving encryption of telecommunications data as well as recent reports on electronic barriers to government information."

News organizations using online research have produced thousands of stories at least partially dependent on this tool in the past decade. Topics are wide ranging. Some examples:

- The *Rochester Democrat and Chronicle / Times-Union* in New York researches breaking stories about automobile accidents and stories about small businesses in its region.
- The *Quad City Times* in Rock Island, IL, investigates businesses by reading annual reports and analyzes the new and growing gambling industry in its Mississippi River region.
- The *Orange County Register* in California researched property descriptions, ownership, assessments, and assessors' maps using online tools when covering the Laguna area fires that became a story of national interest. The library staff also regularly conducts spot online research for major accidents such as plane crashes.
- The *Tallahassee Democrat* in Florida uses online tools to find background information about persons such as candidates for the city police chief position, candidates for the vacant presidency of Florida State University, and developers of real estate projects.

- The *Wisconsin State Journal* in Madison, like many other news organizations, routinely searches other newspapers online to see what its reporters are covering on certain subjects.

From these examples, it is apparent that computers have revolutionized newsrooms in a number of ways beyond writing and typesetting (Aumente, 1989). With news breaking at any time, the instant long-distance reach provided by online computer-based research is increasingly important for news gatherers. For some reporters, editors, and news librarians, online information gathering is the single most important change in news story background research since clip files were first developed. Journalists need only compare the cost of collecting the same information firsthand and it becomes apparent that online research is much faster and less expensive. This argument alone convinced many publishers and general managers to invest in online hardware and software and to budget for online user time each year (Martin, 1986).

DEFINING ONLINE JOURNALISM

Like other computer-based news gathering, online journalism has its own language. Some of the basic terms and their definitions are given in the following.

Online refers to one computer linked to a second computer by a telephone line. The information, which is transferred, is known as *datum* (singular) or *data* (plural). The link is completed by use of modems in each computer. *Modem* is an acronym for modulator-demodulator, the process data go through to be transferred over the telephone line. Technically what occurs is that the data in the computer of an online information provider are converted into an analog waveform by the modem to be transferred to another computer's modem, where the analog wave version of the data is transferred back into data (W. S. Davis, 1991).

Communications software refers to the program used to operate the modem or acoustic coupler. It permits communication between computers. Among the most popular commercial DOS and Windows programs are Procomm Plus, Crosstalk, Smartcom, DynaComm, HyperACCESS, CommWorks, and Mirror. Communications programs provide certain basic features for tasks such as dialing, automatic log-in, uploading and downloading, file capture, repeat dialing, and numerous "invisible tasks" such as transmission error checking.

Communications protocol (settings) refers to the variable settings, or parameters, used in communicating between computers. This transmission protocol is generally standardized, but to establish the electronic "handshake" between computers, these parameters must be in agreement to reduce error as much as possible. The parameters of concern in microcomputer communications include modem speed, parity, data bits, stop bits, and duplex.

To establish communication from one computer to another, a user must know the following information about the second system:

- *Baud rate.* One means of describing modem speed is baud rate. The rate refers to the number of transmission "events" that occur in 1 second, not the number of bits per second that are transmitted. Common baud rates are 2400, 9600, 14400, and 28800, but some modems are even faster.
- *Parity.* This is an error-checking procedure during transmission. Settings are usually "even," "odd," "none," "space," or "mark." For starters, use the "none" or "even" settings. Try "none" when connecting two PCs and try "even" when using a commercial online service.
- *Data bits.* These are binary digits. A communications program needs to know the number of bits—seven or eight—of each eight-bit byte that are going to be used during data transmissions. Some computer programs refer to this as the *word length* or *character length,* but the term refers to the same setting. Most PC-to-PC systems use eight bits. A PC-to-mainframe link, though, most probably uses seven.
- *Stop bits.* Asynchronous transmission operates through PCs using serial ports. Stop bits, or "stops," are marks used by sending computers to determine the end of a byte, or series of bits. The number of stop bits is a user option, either one or two. For most PC communications, one stop bit is the setting to use because it is the default setting in many programs such as Procomm Plus, but this setting must be in agreement with the system on the other end of the link. It is unusual to find a PC using two stop bits.
- *Duplex.* Duplex is the ability of a modem to send and receive data simultaneously. Modems that can do this are "full duplex" modems. Those that can only send or receive at one time are "half duplex." With a full duplex modem, what is typed is echoed back on the display screen. Most communications programs will provide the echo when the computer at the other end does not do so. If a connection results in double characters, change the setting from half to full. If no characters are echoed, change the setting from full to half.

There are a few other practical considerations. Users seeking to go online should consider using a second telephone line, perhaps even a separate line to share with a fax machine, but used only for data. This is especially important if online use is expected to be heavy. Touch-tone line service is preferred, only because it is faster in dialing, especially long-distance and access codes. Modems do work with pulse systems, of course. Some telephone systems, such as ones that do not use direct lines, also may have built-in problems dialing in and out. Persons with call-waiting features can also expect problems. An incoming call on a call-waiting line will disrupt communication and may disconnect the online link. There are ways to temporarily disable the service. For many systems, users can disable the call-waiting by dialing "*70" before dialing to connect with an online service. To disable call-waiting automatically, insert the "*70" before the number to be dialed with a signal to pause for a second or two. A short pause is usually designated by a comma in most communications software (e.g., "*70,,5555555"). Local telephone service providers can offer advice on how this is done.

DATABASE ACCESS AND THE COST OF INFORMATION

The *1994 Gale Directory of Databases* listed about 5,200 publicly available online databases and almost 8,000 total databases worldwide by one expert's estimate (Williams, 1994). These were produced by about 2,200 different sources. The directory also listed over 800 different online services. There are many more private and proprietary databases. However, information, even when it is accessible, is seldom free these days. Valuable, highly useful information is rarely inexpensive. Vendors, the companies providing the services, often charge premium prices for access to the information they have. Governments, at all levels, are offering the electronic data they collect to the public, also, and most services are bargains. But the price is not always as low as might be expected. Certainly the online services most commonly used can be very expensive, but still worthwhile for journalists.

Databases are collections of related information. One computer expert defined a database as "an integrated, centralized collection of an organization's data" (W. S. Davis, 1991, p. 180).

Online access to databases is not only convenient, it is very fast. For journalists, especially those on deadline, speed of access might be the most appealing element of online research. For a skilled news researcher, it may literally take only a few seconds using Lexis or another similar service to find the owner of a piece of property 2,000 miles away, or just seconds to find out the physical description and place of residence of an individual who has a driver's license and who was involved in an serious automobile accident just a few minutes ago.

As the use of database news research grows, so does the amount of information available (Murrie, 1987; Rambo, 1987). For example, at least 125 newspapers in at least 33 states and the District of Columbia have their full-text contents online for public access (Bjorner, 1992; Wall, 1991). There are literally hundreds of databases available to check—Dialog, perhaps the "king" of services, lists hundreds of databases through its massive system, for example. The number grows larger each month.

One of the reasons these full-text periodical databases have caught on is economics. Not only are these services valuable to the newsroom staff, but publishers have found these materials have a *public* market value also. In addition to being tools for their reporters and editors, these services, when sold publicly, are a big source of revenue for news media companies (Donovan & Schalit, 1989; Miller, 1988). Many major newspapers will conduct literature or news story database searches for the public for a per-search fee. The major television networks' news divisions are online through services such as Burrelle's Broadcast Database and will sell transcriptions of their programs as well.

Access seems to be becoming an economic issue, but there are other considerations. Privacy has been a major one in recent years. There are countless ongoing legal debates about access to public records kept in electronic databases. Some could be accessed online, but are not available. Others are available online, but are not available to many users because of high costs set by the providers or because of software, hardware, or other technical limitations. Economic issues involving access and distribution have led some mass communication scholars, such as Emerson College's David Gordon (1993), to anticipate an emerging society of information haves and have nots.

A form of what Gordon called an "informational underclass" may be developing within the news media. Numerous news organizations, especially small dailies, weeklies, and magazines that are not using online research, claim it is because they do not have money for hardware or the monthly online subscription and user fees or the expertise to use the tool effectively even if it were affordable. "We can't afford it and really don't yet know how to make best use of it," said Bill Weaver (personal communication, December 17, 1993), assistant managing editor of *The Macon Telegraph* in Georgia. Similar thinking comes from Sam Daleo, managing editor of the 23,000-circulation Kingston, NY, *Daily Freeman*. "We're a local paper and don't have a need for it," he explained.

Online databases come in two major varieties, *commercial databases* and *bulletin board systems*. Commercial database services contain useful information available to the public for a fee. Bulletin board systems are often free, requiring the cost of only the long-distance call, or charge a subscription or registration fee for users.

Commercial Database Services

The three major types of commercial databases are what Paul (1993, September) labels data superstores, boutique database services, and hybrid services. They are defined as:

- *Data superstores.* These are the major commercial database sellers such as Dialog (Knight-Ridder), Nexis/Lexis/Medis (Mead Data), Dow

Jones, and DataTimes. These companies have assembled large sets, or libraries of hundreds of different databases covering a wide range of content.

• *Boutique database services.* These companies specialize in certain types of data by category. Some, for example, offer public records access (e.g., TML Information Services) or television news transcripts (e.g., Burrelle's Broadcast Database).

• *Hybrid services.* These commercial database services are the ones with the broadest application and best-known names. The five major hybrids are CompuServe, Prodigy, America Online, Delphi, and GEnie. These services offer a rather amazing range of features from news to shopping and from E-mail to gateways to other databases.

Bulletin Board Systems

Some experts estimate as many as 40,000 bulletin board systems in operation in the United States alone. *Online Access* magazine listed more than 3,200 BBSs in one issue and more than 5,000 BBSs in another issue by state and city and how to connect to them. Although these BBSs serve many specialized purposes, they seem to fall into at least three different types of electronic or computer bulletin board systems (Paul, 1993a). These are commercial bulletin boards, linked bulletin boards, and stand-alone bulletin boards.

AN INCREDIBLE RESEARCH TOOL

Computer-literate reporters and news librarians have been the reason use of this method of research has grown in newsrooms in recent years (Chichioco, 1989; Garrison, 1992a, 1992b, 1994; Weinberg, 1991). Yet many reporters have not allowed this new high-powered research tool to substitute for their regular background research for a story. Instead, it has become a supplement for research on a news story (Jennings, 1989). CAR pioneer Elliot Jaspin believes personal computers help good reporters to "become better because they have a new tool for analyzing and building pieces of information into a complete story" (Jennings, 1989, p. 14).

Paul (1991b) believes it is time reporters become aware of the capabilities of their news library professionals. "For too long, librarians have been going to library conferences and talking only to other librarians. We've been writing articles for other librarians. . . . We know what we can do, but we need to do a better job telling our customers (you all) what we can do for you" (p. 3). Paul says good librarians are an important part of an investigative team and this fact is increasingly recognized by wise reporters and editors. "We can lead you through the forest of available databases and efficiently mine the resources that will help give you the background, the statistics and the source documents you need for thorough reporting of your story," she explained.

Luke Clark (personal communication, December 29, 1993), night metro editor and CAR director for *The Press-Enterprise* in Riverside, CA, a 165,000-circulation daily, argues that online skills are a necessity. "I see computer research as something that every reporter should know through regular use," he says. "Reaching that point is my current goal [at our newspaper]." The *Dallas Morning News'* Allen Pusey (personal communication, December 29, 1993) agrees. "It is odd that we in the information business seem to be some of the last to latch onto high tech research and communications tools," he says. "I think we are sometimes too naïve about new tools; we accept too expectingly and reject too habitually."

For those who have toiled long hours in libraries searching for literature on a subject, the computer is the best thing that has come along since movable type. Some news organizations were spending from $500 to $2,000 a month on searches in 1994, others even more if news research staff salaries, hardware, software, and training costs are included. In the 1994 University of Miami CAR study, 69 newspapers that reported their expenditures on online research reported an average of $17,210 a year, or about $1,434 a month. In 1993, 63 newspapers reported spending an average of $16,534 annually, about $1,378 a month. The other newspapers responding in the survey either did not use online services or did not want to divulge their spending habits.

Atlanta's Cable News Network (CNN) also uses databases extensively. But all online searching is conducted by trained news librarians to keep costs manageable. CNN Library Director Kathy Christensen said online research has increased each year since CNN began on-air service in 1980. CNN's librarians usually field requests from reporters by telephone. "When a reporter calls with a question, we talk to them to find out what they really want to know" (Blankenhorn, 1991, p. 18).

The databases have also extended the range and life of local newspaper content and network broadcast content. Users can read stories in newspapers from cities at the opposite end of the country. Network telecasts are now available in full text for use a day or years later, instead of the usual one-time viewing (Miller, 1988).

Commercial databases and BBSs offer access to "read-only" files that allow users to look at information but not modify it in any way. Users can download information into their computers to be printed or stored for later use. Usage fees are not inexpensive. Some run as little as $5 to $10 per hour during off hours, but others reach as high as $200 per hour for more exclusive systems at corporate, prime-time rates. Most searches cost $10 to $25 an hour, however, especially if they are done in off-hour periods. Prime-time premium database searches cost between

$60 to $150 per hour, but these rates may be well worth the investment in terms of time and travel expenses saved. *IRE Journal* Executive Editor Steve Weinberg (1991) said computer and databases are "yielding projects that would have taken years instead of months" (p. 21).

WHAT SERVICES AND BBSs ARE MOST USEFUL?

Popular newsroom database providers are CompuServe, Nexis/Lexis, Dialog/Knowledge Index, Dow Jones News/Retrieval, DataTimes, Prodigy, America Online, and Burrelle's Broadcast Database. These are national commercial services and users pay for the time they are "logged on," although some services such as CompuServe, America Online, and Prodigy offer unlimited use of basic services for a flat monthly fee.

Some databases used for literature searches and news research are electronic versions of indexes that have traditionally been published in hardbound form. The convenience is obvious, if the user is willing to pay for the time to do a broad search. Other databases are full-text abstracts of articles in other publications or newscasts, or indexes of articles. Any of these may be helpful to reporters and editors working on stories.

Many large public and private libraries are beginning to computerize their card catalogs for easier remote and on-site searching. But the scope of the databases is often limited to the last few years, primarily because of the high cost of entering acquisitions prior to beginning the database. Yet these databases are helpful in finding the most recent editions of books, or at least the most recent acquisitions by libraries.

These searches work on the same principle as the database searches: A user searches for the author, the title, or a subject in key words. Terminals set up in the card catalog room or elsewhere make the work convenient. If a user can get the access codes and telephone number, he or she can search the catalog of a local or university library with a personal computer in the office or home. Some libraries, to encourage use of such resources, will provide free access to appropriate individuals, such as students, faculty, and alumni.

Through computers, reporters can access the articles in most major daily newspapers published since the early 1980s. Some larger magazines and magazine groups are following suit. It is easy to find an article through a service such as Knight-Ridder Inc.'s Dialog, Mead Data Central's Nexis/Lexis, or DataTimes. Most major daily newspapers, many nationally distributed magazines, and national subscription newsletters are online in one or more database locations. Many specialized journals, trade publications, and other periodicals are also online. Some publications are not only online in an archival capacity but also are online for "same-day" access to their contents. For example, *The Washington Post* and the *Detroit Free Press* can be read on CompuServe.

A number of other newspapers and magazines are beginning to make immediate online access to their contents available through other services.

A computer database of periodicals called Info Trac is available in many libraries, but it operates with a CD-ROM drive reader and is not online. It includes newspapers and magazines and is comprehensive in scope. The service includes recent reviews and uses the Library of Congress subject headings. The service is provided by Information Access Company and encompasses its Magazine Index. A growing number of newspaper full-text databases are being sold on CD-ROM discs for unlimited access also.

TURNING ROUTINE STORIES INTO SOMETHING SPECIAL

In Rochester, NY, the *Democrat and Chronicle* uses online research regularly, says assistant metro editor John Reinan (personal communication, December 19, 1993):

> We use it nearly daily. Metro and business are really the only users. There was a fatal car crash last summer in which five people died. The driver was accused of running a stop sign and hitting another car. By logging onto the New York Department of Motor Vehicles database, we found that the driver had a previous conviction for running a stop sign, and we included that info in our first-day story. We had a business reporter doing a story on starting a small business which used a lot of information obtained from an SBA [Small Business Administration] bulletin board.

Griff Palmer (personal communication, December 19, 1993), who helps find online sources for Oklahoma City's *Daily Oklahoman,* says his newspaper uses online services such as DataTimes to take stories to a higher level of completeness:

> We use online research daily to supplement our reporting. We constantly use DataTimes and our own electronic morgue, which is stored as a full-text database. As a recent example, we used DataTimes to research allegations of improprieties in other states against a contractor under local consideration. We also used the Texas Ethics Commission BBS to download registration information on a company under investigation in Oklahoma for campaign contributions violations. We have also downloaded census data from the state commerce department BBS for use with analysis of voter registration data.

As these examples demonstrate, searches such as those in Rochester and Oklahoma City can turn routine news into highly effective stories.

Reporters and news researchers who incorporate online tools into their work find their stories are more comprehensive. Online tools permit more depth and breadth of information. It becomes easier to find similar situations elsewhere. Generalizations about situations, a tradition common among news and feature writers, without examples or other forms of evidence in stories are less common when online research is a regular part of reporting.

Reporters and editors also find they have a wider range of sources, because they can use online sources, such as articles from newspapers halfway across the country, to identify and locate these experts and other sources that enhance a story. Not only do sources used in other stories become easier to find, there are even online services designed to link reporters and news sources. Often these are public relations services—such as ProfNet, the computer-based network of universities and colleges that have hundreds of experts on virtually every subject on their faculties who are willing to help journalists. ProfNet is an Internet- and commercial service-based collection of over 640 public information officers (PIOs) at more than 300 research centers and universities. Reporters and editors seeking sources with specializations or expertise in a certain area can make requests through ProfNet to find their sources. And the sources are not just in the United States: The system is global. Reporters making requests within ProfNet can post queries about sources and usually get a response of some sort within 1 day or so. The service is hosted at the State University of New York at Stony Brook. Through the PIOs, reporters and editors have access to approximately 300,000 experts on ProfNet (Noack, 1993).

Reporters are also more easily able to find officially released information. Government agencies, corporations, and other organizations that want their word to be spread have discovered that computer-wise reporters and editors will use such online sources when they are available at low cost or free. PR Online is one such service. For the 1994 Winter Olympics, the United States Olympic Committee set up a sophisticated high-speed BBS—complete with downloadable text files, regular team announcements, information about the games, news, and E-mail—for sports writers and others interested in following the U.S. team's efforts. The only cost to use the service was the toll of a long-distance call to Colorado.

THE INFORMATION HIGHWAY

It is a very tired metaphor after the burst of media attention it received in the early 1990s, but just about everyone in the communication industry has heard the expression "information highway" used. Some critics have written that it has been used so much and so carelessly that it now carries little specific meaning. Discussed for more than a decade, the concept of an information highway has come to represent many things to many people. It is not a single proposal. Instead, it is a term representing different approaches to computerizing communication around the world. For most computer users and information "techies," it simply describes a national and international network of people and computers. This nationwide computer system would provide a wide range of up-to-date and practical information to users, entertainment such as digitized television, films, and music, and other similar content. It is expected to link homes, businesses, libraries, schools, factories, and any other place where people seek or provide information in many different digitized formats.

The on-ramp to that system at present, naturally, is the ability to go online. That may change in the future to include cable, microwave, or satellite connections, but telephone lines are up and running for those wishing to use the massive system. "This is more than just cable TV on steroids. Think of it as a level of interactivity not seen since the invention of the telephone," wrote *Popular Mechanics* Electronics Editor Frank Vizard (1994). "Multimedia communication—image, sound and text combined—can happen in the blink of an eye" (p. 29).

"The information highway as conceived in both public- and private-sector proposals is more a framework than a working system, but it raises important questions about what kind of information people need and who will deliver it," writes Everette E. Dennis (1993, p. 1), executive director of The Freedom Forum Media Studies Center in New York.

Some government officials and industry experts expect the information highway to serve 1 million or more households in 1995 and to be completely in place at some point during the period from 1999 to 2003 (U.S. Government Books, 1994). Other estimates by experts at a national communications summit held in 1994 said it would take 20 years and $400 billion to put the system in place (Elber, 1994).

"What emerges is a sort of Wild West of Infotainment," cautions one writer (Morse, 1993, p. 24). "If we're not careful, we could get stuck with another hodgepodge of mostly useless and boring services. . . . So we face a challenge, and given how much the government intends to spend, we also face an opportunity."

There is concern about the lack of federal policy regarding the information highway. A 1994 Freedom Forum Media Studies Center symposium gathered experts who expressed concern about the lack of "rules for the road." Two areas of concern, according to Attorney Anne Wells Branscomb at Harvard University, are copyright law and liability for content of information riding down the highway (Grady, 1994).

While information and communication industries and federal government leaders sort out the policy that will be the map for this 21st-century highway system, millions of individual users are already on the road.

THE INTERNET

One big part of the information highway is growing exponentially in the mid-1990s. It is called *the Internet system*. The Internet is a massive computer network often associated with any serious discussion of the information highway of the coming century. One estimate says at least 17 million people in 20 countries are already using the Internet (Herz, 1993). The Internet has become a model for what a worldwide computer system, with any computer as an entry point, could become. Figure 3.1 shows the remarkable growth of the Internet host computer systems over the period from 1988 to 1993.

The recent Internet explosion has both immediate and unimaginable potential for journalists in gathering and distributing information. It demonstrates the online future in this tiny piece of the online present. A nationwide computer network for information storage and retrieval will not just be used for E-mail, a common purpose of many users in the mid-1990s. For sophisticated drivers on the information highway, it also means movement of significant information from source to reporter and use of distant computing resources. Although this is a selling point of the major commercial services in the 1990s, the Internet is expected to

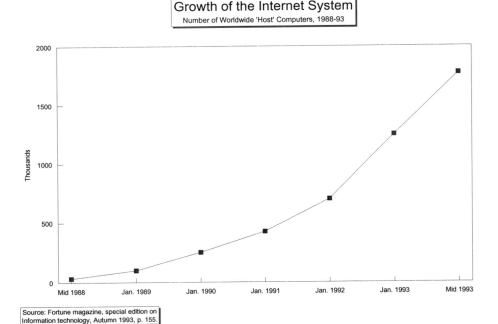

Growth of the Internet System
Number of Worldwide 'Host' Computers, 1988-93

Source: Fortune magazine, special edition on Information technology, Autumn 1993, p. 155.

FIG. 3.1. The rapid growth of the Internet.

link more users in more locations at less or no cost—what most experts feel will be an unsurpassed degree of participation.

What exactly is the Internet? It is a global collection of computer systems and networks, all linked with a common goal of sharing access and information. Tracy LaQuey and Jeanne C. Ryer (1993) describe the Internet as "a loose amalgam of thousands of computer networks reaching millions of people all over the world" (p. 1). LaQuey and Ryer note that the Internet has grown well beyond its original purpose of permitting researchers access to expensive mainframe computer systems at distant research sites. "The Internet has demonstrated such speed and effectiveness as a communications medium that it has transcended the original mission" (p. 1) they wrote.

The immediate value of the Internet to journalists is only now being realized. Some reporters, editors, and news researchers are using it to find information for stories in the same manner that commercial online services and bulletin board systems are being used. Clearly, this is an instant and familiar use for online "junkies." The libraries of information are a virtual gold mine for journalists. Many of these are:

- *Institutional library card catalogs.* Many major institutional libraries' card catalogs have gone on line.
- *Full-text periodical databases.* These include journals, newsletters, newspapers, and so forth.
- *Index databases.* A number of specialized index databases that have been created by organizations are available.
- *Internet-based bulletin board systems.* These are similar to BBSs discussed earlier.
- *Campus and institutional information systems.* Events calendars, telephone directories, local weather, job openings lists, policy manuals, and so forth that are related to a particular institution such as a college, university, or research institute.
- *Data archives.* Some organizations make databases created during research studies available for public access. These include a wide range of studies, but include such things as public opinion polls, crime data, population data, and so forth.
- *Software archives.* Many institutions and organizations archive public domain and shareware software designed for specific purposes. These can be accessed and downloaded.
- *Supercomputer access.* Some major computing centers are accessible through the Internet, but these require accounts and passwords and a reason to use them, of course.

Access to the Internet can literally be gained from any personal computer connected to a telephone line with a modem. It is the Internet's file transfer protocol capabilities that appeal to many users. There are

---

USING NICAR-L AND IRE-L ON THE INTERNET/BITNET

Journalists wandering around the Internet may encounter numerous information-filled features such as list servers. Two of them are designed expressly for journalists interested in computer-assisted reporting. IRE-L is an acronym for the Investigative Reporters and Editors List, and NICAR-L is the National Institute for Computer-Assisted Reporting List, services started in 1994 and owned by IRE and NICAR at the School of Journalism at the University of Missouri.

The lists' scope includes postings, correspondence, and other information pertaining to use of computers by journalists. List subscribers trade information, offer comments, and use the locations as gathering spots for discussion of common interests.

Individuals need only an electronic mail address and access to the Internet to join the list. To subscribe, send only the following E-mail messages:

SUBSCRIBE IRE-L *<your real first name and last name>*
SUBSCRIBE NICAR-L *<your real first name and last name>*

Send the brief one-line message to the list server and it will automatically pick up the sender's electronic mail address. You will receive a confirmation and should begin receiving messages from the list server within hours. The lists' addresses are:

LISTSERV@MIZZOU1.MISSOURI.EDU *(for both IRE-L and NICAR-L)*

---

numerous commercial database service providers, such as the hybrid services, that have already made access to the system, at least for E-mail purposes. Some, such as Delphi, have made complete access to the Internet possible. Others such as CompuServe, America Online, GEnie, and Prodigy, are expected to offer it as well.

Freenets are a popular means of Internet access. These are public bulletin board systems that are funded by individuals and organizations that are part of the National Public Telecommunication Network based in Cleveland. A growing number of these are connected to the Internet.

Access to the Internet through Delphi and BIX (its sister service) and other commercial vendors will cost the user whatever online charges are amassed. Access in other manners may not cost users at all. For instance, a journalist who is affiliated with a local college or university as an adjunct professor may have access to the institution's computer system. Or the news organization may purchase or lease access to a local college or university's information system and thus open the Internet door.

There are numerous other ways to access the Internet. The Berkeley, CA-based Information Access Technologies Holonet provides access for businesses and individuals. BIX, Portal, CERFnet, Telnet, IDS World Network, and numerous local BBS connections such as Halcyon (Seattle), Panix (New York), and Cyberspace Station (San Diego) are examples of other network service providers. There are also numerous regional and statewide networks that provide access. Examples of these include Colorado Supernet, OARNet in Ohio, and VERnet in Virginia. There are other systems already in service and simply too many others adding on monthly to list.

Cost factors are always a concern. Many services permit access for a monthly or annual rate. Connection may cost under $10 a month, but access time charged by the hour or fraction of an hour is the big cost, of course. This can be very low in off-peak times.

GROWING ONLINE USE AND APPLICATION

Contemporary journalists are part of an information generation. More and more information is being preserved and is available to the public. It may take a generation or more, but this enormous amount of public and private information is gradually becoming more usable. Information is entering the hands of the masses and, as this happens, there will be more applications of this information explosion.

One obvious manifestation has been the increase in the computerization of public and private information and the growth of an industry to make that information more easily available to the public, especially journalists. Online services growth has been rapid. In 1992, one study estimated the online services industry to be worth $9 billion annually and involving more than 4 million subscribers (Rosenthal, 1992). Just as the number of users is growing, there is an increasing number of information providers. These are third-party organizations or individuals who serve the public by searching and retrieving information that has been requested. News organizations have offered a variation of this for hundreds of years, of course. But newspapers and other information companies are also making databases and other information they have developed available for the public.

Aside from news companies, there is an increasing number of *information specialists,* or *information brokers,* who make a living by finding information for people. Information brokers create, obtain, retrieve, and use information for clients (Burwell, 1992). This industry has developed because some people do not want to find information themselves or have such rare occasions to search for it, they would rather pay an expert to search and retrieve it for them. To a certain extent, this "let someone do it for me" attitude prevails in some newsrooms. A form of information broker has emerged there also. These are individuals such as reporters or editors known to be able to master the computer to find information. At larger newspapers, it may be news librarians who have developed a specialization as online researchers using these tools.

ONLINE SEARCH STRATEGIES

Jean Ward and Kathleen Hansen (1993), University of Minnesota journalism professors, have developed an orderly approach for searching for information. "The essence of the information age is a constantly rising quantity of information, matched by increasingly sophisticated methods of making that information available," Ward and Hansen believe (p. 3). "Communicators need a conceptual tool that can help them learn where information is located and that offers them a routine for collecting it. . . . *Search strategy* is a systematic means of acquiring and appraising information that will illuminate a subject."

Ward and Hansen acknowledge that the new technologies of information storage have introduced new potential sources that require new research skills. Their model is a general approach, one that offers an overview to how to find what is needed for a news story or any other form of mass communication. The model offers five layers:

- *Question analysis.* Refers to the step of narrowing down and defining the information needed.
- *Potential contributors.* Indicates the three major types of information sources that can be used. These include informal sources (discussions, observations, experience), institutional sources (private and public organizations), and library and database sources (most important, this includes online sources).
- *Interviews.* Discussing information found in the preceding stage to glean meaning and further information about the subject.
- *Selection and synthesis.* Making sense of all the information by bringing together facts, ideas, interpretations, and points of view.
- *Message development.* Producing the news story.

This model is a useful map for where to go when researching any story. The focus of this book, of course, is on one part of one level, but this model places online news research in its greater, more sweeping context of the information-gathering process reporters often use.

Information consultant Tom Koch (1991), who is also a journalist, strongly believes that online news databases have changed how reporters approach information gathering. Koch feels "electronic libraries are a unique information source that empowers writers and changes their relations to the subject" (p. 186). The traditional research model, he argued, was geared to finding one particular piece of information that could be used immediately by a reporter or editor in preparation of a story, perhaps even on deadline. The system worked well until electronic databases came along.

Electronic database search strategies have developed into both an art and a science of their own. Searchers find information by interacting with software that manages the database contents. Unfortunately for beginners, just about every database service has its own language and command structure for retrieval of that information. Some systems offer two approaches. The first, a more direct approach, requires specific instructions on a command line. Experienced users of a database often prefer to use these because they are faster and more direct. The second is more helpful to beginners because it uses a menu-based system of commands in a "tree" metaphor. Selection of one option leads to another and then another.

Key words are at the heart of any type of electronic searching. Key words are identifiers a searcher uses to find information in a database. These can be words, numbers, phrases, or combinations of words. The computer database software will attempt to match the search command with elements of the database and present these to the user on screen or in printed, offline, form.

Searches can occur at two distinct levels on many services and the user can determine how he or she wishes to conduct the search. One level is called *global*. The other is *local*. Global searches will check all files in a library or all libraries in a database service after the search is defined. Local searches focus on a single database in a library or a single file in a database, or even a single part of a file. Local searches save time and turn up more specific information if enough information is known before the search begins. Global searches are all-encompassing and work best when limited information is known or when a lot of information is needed quickly.

Wildcard searches are a convenient means of finding related information. Two major forms of wildcard searches are commonly used. The

---

HIERARCHY OF DATA ELEMENTS

Stephen P. Harter (1986), a professor in the Indiana University School of Library and Information Science, has developed this table of seven levels of online data elements, from the smallest to the largest element, in an online database:

Data Element	Example	Text Represented
Bit	1 or 0	----
Byte	01001100	&
Subfield	(Place of publication)	Chicago, Illinois
Field	(Publication statement)	Chicago, Illinois: Academic Press
Record	(An ERIC Index Record)	(A full bibliographic citation, abstract, search descriptors, search identifiers)
Database	(The ERIC database)	(Hundreds of thousands of records)
Library	(All Dialog databases)	(Hundreds of databases)

asterisk (*) is used to search for multiple characters following a specific string. For example, "journal*" would find such terms as "journals," "journalism," "journalist," and so forth. The question mark (?) is used for a single character wildcard. Searching with "journal?" would likely find only "journals."

Some database service software and some database programs also offer *case sensitive searches*. These searches distinguish between words which are capitalized. "Brown" could be a name, "brown" could be a color, and "BROWN" could be an acronym representing something, such as the name of a group, completely different from a name or a color. Without choosing for case sensitivity, all three usages would be identified by the database to be retrieved for the user.

There are six major forms of searching online full-text services, bibliographic or index services, and databases in tabular, or table, form:

- *Boolean logic language.* This algebraic approach to searching focuses on three logical operators, "and," "or," and "not." When combining two key words, A and B, with "and," all documents or files containing both terms will be retrieved. Using the "or" operator, the expression "A or B" will retrieve all documents or files containing one or the other, or both, terms. Use of "A not B" retrieves all items containing A, but not B.

- *Proximity searches.* These searches permit users to find information by locating two or more words or phrases within a certain "distance" from each other in a text file. The distance can be designated in different units, but most often it is in words or sentences. Words identified in a proximity search do not always have to be in the same order as requested.

- *Phrase searches.* These inquiries seek only a specific string of words or numbers in that particular order. Usually phrases are identified by use of quotation marks or brackets to distinguish them from proximity or Boolean searches.

- *Numeric searches.* These searches are most often used in tabular or formatted databases in tables. They use numerals as criteria for identifying information. Numeric operators include "greater than" ($>$), "greater than or equal to" ($>=$), "less than" ($<$), "less than or equal to" ($<=$), "equal" ($=$), and "not equal" ($< >$). When these are used with a number, the retrieved data are selected only if they meet the criteria.

- *Field searches.* Fields are columns or variables in a database table. Searches can be designed to search single fields for specific words, numbers, or phrases.

- *Date searches.* Both text and tabular databases can be searched for dates. Some databases can select records or documents for both single ranges, dual ranges, and comparisons. Single ranges will search for records or documents in connection with a single date (e.g., before or after a given date). Dual range searches select records or documents

Saving Money With Smart Searching

- Download instructions and read them offline.
- Clip articles about online research tips for specific services and save them.
- Omit common words (such as prepositions and articles) when devising key words.
- Broaden a search by using "or" in key words.
- Truncate search terms by using wildcard characters (e.g., an asterisk).
- Write several combinations of key words in case the first try does not work.
- Capture your entire session online and read it after the online session ends.
- Read specialized publications before searching.

- Double-check spelling of key words, especially names.
- Take advantage of online help offered by many services. Also use toll-free help lines.
- Post questions about searching on BBSs and databases to SYSOPs. They can help.
- Check out the thesaurus of key words provided by some database services.
- Use technical language of the field from which the database you search originates.
- Limit your search to a specific time span.

SOURCE: Adapted from Cathryn Conroy, "Tips on Making Your Best Research Guess," *CompuServe Magazine*, September 1993, *12*(9), p. 14.

FIG. 3.2. Tips for efficient online searching.

within a range (such as July 1, 1994 to June 30, 1995). Comparison ranges select in relation to a given date (e.g., within 180 days of December 31, 1995).

Searches can be combined as well, but the range of combinations and number of combinations will depend on the software used to search the database. A common multiple search, for example, would be to simultaneously request a phrase search and Boolean search or a phrase search and a proximity search. There are numerous ways to search efficiently. Online expert Cathryn Conroy (1993) suggests several strategies in Fig. 3.2 and online authority Barbara Quint (1991) lists seven stages of conducting an online search in Fig. 3.3.

USING AUTOMATED DIAL-UPS AND SEARCHES

There are numerous ways to access online services. Most users access services through their communications software and use the service based on its built-in command interface for users, but some of the major services have designed and distributed their own software packages that eliminate the need for a communications package. These *information managers* seem to do it all. Popular information managers offered to members are distributed by CompuServe, Prodigy, America Online, and Nexis/Lexis. These programs have features that include automatic dialing, log-in, file download, electronic mailbox checking, printing

Avoiding Online Search Frustration

✓ Conduct a reference interview or reference research

✓ Construct a tactical overview (determine limits)

✓ Select databases to search

✓ Formulate search strategy

✓ Conduct the search online

✓ Review search results

✓ Present final search results

Source: Barbara Quint, "Inside a Searcher's Mind: The Seven Stages of An Online Search," *Online*, May 1991, *15*(3), pp. 13-18.

FIG. 3.3.   Steps in conducting an online search.

output or saving output in other forms such as files, and log-off. Information manager software packages make interaction with the service easier for beginners. These "shell" programs do not require a great depth of knowledge about the service by users and are often preferred by novices.

Script files are another option. Script files offer a different form of automatic online services, often much more customized than information managers can provide. But script files require the user to know a little about computer programming in the communication softwares script language. Many script file users develop these miniprograms for automatic log-in, automatic electronic mail checking, or automatic file uploading or downloading.

USEFUL ONLINE SERVICES FOR JOURNALISTS

Reporters, editors, and news researchers will quickly learn what online databases and their particular services are most helpful to their own particular informational needs. News story research potential is perhaps highest on the list of advantages users experience. Close behind is the people connection online news research provides. Online systems permit communication and contact with sources and other journalists in instant fashion. E-mail is one such example of the fast and effective communication online services provide. Another useful feature is special interest subject libraries, bulletin board systems, or forums. These are small collections of public discussions, downloadable files, reference materials, and other information related to specific subjects.

RISKS IN USING ONLINE DATABASES

Most good things have a down side. With online research for news reporting, there comes a danger zone. Database services can be, and have been, abused by unknowing journalists. Beginners, in particular, often do not think about the quality of the information that is contained in an in-house "electronic morgue" or a commercial service. It can contain errors.

The two most common errors are *factual errors* and *misquotations*. Reporters, especially those under deadline pressure to produce, overlook this potential problem and do not check information to confirm its accuracy. This seems to be a necessity in a digital research world. Another problem is depending on the same sources that other reporters have used. Although online services can be helpful in identifying national and regional experts or other useful sources, some reporters who do not go further only perpetuate use of the same people over and over. This reduces diversity of sources and perspectives, especially on national stories. There is a tendency, as some journalists have described it, for these problems to multiply or "feed on themselves" as the errors are used, reused, and reused again (Rowe, 1994).

4 Commercial Online Services and CD-ROM Databases

When a man went berserk and shot up a Long Island Railroad commuter train loaded with people heading home from work, killing five New Yorkers and injuring 20 more, it was a national story happening in the backyard of *Newsday,* Long Island's award-winning daily newspaper. Utilizing all of its wide range of reporting sources meant quickly assembling a large team of reporters, editors, photographers, graphic artists, news researchers, and others involved in the news-gathering process. The tragic event occurred late on a Tuesday. Within 24 hours, the man accused of the shootings was identified by police and a major story detailing his life and profiling the once-unknown individual was produced by the team of reporters for the Thursday morning *Newsday* edition. Reporter Kevin McCoy wrote the overall story, but he had the help of no fewer than 21 other staffers in the newsroom.

Much of the information in the story came from firsthand interviews conducted by the army of reporters. Their goal was to learn as much about the accused man, Colin Ferguson, as possible. But an important part of the process of discovering the details of the life of Colin Ferguson was to thoroughly check all the available online information sources at the disposal of *Newsday.* McCoy's story integrated the many interviews with online news research to detail the life of this individual who wrought such carnage on a holiday-season train full of commuters.

McCoy and the team of journalists used commercial online database services to access public records and also checked original hard-copy versions of other public records not accessible online. Members of the team learned about Ferguson's several complaints to local government authorities, of his problems at Adelphi University, and they dug into his personal background. They learned where he was born and when, details about the neighborhood where he grew up, and where he went to school. They obtained immigration records, marriage records, his parents' death records, school records, U.S. citizenship records, worker's compensation complaint files and records, telephone call logs in the governor's office, court records of lawsuits filed by Ferguson, and criminal complaint records. A significant part of this document searching was done quickly, using online tools.

According to *Newsday* Editorial Technology Manager Mary Ann Skinner (personal communication, January 3, 1994):

> Our newspaper's biggest success with online research is providing access to information that we don't have room to store or the budget to subscribe to. Reporters have more sources to help them track down experts and people important to stories. Editors at *Newsday* believe that computers should be used as another reporters' tool. They don't look for computer-assisted reporting to be the driving force of a project. They encourage reporters to use it wherever they see a need for it.

For nearly two decades, journalists have enjoyed the advantages of online news research. Nearly *two decades?* Yes, such services have been available since the mid-1970s. Some newspapers have been building their own online full-text electronic morgues since the early 1980s and a few insightful news companies were investigating the possibilities of full-text storage and retrieval in the late 1970s. Some online full-text, bibliographic, and index databases began to appear in that era, but these were mostly devoted to subjects in the physical and medical sciences and designed for academic uses.

Even though online research has been around for two decades, to many journalists, commercial database research is something relatively new. To the newcomers, it is the tool of the 1990s. And it *is* a tool for this decade. Perhaps it is *the* reporting tool of this decade. Online research is experiencing a growth unknown in the past two decades, caused in part, if not entirely, by the personalization of computing. More people have computers and the knowledge of how to use online services.

Some computer specialists feel the world of online services is moving into its third generation in the middle of this decade. The first generation began in the mid- to late 1970s. A user simply connected a video terminal to the service's mainframe computer using a telephone line and modem or acoustic coupler. Output was entirely text and information transfer speeds were quite slow compared to those in the mid-1990s. The second generation of online services developed with the commercial offerings of CompuServe, Prodigy, and America Online. These are the services as most users know them in the mid-1990s—featuring text, greater interaction speed, and graphical user interfaces. The newest generation of services has begun to emerge. These new systems take advantage of the greater computing power at both ends of the system. Third generation online technology should change the way users interact with the systems, says *New York Times* computer columnist John Markoff (1994). The new systems will use the greater speed and other features of the user's computer instead of simply linking it as a "dumb terminal" to another system in a remote location. Among the features will be multitasking, for instance, and using the programming power of the user's computer to search distant computers and use their resources. One example of the new generation, Markoff says, is Ziff-Davis' Interchange, which debuted in 1995.

It is a standard procedure at many daily newspapers and other news organizations, as demonstrated in the preceding chapter, to use online research tools when researching major news projects and, more and more, when covering daily news stories as well. Commercial online database research has taken a place alongside the telephone and fax machine as a contemporary news-gathering tool. For those who use online searching for information, there is no longer an acceptable substitute. "Although some editors are beginning to question whether new technology is helping or hurting the quality of journalistic work, they admit that the computer has become a staple in most newspaper newsrooms, and life for some journalists is easier, or at least faster," University of Missouri researchers Brian S. Brooks and Tai-en Yang (1993, p. 2) wrote.

Virginia Commonwealth University Researcher Cynthia De Riemer (1992) argues that the attraction of commercial database services has been caused by technological enhancements in newsrooms. "The widespread adoption of computer technology in the writing and retrieval of news has led to the availability of a variety of databases useful in the reporting process," she wrote (p. 960). Database access, she observed from her research, is dependent on newsroom management. "[T]he entire issue of database access is a management decision but is linked to database use by news personnel and the development of expertise among news personnel," she discovered. "[U]se of databases . . . by newsroom personnel is clearly not a novel activity which will soon fall into disuse" (pp. 969–970). She found, as logically might be expected, that newsroom use of commercial online databases increases as time passes.

PUBLIC AND PRIVATE COMMERCIAL DATABASES

Online research use is growing at what seems to be an incredible rate. One recent estimate predicted as many as 20 million computer users of all types will be online in the United States by the end of the 1990s (Morgan, 1992). A national news magazine estimated 12 million users already online and 20 million users worldwide in 1993 (Kantrowitz, 1993). Another estimate placed 6 million people subscribing nationwide to the mass market services by 1996. In contrast, fewer than 1 million persons or businesses used such commercial online services in 1988 (Resnick, 1993c). Prodigy, a widely popular commercial online service marketed toward a more general audience of computer users, was posting about 70,000 electronic mail messages daily in late 1992 (Morgan, 1992).

University of Illinois Researcher Martha E. Williams (1994) has studied the worldwide database industry for more than two decades. Williams determined there were 8,261 databases available for public use at the beginning of 1994. Nearly 7,600 of those databases had unique subfiles or represented families of databases rather than single databases or files. More impressive, perhaps, is that this number has grown from only 301 in 1975 and 773 in 1982, and the figure is increasing steadily in the mid-1990s. Furthermore, Williams states that the number of producers—the organizations that develop databases, and vendors, those entities that distribute and add value to the database by providing services for customers—has also increased dramatically. There were only 105 producers and 200 vendors of databases in 1975. In 1994, Williams reported almost 2,800 discrete producers and more than 1,600 discrete vendors. In sheer number of searches, the industry has grown from about 750,000 searches in 1975 to 51.8 million in 1992. To show the amount of recent growth, the number of searches jumped 50.1%, from 34.5 million, from 1990 to 1992.

"While numerical growth is indicated by the statistics, the success of the database industry is largely a result of the transition of the information industry from paper-based services to computer-based services and can be measured in terms of the use of computer-readable databases, or the number of searches," Williams noted.

All this usage and all these databases indicate the increasing commercialization of online access to information. As more commercial enterprises begin, more private databases are entering the marketplace as well. According to information services expert Kathleen Webb (1993):

> The basic lure of going online, as the advertising for any commercial online service indicates, is the tantalizing promise of having the world at your fingertips. Join our service and see the world of information without leaving home! No more unnecessary trips to the library in nasty weather, just cozy up to the terminal, in your pj's if you like, fire up the machine, and explore new realms in the endless vistas of data available at a keystroke.

> The attraction is irresistible for increasing numbers of Americans who want and need to keep up with the rapid pace of change in a global community, whether for business, research, or personal purposes. For those who do not have access to, or do not require, more specialized online database services, popular commercial services are a great value. [H]owever, not all personal online services offer equal amounts and types of access to the world at large.

The idea has caught fire at Michigan's *Flint Journal*. Mary Ann Chick Whiteside (personal communication, January 5, 1994), news media manager for the 110,000-circulation daily newspaper, oversees CAR projects and sets up online staff training classes. "The publisher just approved an electronic library, so I expect more people to become comfortable with online research," she explained. "Reporters are eager to learn. My classes fill quickly. There are times when I could spend entire weeks on computer projects."

Some experts feel commercial online services will evolve much like the early television networks did in the 1950s, through trial and error with the market. Those experts believe online users will manipulate the dialing directories of their communications packages much like dials or remote controls on television sets. Eventually, the strongest will survive (Morgan, 1992).

"Today, the nation's five largest mass-market on-line services—Prodigy, CompuServe, GEnie, America Online, and Delphi—count close to four million subscribers, mostly personal computer users who log on for everything from sending e-mail to managing their investments and businesses," wrote Rosalind Resnick (1993c, p. 20BM), a Florida free-lance business writer and author of *Exploring the World of Online Services*. "For businesses and other consumers of instant data, the on-line information explosion could not have come at a better time. Not only is more and more text and financial data coming on-line every day, but the major services are locked in a battle for market share that can only work to the benefit of savvy subscribers."

Until recently, up-to-date research information had been difficult to obtain. A reporter seeking information about a book or an author, for instance, would have had to check a local library's card catalog or look it up in what may have been a 1-year-old or even older edition of *Books in Print*. Now, that same reporter can check the current card catalog of a local library online or go into a commercial online service to check the regularly updated electronic version of *Books in Print*. Or, at a nearby library, he or she could check the monthly update of *Books in Print* on CD-ROM.

For a novice, the range, depth, and levels of information online can be mind-boggling. Online services are aimed at different markets. Some are oriented to general computer users, such as families, students, and small businesses. Others are designed to serve highly specialized information needs. News reporters, editors, and librarians find information gathering crosses all levels and categories of information, just as the news covered every day does.

There are thousands of public and private databases in the commercial online market and even more in private use, but not for public purchase. There is a growing number of databases that are not only online, but also available on CD-ROM discs or, occasionally, available only on CD-ROM. The growth of the CD-ROM market is as staggering as the expansion of online services has been in the first half of this decade.

Most commercial database vendors are information companies. Many of the major communication companies are building databases as well. Many of these corporations are familiar names: IBM, Knight-Ridder, Sears, Dow Jones, Dun & Bradstreet, Media General, Turner Broadcasting System, Standard & Poor's, Tribune Company, General Electric, McGraw-Hill, Prentice Hall, West, Mead Data Central, and R. R. Bowker.

The industry, as any in a growth mode, is experiencing numerous changes each month. Mergers occur, databases are renamed and combined, and the vendors offer new features to attract users. But many of these database services are not operated by journalists, nor do they devise access systems with reporters and editors particularly in mind. Many of these online systems are designed for either general consumer members or highly skilled users such as professional information searchers and news librarians.

Interactive online communication is changing shape. Most users think of it as a two-way communication street, but most of the traffic goes in one direction—from the information service to the subscriber. The growing use of online consumer and business transactions, such as buying and selling, shopping, finance and banking, and travel arrangements, is changing the online landscape. Even news organizations are getting more involved in making the online world more of a truly two-way interaction by communicating directly with readers, for example. The industry is vast and getting larger monthly.

Use of online services as *gateways* has become a more and more valuable feature. Gateways are computer devices used by some online services that allow connection with third-party computer networks or systems. A gateway, technically, is used to connect systems that are not compatible to make them able to transmit information back and forth in a subscriber-usable form. An example of this is the well-established commercial service, CompuServe, located in Columbus, OH. A member in Los Angeles who has accessed CompuServe can use a third computer system, such as American Airlines' EAASY travel information and reservations system, in a third city (Dallas) to check available flight times and make reservations for a flight, a hotel, and a rental car, and even check the weather while planning an upcoming trip.

The Internet has also stimulated considerable interest in online services in the past several years. The initial excitement and interest began to grow rapidly in 1993 and 1994 as more people became aware of, and could access, the information highway. The combination of the vast array of online services, linking such information gathering tools as online databases and worldwide networks such as the Internet, will make online news reporting tools even more appealing to journalists in the latter half of this decade.

USES OF ONLINE AND CD-ROM DATABASES

There are a number of different applications of online and CD-ROM databases of interest to journalists. These include:

- Full-text databases (including the major subdivision of news services, and news organizations).
- Bibliographic or "reference" databases.
- Patent and trademark databases.
- Dictionary databases.
- Directory databases.

There are also "source" databases that are numeric, alphanumeric, and full text. Although journalists may use all of these categories from time to time, focus is on full-text databases, bibliographic databases, and news services as well as other news organization databases. As Indiana University Library Science Professor Stephen Harter (1986) noted, these database frameworks are convenient for thinking about databases, but these categories are neither universally used nor are they always mutually exclusive.

Full-Text Databases

Full-text databases offer the complete text of a primary document such as a newspaper or magazine article or a transcript of a press conference or speech. Newspapers, magazines, news services, and newsletters are most often archived in full-text form. These offer the entire text of the article, plus other important bibliographic information such as the date published, author, publication name, and page number. In some databases, key words have been added to assist in searching.

Encyclopedias, commonly found on compact discs as well as online, are a good example of a full-text reference tool that can be useful to journalists from remote locations. Some online directories and listings books are full text, identical to the published, hard-copy volumes. Other full-text databases include organizational reports, press releases and other public relations material, and transcription services that provide the full text of television programs and public events such as press conferences and speeches.

Bibliographic Databases

Periodical indexes and abstracts are two examples of bibliographic databases. These online and CD-ROM databases are high-quality reference tools for finding specialized literature.

Bibliography and reference databases such as the Educational Resources Information Center (ERIC) of the National Institute of Education, a government database, are also valuable to reporters seeking information about a wide range of subjects.

News Services Databases

Associated Press and United Press International, the nation's leading news services, offer online access to news as it is distributed through their usual networks to news organization members and subscribers. There are different forms of these services, such as AP's abbreviated service for the commercial mass market online services and AP's full-text national wire, which is accessible through several online services. Dow Jones, which has its own online information service, has many of its news and features from the Dow Jones News Service available.

Reuter, the European-based world news service, is also available online through several services. Most major daily newspapers, many nationally distributed magazines and newsletters, and regularly distributed reports are available in different forms online.

MAJOR COMMERCIAL DATABASES
AND ONLINE SERVICES

Which commercial databases at the national level are the best to use for news research or other information gathering purposes? It depends on who is asked. Different information professionals, such as news researchers, prefer different combinations of sources for each unique situation. Of course, much depends on what the services offer.

There are different classes of online database services. The three major types that Paul (1993a) identifies are data superstores, boutique database services, and hybrid services. For beginners just learning about online services, the hybrid services are the best place to start. For more sophisticated researchers and computer-comfortable users, the data superstores and boutique services are the electronic sources of choice.

"Most professional database searchers we know automatically turn to specific databases when asked for news information. Nexis . . . DataTimes, Dow Jones, NewsNet, and, increasingly, Dialog, certainly are logical places to do comprehensive, retrospective searches for newspaper and news wire coverage," wrote *National Geographic* Assistant Library Director Ellen Briscoe and former *Washington Post* News Research Center Chief of Research Catherine Wall (1992, p. 28).

"What marks the good researcher from the rest of us is knowing what paper is pertinent, how to get it, how to understand it," wrote information consultant and investigative reporter John Ullman (1993b). "Databases, of course, are a great playing field leveler, making information equally available to those with mega resources and those with meager" (p. 1).

The most popular databases in newsrooms in 1994, determined by the national CAR study conducted at the University of Miami, are commercially available services. Among "first choices," CompuServe was the favorite of 18.8% of the newspapers. Other leading services included Nexis/Lexis (15.8%), local databases (12.9%), DataTimes (11.9%), and Dialog (11.9%). For all services named in the "top three" in use in the newsroom, Nexis/Lexis was mentioned by 15.7% of the newspapers. Others frequently named included Dialog (13.9%), CompuServe (13.5%), local databases (10.9%), and DataTimes (10.9%). With no single service being named more than one in six times, the study clearly shows wide variation in use of online services.

Although not all databases or database services used in news research are described in the following sections—there are far too many—there are some that have risen to the top in terms of their value to reporters, editors, and news researchers. The services listed here are the major ones used in news organization libraries and in newsrooms in the 1990s:

America Online (AOL). This fast-growing company with about 1 million subscribers offers a wide range of commercial services and features. In addition to electronic mail, AOL offers communication through bulletin boards, learning tools and reference sources; news and financial information such as full-text news services; computing and software information and references; lifestyle and personal interest groups and information; people connections through electronic "chat rooms"; and a wide range of travel and shopping services, games, and other entertainment.

Burrelle's Broadcast Database. A major database service providing broadcast news program transcript retrieval is Burrelle's. Its online service is still relatively new to the electronic library world, but this full-text service will become more and more useful to broadcast journalists interested in national television and radio reporting about a subject (Ojala, 1991). Burrelle's offers network news programs from ABC, CBS, and NBC.

CompuServe. CompuServe, located in Columbus, OH, is one of the largest and oldest commercial online services, listing about 2 million members in 120 nations. CompuServe provides an extremely wide range of online services from electronic mail and mail-order shopping to news and other information. CompuServe offers about 1,700 databases and services oriented to sophisticated computer users (Magazine joins CompuServe, 1993).

DataTimes. DataTimes provides full-text newspaper and other periodicals files from across the country and certain international locations. As a result, DataTimes is quite popular among news organizations as a research tool. DataTimes provides access to the text files of more than 640 information sources, including national publications such as *U.S. News & World Report* and *American Banker.*

Delphi. Delphi is a general consumer-oriented online service based in Cambridge, MA. Its greatest strength is that it provides complete access to the Internet. It was the first online service to do so. Delphi also offers special interest groups, including one focusing on use of the Internet. These special groups, like CompuServe's Forums, provide access to large amounts of information about special subjects.

Dialog / Knowledge Index (Knight-Ridder Information). Dialog and Knowledge Index are broad Knight-Ridder services containing hundreds of highly specialized databases for subscribers. It is the world's largest full-text and bibliographic service online. Dialog is the more complete and more expensive version of the two systems, offering hundreds of major full-text databases. Knowledge Index is the after-hours version of Dialog with a smaller selection of databases from which to choose. It is available for access through CompuServe, although it is a portion of Dialog.

Dow Jones News / Retrieval. Dow Jones News/Retrieval features databases focusing on business, markets, and the financial world. For some business and finance beat journalists, this database is the definitive source for online information. The most useful databases, perhaps, are the full-text files of the *Wall Street Journal* and the Dow Jones News Service.

GEnie. GEnie is a commercial information service with features similar to those offered by America Online, CompuServe, Delphi, and Prodigy. It provides members with access to a wide range of services such as electronic mail, bulletin board systems, and a wide range of travel databases. Like other similar services, GEnie offers a number of gateways to other services.

Lexis / Nexis. Lexis and Nexis are full-text Mead Data Central services. These are actually two separate services among eight originating from the same company. Lexis and Nexis are two of the most popular and most widely used databases in newsrooms. Nexis provides complete text files of a number of national publications.

Prentice Hall OnLine. This specialized service provides access to public records of interest to journalists and business executives with a total of more than 250 million public records.

Prodigy. Prodigy quickly became one of the largest commercial consumer database services in the early 1990s with an aggressive marketing effort. Prodigy is oriented to the general computer consumer market and is a good introductory tool to online services. It offers some 800 basic features including access to general news, sports, business, and features, reference materials, bulletin boards, and support groups.

Washington Alert. Washington Alert is a Congressional Quarterly service that updates users on legislation, provides full text of bills and resolutions, lists abstracts and text of the *Congressional Record,* the *Federal Register,* and other public domain documents, votes, member and district profiles, staff member profiles, and other information related to the activities of the Congress.

Other useful database services. There are many other databases and database services. The most popular online services at newspapers in the United States are listed in Appendix B.

Broadcast and Government Transcript Databases

There are other online sources of broadcast news and other types of transcripts in addition to Burrelle's Broadcast Database. Not only are broadcast news programs available through online databases, but so are government press briefings, press conferences, speeches by leading government officials such as the president, vice president, and cabinet members, and congressional hearings.

CompuServe provides online access to transcripts of major programs produced by Journal Graphics, but the actual full-text is not on the system. Instead, online users place an order for a transcript and it is faxed or mailed to the user. The advantage is a wider range of information sources, and the "Transcripts" service through CompuServe also includes Cable News Network newscasts. Dow Jones News/Retrieval online includes transcripts of its latest *Wall Street Week* programs. And NewsNet's Hotline provides abstracts of political news from the previous day that features a database known as "TV Monitor." It summarizes television news reporting (Ojala, 1991). Nexis offers full-text transcripts of ABC News and full-text transcripts of the *MacNeil / Lehrer Newshour* from the Public Broadcasting System. Delphi offers full-text transcripts of PBS's *Nova* and *Frontline.*

The Federal News Service, a part of Federal Information Systems in Washington, DC, has been providing transcriptions of major federal government public events for a decade. Press briefings and speeches, for example, from the White House, State Department, and Defense Department are staples of this daily updated database. The service also offers translations from selected events such as press conferences in Moscow (Wall & Williams, 1992).

The Reuter Transcript Report has been provided by the Reuter international news agency since 1989. Similar to the Federal News Service, this database offers transcriptions of press conferences and speeches from major executive branch sources in the federal government in Washington. Reuter also offers international access to selected transcribed world-level news events such as press conferences or speeches by world leaders (Wall & Williams, 1992).

Despite the obvious advantages to finding something that was said by a newsmaker on the air, there are problems unique to broadcast news and public event transcription databases. Marydee Ojala (1991), an information consultant based in Kansas, says the foremost problem is the visual component of television news. It is seldom represented and, when it is, users find only brief parenthetical material supplied. She also says live interviews are a search challenge. "People interrupt each other. They talk over each other. A sentence might begin far away from where it ends," she warns (p. 40). The shorter, more conversational writing style might also cause search problems not encountered in print-oriented databases, she says. Repeated stories in newscasts are also a minor concern. The major future area for development of these broadcast news databases will be major-market local news stations.

ONLINE CREDIT RECORDS

Private commercial credit reporting services are another major source of online information. Credit records are maintained for a variety of reasons on just about every adult in the country. Credit records, because of the personal nature of their information, are highly restricted databases.

The federal Fair Credit Reporting Act sets the rules for disclosure of this information. Usually a user must submit specific legitimate reasons for seeking information such as employment, loan applications, and other credit situations. Credit services managers claim they have worked hard to self-regulate themselves to follow the letter of the law, if not also the spirit of the law. These businesses provide limited forms of their credit reports for more general public consumption that do not violate the federal credit information reporting law. Even in stripped, or restricted, form, these files can be a tremendous asset for reporters or news researchers involved in "people finding" or searching for background information about individuals or businesses. The most common information available to the general user in a credit history will be residential address, birth information, social security number, spouse, and employment history.

The three major national online credit network services are TRW Information Services in Dallas, CBI-Equifax in Atlanta, and TransUnion Credit Information in Chicago (Naylor, 1991; Piller, 1993). NCI Network in Ohio also maintains a massive credit information service of millions of consumer credit reports and commercial credit reports on businesses for qualified users. Each of these services maintains hundreds of millions of credit records in numerous databases.

As with other online databases, caution is necessary in using the credit databases because of errors and because of legal concerns involving privacy laws. Consumers Union, publisher of *Consumer Reports,* says there are numerous errors, some serious in nature, in these reports (Naylor, 1991). Error rates run as high as 43% to 48% of the records, including some errors in 19% of the records that could cause credit application rejections (Piller, 1993). Using this type of information for facts in a story may be risky, if not outright dangerous. Instead, as many reporters and news librarians do, the information should be used to locate additional personal information and people from other sources. Then the two sets of information can be used to verify facts through more conventional reporting strategies such as interviewing and firsthand observation.

Another growing set of concerns involves the unethical, and often illegal, access to information contained in credit reports. Credit services sell certain basic information, such as names, addresses, and telephone numbers, to the general public for a search fee. Other financial records are not supposed to be sold by the services to the general public, including journalists. Some news organizations have been accused of using access to credit databases improperly to obtain credit ratings, credit card balances, mortgage balances, and related personal data that are protected by state and federal laws. Even in cases where access is legitimate, there is growing concern about public access to this information and the conflict with privacy interests.

GROWTH IN CD-ROM AND OTHER PORTABLE DATABASES

The number of news organizations and individuals using CD-ROM drives and discs is growing rapidly. Similarly, the number of CD-ROM-based databases available to the public is growing as fast or even more quickly. As shown in Fig. 4.1, there were about 6,200 CD-ROM software titles published and placed on the market in 1994, about triple the number of the total 2 years earlier. In the 1993-94 CAR study conducted at the University of Miami, it was determined that 40.1% of the nation's newspapers had CD-ROM drives for use in newsrooms. A total of 2.9% had more than one CD-ROM in the newsroom. Both figures, it appears, will continue to increase. Many newspapers that did not have CD-ROM drives indicated plans to acquire them in the near future.

CD-ROM is an acronym for "compact disc, read-only memory." This form of disc storage differs from floppy disk storage in that most floppy disk drives can both write data to the disk and read data from it. CD-ROM technology exists to do both as well, of course, but drives that

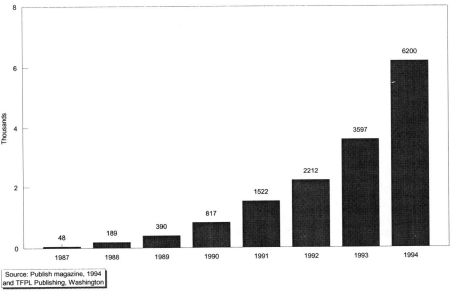

FIG. 4.1. Recent growth in CD-ROM publishing.

can read and write remain expensive and are affordable by few news organizations or individuals.

Read-only compact disc drives are quite inexpensive by comparison and are currently installed in many off-the-shelf personal computer systems, especially those designed for multimedia software. The best single advantage of a CD-ROM disc is its high capacity of data storage. A CD-ROM disc can store about 600 MB of information. This compares to 1.44 MB of storage on a conventional 3.5-inch double density diskette. The CD-ROM disc's capacity makes it ideal for large databases that do not require updating, such as census data or large full-text databases.

CD-ROM drives work by use of laser optics technology rather than the magnetic storage used in conventional diskettes. These units are often rated by access speed time in milliseconds. CD-ROM drives used for loading software or reading databases can also be used by PCs to play music or other audio if the computer system is equipped with a sound card and compatible speakers. For a home system, especially, this gives the CD-ROM drive additional use for the single investment. In addition to the costly optical read and write drives, there are also devices, called optical WORM (write once-read many) devices that permit writing to the disk only one time but unlimited readings from the disc.

Like most other computer hardware, CD-ROM drives have dropped in price in recent years. Users interested in upgrading an office or home system can get a very fast CD-ROM drive and interface kit (cable, card, and device driver software) for $500 to $1,000 and a slower, older technology CD-ROM drive and interface kit for as low as $150 to $200. If speed is not a major concern, then the investment is minimal considering the database advantages that become possible. Someone considering the investment for the newsroom or for home should visit a computer store or a library and try one out.

Users may be accustomed to relatively low prices for CDs that contain music or other audio, but database CDs can be quite expensive, ranging from under $20 to hundreds or thousands of dollars. A typical interactive multimedia encyclopedia—complete with video and sound—on compact disc can cost several hundred dollars. The advantage, of course, of the large initial investment is that there are no recurring access fees or hourly online rates about which to worry.

The most popular databases available commercially that are useful to journalists include U.S. census data; reference works such as dictionaries, almanacs, encyclopedias, and thesauruses; telephone directories; full-text collections of specific authors or collections of topics by subject; periodicals indexes; atlases; specific full-text databases of newspapers and magazines; and other noncensus statistical sets such as sports and finance data.

The most popular CD-ROM titles in U.S. research libraries include PsycLIT, ERIC, ABI/INFORM, MLA International Bibliography, and MEDLINE. These are abstract, index, and reference discs to assist in finding more detailed information in other places (Tenopir, 1992; Tillotson, 1993).

5 Using Government Databases

Why do some communities grow and prosper whereas others deteriorate and eventually die? This was the tough question that reporters and editors at *The Detroit News* wanted to answer when they began research and reporting for a major series focusing on behind-the-scenes political connections and agendas in the Detroit metropolitan area. Editors believed these connections had driven suburban Detroit growth since the late 1940s. Reporters Laurie Bennett and Robert Ourlian spearheaded the project. "*The Detroit News* series 'Hidden Interests' demonstrates the effectiveness of reporting that combined traditional legwork with the use of sophisticated databases," *News* Editor and Publisher Robert Giles (1990, p. 16) told readers. "Reporters . . . utilized these old and new approaches to give readers a revealing picture of the hidden agenda behind two generations of public debate over race, crime, white flight, unemployment, downtown abandonment and suburban overdevelopment in Metropolitan Detroit."

Bennett and Ourlian, both 36 when the 6-day series was published, are experienced reporters. They combined interviews with numerous business, civic, and academic leaders with an in-depth analysis of several local government records databases. These databases came from public sources and were developed from scratch using public documents going back to the 1940s. Databases with information about area real estate and people were either obtained or generated from scratch. The first set of databases focused on elected and appointed public officials, salaried officials, the officers and partners in thousands of companies, licensed real estate agents, building contractors, bank records, political campaign contribution records, political action committee records, and local government financial archives. Another set of databases focused on real estate developments such as subdivisions, condominiums, shopping centers, and office building projects records. The massive project came together when the reporters merged the two major sets of databases to get a master profile of the connections between and among these various groups, their constituencies and interests, and real estate development in the Detroit area.

After combing several metropolitan area government databases, conducting hundreds of interviews, and assembling the project, the newspaper published approximately 15 full-size pages of stories, charts, graphics, and photographs telling readers the ways in which many local public officials routinely mixed their public lives with private real estate interests. Stories described numerous officials who were found to have financial stakes in public growth and development policy. The review of secrets, deals, and contracts might not have been as comprehensive or it may not have been as easy to see the links without use of government databases and personal computing tools. "We are all very committed to what [database-oriented analysis] is clearly becoming a staple of good reporting," notes *News* assistant managing editor Mark Hass (personal communication, January 5, 1994), who supervises CAR efforts at the *News*.

Just less than 200 miles to the southeast, in Cleveland, Dave Davis and Ted Wendling, veteran government reporters for *The Plain Dealer,* got interested in the effects of radiation in trying to report about a radioactive chemical spill at a local clinic. Officials refused to reveal certain information about a nearby school that had been contaminated by the spill. The reporters did not take no for an answer and soon began making federal Freedom of Information Act requests to the U.S. Nuclear Regulatory Commission (NRC) to find out about the school. One thing led to another. About 1,000 requests later, they had a pretty good picture of a significant national problem: People were suffering and dying after being treated with overdoses of radiation therapy.

Davis and Wendling developed a major investigative project idea for the topic and their editors approved. The eventual series, "Lethal Doses—Radiation That Kills," told readers that mistakes in hospitals around the nation, combined with lax NRC standards in investigation and enforcement of safety procedures, led to numerous patients who experienced health problems. It led to the overexposure of at least 413 cancer patients who died from treatment—something that seems unimaginable in the 1990s. Although many of those deaths were of terminal patients, the reporters stated in their articles, the radiation overexposure left wounds that did not heal and hastened the deaths.

To produce the project, Davis and Wendling interviewed 150 sources, reviewed more than 10,000 documents, and used computer power to analyze from 1.5 to 2 million NRC records through the online federal government nuclear document system database called "NUDOCS." Both D. Davis and Wendling (1993) know their project would not have come together without access to those records. "The series could not have been done without access to the NRC's online database, NUDOCS. We spent hundreds of hours searching and analyzing the 2 million records on NUDOCS, looking for leads on radiation accidents and victims," they wrote (p. 1).

Davis, who is in charge of CAR for *The Plain Dealer,* said NUDOCS only provides summaries of the documents. After a document summary is found online, the full document must be obtained in person, by telephone call and return mail, or by return fax, from the NRC's Public Documents Room in Washington, DC. Davis said a project of this magnitude needed ample research and interview time and high-level newsroom support to complete the investigative work. "We get pretty good support. The newspaper recently spent $80,000 on equipment and expectations are high," Davis (personal communication, January 5, 1994) said. "Editors are good about providing time for CAR projects."

There are thousands of local, state, and federal government databases such as those used by *The Detroit News* and *The Plain Dealer.* Governments are the second-largest producer of publicly available databases in the nation. Private commercial and industrial sources are responsible for 75% of databases available for public use. Government agencies produce about 15% of databases, and not-for-profit and academic sources—many funded by government grants—generate 9%. The remaining 1% is from mixed sources (Williams, 1994).

This is a dramatic change from the situation in "pre-PC" days. In the 1960s and 1970s, the government was the leading source of database production, responsible for as much as 56% as late as 1977. But that figure dropped to 21% less than a decade later. Mixed producers, such as more than one government agency or level of government, account for a number of government databases as well. Most prolific in database production, historically, have been the National Aeronautics and Space Administration (NASA) and the NRC (once known as the Atomic Energy Commission). Numerous databases produced by the Bureau of the Census are widely used by news organizations and account for a significant proportion of government databases in use by the public in the mid-1990s. More and more of these databases are available through remote access. Although many remain available only on site, numerous government agencies at all levels are placing their useful databases into public access with online, compact disc, or magnetic disk access.

State and local governments produce and update thousands of useful databases each year. These include such potentially newsworthy subjects as licensing, permits, crime and courts, welfare, automobiles, agriculture, consumer affairs, housing and residences, corporations, voting, pollution, businesses and their operations, education, banking and finance, sports, gambling, lotteries and gaming, taxes, and just about anything else in life that is regulated.

Government database access is achieved using one or more of these distinct methods:

- Direct access to a host computer through a commercial "gateway" computer.
- Copies of databases sold to an information provider.
- Direct access to the host computer provided by the government.
- Records collected and processed into a database by a commercial information provider.
- Synthesized voice databases. (Paul, 1991a)

There are other methods, also. Some news organizations purchase raw data tapes for original analysis or reanalysis by reporters. A second more common method is to access information that has already been processed, analyzed, and prepared for public release. This is done online in one of the most popular trends in the mid-1990s to access government information: electronic bulletin board systems. Most electronic bulletin board systems have menu-driven commands to guide unfamiliar users through the system. Government BBSs usually provide references, news or announcements, message services, question–answer files, press releases, report abstracts or full-text report files, and general background information about the agency. Some are so in-house, however, that they are virtually useless except to employees or contractors (Krumenaker, 1993). Many federal or state agencies have set up their own BBSs. One popular example is FedWorld, operated by the National Technical Information Center. FedWorld is discussed in detail later in this chapter.

A fast-growing application of computer information processing power is to conduct secondary analysis of raw data. This is much more sophisticated, may require high-cost processing, and may be beyond the skills of most reporters. Nevertheless, some reporters are learning these procedures and moving to use a helpful investigative tool.

Some government agencies simply do not have information in computers that reporters need for their stories and reporters still have to enter the data themselves to build an original database for analysis. One example of this problem involved the federal Bureau of Alcohol, Tobacco and Firearms (ATF). James Stewart and Andrew Alexander, Cox Newspapers national correspondents based in Washington, DC, sought to learn about the use of assault weapons in crime for a series for the Cox newspapers. The most important information they needed was not available from local metropolitan police departments, private groups, or even the Federal Bureau of Investigation. Turning to ATF, the two reporters found boxes of noncomputerized records at ATF's massive warehouses, but the agency would not permit the records to be taken from the warehouse. ATF had stopped computerizing its records because of budget cuts. Stewart and Alexander were given a budget by their editors to set up six rented personal computers in the warehouse with six temporary clerks and keypunchers. The team keypunched the 15 months' worth of data. The process took more than a month but resulted in a package of stories that was sent to all of Cox's newspapers. "If they (government officials) tell you that the information is not available, find a way to make it available. Eventually it will pay off," Stewart said (Chichioco, 1989, pp. 20PC–21PC).

State BBSs are growing in number. Most contain the same sort of information, concluded Larry Krumenaker (1994), who compiled a list of major state BBSs for *Online Access,* but there is wide variation in quality. Most state-oriented BBSs offer population data, economic data, tax information, wage statistics, and industrial statistics. Some also offer legislative bill tracking. "Unlike the federal government—which supports over 100 useful BBSs—the states are 50 little drawfs running around in different directions," Krumenaker wrote (p. 32). "We couldn't even find electronic services for 11 of the states. Several states we questioned were downright hostile to the idea that mere 'people' have the right to know how things are going at the capitol." Among the 79 services he listed, Krumenaker found three trends that were surprising. First, he said states that are supposedly high tech are not necessarily the best and those that are not known as high-tech states often have the best BBSs (e.g., Montana, Nebraska, and Kansas). Second, he determined that nearly half the public services charge user fees. Third, only one state service, "Kansas INK," offered access to the Internet.

TYPES OF INFORMATION AVAILABLE
TO THE PUBLIC

There is an enormous amount of federal, regional, state, and local data about human behavior and other aspects of the world around us that is being collected. Census and crime data may be two of the most used databases by journalists, but there are other types of information being collected, compiled, and processed each day. Yet much of that information is just collected and remains in a warehouse or on a magnetic tape somewhere, never released to the public. Some data are retained by government agencies in paper form and never entered into computer databases. But the data could be used if they were viewed as possibly newsworthy by a reporter. Great quantities of other government data stored in electronic form remain unused by even the bureaucrats and agencies that collected the information.

There are at least eight different types of federal, state, or local government information available online, on compact disc, on magnetic tape, diskette, and in other archival forms that may interest journalists. Records, quite simply, are kept on almost all aspects of our lives. The major types of government records include:

- Corporate records (state level).
- Uniform Commercial Code filings of business data such as debtors and secured parties (state level).
- Motor vehicles, accident reports, and driver's license records (state and local level).
- Bankruptcy filings (state and federal level).
- Official Records Index, a locator for documents (state and local level).
- Real estate records (local level).
- Tax liens (state and federal level).
- Civil courts cases (local, state, and federal levels). (Paul, 1991a)

Among those most able to recognize the potential of this sometimes amazing, sometimes baffling, collection of information are investigative reporters. According to *The Miami Herald's* Steve Doig (personal communication, December 16, 1993), who directs CAR at his newspaper:

> To me, the real sad thing is that most government agencies have been computerized for a long time. So much data now is routinely collected and never studied by not only people on the outside, but by the agency itself. Invariably, when we do one of these computer-assisted projects, on drunk driving or whatever, the agencies are as amazed as anybody else—"My God, are we doing that?" they'll say. They don't know what's there either. They don't have time to do it. Just being able to generate statistics out of their data is not something that they're doing. Maybe it's not their mission or whatever.

The big problem in depending on government agencies to release information is that it has to be analyzed and interpreted by government statisticians who may be looking for something different from what a reporter seeks. One such situation may be that a federal government official looks at a database from a national or regional perspective, whereas a reporter wants a more localized point of view. Many times this is not available if news organizations wait for the agency to report certain statistics or other information gleaned from a database. In fact, this scenario seems typical on many stories. There are occasions when interpretations will vary or, simply, an agency representative will not acknowledge that a particular phenomenon exists.

This occurred to reporters at the *Lexington Herald-Leader* in Kentucky. Reporters and editors were anxious to learn about the spending patterns of the Appalachian Regional Commission (ARC), a federal agency that distributes aid to poverty-stricken regions of the several states in the Appalachian Mountains area. A *Herald-Leader* reporter discovered the ARC was spending twice as much money in one Pennsylvania county than it had budgeted for the entire state of Kentucky. News researcher Robin Luger (personal communication, September 9, 1993) recalled the problem and how the newspaper's own analysis of data got to the issues quickly:

> There was a debate about what the ARC had done in Kentucky. How much had been spent? What did they spend it on? What were they doing? When our reporter made the phone calls, he had solid numbers in front of him about the spending, compiled in a way that even the ARC had not compiled it. It was ammunition for background. He wasn't depending on other people's interpretations. If you had called the ARC's press office and said, "Are you doing this?" they would have said "No." So that's the joy of using CAR, to be able to say, "Well, here's what you're really doing compared to what your press release says you're doing."

FEDERAL AGENCY DATABASES

For several decades, getting either original or processed databases out of Washington or the many other locations of the federal government's bureaucracy meant a reporter or editor had to pick them up in person, order them by telephone or mail, and then, perhaps, load them onto a mainframe computer using nine-track tape. Or, for those fortunate reporters and editors with a budget, it meant going to a third-party commercial information vendor for the "value-added" database product—usually at a much higher price. Changes in computing and the way reporters use computers have turned all that into what seems like ancient computer and investigative reporting history.

Washington correspondent Craig Webb (1989) saw it coming before most journalists did, and it led him to write:

> Proliferating computer links to federal agencies are redefining what it means for a reporter to cover Washington, D.C. The links enable anyone with a personal or office computer, communications equipment and the requisite software to hook up to government-run information banks. These services—electronic bulletin boards or more detailed databases—typically contain press releases, texts of reports and background information from an agency. The information is not very different from what a Washington reporter could get by stalking federal hallways, but acquiring it via computer has two advantages. First, it goes directly into the writer's computer, slashing the preparation time for stories. Second, with a bulletin board a reporter doesn't need to be in Washington to cover what happens. (p. 18)

Miami's Steve Doig (personal communication, December 16, 1993) believes there is no better place than Washington for locating databases. "Washington is the motherlode of *unexamined* databases," he proclaims.

PROJECT REPORTING: USING GOVERNMENT DATABASES

The Miami Herald told residents of South Florida a lot more about the damage caused by Hurricane Andrew than even local and federal government officials knew. Within just a few months of the storm, which destroyed thousands of homes, CAR Editor Steve Doig and a team of reporters and editors began searching for reasons for what seemed to be patterns of extensive damage in some localized areas and less damage in other nearby areas. Combining several government databases with computer analysis, they found some revealing explanations: Building codes, lack of enforcement of codes by officials, and use of certain high-risk construction materials and styles were to blame. Doig (personal communication, December 16, 1993) explains:

A month or so after the storm, while most of the staff was still dealing with the day-to-day stories . . . Jim Savage, the investigations editor, his group, some other editors, and I sat down and looked at some of the questions floating around. At the time, there was a big, acrimonious debate going on between the developers and the homeowners in Dade County. Some developers said this was "an act of God and no home could have withstood this sort of storm." So we said, "Gee, maybe that's a testable premise."

So I spent much of the ensuing couple of months—I think we started in early October and we got the sixteen-page section published December 20. Much of it dealt with the things we [the computer analysts] found.

We used a variety of techniques—and maybe this is a good thing to raise when talking about CAR—certainly a core element of that sixteen-page section was the result of our computer-assisted reporting. But a great deal of it also was good, traditional, on-the-ground, talk-to-people, go-to-the-site kind of journalism. We studied documents, too. We didn't just sit in a room with a computer and produce all of that.

What "precision journalism" does is turn anecdotal evidence into statistical evidence. Instead of saying, "We found a home that's all beat up" and then talk about it, which is the approach you always had to use before, now we can say, "Here's the horrible case of a drunk driver and there are 172 cases like it." You couldn't do that kind of thing before.

CAR adds authority to what you are doing. We did it by building a database out of a variety of other ones. By the end of the time we were working on this, they [county officials] had done 60,000 inspections. They varied wildly in quality. We took that database, the county property tax roll, which I was familiar with, which contained a lot of housing variables such as cost, age, and location. We got another database with more details on the construction, type of walls and things like that.

I built all those things together into a database . . . literally millions of records by the time I pulled these different things together. The ultimate step was a very simple frequency count.

The property damage project was a part of the months-long package of hundreds of news and feature stories that helped earn *The Miami Herald* numerous national awards, including the 1993 Pulitzer Prize for meritorious public service for its overall coverage of the storm and its aftermath.

"There is so much that just has not been looked at and, with the Freedom of Information Act, you have decent access."

Perhaps Doig's perspective can be expanded to include not just Washington, DC, but the entire federal government. The federal government is certainly the ultimate U.S. data collector and a major database producer. In fact, the federal government not only generates its own data, but also creates national databases by collecting and merging data and reports collected from the states, territories, and other regional and local sources.

> The U.S. government—one of the most fertile sources of business, legal, and financial information—currently provides the public with access to many of its databases through the Government Printing Office, which takes weeks for delivery. Some of this information is also sold through private on-line services, which can cost more than $250 an hour for connect charges. But as the information highway unfolds, much of this data is becoming accessible at no charge or at very low rates. For example, EDGAR, a giant Securities and Exchange Commission database that contains information on public companies, was recently promised for availability over the Internet sometime in the future. (Patch, 1993, p. 20)

There are hundreds of government-sponsored bulletin board systems, and current lists of these BBSs are fairly easy to find on both public and private BBSs in most communities or in any of several magazines that devote their space to online services and BBSs. Reporters in many professional groups, such as the Investigative Reporters and Editors and the Society of Professional Journalists, also swap BBS lists at their meetings. For many reporters, there are some fairly standard locations for government BBSs and computer databases. The departments of Commerce, Agriculture, Defense, Education, Labor, and Energy are particularly helpful to computer-oriented journalists on those beats. The Securities and Exchange Commission, the General Services Administration, Federal Communications Commission, Federal Aviation Agency, Federal Election Commission, the federal courts system, National Aeronautics and Space Administration, the Federal Reserve, U.S. Customs Service, and the National Oceanic and Atmospheric Administration are also major sources of information.

PACER is a good example. PACER is an acronym for Public Access Court Electronic Records, the U.S. District Court public records database system. PACER contains two types of information for online users: one for district civil and criminal court records and one for bankruptcy courts. Each system is accessible through different telephone lines, although the interface for both systems is the same. Its databases focus on individual judicial districts. Users are charged a relatively high hourly fee, $1 per minute in 1995, but PACER is available to the general public for use at all hours, including weekends. Users can search court dockets by name of the person, institution, or organization involved in litigation and the docket for an individual case is scrolled on-screen for review. The database does not include full text of most court documents, only the docket summary of court action in a case in reverse chronological order.

Two other court system databases are useful to reporters, too. The federal appeals court system has a service called ACES, an acronym for Appeals Court Electronic Services. EDOS is the Electronic Dissemination of Opinions System, which provides full text of appeals court decisions, usually within 24 hours of the decision announcement. The service also includes court rules, press releases, calendars, and public notices. These are part of the same service and are also available for public access (Griffith, 1994).

Another example is the Federal Election Commission's (FEC) online service. It is immensely popular among journalists working in politics and elections. The FEC offers a large number of useful databases, but perhaps the most popular are the constantly updated campaign contributions databases. These databases allow users to check lists of campaign contributions reported to the FEC for candidates for federal-level offices. Required by law, the lists are comprehensive and easily accessible. The National Library on Money & Politics uses the public FEC data as well as databases assembled from a variety of other public and private sources for its online services.

Some government BBSs are free and require only the cost of the telephone call. Others require subscriptions on an annual basis and/or an hourly user fee. Generally, however, government databases are less expensive to access and use than services in the commercial world. Of course, some of those databases in the commercial sector are the same government databases with certain enhancements—such as easier to use interfaces—that are often labeled "value-added."

"Not all government information banks are worthwhile to reporters," cautions Webb (1989, p. 18). "The computer services set up to be bulletin boards sometimes are little more than just that: a place to post notes and read comments left by others. Databases tend to be more formally constructed and usually are meant primarily to be repositories of information, but they often include message sections as well."

STATE GOVERNMENT DATABASES

Perhaps the first, and most frustrating, observation by participants during any conferences that feature discussions about government databases and CAR is that there is considerable variation in access to, and quality of, state government information. Some states still seem to be in the Jurassic Age of computer database development and public access to that information even in the mid-1990s. Others, which have enlightened legislatures and senior bureaucrats, have gone into electronic databases with enthusiasm and forward thinking about how the public can most easily locate and use the information contained in the databases.

Barbara Palladino (1992), a New Jersey online research specialist, recently surveyed state online databases and found that about half maintained public access online database services of one type or another. Although the number will rise as more states go online for public access, it is important to consider what types of information are available for access. "These databases contain a variety of state-specific data which is usually available free (except for long-distance telephone charges)," Palladino wrote (p. 20). "Only a handful of states charge a subscription or online fee. Most operate 24 hours a day, seven days a week. Some systems . . . restrict the length of time that users may remain online."

Palladino found that typical state-run database services provide bulletin board system-type interfaces. Users will find demographic data such as income and employment, taxation data, general population data, labor data, government activities such as schedules and calendars, environmental records, education, and business activity statistical databases. Some state services contain archival, historical, and reference content such as state constitutions, historical documents, and state statutes. In short, these can be very useful reporting tools.

A major source of online information about business activity in any state is the office of the secretary of state. One state official estimated that at least 26 states had placed corporate or centralized Uniform Commercial Code—databases containing information about businesses such as ownership, officers, agents, and debt—available online (Griffith, 1994). These online databases are available directly from the states involved through their own systems or from commercial services such as Lexis and Information America. Online costs vary from state to state and service to service, but it is generally cheaper to establish accounts directly with each secretary of state office that will be frequently used. For occasional users, the commercial services may be the best and least expensive over the long-term alternative.

Some databases are specific enough that they provide county- or city-level statistical data as well as state figures. "These state sources are even more attractive when you consider that they may contain information that is simply not available through any other online source," Palladino (1992, p. 20) stated. "The bulk of state data is drawn from sources such as government agencies, educational institutions and private research organizations" (p. 21).

Access and use of online state database services will vary. Some are easy, some difficult. Many use menu systems that require little or no training for use. Some may require user's guides to navigate in the beginning. These guides are usually available in the downloadable files library/directory or can be requested from the system operator online using the messages or electronic mail services or by telephone.

Some states, such as Florida, offer online directories of state databases that may not be online but are available in one electronic form or another. These lists describe the databases, which agency maintains them, and where they can be found. The lists are often available online or by request from a state agency or department such as the state data processing or information systems department or the secretary of state, department of commerce, or department of labor offices. There is clear movement toward more access to state databases using online technology.

CITY AND COUNTY GOVERNMENT DATABASES

An increasing amount of government data is being entered into computer systems at local administrative levels. County, city, town, village, and even quasi-public neighborhood and condominium associations keep some data, such as budgets or name and address lists, in computers. The key is knowing what is out there and where to find it. One way is to identify the county or city information systems department director and meet with that person. The information systems people should know what databases are maintained, where they are kept, the format of the database, and other details. These persons may also be able to arrange for ongoing online access if it is not currently available. These individuals also set prices and other access policies not prescribed in ordinances or statutes.

Local government databases in the mid-1990s that are the most commonly used by reporters are municipal and county-level civil and criminal court records, occupational licenses, school system records, budgets, crime reports and statistics, employment records, real estate transaction records, and construction permits and licenses.

Often, individual government records, or even entire databases of government records, do not reveal as much meaningful information alone or as a single dataset. But enterprising reporters, such as those from Detroit and Cleveland discussed at the beginning of this chapter who combined two or more databases to obtain a higher level of analysis and meaning from seemingly unrelated sets of information, are finding the ultimate way to use government information to permit people residing in a community to learn more about themselves.

Just as many journalists have observed at state government levels, there is tremendous unevenness in access to the databases kept at local government levels. Similarly, there is also variation in methods of online access, pricing policies, hours, and type of information in the database. It may be obvious to some veteran reporters, but it is important to remember that not all databases that may appear to be the same contain the same information.

Although there seems to be a need for some kind of standardization, no government-down efforts have been successful so far. It seems that any uniformity that exists has been created by the software and hardware industries, but there is not much standardization from those quarters either. For example, crime databases kept by local law enforcement agencies are not all the same. Often, the legal and database category definitions of crimes are quite different from jurisdiction to jurisdiction even though there are efforts on the federal and state levels to create a degree of uniformity in databases. Even if there were uniformity in categorization and other areas, the variety of approaches taken by database programs on the market prevents any immediate hope for consistency.

Perhaps the most important consideration in using local government databases, however, is the overall approach local officials take toward online access. Some officials feel online access is an enhancement of "government in the sunshine" and have been extremely cooperative in preparing remote access ports to use with public computer systems. Others have made access as difficult as possible while still remaining within the letter of prevailing state or local open records laws. The result is that some municipalities and some counties are electronic database gold mines whereas others have yet to allow any useful prospecting by citizens. Reporters encountering reluctant city or county clerks, or information systems specialists will, with some effort, probably obtain access, if permitted by law. The process may require some old-fashioned negotiating, technical giving and taking, some price haggling for services and the data, and some legal maneuvering. In some communities, it may be reporters, with the support of their editors and publishers, who initiate changes in local or state laws. The process may become complicated to some people, but it does not have to be. Electronic access to government can happen. And it might not take so much, if officials just tried, argues Dale Morrison (1994), a former government bureaucrat and a former journalist living in the Seattle area. Perhaps Morrison summed the situation up when he questioned why online access to Puget Sound government records and public officials was not already a reality. For example, Morrison wrote:

> [A]n E-Mail system adequate for most or all of the correspondence between all local members at the State Legislature, the Seattle City Council and the King County Council and their constituents in the Puget Sound area could easily be set up and run by a reasonably bright high-school sophomore using a couple of used 286's and free RBBS-PC software. In contemplating the information future, taxpayers should ask themselves these questions: Are public records of interest already maintained on computer? If so, are they accessible online? If not, why not?

USEFUL GOVERNMENT DATABASES

Dave Davis and Beth Marchak (1993, 1994), reporters at *The Plain Dealer* in Cleveland, recommend 20 government databases that they say journalists "can't live without." These are their suggestions:

Energy and Environment
- NUDOCS (Nuclear Document System), U.S. Nuclear Regulatory Commission, Washington, DC.
- TRANSNET (Transported nuclear materials reports network), Sandia National Laboratories, Department of Energy, Albuquerque, NM.
- TOXNET (Toxicology Data Network), part of the National Library of Medicine (MEDLARS), National Institutes of Health, Bethesda, MD.
- Nexis Environmental Library, Nexis, Dayton, OH.

Medicine
- MEDLARS, National Library of Medicine, National Institutes of Health, Bethesda, MD.

Workplace Safety
- OSHA Data, Occupational Safety and Health Administration, Washington, DC.

Companies/Corporations
- CompuServe's IQUEST, Columbus, OH.

Campaign Contributions
- Federal Election Commission Direct Access, Washington, DC.

Census
- CENDATA, available through CompuServe, Columbus, OH, and Dialog, Palo Alto, CA.

Aviation
- Aviation Database, Federal Aviation Administration, Washington, DC.

Courts
- PACER, Public Access to Court Electronic Records, Administration Office of the Federal Courts, Washington, DC.
- U.S. Supreme Court, full-text decisions, the Internet, Telnet, "marvel.loc.gov."

Education
- EDSEARCH, National Center for Education Statistics, Department of Education, Washington, DC. (diskettes only, not online).

U.S. Government Business, the Congress
- CompuServe's Commerce Business Daily, government contracts, Columbus, OH.
- Lusknet, real estate records for Washington, DC, area, Silver Spring, MD.
- Dialog CIS, Congressional Information Service, Palo Alto, CA.
- Library of Congress, the Internet, Telnet, "locis.loc.gov."

Military
- Periscope, the military database, U.S. Naval Institute Military Database, United Communications Group, Rockville, MD.

Patents
- Dialog, Derwent's Patent Database, Palo Alto, CA.

People
- IRSC, Individual records for U.S. residents, Fullerton, CA.

GOVERNMENT BULLETIN BOARD SYSTEMS

Some government agencies have tried to be more accessible and have sought new ways to disseminate information and provide services to the public. Partly because of the low cost and the ease in setting up a bulletin board system, some agencies have found BBSs to be fast and convenient and to be one of the best ways to make current information available to the public.

A 1993 study conducted by the Office of Technology Assessment (OTA) of the U.S. Congress stated there were approximately 175 federal BBSs in operation (U.S. Congress, 1993). The "mother" of those BBSs, perhaps, is the FedWorld BBS operated by the National Technical Information Service in Springfield, VA. Other federal BBSs are much more specialized, depending on the agencies operating them.

Typical government BBSs offer much of the same type of content that is found in private or commercial BBSs, such as electronic mail, messages, direct online contact with agency officials, announcements, news, reports, press releases, downloadable text and data files, and readable or searchable databases. Perhaps the biggest problem of these services, the OTA notes, is that they are not always easy to locate. But once these services are found, they are used. OTA reported that in 1993, for example, the Department of Commerce's economic BBS received about 10,000 calls a month.

Federal, state, and local government BBSs are generally free, except for any long-distance tolls involved. Some charge hourly fees or require subscriptions or one-time connection fees. Some may require special software that has to be purchased as well, and some may, for security reasons, require dedicated telephone lines for *call-back* log-in procedures. Call-back systems require the remote user to dial into the system, identify the user, and hang up. The BBS then calls back to the telephone line of record for a particular user to make the accessible connection.

More and more access to government BBSs will undoubtedly be made available through the Internet in the remaining years of this decade. Combined with access through linked computer networks such as FedWorld, access is becoming less of a problem. Some government agencies consider the long-distance tolls a barrier to certain members of the public

FEDWORLD: ONLINE GOVERNMENT INFORMATION

FedWorld is the premier electronic access service for locating, ordering, and acquiring federal and foreign government information. The online bulletin board, begun as a pilot program at the National Technical Information Service (NTIS) in November 1992, has been, according to NTIS, a "success" and has led the service to become, in NTIS's own words, "the electronic hub for public access to U.S. and foreign government documents, directories and information services" (NTIS, 1993, p. 1).

The service is the front door to more than 100 government bulletin board systems and offers access to thousands of information resources. Users will find inventories of recently published reports, federal government databases, software, bulletin board systems, and names of sources and contacts for information providers. The service permits access to other federal BBSs through a network of computer links. FedWorld officials say it attempts to keep the information on the service as timely as possible. According to the NTIS catalog:

> As resources are updated, they are made available instantaneously to users around the nation. FedWorld is currently accessible via modem or through the Internet. Current FedWorld features include walk-you-through prompts, a simple online help system and electronic mail services.

> FedWorld is expanding its online government-wide information locator, which allows users to search databases online, connect to other agency online computer systems or transfer any of hundreds of files that facilitate location of government information. As a distribution mechanism for other government agencies, FedWorld houses substantive U.S. Government databases and makes them available online to users around the world. (pp. 1–2)

FedWorld received almost 100,000 calls from 25,000 users during its first 9 months of operation in 1992–1993. With the high demand by users, NTIS has expanded incoming telephone lines, Internet access, and easier search interface.

"Plans for the near future include online credit card ordering of NTIS products, instantaneous delivery of U.S. government computer products, a graphical interface that will allow the user to point and click with a mouse and connection to U.S. government databases available currently only via the Internet," NTIS stated (pp. 1–2).

Users of FedWorld will find:

- Dozens of catalogs listing thousands of federal documents.
- Documents released in electronic form by the White House.
- Abstracts describing NTIS-published searches.
- Summaries of the Government Results and Performance Act of 1993.
- Federal job opening lists from across the nation.
- Weather satellite images.

The NTIS has noted:

Users have found much of FedWorld's current information beneficial. There are thousands of useful downloadable files available, with others becoming available daily. Some of the most popular information products made available through FedWorld are White House documents. FedWorld has served as an archive for White House documents released electronically since January 1993. The documents include transcripts of press conferences, briefings, remarks by the president and executive orders. (p. 2)

FedWorld online time is free. However, users must pay the long-distance charges. To connect with a modem, dial (703) 321-FEDW (3339) or (703) 321-8020. Set parity to none, data bits to 8, and stop bit to 1. The terminal emulation should be ANSIBBS, but VT-100 also works. FedWorld accommodates modem speeds up to 14400 baud. For users seeking to connect through the Internet, Telnet to "fedworld.gov."

and are pushing for government-supported toll-free "800" numbers to eliminate the cost of access problem (U.S. Congress, 1993). It should also be noted that some local governments, such as those in California, are finding online access to government records to be a desirable alternative to using the automobile to travel to the source. A recently passed California law, for instance, requires municipalities to find ways to reduce automobile use to enhance air quality. Online databases are viewed by some officials as a contribution in that direction. Appendix C contains a list of the major online government bulletin board systems.

ONLINE AND CD-ROM CENSUS DATA

The U.S. Bureau of the Census is a function of the Department of Commerce. It is headquartered in a massive federal complex in suburban Suitland, MD, a few miles outside Washington, DC. However, there are 12 additional regional offices, as well as data centers, in each of the states. Some state data centers are in state capitals, whereas others may be associated with universities, departments, or major libraries in communities outside the capital. The bureau has also opened business and industry data centers in 16 states.

For many years, census databases in electronic form were usable only on magnetic tape and readable by a tape drive interfaced with a mainframe computer system. All that began changing in the early 1980s with the advent of personal computers and PC-related technology. In fact, in 1994, the Bureau of Census announced it would phase out all of its mainframe computers by 1996 in planning for the next census in 2000. The bureau will move to minicomputers, but it is also studying options for its archive of nine-track tapes generated over the past three to four decades.

Reporters in the mid-1990s can still access large census databases on nine-track magnetic tape, but they can also find the data on CD-ROM discs and floppy disks, and data are downloadable online. Census data are available in easily accessible forms in addition to the traditional printed reports available through the U.S. Government Printing Office (USPGO) bookstores or directly from the bureau.

Two of the most popular electronic forms among journalists are direct online access and CD-ROM discs. Some reporters use nine-track computer tape if they prefer to access the data with a mainframe computer, minicomputer, or a PC interfaced with a nine-track tape reader.

When census data were available only on nine-track magnetic tape, all but the most computer-skilled journalists were discouraged from using the data. One of the reasons for the growth in the number of census-related CAR stories in the past several years is that the census bureau has made its numerous databases available on other storage media such as CD-ROM and diskettes. With the 1990 census reports, individuals with personal computers are able to read and use census files for the first time.

Users can access census data online through two major commercial online services. Both CompuServe and Dialog offer access to the census data through a database called CENDATA, but both require membership accounts to permit access. For persons with one or both of those accounts, or news organizations planning to open memberships in one or both of the services, it makes sense to explore CENDATA. CENDATA, available online since 1984, contains portions of the Public Law tape file and Summary Tape Files 1 and 3. Public Law data files are the counts used by states for Congressional redistricting and were among the first 1990 census results to be released in 1991. This database includes general population characteristics such as race, ethnicity, housing unit counts, and population age 18 and higher.

The census database library covers an impressive range of subjects. The organization collects data constantly, not just each 10 years. Every 5 years, other censuses are taken by the bureau. For example, economic, agricultural, and government censuses are taken in years ending in 2 and 7. In addition to basic population data, the census collects data about agriculture, construction, foreign countries, foreign trade, governments, housing, personal income, manufacturers, mineral industries, retail trade, services, transportation industries, and wholesale trade.

Many news organizations just beginning to conduct CAR projects find census stories manageable. Those reporters who routinely use census data for news stories have opted to purchase compact discs covering their state or region and read the data using CD-ROM disc drives because the CD permits unlimited access and no online tolls or other restrictions. Census CDs are shipped with software that permits data to be downloaded in formatted tables for spreadsheet software such as

Lotus 1-2-3, Microsoft Excel, or relational database systems such as Borland's dBase and Paradox.

What census discs should a news organization consider acquiring to get started? For most newsrooms with reporters and editors unfamiliar with the census, there are two basic pieces to the puzzle. Discs are distributed in sets by state, so the best place to begin is probably the news organization's own state or states, if more than one is involved. Summary tape files provide statistics with sufficient detail for specific geographic areas for most journalistic analyses, and far more depth than offered in the published census reports.

The first choice is the summary tape file (STF) 1 versions A through D, which contain very general information from the short form filled out by all U.S. households. STF 1 contains population statistics including variables broken into categories such as sex, age, race, marital status, and housing characteristics. The second is STF 3, which contains sample data from the long form that was distributed to every sixth household. This contains much more detailed economic, social, and housing data. Among the many variables are birthplace, educational level, ancestry, migration, language spoken, disability, work commuting, occupation, and income. For the 1990 census, the Public Law tape file and STFs 1A, 1B (extract), 1C, 3A, 3B, and 3C are available on CD-ROM discs.

There are easy ways to keep up with the fast pace of census data releases and other data developments. One means is to contact Census Data User Services (301-763-4100) or go online with the Census Bureau's BBS through CompuServe or Dialog (for information, call 301-763-2074). Data User Services will take requests to be placed on the free *Monthly Product Announcement* mailing list. An annual *Census Catalog and Guide* is also published and is sold through the USGPO. For more information, subscriptions for the monthly newsletter, *Census and You,* are available from the USGPO. Individuals who are not yet using census data for news stories but who may be interested in the census should read:

- *Census, CD-ROM, and You!: New Horizons for Microcomputer Users of Census Bureau Data,* published in 1993.
- *Census '90 Basics,* revised in 1993.
- *Hidden Treasures: Census Bureau Data and Where to Find It!,* published in 1990.

OTHER GOVERNMENT DATABASES ON CD-ROM

Including census data on CD-ROM, there were more than 300 different CD-ROM products sold by the USGPO, private vendors, or the agencies in mid-1993 (U.S. Government Books, 1994; York & Haight, 1992). Perhaps census data focused on local or regional areas are the most widely known form in which government data are found on CD-ROM discs. There are, however, numerous other federal and state sources for both unprocessed and processed data and statistics. The federal government is certainly one of the nation's largest producers of databases on CD-ROM and it will continue to be so since the Office of Technology Assessment of the 103rd Congress strongly feels CDs reduce publishing costs and "are particularly effective for reference materials and searchable databases that can be updated monthly or over longer periods" (U.S. Congress, 1993, p. 40).

Although CDs are highly useful database storage tools, the biggest problem is that there is no single official listing of government databases available on CD-ROM. Perhaps the closest thing to a complete list is the SIGCAT CD-ROM Compendium. SIGCAT is the acronym for the 6,500-member Special Interest Group on CD-ROM Applications and Technology. The compendium may be purchased from the USGPO in printed form for about $11. The compendium contains an annotated alphabetic index of the CD-ROM products offered for sale by the federal government. The index describes how the databases can be obtained. A group of avid government CD-ROM users, SIGCAT is sponsored by the U.S. Geological Survey and "provides a forum for federal government agencies to exchange ideas, information and experiences on CD-ROM," note Montana State University librarians Vicky York and Audrey Jean Haight (1992, p. 14).

At the federal level, reporters can find numerous types of data on CD-ROM. Although it is difficult, if not impossible, to discuss all government databases available on CD-ROM, it seems necessary to describe the major data sources if this chapter is to be complete. Some general categories, with examples, for which CD-ROM discs containing databases are available include:

- Congress (e.g., full-text of the *Congressional Record*).
- Education (e.g., Department of Education comprehensive national education statistics and student survey data).
- Environment (e.g., Environmental Protection Agency Toxic Release Inventory).
- Federal laws (e.g., U.S. Code full-text database).
- Foreign affairs (e.g., State Department's full-text official public information database).
- Health care (e.g., National Center for Chronic Disease Prevention and Health Promotion databases).
- Labor and jobs (e.g., *Occupational Outlook Handbook*).
- Library of Congress (e.g., catalogs and other reference lists of holdings).
- Occupational safety (e.g., Occupational Safety and Health Administration's regulations and documents full-text databases).

One major, but often overlooked, source of databases on CD-ROM is the Department of Education. An example of educational databases is ERIC, the Educational Resources Information Center, a database of educational research citations and abstracts.

The Environmental Protection Agency (EPA) distributes several valuable databases on CD-ROM. One example is the toxic releases database produced by the Office of Pollution, Prevention, and Toxics, which lists comprehensive information about more than 300 designated toxic chemicals. Another example is Air Chief. This is a database of current air emissions compiled from EPA reports from around the nation.

The U.S. Geological Survey has several divisions that generate and distribute discs. The Earth Resources Observation Systems Data Center, the Joint Office for Mapping and Research, the National Earthquake Information Center, the National Energy Research Seismic Library, and the National Mapping Division of the Earth Science Information Center are examples.

The Library of Congress is also a CD-ROM database producer. The National Aeronautics and Space Administration, U.S. National AIDS Information Clearinghouse, U.S. Forest Service, National Institute of Justice, National Library of Medicine (MEDLARS), National Oceanic and Atmospheric Administration, National Technical Information Service, U.S. Navy, and the U.S. Patent and Trademark Office are also common sources for databases on CD-ROM (Marcaccio, 1993a, 1993b).

For an up-to-date list of available databases on CD-ROM, contact each agency, bureau, or department separately. Prices vary, but compared to prices of CDs sold by commercial vendors, most federal government databases on CD are real bargains. Some offices maintain nationwide toll-free order numbers. Some agencies permit orders to be submitted by fax or by telephone once accounts are set up. Most government customer assistance numbers are set up to permit major credit card orders by telephone for purchasers who know what they need. Catalogs and order lists are available at no charge.

GOVERNMENT DATA PROBLEMS

The benefits of using online and CD-ROM government databases have been outlined, but there are certain difficulties that come along with the advantages. With any database, from the public sector or from the private sector, there can be errors and other flaws that can cause inaccurate analyses. Limitations to government databases, says the Poynter Institute's Nora Paul (1991b), come in three main areas:

1. *The purpose of the database.* Some databases simply do not provide the information sought. These types of databases are not designed for archival purposes and have short electronic lives, like 1, 2, or 5 years.

2. *How data are entered in the database.* Most data are keypunched from hard copy forms by clerks. These will naturally contain keypunch errors and other inconsistencies. Even scanned "bubble-sheet" data can have machine-caused errors if sheets are not used properly.

3. *How (or if) searching is monitored.* Some systems monitor how they are being used. This can reveal to individuals being searched, especially public officials, that an investigation is being conducted.

Errors can be caused in several ways. Simple keypunching errors occur often, especially in large databases or those with complicated coding schemes. In some agencies, keypunching is not meticulously checked, if checked at all. Machine, or hardware, errors or system operator errors are two other sources of problems. Data that are "read" into the computer by optical scanning devices can contain errors if alignment or formatting is out of adjustment.

"Dirty" data are another problem. Whatever the cause of the errors, some databases are described as dirty because they are not properly formatted, contain missing information, have values out of the correct range, have values in the wrong positions in the data matrix, or have other problems that need to be "cleaned up" before they can be analyzed. This process can be time consuming and expensive.

John C. Sparhawk (1993) of *Government Computer News* wrote:

> Until the last few years, the nature of mainframe data processing kept most of the public from examining government data closely. Today, the cost of both access and analysis is reasonable. Thanks to the Freedom of Information Act, the public can graze at large on our data. Unfortunately, open systems and common interfaces don't guarantee the quality of data—that remains the responsibility of the collecting agency. The government seldom questions the accuracy of its databases, and the commercial world is only beginning to realize the true cost of such misperceptions. (p. 38)

Sparhawk argues there is need for federal policy regarding the quality of its databases. "Although we have many regulations and circulars on systems acquisition, data security and records management, nowhere does the government directly address the quality of data it collects and provides," he said (p. 38). The short-term responsibility, he observes, rests with the collecting agencies.

In addition to concerns about database management on the part of the collecting agencies, it is also important to ask the agencies about the system requirements before ordering databases on magnetic tape, diskette, and CD-ROM disc. Many diskettes and CDs, for instance, sold through the USGPO are not Macintosh compatible and can be read only by IBM or IBM-compatible PC systems.

6 Bulletin Board Systems as Reporting Tools

The *Santa Cruz County Sentinel* in California is typical of many small daily newspapers that use online resources for reporting. With no real budget for commercial online services, the newspaper's reporters, editors, and news librarians use the best resources available within their budget. That means resources with virtually no cost. *Sentinel* Editor Tom Honig (personal communication, December 31, 1993) says his newspaper spends about $500 a year for online services. To make the online research efforts go farther, Honig says the reporters and news librarians for the 30,000-daily circulation newspaper, which serves a coastal area community about 80 miles south of San Francisco, use local bulletin board systems as reporting resources. "It's a new thing here," he observed. "We use online research about three times a week. Our most recent uses include using local private bulletin boards. Our next move is to train people. We have no organized approach—we're all learning. Our successes are in front of us."

Electronic bulletin board systems are becoming increasingly valuable resources for reporters and others seeking information and sources in the online world. Although the use of online commercial services is more widely practiced, reporters are also discovering the value of local, regional, and even international bulletin board systems. There clearly is informational gold in the hills of privately managed bulletin board systems, but there might be greater treasures in institutional and other nongovernment public BBSs. All that is needed for most journalists to benefit from those resources is for them to use their PCs to look around and explore the local online territory.

Pennsylvania online computing authority Alfred Glossbrenner (1990) wrote:

> Bulletin board systems, like the electronic universe as a whole, offer you information, adventure, and a sense of community. Dialing up a board is an ideal and virtually cost-free way to enter that universe. And it's easy, particularly if you follow our advice and put several board numbers in a

dialing queue so your comm program can cycle through them seeking a connection. . . . And you'll find that the BBS community is so diverse that it can answer virtually any question on any topic. It's simply a matter of locating a board frequented by the kind of experts you seek. After a while, you yourself will probably start to visit the same boards again and again. (p. 348)

Compared to the slick online world of commercial information services such as America Online, CompuServe, and Prodigy, bulletin board systems are a different planet. Online browsers accustomed to the commercial services will find most BBSs to be technically crude by comparison. However, access to the major services often is enhanced by special software called information managers. Users will not find these very often in the world of bulletin board systems. "Bulletin boards are not fancy. . . . They are operated by people who enjoy sharing information with others," said Elizabeth McGinnis (1993a, p. 6), a software producer and marketer. "One of the greatest attractions to BBS-ing is the opportunity to interact with other callers. This is usually done by means of a message base where callers exchange ideas, solutions and opinions."

Some reporters and editors at daily newspapers are already using local BBSs and national BBS networks for information gathering. For many, the information found on BBSs serves as strong backgrounding on issues and subjects for major stories. For others, BBSs are a way to find local sources—both people and documents—that might not be easily found through more conventional reporting channels.

There are plenty of examples of newspapers using private BBSs for reporting. Metro Editor Jack Lail (personal communication, December 20, 1993) says he regularly uses private BBSs to supplement reporting at the *Knoxville News-Sentinel*. Using BBSs found in the Internet, Lail (1994) helped develop a story another reporter wrote:

A message circulated through Martin-Marietta's Oak Ridge operations and at the University of Tennessee about a Blue Tattoo LSD problem. We started getting calls about it and people wanting us to do a story. It turned out this was a bogus thing, an urban legend. I checked "alt.folklore,urban" (a Usenet newsgroup). I found some information about how old this tale is and [was given] a point to a FAQ [frequently asked questions] file just on Blue Tattoo. I E-mailed the author of the FAQ and got mail back from him. Not much of this made it into the story, which was written by one of our reporters, not me, but it did add greatly to our understanding.

Mark Ridolfi (personal communication, December 20, 1993), city editor at the *Quad City Times,* says some of his newspaper's reporters, the business editor, and news librarians frequently find government and privately operated BBSs helpful. At the *Eugene Register Guard* in Oregon, Assistant City Editor Tom Detzel (personal communication,

January 10, 1994) said his newspaper cannot use much online news research because of budget limitations. The newspaper had $1,000 budgeted for online services in 1994, but that does not go far for a newspaper with an 80,000-daily circulation. "We've failed to acquire serious online services because of cost," Detzel, who calls himself the newspaper's computer "coach," explained. To solve the problem, the newspaper uses low-cost online tools such as private BBSs, as well as the Internet.

Rosalind Resnick (personal communication, February 11, 1994), a journalist who specializes in online research and business reporting and author of *Exploring the World of Online Services,* finds BBSs helpful in her research.

> For me, the primary use of computer bulletin boards and online services has been to find sources. You just post a message online and—*voila!*—instant sources. It's important to caution your readers, however, that they shouldn't just pluck off an online message and pop it into their story. As they say, on the Internet, nobody knows you're a dog! A good reporter should contact the person by phone before sticking an online quote in a story—it's harder for people to lie (or invent a fictional identity) voice-to-voice than through e-mail.

Resnick also noted that there are many options for journalists on low budgets who still want to go online when reporting for an assignment. "As for free BBSs, there are something like 50,000 (or more) mom-and-pop BBSs nationwide that don't charge anything to join. Plenty of them are within local dialing distance of any given reporter. A good source of BBS listings is *Boardwatch* magazine, which is widely available at bookstores."

WHAT ARE BULLETIN BOARD SYSTEMS?

Sports journalists in the United States and even sports fans interested in news about the 1994 Winter Olympic games had their own online bulletin board system to keep up with the developments of the U.S. Olympic Team in Norway. At the end of 1993, the U.S. Olympic Committee (USOC) opened an electronic bulletin board for access on a 24 hours a day, 7 days a week basis. The only cost to users was the long-distance charge for time online. When sports writers logged onto the USOC BBS's main system menu, they found almost two dozen different areas, or sections, from which to choose. These were the options from which a user could select online:

1 Daily Olympic News Briefs	A Paralympic Games News
2 Current Sport News	B U.S. Olympic Festival News

3 Media Advisories	D World University Games News
4 U.S. Olympic Committee News	F Pan American Games News
5 Internat'l Olympic Committee News	H Goodwill Games News
6 Other National Committee News	
7 Sport-By-Sport News	
8 USOC, Olympic Movement TV News	
9 Olympic Summer Games News	E Electronic Mail Services
0 Olympic Winter Games News	S Submit to *Olympian Magazine*

Most people refer to these online computer systems as *bulletin board systems*. Some users call them *bulletin board services*. Others prefer to use the term *electronic bulletin boards*. There is a movement in the growing industry to refer to certain BBSs as "online information services" or "public online services" to reflect the differences in multiple-line for-profit systems and those systems that do not seek commercial gains (McCabe, 1993). Whatever name sticks, these online tools are finding growing popularity with reporters, photographers, information graphic artists, editors, and news librarians.

The authoritative *Microsoft Press Computer Dictionary* (Woodcock, 1991) defines a BBS as simply "a computer system equipped with one or more modems that serves as an information and message-passing center for dial-up users" (p. 33). There are a number of common features found on most bulletin board systems. The features are generally a function of the software that the system operator chooses to use, but BBS software developers have found some common ground for these packages in recent years. The most common features include electronic mail (communication that remains private), messaging (which, in contrast to mail, denotes public postings), conferences, public forums, libraries of files that can be copied, libraries of submitted programs and files from users, full-screen message editors, and online user help (Weintrob, 1993).

BBSs are highly specialized in most cases. The three major categories of systems are commercial bulletin boards, linked bulletin boards, and stand-alone bulletin boards (Paul, 1993a):

- *Commercial bulletin board systems.* These are found on the commercial online services such as America Online, CompuServe, Delphi, GEnie, and Prodigy. These "forums" or "interest groups," as they are called in some systems, reflect highly specialized focus—such as pets, WordPerfect, UFOs, or journalism. There are also a growing number of independent pay-as-you-go BBSs, some with thousands of regular users, that offer some of the same features as the major commercial information services but are not as large or as expensive to access.

• *Linked bulletin board systems.* Some individually operated BBSs are connected to other systems in a network. This permits national or even worldwide connections through a single local BBS. One of the largest systems is FidoNet. There are also linked BBSs on the Internet. Most of these systems require some sort of user fees to help pay for network costs.

• *Stand-alone bulletin board systems.* Most BBSs are operated by an individual or an organization for a singular purpose. Some operate out of a single PC in the system operator's home or office, and others are complex systems of PCs operated by private companies, organizations, or government agencies. In just about any community, there are dozens, perhaps hundreds, of stand-alone BBSs. For those users willing to pay connect time for long-distance, thousands are immediately accessible. Some BBSs require one-time registration fees, and others are free. Some organizations even offer toll-free "800" number connections to encourage use.

Paul (1993) gives four main features of BBSs, listed in Fig. 6.1. The best features include libraries of files, conference areas, electronic mail, and public message areas.

Mastering BBS Terminology

Most bulletin board systems do not come with users' guides and a few do not even offer much online help. Most people just log in and read the on-screen instructions. Getting started is that simple. To understand the world of online bulletin board reading, there are a number of BBS-related terms found often in the literature or heard in conversations between BBS regulars. They include the following:

Access time. Because of their often-strained hardware resources, such as the number of telephone lines connected to the BBS, many system managers limit the amount of online time for each user by hour per day or week. The BBS software keeps track of this usage time.

BBS. Bulletin board system.

Browsing. The act of scanning the contents of a BBS. This includes casually checking and reading file libraries or message areas for something that might be appealing to the user.

Bulletins. These are important messages for all users of a BBS that have been posted by the system operator. They frequently include system information, news about new files or procedures, or other information the operator feels users need to know. Not reading bulletins and not following instructions may result in disconnection on some systems.

The Four Best Features of BBSs

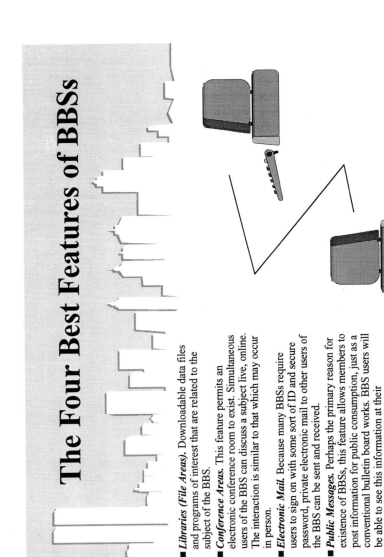

- *Libraries (File Areas).* Downloadable data files and programs of interest that are related to the subject of the BBS.

- *Conference Areas.* This feature permits an electronic conference room to exist. Simultaneous users of the BBS can discuss a subject live, online. The interaction is similar to that which may occur in person.

- *Electronic Mail.* Because many BBSs require users to sign on with some sort of ID and secure password, private electronic mail to other users of the BBS can be sent and received.

- *Public Messages.* Perhaps the primary reason for existence of BBSs, this feature allows members to post information for public consumption, just as a conventional bulletin board works. BBS users will be able to see this information at their convenience.

Source: Nora Paul, "Database & Bulletin Board Services: A Guide to Online Services," *The Quill, 81*(7), September, 1993, pp. 18 -20.

FIG. 6.1.   Some of the best uses for BBSs.

Chatting. Real-time, live, and spontaneous discussions online with other BBS users or directly with the system operator.

Compression. Moving files between systems is time consuming, so many files are compressed or a group of files is combined and compressed for uploading and downloading. This is done using one of several utility programs in the public domain or in shareware. Two such popular programs are called Archive and PKUnzip.

Conference area. This is a "group meeting" section of a BBS, where several online users can get together at the same time to hold live discussions or meetings.

Customer. User of the BBS.

Downloading. This is the process of moving a file from a remote computer to the user's computer using a modem and communications software. The procedure usually requires requesting the transfer by file name from a library of files for public use.

Handle. An alias or nickname used by an individual when posting messages on a BBS.

Library. A collection of downloadable public-domain files in a designated section of a BBS.

Message boards / areas. Like the bulletin board at the corner grocery, this is the public location of many BBSs where messages can be posted for all customers to read.

Menu. This is the list of file areas or activities and options within the BBS. There are different levels of menus.

Network. Some BBSs are linked together, forming a network that shares information such as mail and files.

SIGs. These are special interest groups. On larger BBSs, some subdivisions or areas have been created to reflect unique concerns.

Password. For security, most BBSs require some sort of unique identification word (or number) that is stored in the BBS memory and matched against names when users sign on.

Pay boards. Systems that require fees for access to the entire board or certain areas of the board. Some BBSs are subscription only.

Registration. BBS operators want to know who is using their services and often require new users to sign on with their legitimate name, address, and telephone number—and some operators verify identification by telephone before permitting access. For some BBSs, registration may include a user fee. Some registration procedures also require the user to provide information about his or her system configuration, such as color/monochrome, the number of lines per screen, and the number of characters per line, to enhance communication between the two systems.

SysOp. System operator, the person who owns or is in charge of the BBS.

Uploading. The reverse of downloading, it is a process of transferring a file from the user's computer to a remote location BBS using a modem and communications software.

SCOPE AND NATURE OF BBSs

Just about every community has private and public BBSs of some sort. In metropolitan areas, there are dozens—perhaps hundreds—of private BBSs, dozens more commercially oriented BBSs, and perhaps a growing number of local government BBSs. Most homegrown BBSs are very small and specialized, and they typically offer only one line in and a single computer, modem, and port for communication. A few commercial BBSs and government BBSs may be as small, but most are larger, involving much more hardware.

There are different estimates of the number of bulletin board systems online in the United States. A writer for *Newsweek* magazine estimated the number of home-based noncommercial bulletin board systems at about 53,000 (Kantrowitz, 1993) and a writer for *Online Access* estimated the figure at more than 50,000 public and private BBSs (Weintrob, 1993). While early growth in BBSs was mostly private and by hobbyists, BBSs have entered the domain of institutions, associations, and big business in the 1990s. One computer magazine estimated that about 70% of all new BBSs are being set up by businesses (Weintrob, 1993).

There are a number of different and specialized BBSs accessible through the Internet. These are very similar to those that stand-alone or those that are on a smaller network. Internet experts Tracy LaQuey and J. C. Ryer (1993) say Internet BBSs vary in purpose and content: "Most BBSs [on the Internet] offer a menu of services. Some provide conferencing capabilities, while others provide 'read-only' information, similar to regular bulletin boards at a library where information is tacked up for everyone to read and taken down when it's no longer relevant" (p. 84). Bulletin board systems on the Internet take two main forms, LaQuey and Ryer stated. These are freenets and campus-wide information systems (CWISs). Freenets are good local BBS systems that allow access to the Internet. CWISs are "digital kiosks," to use LaQuey and Ryer's words, with information related to the institution it serves.

BBSs take on a wide range of looks and attitudes. These are a manifestation of the system sponsor, the system operator, the system software, and the system's subject focus. Veteran BBS browsers know that some systems are bright, animated, colorful, sound-oriented, multimedia experiences. Others are low key, offering simple text, very little in graphics, and few features other than the basics. A BBS will often have a catchy name that reflects the interests of the system operator or the subject matter. A look over any list of the thousands of BBSs will verify the extremely wide range and high level of specialization of many public boards.

Wrote author Rosalind Resnick (1993a):

> The real value of online bulletin boards is their specialized focus. Unlike the community bulletin board at your local supermarket, online bulletin boards typically appeal to a niche audience—for example, people who use IBM-compatible, Macintosh, or Amiga computers, or people with a particular interest such as home-based business, desktop publishing, or horse breeding. . . . Some online bulletin boards are strictly local, targeting computer users in a particular city or town; others are national, offered through major online services. (p. 123)

Most BBSs operate 7 days a week and 24 hours a day. Some systems shut down for short periods of time each day to permit maintenance, file updating, or other necessary work to occur. There are certain conventions, or rules, that each BBS operator employs. These rules are usually placed in a conspicuous location that a user cannot avoid seeing, such as during log-in or registration. "It is a good idea to familiarize yourself with these rules because violating them may cause your account to be deleted from the board, depending upon the severity of your offense," veteran BBSer Jeff Russell (1993, p. 60) wrote in *BBS* magazine. Russell advises novices to remember:

- *Don't post messages in all capital letters* (online regulars consider that to be the equivalent to screaming) and use the rules of grammar in writing the message.
- *Stay on the topic* in posted messages or during chats and conferences.
- *Use handles.* If someone uses an alias or handle, address him or her with the handle even if you know the real name.
- *Minimize "flaming" or insulting.* Some individuals do this to get attention, but it is seldom appreciated. Similarly, use of profane language is often not permitted, especially if the board is used by minors.

System sizes vary wildly. The largest systems around the country are, in reality, small businesses. The king of BBSs, perhaps, is EXEC-PC, a system in suburban Milwaukee. EXEC-PC is truly massive by any BBS standard. EXEC-PC, in 1993, had 280 inbound telephone lines, 25 GB of storage capacity, 12 CD-ROM drives, and more than 120,000 compressed files ready for downloading. EXEC-PC, which has a wide range of content and subject areas and which requires a subscription fee for access, receives about 6,000 calls a day. Its message area is reportedly quite active. "These huge multi-line boards are well-run and reputable," wrote computer expert Elizabeth McGinnis (1993b, p. 31).

There are other large systems around the country and many more that are closer to the single-PC model. "Bulletin board systems have been around for a number of years now. Many started as, and remain, small operations with one computer connected to a single phone line," wrote Janet Balas (1991, p. 31), a library information systems analyst in Pennsylvania. "These systems often choose to devote themselves to a specific area of interest or expertise. Other BBSs are sophisticated networks with gigabytes of disk storage and multiple phone lines. These larger systems are so diversified that they can be attractive and less expensive alternatives to the more widely known commercial online systems."

Many systems are stand alone, but some have come together in networks. The most widely known BBS networks are FidoNet, RBBS-Net, GlobalNet, and WorldNet. These networks are inexpensive, some even free, to use. The networks are not closed organizations, nor are they restricted in membership. They are not very similar to the Internet. The major difference is in protocol, the means by which the parts of the network "talk" to each other. Internet network computers must use one particular protocol and operate the serving computer by a form of remote control. "By comparison, the other [BBS] networks are more like relay stations. Messages are passed along the line," wrote New Jersey free-lance writer Jack Germain (1993a, p. 17). "Requested files are sent the same way. There is no remote control of one computer via another [as happens with the Internet]."

Many of the major BBS networks in the United States are modeled after FidoNet, which was started in 1984 by BBS operators in San Francisco and Baltimore. FidoNet originally just moved private E-mail between *nodes*—the local outposts on the network. The developers found a way to move posted public messages to various topic groups, a capability called "echomail," which is appealing to many users. These echoes can be regional or international. BBS networks also host conferences on any and all varieties of topics, just as the commercial services offer their members. File transfers between BBSs that result from user requests are common tools for users also (Germain, 1993a; Savetz, 1993).

BBSs AND SPECIALIZATIONS

System operators give their BBSs a bit of their own personalities in the form of their own "flavor" for content and operation. One of the ways the personality is communicated is through the software the system operator has chosen to use to manage the BBS. There are numerous BBS software packages on the market, so BBSs are not all set up the same way and are not operated in the same manner by users. BBS software

---

BBS USER PUBLICATIONS

There are several periodicals that have begun publication in the past decade that are geared toward bulletin board system users. Among them are:

- *BBS,* published monthly by Callers Digest, Inc., Medford, NJ, 800-822-0437.
- *Boardwatch Magazine,* published monthly by Boardwatch Magazine, Littleton, CO, 303-933-2090.
- *Connect,* published bi-monthly by Pegasus Press, Ann Arbor, MI, 313-973-8825.
- *Online Access,* published 10 times a year by Chicago Fine Print, Inc., Chicago, IL, 312-573-1700.
- *Online* magazine, published six times a year by Online Inc., Wilton, CT, 800-248-8466.

---

controls access to persons who dial into the system, what areas of the system can be visited, what files can be read or changed, virus detection, file transfer, file backup, and correspondence, such as systemwide messages and private electronic mail for other BBS members.

> A real computer bulletin board system consists of the same components everyone uses to go online: a computer, a modem, and a telephone connection. The difference is in the software. The sysop is . . . responsible for the board's personality. Indeed, most sysops view their boards as their own unique creations, and they are forever tinkering with them the way some people tinker with souped-up stock cars. Thus, even if you are an experienced user, you never know what you'll find when you sign on. (Glossbrenner, 1990, p. 338)

A good way to identify specialized bulletin board systems is to check the most popular online computer user magazines. These publications publish lists of thousands of BBSs several times a year, often according to specialization and interest areas. At other times, these publications will publish lists according to geography, such as by state or by telephone area code. Many BBSs, of course, also contain such lists in their files libraries. Downloading a BBS file list may take only a minute or two, depending on transfer speed and file size, and the list will provide dozens of specialized BBS prospects.

FINDING THE BEST BBSs

There are two different types of bulletin board systems that may appeal to a reporter or editor. One is the specialized BBS that focuses on topics of interest for news stories or news projects underway or to be completed in the near future. The second is the personal interest or local BBS that is available just for fun or online entertainment. There are a number of ways to find BBSs, no matter what the purpose might be:

- *Word of mouth.* Most computer users know other users. Most individuals using online services will know others, such as colleagues around the office who use bulletin board systems. The same goes with BBSs. Ask around. Often people around an office will know about local BBSs or keep lists that can be shared. Most people who maintain dialing directories in their communications software will have one or more BBS numbers listed. Ask for recommendations.
- *Computer stores.* A favorite computer store or office products store may keep lists handy for distribution to customers. It makes sense to ask for such a list at a nearby store.
- *Computer and other specialized publications.* There are dozens of computer magazines on the market and a handful are devoted to online users. A list of some of the leading online and BBS magazines is offered elsewhere in this chapter. These publications frequently publish updated national lists of BBSs—some general by area code and some specialized by topic. On occasion, some commercial and institutional BBSs even advertise their existence.
- *Online BBS lists.* If a user can connect to one BBS, chances are good that he or she can find other local BBS lists in the files library of that system. Once one list is in hand, other contacts will lead to other lists.
- *News sources.* Often, some news sources will be able to suggest certain online connections that relate to specialized subjects. It makes sense to ask as a matter of habit, especially if it is clear that a source is a computer user.
- *Organizations and institutions.* Because many organizations and institutions, such as special interests groups and the government, maintain BBSs, these also become significant sources of BBSs.

It is important to remember that BBSs change. Some start up overnight and others shut down just as quickly. Thus, any lists can be quickly outdated. This means that lists should be checked for the date on which they were distributed. Old lists can be troublesome. "The ephemerality of bulletin boards is a fact of online life, however, and it simply means that you must pay particular attention to the freshness of the BBS lists you use," said Glossbrenner (1990, p. 341). "Because of this, books and magazines are not very good sources."

ELECTRONIC MAIL AND BBSs

One of the leading advantages of regularly using one or more bulletin board systems is the ability to send and receive electronic mail for very little cost. For most reporters and editors, this is a highly useful communication tool that can be used at no additional expense or for only the cost of a long-distance telephone call.

Some reporters, photographers, informational graphics specialists, and editors have no other access to electronic mail than through bulletin board systems. By logging on regularly and by developing relationships with other persons who have computers and modems, and who contact the same BBS, electronic mail becomes a possibility. Even two reporters can correspond, or a reporter and editor can communicate, through a single local BBS. A BBS serves as an excellent personal message service, just as an answering machine might do. The advantage is that letters, memos, and other correspondence can be sent, of course, but so can other files such as lengthy reports and other useful documents. The similarity is to that of a fax machine with a memory and a "mailbox" for the user.

For reporters, a BBS is an essential tool in contacting and finding new sources, maintaining those sources, and even interviewing them online. Regardless of how it is used, E-mail is different from conventional mail, often called "snail mail" because of its comparative slowness in delivery. Not only is E-mail much faster—nearly instantaneous, in fact—it is more casual in nature on most BBSs and other E-mail systems. E-mail is also growing in popularity because it is easier and cheaper than other forms of mail.

"E-mail is also different in tone from regular printed letters. E-mail is casual and informal. We write e-mail the way we talk," observed *BBS* magazine writer Lance Whitney (1994, p. 36). "We write e-mail in a very free, loose, stream-of-consciousness way. . . . If writing e-mail is easy, addressing it is the hard part. An e-mail address is not quite as simple as a street address."

The issue of addressing E-mail is simplified if the correspondence remains within the same BBS. But when users begin to ship electronic correspondence and files from BBS to BBS or from a BBS to another computer system through the Internet or a commercial online service, Whitney's point is well taken. "But e-mail addresses must be precise and accurate. One typo in the address, and your message winds up in some dead e-letter office."

ATTENDING ONLINE BBS "EVENTS"

An online BBS event is a scheduled gathering of BBS members for a single purpose. These can be online discussions in the form of conferences or meetings devoted to a single topic. The major commercial online services, with their BBSs in the form of special interest groups, forums, and areas, often offer such online events. In fact, for most of the services, there are regularly scheduled gatherings. Some special events take place, such as when Vice President Al Gore discussed the information highway with members of a service or when computer company executives—Microsoft Chairman Bill Gates, for example—answer questions in an electronic question and answer session. BBSs often offer the same events. Although these are more frequent with networked BBSs, even the smallest BBSs will have gatherings from time to time.

Online events can include insightful discussions by experts that might be excellent resource sessions for reporters, editors, or news researchers seeking background on a subject. Topics range from health and medicine to fun and games. There is a significant how-to dimension to these events, in which experts lend a hand online to solve computer problems, research difficulties, tutoring, and other similar situations.

Events seem ready-made for beat reporters to gain fast insight into current interests and trends. It is a new form of grassroots contact with persons interested in a topic or issue. The debate environment of some events, an often free-wheeling interchange of thoughts and ideas, can be eye opening and lead to story ideas, source identifications, tips, and more reporting benefits.

Some events are very practical for beginning computer users. Some organizations offer online workshops that provide training and tutoring that focus on use of their particular software or hardware. Events may not require any advance planning other than to decide to join into the fray. Others, such as the online session with Vice President Gore, or an online training program offered by a software producer, require reservations or special qualifications such as registered ownership of a product. Some online computer magazines publish event schedules, but because these change frequently, it is probably best to consult online schedules with the BBSs themselves.

HOW BBSs ARE OPERATED

Who runs BBSs? How is a BBS set up? These are questions that novice BBS users often ask. It is probably clear that there are several answers. BBS operators are individuals interested in computing and the communication power of computing. Some are computer hobbyists. Some operators are professionals who serve an organization or who have set up their own BBS for commercial purposes. The set up is simple, actually. The small BBS operator has a single PC, a modem, a telephone line, and BBS software. The process of setting up and operating a BBS is described in more detail later in this chapter.

BBS goals and purposes also vary. They are usually a function of the organization or the individual who owns and operates the system. Some are a means for people of a common interest area to get together without leaving the home or office. Most BBSs are specialized in some manner;

some of the largest privately operated BBSs, nonprofit BBSs, and commercial BBSs are highly specialized. A look through any list of BBSs will confirm this fact: There are literally hundreds of different topics— for instance, people, the sciences, animals, occupations, the arts, politics, small and big businesses, games and recreation, hobbies, organizations, and personal finance—that are the focus of nongovernment BBSs.

Regardless of the focus, the size, or the purpose of a BBS, bulletin boards must follow state and federal laws regarding content. Therefore, there may be some restrictions regarding the types of material permitted on the BBS as well as some restrictions about the age of the user. Some types of "adult" material may be illegal in some areas. The comments of occasional "flamers," who say things that could be offensive, or even libelous or slanderous, are often not permitted by operators.

Of course, there are immediate legal concerns whenever copyrighted commercial programs are being uploaded or downloaded without permission on a BBS. It pays to be alert and to know the law. "A BBS of any size will have problems with pirated software and adult files from time to time," said Hank Hurteau (1993, p. 10), a BBS operator and software reviewer for *BBS* magazine. "Even the most diligent Sysop might unintentionally miss the rare unwanted upload." For both operators and users, it pays to be aware and to avoid potential problem areas.

NEWSPAPERS, MAGAZINES, AND BBSs

Many newspaper and magazine news managers are discovering BBSs as a means to keep in touch with and provide additional services to readers. In 1993 and 1994, there was a major rush by newspapers and magazines to move to online accessibility, including *both* larger and smaller publications (Resnick, 1994, February 12). The *Albuquerque Tribune* has its Electronic Trib that focuses on nonbreaking news such as features and news analyses. *Popular Mechanics* has offered its New York-based BBS after hours for a number of years to its technologically advanced readers. "You can call the *PM* computer. . . . Once you're on line, you can leave messages for specific editors, or direct inquiries and comments to a specific department. The department bulletin board also allows you to share your thoughts with other readers who call in," *PM* editors tell readers ("PM Hotlines," 1994, p. 12). Other newspapers and magazines are adding similar services for readers each month as they discover BBSs to be an inexpensive means to broaden the reach of the news organization.

The *Florida Today's* Newslink Forum on CompuServe, launched in 1993, represents what some newspapers are doing online. This is the Gannett newspaper's own BBS, but it is hosted on CompuServe. This makes the BBS accessible to anyone, worldwide, who is a CompuServe member. For the newspaper, of course, the service offers an existing subscriber list and a network of worldwide access. Newspapers or other publications are then paid a royalty by the service for online time used to access the publication's BBS (Resnick, 1994). To be a member of a forum such as Newslink, a user needs only to give a name. Once in the BBS, users find message boards, file libraries, conferencing, various announcements, a member directory, online help and reference, and a forum user's guide.

Because *Florida Today* serves Florida's "space coast" and many tourists interested in Central Florida's attractions, some users of the forum find it helpful as a timely source of space and other science reporting by the newspaper. For many users, the files of selected articles from the newspaper are appealing. The BBS's file library includes such topics as space, leisure and tourism, money and real estate, Florida sports, Florida gardening, the environment and Florida outdoors life, the weather, senior citizen and "snowbird" news, family life, health and fitness, Florida politics, Florida education, and feedback.

System Operator Mark DeCotis (1994) explains to new users: "The *Florida Today* Newslink Forum has four main areas: announcements (notices), messages, libraries and a conference area. Each has its own function, but all are designed to help you get the most out of *Florida Today* Newslink Forum."

The files library is also a functional part of the BBS, the sysop says:

> The Libraries primarily contain stories from *Florida Today* and GIF (graphics) [Graphic Interchange Format] files which contain the best pictures and graphics from the newspaper. The Libraries contain valuable archived information for both Florida residents and non-residents. We have chosen stories from *Florida Today* that have wide appeal. The stories are generic text (ASCII) files that can be displayed . . . or downloaded directly . . . for viewing offline. . . . Keywords and file descriptions are maintained for each file.

Conferences are a significant part of the BBS's activities. Conferences frequently involve politicians and politics, aerospace experts, space policymakers, scientists, and "live" online coverage of launches of space shuttles. Space-oriented users will find files that include not only news story text, but photographs in GIF form also.

"Members of the *Florida Today* Newslink Forum can communicate with each other in the forum's 'real-time' conference area," the sysop stated. "Spontaneous and informal chats can occur anytime. Scheduled conferences will be held with occasional presentations by special guests. . . . Often members prearrange, using messages or electronic mail, to meet in the forum at a particular hour, on a particular day. Any number of people can participate in conferences."

This discussion by no means contains a comprehensive list of newspapers using BBSs. These are some of the early birds that saw online BBS opportunities. Other news organizations are considering such features and new services are announced almost monthly. Even if an arrangement with a national or international online service is not needed, a local BBS may be an appealing and less expensive option.

Setting Up a Newsroom BBS

For news organizations interested in starting a BBS for internal use or for public access, there are some basic hardware and software considerations. There is no doubt there could be many uses for an internal BBS for employees only, especially if there is no other electronic mail system in the newsroom. It is an inexpensive alternative for small news organizations. For external purposes, it is an excellent way to get readers involved, to receive "feedback" from readers on a wide range of concerns, to receive letters to the editor, to be sent free-lance submissions, and to distribute information that may or may not be included in the newspaper. It seems to be an obvious readership recruitment device to be aimed at young people as well.

The first step is to identify a person in the newsroom who will serve as system operator. There may be need for assistants also, depending on the size of the online operation. For the individual running the BBS, it is strongly recommended that assigned time be given to the person on a daily basis to attend to related chores. John S. Makulowich (1992), writing in *Online Access,* advises individuals or organizations planning to start a BBS to develop "a mission statement, some objectives and clear measures to determine the board's success" (p. 32). The statement should focus on users, he recommends. Decisions about the goals of the bulletin board system will determine the set-up cost. Acquisition of the right hardware and software is the next step and must relate to the goals. A new computer system is neither required, nor always the best choice, for low-budget BBSs.

Hardware can be acquired at either small-time or big-time levels. The basic hardware includes a personal computer with a hard drive, a modem, a telephone line, and a surge protector. The system should be dedicated to the BBS and not be used for other purposes. This reduces conflicts and increases service quality to users. A printer is optional, but it would be convenient for certain system management chores. A used system from the newsroom, liberated from another purpose, allows for a meager beginning, but it also keeps costs low. There may be limitations in storage and speed with an older system, of course. Using an existing system, a complete BBS hardware set-up could be put together for well less than $1,000, perhaps as little as $500. A new set-up, complete with room for growth, will be more expensive. Hardware ideal for BBS operation will cost from $3,000 to $5,000 and more. Some experts recommend at least a 386-speed PC system, but a 486 or 586 (Pentium) is preferred because they are much faster processors. The system should run at least at 33 to 66 MHz in speed and have a 200 MB to 500 MB hard drive as a minimum BBS configuration. Clearly, as file storage grows so will the need for a larger hard drive. It may be best, if a new system is purchased, to begin with a larger hard drive, from 500 MB to 1 GB in size. Furthermore, a BBS hardware configuration, Makulowich (1992) recommends, should have both 5.25-inch and 3.5-inch floppy drives and two serial ports. A fast modem will be needed to satisfy users. Ideally, a 9600, 14400, or 28800 baud modem should be installed, but a minimum 2400 baud modem will also do the job. Modems range widely in price, but an internal modem card can be obtained for as little as $50 to $100.

Software is not a major problem, but at least one new program will have to be acquired in addition to the operating system software. This is the host software used to operate the bulletin board system. There are a number of major packages on the market and most are sold in major computer stores or through national mail-order services. Makulowich advises acquiring the BBS host software first, if possible, because this often determines the minimum hardware needs. Some of the leading BBS packages in 1994 were MMB TEAMate, PCBoard, RBBS, Searchlight, Synchronet, TBBS, The Major BBS, Undetermined, and Wildcat! Two other easy-to-use BBS host programs often recommended for beginners are Sapphire and Free Speech (Germain, 1993b).

Decide on a location for the system. Make certain at least one telephone line—preferably several, depending on the size of the BBS and the community it serves—is dedicated solely to use by the BBS. It is not a wise decision to share the line with voice or fax users. Makulowich (1992) advises these basics for beginning sysops:

- Allow time to test the system and to establish a core of users.
- Line up a core of committed users.
- Set up goals for users and explain these to the users at the beginning.
- Define the level of service for users.
- Join a club for sysops.
- Seek continuous improvement in the system.
- Be responsive to complaints and be user driven.

LEADING COMMUNICATIONS PACKAGES

For use with a bulletin board or for simply linking to a commercial database service, a communications package is an essential tool for the digital journalist of the mid-1990s. Once a computer is available with a reasonably fast modem, at least 2400 baud, some consideration can be given to a communications package. Some people never think about the choice because they simply use the software that came with their computer. This is fine in most cases, but not all software does the tasks needed in the database and BBS world of information gathering.

Communications packages allow computer users to link their computers with other computers. There are programs for all types of platforms and systems. Like other software decision making, the program should cover the basic features, be affordable, and be easy to use. Major features of communications packages include:

- Compatibility with the modem being used.
- Flexibility in information transfer speed.
- Parity checking for transmission integrity.
- Error checking and error control during transmission.
- Data compression and decompression.
- A range of the most popular upload and download file protocols.
- Automatic log-ons and other time-saving "script" file programming tools.
- A host mode to permit other users to dial into the user's PC.
- Dialing directories to list frequently used numbers and services and their communications settings.
- Terminal emulation and keyboard customization.
- On-screen data capture capability.
- Printing capability.
- Manual modem command control.
- On-screen help.

COMMUNICATIONS PACKAGES IN NEWSROOMS

The 1994 University of Miami national CAR study found a range of communications packages in use in U.S. daily newspaper newsrooms (n = 208). Of those in use, Procomm, used in both DOS and Windows versions, is by far the most popular in newsrooms and news libraries:

Circulation	Procomm	Crosstalk	Smartcom	Other	None
Under 50,000	9.6% (7)	23.1% (3)	27.3% (3)	25.4% (15)	67.0% (59)
50,001–100,000	31.5 (23)	7.7 (1)	54.5 (6)	25.4 (15)	20.5 (18)
100,001–250,000	34.2 (25)	30.8 (4)	0.0 (0)	35.6 (21)	15.5 (9)
250,001–500,000	15.1 (11)	23.1 (3)	9.1 (1)	13.6 (8)	3.4 (2)
Over 500,000	9.6 (7)	15.4 (2)	9.1 (1)	0.0 (0)	0.0 (0)
Totals	100.0% (73)	100.0% (13)	100.0% (11)	100.0% (59)	100.0% (88)

Note: Percentages are for columns. Frequencies are in parentheses. Some newspapers reported using more than one type of communications package.

The most popular asynchronous communications package on the market among newspapers is the DOS and Windows versions of Procomm Plus. Crosstalk and Smartcom are also common at daily newspapers. Some users find Terminal in Windows, which comes with the basic Windows package, to be useful although it offers only minimal features. Among newspapers using Macintosh systems, MicroPhone, White Knight, Z-term, Claris Works, and Red Ryder are used. Some users, who do not access online services often, find the communications tools provided in integrated packages, such as Claris Works, to be quite sufficient for their needs.

BBS USER ISSUES AND CONCERNS

There are several issues that BBS users may think about from time to time. For example, should a user be obligated to help pay for operation of a BBS by paying memberships or access fees to a BBS operator? Some people argue this depends on the purpose of the board. Commercial boards require fees to keep the system in business. Organizations seeking to promote or publicize their interests give away access and some even pay for the long-distance telephone call. There is no single approach and as the world of BBS matures some of the fee issues will sort themselves out.

There are clearly copyright and other legal issues that are part of BBS use. Many of these issues have already been discussed, but it is clear that software piracy is a serious concern whenever BBS libraries are discussed. Users should be as concerned about illegal software as sysops.

Registration is almost always required by BBSs although some do not need identification to serve their purposes. Some BBS users register with false identifications, which raises ethical, if not legal, issues. There is ample opportunity for misrepresentation in the rather anonymous world of online conferencing, electronic mail, and messaging. Just as journalists must be concerned about misrepresentation in their conventional relations with sources, it becomes a focal point of online communication, as well.

Privacy and other security issues have come to the forefront of online research in recent years. Many people are concerned about invasion of their privacy by online research, but there are also online users, such as those who regularly visit BBSs, who worry about the privacy and security of the systems they frequent. Most sysops are honorable and do not violate the privacy of electronic mail, but BBS users should always be careful not to write or send files that contain sensitive information of any type. In the online world, just as on the street, users cannot be sure of who is on the other end of the line and caution is always a wise stance to take.

Security through encryption is one way to enhance privacy (C. Lang, 1994). Encryption is a method of "making information indecipherable" (Woodcock, 1991, p. 128) by translating messages, such as E-mail or stored data, into sophisticated digital code. Computer users seeking increased privacy of their data and data transmissions frequently find encryption useful, although some government officials would prefer a standard that would allow their interception and decoding of messages and other files. Officials say the standard exists for law enforcement purposes, but computer users feel it could lead to invasion of their privacy (Strauss, 1994). There are various encryption software packages on the market for users if high security is a concern. Some news organizations, for some stories such as sensitive investigations, may require it. For most users, it is not necessary. It is always a good idea to know the option is there if it is needed.

Time limitations are a real problem for some BBSs. Because of the limitation of lines, or because of the high number of callers in a 24-hour period, many boards place time limits on use. Some are as short as 10 or 15 minutes; others as long as 1 or 2 hours in a single day. It makes good sense to have communications software that monitors connect time when this is an access factor.

Software viruses are also a concern. Viruses are usually a minor problem, if one at all, for most BBSs, but user systems can be infected if downloaded files are stored on a hard drive instead of a floppy disk. BBS sysops are diligent in checking files for viruses, but, as *Online Access* magazine likes to remind its readers, there are some "sickos" out there and online users must be alert to the risks. Most experienced online users have an antivirus software program installed and running on their computers. These detection programs will warn against the most common viruses but may not detect all viruses, especially the most recent versions.

7 Access and the Cost of Using Databases

When a visitor recently stopped at his desk in the *St. Petersburg Times* newsroom, investigative reporter Bob Port described how he often has to fight Florida state officials to obtain public records kept in databases. It has been his experience, he says, that bureaucrats in Tallahassee, the state capital, do not want his newspaper to possess some computer databases. He has at least five or six different stories about his attempts to get one public database or another from the state, but an experience in 1991 is probably his favorite.

Port, who served as the newspaper's computer-assisted reporting director, before moving to the Associated Press in 1995, wanted to acquire the nine-track tape of the state payroll database kept by the state's Department of Administration. The database is saved on tape once a month as backup by state programmers, and Port requested a copy of that backup tape under Florida's liberal open records law. The database would be a highly useful reporting tool, Port and his editors believed, because it included names, addresses, job descriptions, salaries, and other information about all state employees. Port said he planned to take the copy of the database and, using his own nine-track tape drive and the newspaper's mainframe computer, access the database whenever the need occurred. Port (personal communication, January 25, 1994) recalled:

> I asked the governor's office for a copy of the state's payroll database and they said they could give it to me for $1,600, including the cost of programming, CPU, and other time costs to spit it out. Then they discovered they would have to include code to eliminate the legally exempt addresses, such as those belonging to police officers. So I told them to just forget the addresses and that I would come up there and copy the tape myself with my own tape and tape drive. They said it would still cost $1,600. So, I rented a Pontiac, took my computer and portable nine-track tape drive in the car, and went to Tallahassee. I drove right up to the front door of the state office building, went inside, and said, "I'm here to copy the payroll tape." Well, that set off a week's worth of meetings with their lawyers, our lawyers, and me. In the end, we got the tape for $50.

Port explained that barriers to access to public information are a regular problem for database reporters seeking to copy open public records in electronic form, especially in most states where laws about access are not clear. Port recalled that he was quoted a price of $150,000 for a death certificates database from the state's Health and Rehabilitative Services department at a base rate, permissible under the law, of 25 cents per record. He also remembers when officials in Pinellas County, where St. Petersburg is located, quoted him an access and duplication fee of $360,000 for a highly detailed database of all cases handled by the county medical examiner's office. After negotiating to eliminate the names of deceased persons from the ME's database, the price went down to $400. "They [county officials] were worried about the legal problems related to releasing names in connection to causes of death such as AIDS, but this is public information," Port explained.

Officials from the Florida Department of Highway Safety and Motor Vehicles quoted, on separate occasions, a $3 per record fee both to Port and to Steve Doig, *The Miami Herald's* associate editor for research. Considering there are approximately 11 million records, the cost would be $33 million. Needless to say, the newspapers did not purchase the database. "I know they have cut deals with commercial database vendors for much less—prices more like $750,000," Port explained. "But for newspapers, the price is $33 million." In Ohio, the *Dayton Daily News* was offered a deal in 1989 by state officials for 7 million Ohio driver's license records at $3 each, or $21 million. It took a year, but the newspaper finally got the records on nine-track magnetic tape for $400 (S. D. Scott, 1991).

In Houston, there have been similar experiences. A reporter for *The Houston Chronicle* requested public information contained in a computer database from the Harris County Appraisal District. The large number of records was printed out by an employee of the office responsible for collecting and maintaining the information. The official then proposed that the reporter view the long computer printout in the appraisal district office at no cost or the newspaper reporter pay $600 for the privilege of taking the document back to the office to read it. After some discussion between the agency and the newspaper, the agency withdrew its fee requirement and gave the reporter the paper copy at no cost (Hunt, 1993). That scarcely compares to another request by *The Chronicle*. In response to a database purchase request from *The Chronicle,* officials of the Texas Department of Public Safety said it would cost about $60 million—$5 each for 12 million individual records—to obtain a magnetic tape copy of the state's drivers' license records database. The newspaper argued the tapes should cost no more than the actual cost of copying the tapes. "With most government agencies, however, if a computer is involved, so are costs," wrote *Chronicle* staff reporter Dianna Hunt (1993, p. A1). "Charges of $1,000 or more are not uncommon even for routine information. And it is those stiff fees, perhaps more than anything else, that threaten to close the door on public access to computerized information, open government advocates warn." Hunt and others who write about the subject like to point out that many citizens cannot pay $5, $10, or whatever may be considered nominal costs for access, much less pay outrageous fees such as the $60 million demanded in Texas.

What happened in Florida, Ohio, and Texas occurs often throughout the United States. News organizations with the resources of a *St. Petersburg Times* or a *Houston Chronicle* choose their fights carefully, but they are willing to discuss, debate, bargain, and even plead for access to records in electronic form. Timid officials often refuse. If negotiating does not work, then the news organizations' managers are not shy about filing suit for access under state and federal open records or freedom of information laws. What Port and the *St. Petersburg Times* did to obtain the state payroll database is typical of the effort required. Unfortunately, many news organizations do not have the necessary resources to accomplish so much. When budgets are tight, or when legal expertise is not available, some news organizations team with others who have some, or all, of the needed resources to fight for access to public records. Costs can be shared as much as possible.

There are two major focal points about access and costs of using online services and electronic databases:

- First, attention is given to the group of issues that relate to basic access. Included in the discussion of access issues are legal concerns, rights and freedoms, and privacy issues.
- Second, the discussion focuses on a number of concerns that relate to the economics of online news research.

There is no doubt that the computer is changing access to public information, such as government records, at all levels. But the new technology means potential new problems. "[I]f proponents of public access are not careful, government officials could use the most advanced information processor [the human brain]—under the cloak of such reasons as privacy or financial constraints—to reduce the amount of information made available to the public," wrote media law scholars Bill Chamberlin and Sigman Splichal (1993, p. 339). "Government officials who wish to keep information from the public have discovered a new weapon. Public policies of openness that have guided government record keepers since the 1960s can be effectively stifled by sophisticated use of the computer as an excuse for nondisclosure."

Perhaps the single most significant concern in the mid-1990s that involves access to computer-based public records is an economic issue. These two subjects, access to information and the cost of that access, are inextricably linked. The best example of the connection is the recent efforts by many government agencies, at levels from federal to local, to sell the information to the highest commercial bidder. In an era of tight public budgets, many agencies have discovered that the information highway can be a toll road. Some critics have even called public records databases the latest "cash cows" of government. Bureaucrats subscribing to this philosophy view the sale of records to vendors, or to the public directly, as a new revenue source. "[S]ome governments eager to cash in on their records are proposing steps that would fundamentally change the public nature of the records altogether," wrote *Editor & Publisher* Reporter Mark Fitzgerald (1993, p. 9), referring to sale of databases to private vendors for eventual resale to the public. An article in *PACs & Lobbies* ("Rep. Major Owen," 1991) pointed out the sometimes dramatic differences in what the federal government charges and what it costs to generate data for the public to use. For example, in 1991, the Bureau of the Census charged $250 for a compact disc that cost about $2 to produce and the Federal Reserve charged $500 for a copy of a banking report that could be put on a computer tape for about $10. Private sector information markups are often equally high.

"The public's right to know is increasingly being defined in terms of an ability to pay, as valuable government databases are rationed to the most affluent citizens," argued Steve Farnsworth (1993, p. 19), a researcher at Ralph Nader's Taxpayer Assets Project in Washington, DC. "A democratic society deserves better. Citizens should have convenient and affordable access to this information."

ACCESS TO PUBLIC INFORMATION

Sigman Splichal (1993), a University of Miami journalism professor, identifies three distinct categories of conflict involving access to public information and the privacy of individuals. The categories are (a) technical and mechanical issues, (b) definitional or interpretational issues, and (c) public policy issues. Access difficulties for journalists and other citizens often arise from computer hardware and software problems. There are occasions when some agencies cannot provide information because officials do not know how to provide it or the system is not capable of fulfilling the request because of its design. However, still other access barriers exist because of unresolved debate over what is included and excluded by laws and departmental policies. Policy controlling collection and storage of data is also a major concern, Splichal noted.

For some journalists, the most central concern about access to information already collected by a governmental body is *control of information*. There is no doubt policy affecting control is an individual privacy matter as well. Discussions about who is able to collect information, what that information can and cannot include, and how it can be distributed surface in most discussions about access and privacy.

There is a growing public discussion about when and how the federal, state, and local governments should make their computer databases available to citizens who request them. Although this debate is primarily focused on the federal government, it will eventually grow to all state, county, and city government levels as well. The issues include economic matters as well as *privatization* of public data. During the Reagan and Bush administrations, the federal government made conscious efforts to reduce its size, including developing policy that made privatization—turning over former public governing processes to private enterprise—possible. This policy, combined with the growth of personal computers and advancements in remote access hardware, set up a potential collision in priorities at one of the major intersections of the information highway. "The elitist franchising of government information is a strange byproduct—make that unintended consequence—of America's computer revolution. Even in the logy federal government, information once stowed in binders and gunmetal files is now neatly ensconced on computer diskettes, magnetic tapes, and CD-ROMs. . . . But while the government can store data in these configurations, most ordinary personal and business computers can't read it," wrote Daniel Gross (1991, p. 37) in *Washington Monthly*. "What private vendors do is mold the raw data into a form that their customers can use. In doing so, they 'add value' to public information and gain the right to copyright the final 'product' and charge high prices for its use."

Writer Mary Jacoby (1993) described this as the *selling of government:*

> [R]esale by private companies of taxpayer-financed materials has been a point of contention over the years, most recently flaring up in debate over House legislative service organizations [LSOs]. Should private foundations affiliated with LSOs be allowed to resell for profit reports produced by the LSOs with taxpayer funds? There's no law against it, as critics found. In fact, government documents are not copyrighted and thus fair game for private firms that wish to resell them for profit. A small industry has sprung up around this practice. (p. B33)

Journalist Patric Hedlund (1992), a computer access proponent, strongly advocates that computer users be aware of the threat of governments selling their vast electronic information libraries to the highest bidders. This trend has already begun as many federal and state agencies have contracted to make databases available through commercial vendors. Fortunately, this access is not exclusive in most cases. There are situations, however, where some agencies have made arrangements that the electronic information is made available only through the vendor, at high prices as well.

One federal government example is EDGAR—an acronym for Electronic Data Gathering, Analysis, and Retrieval—the $50-plus million Securities and Exchange Commission system that began operation in 1993. Before EDGAR, any citizen could go to an SEC office and look at public company filings, required by law on paper. The electronic conversion will eventually place all 15,000 publicly owned companies online. If the government made this information available to the public online itself, the cost would likely be minimal. It could be similar to dialing into FedWorld, costing only pennies per document to retrieve. But because the SEC has a contract with an independent vendor and the vendor has the right to sell the database to other vendors, the price has gone way up. Perhaps because of consumer cost, general public access to public information such as the filings on EDGAR, has gone down (Kerber, 1993; Middleton, 1993).

Some computer-handy citizens are angered by the act of *double billing* for access. Taxpayers funded creation of these databases in the first place, these individuals contend. With the current vendor–contractor system and with the vendor's "enhancements" to the same database, the computer user winds up being charged a second time for information some critics say the user, a taxpayer, paid for in the first place. In worst-case scenarios, some federal and state agency employees find themselves literally buying, by the hour or by the document, the same public information they originally worked to create (Nader & Love, 1991).

Situations such as this have led some consumer organizations to take positions advocating greater public access to government information. Consumer watchdog Ralph Nader and his associate, James P. Love (1991), described the 1980s as:

> An era of towering potential and diminutive accomplishment. The potential was created by staggering advancement in computer and telecommunications technology. The principal roadblocks to exploiting the technological advancements were pressures to privatize access to government information resources. Now, after years of the federal government getting things wrong, Congress is undertaking a promising review of technology and public access to government information. (p. 25)

Nader and like-thinking individuals have argued that most taxpayers, schools and students, and other participants in society cannot, and should not, pay the high online fees of commercial services. Steve Farnsworth (1993), a research staff member for Ralph Nader's Taxpayer Assets Project, which actively campaigns to open federal databases, argues, "Citizens paid for these data bases. The public should be entitled

to use [them], and in a form far more convenient than paper copies. . . .
Citizens should not have to pay twice for this important information:
once as taxpayers and then again as captives of high-priced data
vendors" (p. 15).

Free speech issues are a major part of the electronic database access
debate. When the Constitution and Bill of Rights were written, no one
imagined the technology that is commonplace in the late 20th century.
Even the legislation and related documents that are the foundation of
broadcast regulation do not address electronic communication or information storage using computers. Journalists and others who use computer-based information are often left to court interpretations and
one-on-one negotiation. Does the First Amendment, for example, give
any protection to communication using telephone lines and computers?
If so, how much? In what circumstances? Are electronic mail communications of government officials, such as letters or memos, public records
or are they more like telephone calls—all made of electrons that come
and go—with no permanent form? Or are they a new form altogether?

Numerous critics suggest that governments are erecting the *barriers*
of high cost and general inconvenience to prevent access. One such
barrier is the lack of compatibility of online computer systems, making
use by citizens less knowledgeable about use of computers difficult, if
not impossible. In the Philadelphia metropolitan area, for example,
county courthouses and city halls have placed the most critical public
records into computer databases and many are available through remote access. The problem arises from the fact that just about each
jurisdiction uses its own software and unique access commands. This
requires users of more than one system to learn each one. Few citizens
would be willing to do this on their own time, it could be argued, and for
individuals who must access these databases as part of their work, there
will be an extended learning period (Grezlak, 1993). Without independent computer programmers and commercial interests willing to devise
an interface that makes access to all systems easier, access is a challenge
for most citizens. But that third-party involvement—such as one in
greater Philadelphia and in dozens of other states and metropolitan
areas across the country—comes with a usually high price tag for the
service rendered.

FIGHTING NEW ACCESS BATTLES

Access battles will be fought at the federal, state, and local levels for the
rest of this decade and well into the next one. The battles will be fought
in government offices, in courtrooms, and in legislatures. The debate
over what should be available and in what form will take years in some
parts of the country, it seems. All of this leads some people to conclude

that computers have not helped make public and some private information more accessible but have instead made it more difficult for citizens to get information conveniently, in a timely manner, and inexpensively. Dianna Hunt (1993), a reporter for *The Houston Chronicle*, co-authored a three-part series about "Computer Inaccess" that was published by her newspaper. Computers, Hunt wrote, should have made access easier. But she found that "computers have stymied public access to government information. While some information that was already accessible can be obtained more easily by those with the talent and technology to tap government files, routine requests for information in many cases have become more difficult in the age of computers. Indeed, where government is concerned, computer access is threatening to become a contradiction in terms" (p. A1)

It is clear, then, that not all databases are public and accessible. Even public records are not always available. In most states, for example, drivers' records are public, but they are not in California. Even public records in some jurisdictions, which are made available directly through the government or indirectly through a commercial vendor, are not always easy to access. Some companies that have made public databases available for sale (e.g., Knight-Ridder or Mead Data Central) have a vested interest in maintaining control over the government data. It is a big revenue source.

Even some databases that are available directly from the government at low cost are difficult to find and access. For some persons, adding the complication of a computer makes access harder, not easier. "The very tools that make it possible to store and sort enormous amounts of information also make it harder to get to," wrote *Houston Chronicle* staff reporter Dwight Silverman (1993, p. A1), who worked with Hunt on the *Chronicle* series. "Even experienced computer users . . . find the task daunting."

Tom Koch (1991), a journalist and online information consultant, feels there is a need for public libraries to make commercial databases more accessible at a more affordable price. Koch is not alone in his thinking. Former journalist and United States Information Agency staff member Dale Morrison said greater low-cost public access is a necessity. "For most citizens—and for most of our civic leadership—these issues [public computer access to government information and services] appear dauntingly complex because they involve the impenetrable mysteries of the computer," Morrison (1994, p. 2) stated. "In fact, the computer stuff is easy. Really sticky are the political, organizational and commercial interests at play in making public information available online at little or no cost."

Others in the Pacific Northwest, where Morrison resides, must agree with him. The Seattle–Tacoma area of Washington state is moving toward a complete online government system, what some writers have called "virtual government." Katherine Long (1993), a reporter for *The Seattle Times,* wrote that the concept could put the area "light years ahead of the most areas of the nation" (p. A1). The system is high tech, but it will truly put government access online. With existing technology, the area's officials are working to put interactive links between citizens and their governments to work. Such interactive online access to government, according to the Puget Sound region's model, would permit electronic mail to local government officials, discussion about government proposals, and the ability to complete transactions with local governments—such as paying parking tickets or property tax bills—online.

Some persons, including those who fear computers and the misuse of the power of computers, prefer that government not take on a dimension of George Orwell's "big brother" form of government. Officials in Washington seem to feel an Orwellian government will not develop. Other critics seem more concerned about the cost of becoming part of the online network. They feel that individuals on limited incomes cannot afford to own and use computers and those without computer skills will be effectively shut out. Officials in communities like Seattle hope to give everyone access by placing terminals in public places such as city buildings, schools, and libraries (Long, 1993).

COMPUTERS AND PERSONAL PRIVACY ISSUES

For a generation or more, the open government–privacy pendulum has swung toward open government and open access to public information. However, some segments of the U.S. public would like to push the pendulum back toward less openness of government and personal information. The reason? To protect and increase levels of individual privacy. These persons and their interest groups view invasion of privacy as a major concern. "The most imminent threat from electronic progress may be to personal privacy. Safeguards on personal information already have been nibbled away as data 'puddles' on financial, medical and tax records have been stored on scattered computers," Vic Sussman (1993, p. 68) wrote in *U.S. News and World Report.* "The fact that these various computers have been unconnected has made it difficult, until recently, to gather and collate information on any individual. But the phenomenal increase in the power and connectivity of computers is rapidly eroding whatever *de facto* protection may have existed."

In 1991, Patric Hedlund (1992), a journalist and television producer, attended a conference on computers, freedom, and privacy. One of the purposes of the meeting was to discuss ways to prevent overzealous law enforcement from being applied to the growing electronic information networks. Organizers wanted to advise computer users to be careful not to sacrifice traditional U.S. freedoms, such as access to public information, to the government, or to large information companies. "There was widespread agreement on two concepts: First, the evolution of human technology seems to move at a faster rate than the evolution of truly democratic governance. Second, social policy has a way of twisting technology to its own ends, for better or for worse," she wrote (p. 12). "The process is filled with intangibles and conflicting interests that are especially complex when applied to the developing domains of digital telecommunications."

Individuals who have taken the time to contemplate the public records access situation have concluded that computers have given the idea of government in the sunshine a new dimension, a new level of complication. "[C]omputers have complicated the concept of open government like never before," Hunt (1993, p. A1), wrote. She concluded that, in Texas, this was caused by four major categories of access problems:

- *Vague laws.* Many laws do not even consider electronic forms of information or storage of it. This means legal interpretations are necessary, sometimes by the agencies that keep the records.
- *High costs.* Paper copies cost only a few cents per page, but even routine requests for data can cost hundreds or thousands of dollars when computer time or programmer time is passed, by law, to the requester.
- *Loss of access.* With paper records, browsing was free. But direct access to browsing some electronic records is not easy or cannot be done at all.
- *Government indifference.* Some state agencies have not done anything about computerizing records and some have even found ways to avoid it within the law. Some bureaucrats feel open records are very important but that computers are not necessary to have open access.

The federal Freedom of Information Act (FOIA) does not address electronic records or databases. It was written and passed in an era, the 1960s, when electronic databases were maintained only on mainframe computers and access to this information was a minimal, or perhaps nonexistent, public concern. Similar legal situations exist in most states, which may have very strong and clearly worded freedom of information laws, including open records statutes, that rarely consider electronic public records. Few states have amended their public records laws to include such technological advances in record keeping in the past decade or so. The existing laws need to be changed, argued *Houston Chronicle* reporters Dianna Hunt and Dwight Silverman (1993). The most important areas of concern, Hunt and Silverman believe, include specific mention of computerized records in the laws themselves, a mandate to agencies to provide public access to the information, and a right of citizens to obtain copies of the records in computer-compatible formats.

Marketing professor Ellen Foxman and political scientist Paula Kilcoyne (1993) concluded that:

> Two major ethical conflicts relating to marketing practice and consumer privacy involve (a) discrepant views between businesses and consumers about who should control consumer information and (b) friction between consumer privacy and other consumer or business entity rights. These conflicts are exacerbated by consumers' lack of information about the uses to which information pertaining to them may be put and their lack of resource when information pertaining to them is misused. (p. 106)

IS PERSONAL PRIVACY UNDER SIEGE?

With the growth of privately operated mainframe computers and electronic databases, individuals became more and more concerned about loss of their privacy. After all, there is no explicit guarantee of personal privacy in the Constitution (Piller, 1993). Pressure on the federal government led to laws assuring certain levels of privacy to citizens. Sound like a mid-1990s story line? It happened in the late 1960s and early 1970s. The federal Privacy Act of 1974, driven by computer/privacy concerns, limited how much information the federal government could collect and how it could be combined in interagency efforts (Rothfeder, 1992). Things have changed in the past two decades and the private sector has caught up and gone beyond, in some cases, what government agencies collect. The rapid and seemingly all-encompassing growth of data collection in the private sector has returned public attention to privacy issues, even though many professional information gatherers, such as journalists, find public and private databases to be extremely valuable tools in their work.

Depending on how a person views the situation, the availability of online information can be a curse and a nightmare or it can be one of the most exciting developments in news reporting since the telephone came along. In recent years, just about every major news network, national news magazine, and daily newspaper has prepared some sort of article or series of stories about the so-called assault on personal privacy. It is the stuff of sweeps week programs, cover articles, and classroom discussions. It is a topic of interest to most everyone. Journalists certainly have a stake in the public discussion and any legislative action or bureaucratic policies that result.

Most Americans, particularly newsmakers and potential newsmakers, value their privacy. Polls have shown that privacy is a high priority or, at least, a personal concern of citizens—ranging from 76% to 93% in different national public opinion studies (Foxman & Kilcoyne, 1993; Piller, 1993). "Consumers have expressed increasing concern about the erosion of their personal privacy resulting from the collection and use of personal information by state and federal government agencies and business institutions," Foxman and Kilcoyne (1993, p. 106) concluded. The concern has led to some action, they wrote, by legislators and computer professionals, in the area of public policy. When information can be found easily, or more easily than it once was found, there is cause for concern.

Some state legislatures are closing records that were once public. If they are not closing records, they are restricting certain categories within public records databases. California, for instance, once opened its drivers' license records. However, the state legislature recently changed the law and closed access to outsiders (Eckhouse, 1993). This may have been caused, in part, by the 1989 death of television actress Rebecca Schaeffer, who was stalked and murdered by a man who obtained her address from a public records database (Rothfeder, 1992). For many journalists, the scenario of closing records in reaction to isolated incidents is difficult to imagine, but for the average citizen, the view is that investigators—even reporters or news researchers—should have no legal "right" to be prying into their private lives.

The advancing technology that made "people-finding" and personal information finding easier did not change the laws. It only took advantage of information that was already available to the public. As most journalists and news researchers know, bits of information ultimately can add up to a fairly complete portrait of a person, an institution, or a company. For many citizens, the accumulation of such information, acquired for just a few dollars and a few hours of time, is shocking. Many citizens feel the bounds of privacy are being stretched by the new technology to a level with which they feel uncomfortable.

Some legal arguments have been advanced against use of computers to merge various bits of information to create "profiles" or "composites" of individuals, organizations, and neighborhoods (e.g., by zip codes) even under existing open records laws. The "practical obscurity" doctrine assumes that computers only make matters worse, in a matter of speaking. Computers, the doctrine explains, eliminate the distance and time that naturally separate much personal information about individuals contained in public records. Individuals, advocates of this doctrine argue, have the chance to distance themselves from their pasts and, in essence, start over. The composite picture, painted by a computer's access and its relational processing abilities, is far more threatening than any individual piece (Splichal, 1993).

BusinessWeek investigative reporter Jeffrey Rothfeder (1989, 1992) demonstrated this concern involving loss of privacy and, at the same time, alerted many Americans about the growing amount of information kept in private database services often called "superbureaus." His magazine articles and book, *Privacy for Sale,* offered countless examples of the extended limits of personal privacy. He made his points with a bang, using large amounts of personal information collected online and through information "superbureaus" about then-Vice President Dan Quayle and CBS News Anchor Dan Rather. Rothfeder described how large computer services, unethical and law-breaking information "cowboys," and certain government policies and laws had led to a fundamental change in the United States. Privacy was eroding, he said. "Key privacy issues that have been ignored for decades are now on the national agenda," Rothfeder wrote (1992, p. 209).

A reporter for *The Ottawa Citizen* also demonstrated how much information can be obtained about individuals under Canadian laws when he searched legal sources for information about three individuals who "volunteered" for the experiment. The investigation found long lists of personal information on the individuals such as occupation, education, birth date, home address and telephone number, minimum salary, marriage and divorce history, automobile type and loan amount, criminal past (if any), and even some hobbies. The newspaper did not use any special services or misrepresentation, remained within the law, and did no interviews. Because of strong Canadian privacy laws, the journalists could not find medical, banking, credit, or national social insurance information (Hum, 1993).

Newsday Reporter Bernie Bookbinder did the same sort of story—back in 1967. Although it was written in an era before personal computing, the results were much the same. The main difference is that it probably took a lot longer to get the information. Reporter Kinsey Wilson, writing for *Newsday* 26 years later, did an update on the same individual, his family, and the residential address by using personal computers. Not only was it faster—it took only a few hours and Wilson said he never had to leave his newsroom desk—it was undoubtedly more thorough in many regards, although some of the original databases used in 1967 by Bookbinder were not available to Wilson online. "What has changed . . . is the speed and ease with which a computer-assisted dossier can be assembled," Wilson (1993a, p. 27) concluded.

A major reason for the attack on open access to information is the occasional misuse of it. John Eckhouse, a staff reporter for the *San Francisco Chronicle,* made this point when he described to business section readers how people can use online information to commit crimes, to market products, or to target individuals for sales pitches for certain services. Wilson (1993b) detailed similar scenarios for readers of *Newsday* on Long Island. Wilson argued that when private information obtained by major marketers, such as purchasing habits or reservations, is combined with public records, such as voter registration or auto license information, "these scattered fragments assume the dimensions of a powerful dossier. And it's all quite legal and largely unregulated" (p. 24).

Eckhouse (1993) detailed how a basic combination of driver's license record information, such as a person's height and weight, and property tax records, such as an address or value of a home, could be used by a clothing store to pitch its products to people of certain sizes and socio-economic levels. "More and more personal information gets entered into computer databases every day. When an enterprising individual—whether a salesman, police officer, or criminal—cross-tabulates these reservoirs of information, it makes for some interesting—and perhaps unanticipated—results," Eckhouse (p. E1) wrote.

Eckhouse noted that "[t]oday's technical innovations are a double-edged sword, creating efficiencies for consumers and companies alike yet threatening personal privacy. It's a public policy dilemma that has baffled legislators, computer professionals, privacy advocates and law enforcement officials for years—and will become more complex with the proliferation of huge databases" (p. E1). The Direct Marketing Association helps consumers' names and addresses to be taken off "junk mail" lists; about 3 million persons have requested the service. This is strangely puzzling in itself: What uses, it could be pondered, are there for a database of 3 million names and addresses of individuals who do not want to be part of a database?

Eckhouse also predicted that medical records will be the next battle-ground for the war on privacy. Expected major changes in the national health program combined with computerization of national health records will lead to massive medical databases in private and public hands. Access issues related to those databases will be debated, but the outcome remains unclear. Outsider access to such records, Eckhouse

---

PERSONAL INFORMATION IN PUBLIC DATABASES

For anyone who has tried to find information about another person online, there is a vast list of personal data at the other end of a keyboard and modem. Some of the most easily found legal information in public records and private commercial databases includes:

- Motor vehicle registrations, driver's license records, accident reports, and driving history data such as vehicles and personal descriptions.
- Voter registration and voter participation data.
- Criminal, civil, and bankruptcy court records.
- Business and corporate information and Uniform Commercial Code data.
- Property information such as ownership, taxes, legal descriptions, and mortgages.
- Telephone listings.
- Boat and airplane registrations.
- Permits and other operator's licenses.
- Occupational injury claims.
- Social security death records.

predicts, could be "devastating" to some individuals for a wide range of ordinary reasons such as job seeking and insurance applications.

Charles Piller (1993), a senior editor for *Macworld* magazine, may have summed up the situation best. Discussing both sides of the matter, he wrote:

> The new standards of electronic intrusion upset the balance between two distinctly American values: an open and accountable society, and the right to be left alone. As online services become increasingly interconnected, affordable and fast, the ability to build electronic dossiers may quickly become the hottest privacy issue of the next century. Then again, there are so many pressing privacy issues and such widely divergent sensibilities about personal privacy, even professional privacy advocates have trouble deciding what's most important. (p. 6)

FEDERAL AND STATE LAWS AFFECTING ACCESS

It is a rather common, and perhaps exasperating, example in the literature about privacy and computers: Privacy laws protect videotape rental information more closely than personal medical records. After the confirmation hearings of U.S. Supreme Court nominee Robert Bork revealed his videotape rental habits, those laws were changed by Congress. Yet, despite the assumed need for greater privacy involving individual medical and health information, those records are more easily—and legally—available than data about who rents what videotapes.

Federal and state laws attempt to resolve many issues involving access and privacy. Yet, there seems to be an inherent conflict. There are simply no laws covering many of these high tech data situations. How such activity will be regulated in the future is the major question, not whether it will be governed. Some computer journalists, such as *Macworld's* Piller (1993), seem to think that although the stakes are high, no sweeping changes are on the horizon. "[T]he privacy implications of new technologies are likely to be confronted by government on an *ad hoc* basis, and only after the public has cried out," he wrote (p. 6).

As noted earlier, technology is far ahead of the law involving computers and government records, electronic databases, and privately assembled records. "Law has a hard time keeping up with technology. Nowhere is this truer than in the area of access to information. Government information increasingly is stored in computers, but many states' laws do not adequately reflect this fact," wrote Sandra Davidson Scott (1991, p. 8PC), a Missouri newspaper attorney and journalism professor.

States can expand constitutional rights, but they cannot restrict them. As a result, some states have passed legislation that does increase privacy rights. Some laws restrict telemarketing, for example, using computer-based dialing systems. The telephone service known as Caller

ID also has been a focus of privacy legislation in numerous states in the 1990s. Some states are exploring, and even passing, legislation that prevents data from being used for "commercial" purposes—whatever they may be (Foxman & Kilcoyne, 1993).

The U.S. Supreme Court has determined that, under the First Amendment, there are certain rights to receive information and limited rights of access to government information (Bunker, Splichal, Chamberlin, & Perry, 1993). Where the Constitution and judicial interpretation have not made matters clear, some state and federal statutes have done so. Existing federal laws offer some guidance, at least, about what is accessible and what is not.

Beyond the First Amendment, the most significant legislation on the books are, perhaps, the Federal Administrative Procedures Act (enacted in 1946), the Freedom of Information Act (1966), the National Privacy Act (1974), the Electronic Communications Privacy Act (1986), and the Computer Security Act (1987). There are others, of course, including several federal laws involving fraud, that are also helpful to those seeking to keep access to both public and private information legal.

Each state has some form of public records access law. As some scholars note (Bunker et al., 1993), "[t]he comprehensiveness of these open records statutes varies significantly" (p. 555). At least four states have references to public records access in their constitutions, and others handle the issue in a statutory manner. An analysis of access to computerized government records at the University of Florida determined that public access has had a "low priority" because many agencies have barely been able to keep the records accessible to agency employees.

Types of access to information can vary under existing laws. Paper records can be viewed in an office or faxed to a different location for viewing. Electronic records take forms in addition to paper, such as online, magnetic tape, diskette, and compact disc. When viewed online, most, if not all, systems are read-only format. There are also different variations of arranging the information into whatever format in which it is viewed.

What should state and federal public records access laws include? Few current state public records laws define records in terms of computer formats. Although it is often presumed electronic records are open, this needs to be made clear in any state or federal laws. Then, attorneys argue, certain exceptions can be approved as needed. Among other characteristics, Scott (1991) believes contemporary laws should also include access for all, regardless of the purpose. Cost, which is a concern for almost all online users, should also be contained in some form. In addition to the ability to tailor requests to formats needed by citizens, Scott feels access and retrieval of *all* records should be possible under state laws.

Four attorneys working on behalf of the Society of Professional Journalists' Project Sunshine, through which the organization proposed a model open records law in 1993, make two important points about computerized public records. First, they noted that because of copyright law limitations, data created with proprietary software cannot be given to the public along with that software necessary to use and understand the database. Second, and perhaps more important, they recommend the:

> Best statutory scheme is one which prohibits public offices from recording information electronically except with application programs that include options to reproduce the data in the nonproprietary printable character form. Generally, the state of the computer industry today [April 1993] is that, where data is recorded in encoded form via a proprietary application program, the data can be put into nonproprietary printable character form through an option that is part of the program. (Sanford, Hoberman, Lystad, & Marburger, 1993, p. 11)

There is no doubt, as Splichal (1991) recommended, that greater awareness about access issues involving computers needs to be created among journalists. Splichal also called for a more systematic approach to solving the access problems, perhaps including an informational campaign aimed at government officials and record keepers. "This would ensure that public access is a priority as more and more agencies adopt computer technologies or upgrade existing systems," he stated (p. 22). "If computer access practices and policies continue to develop piecemeal, a new technology that should enhance public access to government information could ultimately have the opposite effect."

COSTS OF ONLINE AND DATABASE RESEARCH

Most online research has a price tag, even if it is only the cost of the long-distance call or the time of an employee to conduct a search. Access to online services and to databases is expensive. Necessarily, many news organizations are concerned about the costs of access to online and database research. The national CAR study conducted at the University of Miami found that daily newspapers spent an average of $17,210 a year in 1994 and $16,534 in 1993 for online services of all types. Many of the newspapers did not spend any budgeted funds on online services and some news organizations regularly reimbursed reporters and editors for their business-related search expenses using personal accounts. Some dailies reported spending hundreds of dollars a year on online services, whereas others spent thousands and a few soared into the budget stratosphere with tens of thousands of dollars for online services. Smaller newspapers, such as the *Battle Creek Enquirer* and *Santa Cruz County Sentinel,* get by spending less than $1,000 a year. Middle-range spending is exemplified by the *Cape Cod Times* and *Elmira Star-Gazette,* which spend about $5,000 a year on these services. *The Greensboro News*

& *Record, St. Cloud Times,* and *Seattle Times* represent the next tier, spending between $20,000 and $25,000 each. Among the major league spenders in online services—reporting more than $40,000 a year—are the *Anchorage Daily News, Arizona Republic, Dallas Morning News, Atlanta Constitution, Detroit News, Daily Oklahoman,* Fort Lauderdale *Sun-Sentinel, Memphis Commercial-Appeal, Houston Chronicle, Camden Courier-Post,* and *Eagle-Tribune* in Lawrence, MA.

Although CompuServe, Prodigy, America Online, or another popular commercial online service will cost a basic services user a minimum of $100 to $150 a year, many newspapers still are not spending even that much for online news research. This may be the most curious finding about online usage in the 1994 study. When pressed about why online services are not used, most editors cite the cost or lack of appropriate hardware and software, and then respond that their budget priorities are in other directions. Some individual journalists, already committed to CAR, reported in the Miami study that they use their personal online services accounts for their news stories and hope they will be reimbursed for the costs.

The price of finding useful information online varies with the database and the provider, of course. Specialized services are expensive compared to the consumer services. Commercial online services and databases are generally more costly than similar government services. Pricing systems vary greatly also. Most specialized vendors charge by the search or by the time used. When time is the pricing unit, it is most often priced either by the hour or by the minute. Hourly rates are usually billed in fractions rounded to the nearest full minute. To encourage new customers, the most popular commercial services offer basic services with either unlimited or considerable duration of online time per month for a flat rate. Additional services, such as premium databases or unique searches, add additional costs.

Pricing structures are not unlike those used by many cable television systems in which a basic set of channels are provided. Premium channels, such as movie or other specialized entertainment programming, add to the monthly cost at varying prices. Special services, such as one-time special event programs, impose a separate additional charge. Despite what may intimidate some news managers as a potentially runaway cost for locating information online, Koch (1991) concluded that database technologies are cost efficient, especially if compared to the cost of obtaining the information firsthand or through intermediaries of some type such as information brokers.

Fee Systems

"Per search" price structures can become expensive for repeat users, but for individuals or news organizations conducting a one-time or rare search in a database, the cost plan may be preferable. It is important to note that some searches are billed at the per-search rate regardless of whether anything is found. Some searches are billed by the number of "hits" (items found), but additional costs result if the user wishes to see a full record on screen. Some services that provide per-search services also will provide printed output and mail it to the user, especially if the output is lengthy. This reduces online time but does add extra costs for printing and mailing.

Most services advertise rates by the hour and some of these rates can run anywhere from just a few dollars an hour to hundreds of dollars an hour. As some costs have become quite high at an hourly rate, some commercial services have begun to market prices on a per-minute basis. Recalculate it as an hourly rate for comparison, if needed. It is sensible to make certain, when reviewing a service and its costs, that there are no larger fractions of an hour or the entire hour billed. This is sometimes done as a minimum cost for initial connections regardless of the duration of actual connect time.

Flat fee monthly rates or, as CompuServe calls it, standard pricing plans, give users a set of constant services available at any time for unlimited access. In 1994, services that offered these plans charged about $10 a month. For CompuServe, for example, the basic plan included unlimited access to news, weather, and sports information, access to several databases that are part of the reference library, online shopping, certain financial databases and money-related features, a dozen or more games and entertainment databases, online customer support, user support forums, membership directory access, a handful of travel- and leisure-related databases, and CompuServe E-mail. For traveling journalists, there is no change in the basic cost for accessing the service if the access location changes, unless a different baud rate is used or if a special surcharge is involved. Access to many user interest groups, advanced and specialized databases, and links to many other computer systems and services are available at the hourly rate in effect, depending on the speed of the modem used. CompuServe charges higher hourly rates for faster modems, so there may or may not be a significant savings for users with 9600 and 14400 baud modems—unless the user is downloading large files. America Online and Prodigy offer similar options. For services offering more highly specialized data, such as hard-to-locate financial information, the rates often seem to skyrocket.

Premium Fees and Service Charges

Services assess surcharges on users needing to use certain features of the system. Access to exclusive databases such as the census' CEN-DATA, certain types of mail and fax services, access to particular electronic reference libraries, and some financial services can result in premium fees or service charges. Usually, the systems will notify users if they are entering a feature that will result in additional costs.

Some services also offer users the opportunity to store and retrieve data online. This is not always an inexpensive option, but it is an alternative when other options are not possible. There are also various printing services available from some vendors.

ECONOMIZING WHILE ONLINE

Online services sometimes have highly complicated pricing structures. It pays to check them carefully before signing up. Basic plans are often simple enough, if users stick to them, but few users can do that once they get "hooked." The list of premium costs and surcharges gets long for the major commercial services. Yet there are ways it economize while online. Experienced online users have their own favorite ways to save time online (which, of course, means saving money).

Planning the online session ahead of time makes a big difference in keeping online charges down. For many users, this means at least two things: First, think about which databases will be searched. Most services offer printed catalogs of databases, updated annually or more often, which can be kept next to the PC and used *before* going online. Second, it makes sense to list key words and subjects within the selected databases *before* dialing the number to connect. Once the "meter" is running online, it costs money to let the terminal sit idly while new key words are considered if an initial search fails.

Similarly, prepare as much of the necessary work that will be done online offline. For instance, some individuals prepare electronic mail online, with the connect time charges adding up. It is much more cost-effective to write memos or letters in advance and upload them to the electronic mail system while online. Unless the time is not directly billed, such as that covered by flat rate arrangements, this approach for mail, report preparation and transmission, and so forth, is a time and money saver.

Another way to save is to use databases that offer toll-free "800" or local access numbers. Some BBSs offer users toll-free access to their services because that want to encourage user access. Although there are not many of these toll-free online services of high value to journalists, some are useful to reporters. Most BBSs and online services build long-distance costs into the basic connect charges that are paid no matter where the access is made. Most commercial services are part of networks that permit local access to their systems and this facilitates the flat rate toll costs at a national level. Any long distance involved in connecting to the base computer system is then included in the basic charges assessed by the vendor. Some users who live in areas not served by "nodes" that permit local access may still have to pay for a long-distance call to connect to these services. Depending on local long-distance rates, it could even be cheaper to connect to an out-of-state node than one in state.

One method for individuals using personal accounts with commercial online services for news stories or other business-related purposes is to use employer-paid long-distance telephone lines from the newsroom. Some companies provide reporters with remote long-distance dialing through switchboards or permit reporters to use company calling cards for online access fees.

Make access calls during off-peak hours. When users pay for long-distance calls, the tolls are lower in off-peak periods. For the telephone company, this means evenings and weekends. For the online services themselves, there are also less expensive periods (sometimes called "nonprime" hours or rates) for some services. These hours usually depend on demand, but the major services get most of their business during normal business hours, Monday through Friday. Generally, if discounts are offered, they are given for usage at night, on weekends, and on holidays. CompuServe, for example, considers 8 a.m. to 7 p.m. local time to be prime/daytime service. From 7 p.m. to 8 a.m. Monday to Friday, all day Saturday and Sunday, and holidays are CompuServe's standard/evening service hours. Unfortunately, for most reporters on deadline assignments, online searching cannot be done at scheduling convenience to save money. For stories that are less deadline sensitive, off-peak dialing can be smart use of limited online or long-distance resources.

Sophisticated users of communications software can automate the process of logging on and checking routine information, such as electronic mail or electronic wire service capture or clip files online. These "script" files work faster and therefore reduce online time for persons who use the service frequently and whose costs are based purely on connect time. This feature of programs such as Procomm and Crosstalk takes a little patience on the part of users to learn and does require some introductory programming skills.

Furthermore, use online service information managers. Some services offer their own software for online access and information management, providing features that save time online. For instance, it makes sense to download files and electronic mail and read the files offline to reduce connect time. Information manager programs automate many of these ordinary online tasks and do them faster than most users could do them. "The best way to save money online . . . is to stay off-line as much as possible," wrote Rosalind Resnick (1993a, p. 7), author of *Exploring the World of Online Services*.

Some services offer preferred customer volume discounts or bulk time pricing, depending on a news organization's specific needs. Usually, these can be discussed with the marketing and sales representatives of the services and even written into the contracts when registration for online service begins.

Educational institutions are frequently offered discounts as well. These discounts can include lower rates or flat rates. This is particularly valuable for campus newspapers and other news organizations at colleges and universities, for example, that seek to develop increased use of online research in their reporting. During all of calendar year 1993, for example, the University of Miami's School of Communication paid Mead Data Central a total of $6,001 for its Nexis/Lexis database searches and telecommunication services used by journalism students. If the conventional rate had been paid, Mead Data Central officials estimated the cost would have been more than $67,000. During calendar year 1992, the University of Florida paid $20,253 for Mead Data Central services that would have cost $1,009,498 at the standard commercial rates. For flat rate arrangements for some institutions, some access may be restricted—such as the time of the day of use or the libraries or files that are available.

Online commercial services make it possible to monitor costs as users go online. Most services allow ongoing account monitoring online or the service will provide a billing statement for each session at the point a user logs off the system. It makes sense to keep track of these costs if budgeting is a concern.

Many communication software packages offer a "clock" or "timer" feature that permits a user to also monitor total connect time during a session. This is convenient for cost-conscious online database users to know how long a session has taken. This is similar to the practice of some individuals who watch the meter run in a taxi cab or persons who keep a timer near the telephone to use when long-distance calls are made.

8 Using Computers for Reporting on the Road

Computers are rapidly becoming portable tools. Reporters frequently have to go far from the newsroom to cover their assignments. In political reporting, for example, success of reporters working on tight deadlines on the campaign trail often depends on the ability of reporters to master their high-tech tools (Bunch, 1992). "A herd of reporters trails the candidates through an exhausting parade of rallies, tours, fairs and dinners from one end of the country to the other. The days dissolve into a surreal blur, a dash from plane to bus, through seas of screaming crowds and chanting hecklers, then back to the bus and again the plane. In between, somehow, reporters write and file their stories," wrote *Miami Herald* Washington correspondents Reed Karaim and Mary Voboril (1992, p. 22A). "Fuselage journalism, it's called."

For these reporters, the road is a way of life. With recent portable computing technology, it no longer matters where journalists do their jobs. They do, however, need the best technological tools to do those jobs in an era of instantaneous worldwide communication. For most reporters who frequently work on the road, the tools include cellular telephones, cellular modems, beepers with regional or national range, and portable computers equipped with modems or fax/modems. For those reporters, it is a lifestyle of filing stories from hotel rooms, telephone booths, airport concourses, and office building hallways. For those reporters, too, it is a life of writing stories during a flight or a bus ride, talking to editors on in-flight radio telephones, and getting the job done just about any time there is a pause in the schedule and any space large enough to set up a portable computer.

There is also a type of remote reporting that does not have the same glamour of the national press corps or those journalists who move from big event to big event. There are thousands of other reporters and editors who never leave their home communities, but still work much of their time out of the newsroom to cover assignments. These reporters need many of the same tools as those who work on major breaking stories. With some of the extraordinary technological leaps in the past generation of reporters, road reporting is much different from the 1970s *Boys on the Bus* days—chronicled by Timothy Crouse (1973)—of portable manual typewriters, nickels or dimes for pay telephones, finding Western Union Telex operators ready to send a dispatch, and ability for fast, error-free dictation to a copy desk.

The first portable computers, those of true laptop size, were introduced in the United States in the early 1980s by Epson, NEC, Osborne, and Tandy, but were being conceived on the drawing board in California design labs in the early 1970s (Press, 1992; Walter, 1993). The widely popular Tandy Model 100 was Japanese built, and it changed on-the-road news reporting on a worldwide level forever. Its light weight, easy use, low price, small size, and extensive availability helped it catch on quickly in many newsrooms. The Model 102 followed with more features, less weight, and other improvements, but the Model 200 series eventually replaced the 100 series. Early portable systems did not even have disk drives, so storage of a story or notes was not possible. Later systems, of course, had increased capabilities. Osborne produced its commercially successful portable, the Osborne 1, at about the same time as the Tandy Model 100 debuted. Whereas the Model 100 was a complementary machine—it ran with a desktop—the Osborne 1 ran the same software as its desktop mate. Both models were instantly popular with reporters (Press, 1992) and there are still many of the durable original units still in use in the mid-1990s.

A survey by J. D. Power and Associates in 1994 determined that 54% of all notebook computer use by businesspeople occurs at home (24%), at a remote work site (20%), or in transit (10%). The study also found that because of increasing speed, power, and storage capacity, 45% of respondents use their notebooks in their offices (Caldwell, B. Gillooly, & C. Gillooly, 1994). It is likely, of course, that journalists may use their portables less in the office and even more on the road or in transit than the average businessperson who uses a notebook PC. This is because of the nature of the work reporters and editors must do and because newsrooms have desktop PCs or other computers dedicated to word processing connected to a LAN.

Road reporting in the mid-1990s requires much more computer power than the original Tandy laptops could ever offer. Road journalism requires portability, of course, as well. Combine computing power and portability with equally significant advances in telephone technology, such as the cellular telephone and beeper, and reporters are literally unleashed. Road reporters have the potential to be faster, more thorough, and more accurate than ever before because of these improved high-tech tools.

BASIC COMPUTER HARDWARE FOR THE ROAD

Reporters going into the field in the mid-1990s are equipped with a varying collection of hardware tools. Many newspapers and magazines continue to use mid-1980s portable technology or no computer technology at all. A handful of respondents to the CAR study conducted by the University of Miami considered remote reporting to be the least advanced aspect of the news business. Some editors proudly reported that their road reporting technology was a pencil and notebook.

For most traveling journalists, portable computers are as essential as telephones. Portable computing is often a balancing act between power and portability. Often, computer power is sacrificed when portability is enhanced. Similarly, when portability is increased, computer power may be lost. There are five general categories of portable PCs in the mid-1990s: laptops, notebooks, subnotebooks, palmtops, and personal digital assistants (Lauriston, 1994). Journalists most commonly use laptops, notebooks, and subnotebooks because of their mix of power and portability. Palmtops and PDAs are just not powerful enough, although they are quite convenient to use in their current configuration. PDAs, in fact, seemed to be slow in catching on in 1994.

"Laptops and their smaller brethren, notebooks . . . are journalists' life support at the office and on the road," wrote Cleveland *Plain Dealer* Washington correspondent Beth Marchak (1993, p. 1C). Thus, using the right laptop, notebook, subnotebook, or palmtop computer is a major equipment concern for traveling journalists in the mid-1990s. "Sadly . . . most users simply buy the most powerful portable with the biggest hard disk they can afford. But power often does not mean more productivity. Other trade-offs have to be taken into account for portables," commented Steve Homer (1992, p. 25), a writer for *The Independent* in London. "There are six important factors to consider: weight, size, keyboard, display, battery life and computing performance. For most users, the least important aspect is performance."

RAM is important for most portable PCs, especially if a graphical user interface environment such as Windows will be used. It is less important if the system will run only DOS. For Windows or other environments that can run several programs at once, 4 MB of RAM is a minimum and 8 MB to 16 MB or more is advisable for greater speed and fewer system resource problems.

Portable PC screen/video display must be able to handle the varying locations that road reporting demands. This must include sufficient screen lighting for minimal outdoor daytime display. In daytime lighting, some portables are virtually impossible to read outdoors, even in the indirect light of an automobile or bus interior. Color display—there are several types for portables—is an additional expense that may not be necessary for some remote reporting.

Storage is another key. Storage needs are mostly based on individual use. A portable that will be used for writing stories and filing them by modem will not need much hard drive storage space. A system with 100 MB to 200 MB will be more than adequate for even the most sophisticated word processors, communications software, and an operating system and environment. If the system will be used for more than just these basics, such as extensive database creation or error cleaning and editing, a much larger storage medium is needed. Planning is a key. Determine the fully installed sizes of the programs to be used, including the operating system, then add sufficient space for data files to be stored, and this should provide some indication of minimal storage need.

Battery strength is also critical for traveling journalists. Some notebooks advertise battery power of 3 to 8 hours or more. However, users of portable systems know from experience this is not always the case. Some systems get from an hour to 2 hours because the user is constantly accessing the drives or power-draining peripherals such as a modem. It makes sense to purchase one or more extra batteries for extended use. This way, of course, a journalist on assignment will be able to use his or her computer on the road without taking the power pack-recharger. That unit can be left back in the hotel room for in-room computer use without weakening batteries and for recharging at the end of a day. Some portables, it should be noted, can also use regular nonrechargeable batteries, such as four to six AA size, for one-time emergency power if a rechargeable battery runs down.

Batteries are a major part of a portable's total weight. When a computer has to be carried in a shoulder bag all day, the unit weight becomes a major concern among traveling journalists. Bret Hume, chief ABC News White House correspondent who often travels on assignment, also writes an occasional computing column for the Washington Post Writers Group. Hume (1993) aptly reminds portable users that computers are not the only thing traveling journalists will bring along on assignment. "You may need to carry an extra battery, AC adapter or a battery charger. These can add a half a pound to a pound. You may also need to carry an outboard floppy disk drive, since many of the smaller notebook systems have no built-in floppy drive," Hume (p. F26) wrote. "You may need an external modem and cables. Not to mention a printer. A serial cable may be needed, and for Microsoft Windows users, a mouse as well. By the time all of the above paraphernalia is included, you may find that not everything fits in your briefcase, forcing you to carry your computer gear in its own case. At that point, the computer has become luggage."

Some reporters and editors, especially those working out of automobiles, have discovered the on-the-road benefits of *portable power inverters*. These electrical devices change 12-volt DC current, such as that produced by an automobile battery, to standard 140 watts of AC current. The devices are most commonly used for changing DC to AC in automobiles, RVs, or buses. These units will power one AC appliance such as a personal computer or printer in a vehicle by plugging into the cigarette lighter socket. The advantage, for certain, is to extend the use of the portable computer and to reduce the dependence on batteries. Furthermore, the inverter will also allow personal computer users to recharge the PC batteries while in transit, without returning to home, hotel room, or the newsroom for a conventional outlet.

Portable power inverters cost anywhere from $60 to $200, depending on the features of a particular unit and the manufacturer. Higher quality units will offer electrical grounding to reduce the chance of power surge damage to the computer or appliance. Another desirable feature is the ability of the unit to cut off when the car battery power drops below 10 volts, preventing complete vehicle battery discharge. Most do not weigh much, about a pound or so. Some units are designed with only one power outlet, and others have two outlets. The units can be purchased at many electronics or recreational vehicle supply businesses.

EQUIPPING JOURNALISTS FOR FIELD WORK

Road reporters have entered the portable computer and cellular telephone age. This is the case for some reporters, at least, at the leading daily newspapers and news magazines in the country. For other smaller organizations, reporters are still working with older technologies such as beepers and early-generation laptop computers. A few news organizations continue to linger in the technological dark ages, with reporters working in the field with only pads, pens, and pay telephones.

Using State of the Art Tools

The most technologically sophisticated news organizations use state-of-the-art electronic tools. Reporters in this idyllic electronic remote reporting world in 1995 used lightweight notebook and laptop computers with fast Pentium (586) or 486 processors, active color matrix screens,

---

WHAT'S IMPORTANT IN CHOOSING A PORTABLE PC?

David Strom (1993), a business consultant in Port Washington, NY, offers these criteria, in descending order of importance, for selecting a new portable computer for remote use:

- *Availability*—It should be in stock, with all the accessories.
- *Lightweight*—Under 4 pounds.
- *Battery life*—At least 3 hours.
- *Storage capacity*—Enough space to store all data and programs.
- *Screen and keyboard*—Close to full-size keyboard and a bright screen.
- *PCMCIA*—At least one card slot.
- *Expansion*—Capability to do other things besides the usual computing.

extended battery power, built-in pointing devices, high speed fax/modems, built-in CD-ROM drives, 8 MB or more RAM, and 500 to 700 MB hard drives. These systems are loaded with software comparable to what is available in desktop systems back in the newsroom, including powerful feature-laden word processors, spreadsheets, personal information managers, communications, and a database package.

Some journalists are venturing into a newer class of portable computers known commonly as *subnotebook computers*. The major advantage of these systems is their remarkably small size and light weight. Smaller than laptops and even notebooks, these systems weigh under 5 pounds and have much of the same capability of notebooks. The main disadvantage is that some subnotebook PCs do not offer floppy disk drives, a main reason for the lower weight. Instead, the newest systems use PCMCIA slots, which permit exchange of data with desktop systems or larger portables without going online. The PCMCIA slot also allows use of a high speed fax/modem card for communication such as file transmission on the road. External floppy drives can be connected through PCMCIA slots, too. These systems are powerful enough for most journalists' road work, offering 486 processor chips, 33 MHz or faster speed, 4 to 12 MB of RAM, and hard drives in the neighborhood of 200 MB. Some computer companies are marketing these handy systems to frequently traveling professionals such as journalists. Base list prices were about $1,500 to $2,000, without color displays, in 1995.

Those news organizations at the cutting edge are also offering reporters complete wireless remote technology by linking their powerful portable computers with cellular telephones. Having the right technology permits stories to be filed from anywhere at any time. It also allows reporters to access online news research resources anywhere at any time. Not all types of cellular telephones will permit data to be transmitted, however. This should be considered when purchasing a cellular telephone if remote PC connections will be used upon purchase or at any point in the future. A special modem and direct connection to the cellular phone bus is required. If this is not available, a more complicated and cumbersome hardware connection must be used (Conroy, 1994). Most cellular PC connections in 1994 were from 2400 to 28800 baud. These tools, when properly set up, enable field reporters to be as well equipped as they would be in the newsroom itself.

A related communication device is a *cellular modem*. These units allow users to transmit directly from a portable PC. Cellular modems run at up to 28800 baud, even faster than most conventional portable PC modems. Cellular modems are connected to a data coupler and the unit is, in turn, attached to a cellular telephone. Such a unit allows the user not only to transmit files such as news stories written in the field, but also receive files, such as research information or memos from editors. Sometimes these tools are available from news sources. For example, the U.S. military can make satellite-linkable modems available to reporters on assignment who do not have them but who need to file stories from PCs while on a ship or remote battlefield (Offley, 1994).

Some national and international telecommunications companies also offer wireless communication using beeper, or paging, technology. Operating on the same principle as wireless pagers, these wide-area satellite-relay-based technology systems permit messages, documents, data files, and similar information to be downloaded. Although these are one-way systems that can be received by a journalist using a portable computer, they are a more sophisticated way for editors to communicate with reporters and photographers than pagers and are more efficient, cost much less, and weigh less than cellular systems connected to telephones.

Informational graphics specialists are as well equipped as reporters. Portable Macintoshes such as the Powerbook line provide the needed computing power, in terms of screen display, RAM, and mass storage for creation of graphics on site during deadline reporting. Just a few years ago, these same graphic artists had to go to the scene, take notes or photographs, and then return to their newsroom systems for their final creative work. No longer. With these portable tools, the needed news graphics can be developed on location and transmitted online to the newsroom. In both cases, taking computing power to the story site ensures speed and accuracy in reporting what has occurred.

Some U.S. airlines are making it easier for computer-carrying passengers during long flights by offering links to the ground. These air-to-ground systems, such as the one offered by USAir on some flights, permit passengers to connect portable PCs into the armrest of the seat with an "RJ-11" telephone jack to transmit faxes or to use online services in the same manner as passengers would use them on the ground. This may be helpful to a reporter on deadline who needs to file or a reporter who seeks to upload data such as important E-mail. The system works in both directions. Passengers are also able to receive incoming transmission calls. These new digital systems offer more reliable service than analog systems in conventional airphones by reducing transmission errors. Air-to-ground transmission is completed using radio waves, making these services expensive—running $2 a minute in some systems. For convenience of some deadline-oriented journalists, it may be worth the price (Perenson, 1993).

What News Organizations Are Using

Not all news organizations can afford the thousands of dollars per computer required for a state-of-the-art remote reporting setup. Even though many news organizations invested in portable computers when the technology was first introduced in the early 1980s, some of these organizations are still using the same technology. The cost of upgrading is simply prohibitive for some newsroom budgets.

The 1994 national CAR study conducted at the University of Miami found that there are a surprising number of daily newspapers (35.6%) that still have no portable computing resources. Some dailies have not expanded their remote reporting to include beepers or cellular telephones, either. A majority have not expanded their reporting tools to include out-of-the-newsroom online news research, although the technological capability has existed for a decade or more.

"We have not found extensive in-field use for many of the [reporting] gadgets available. With a condensed coverage area, it is not often necessary for us to go far afield," explained Mark Lukens (personal communication, December 19, 1993), systems editor at the *Reading Eagle and Times,* a 78,000 combined morning and evening circulation news organization in Pennsylvania. "When it is, the Radio Shacks have been adequate, although I plan to update with Toshiba this coming year."

The Observer-Reporter, a 40,000-circulation daily located in Washington, PA, near Pittsburgh, may be typical of remote reporting technology in use at many medium-size dailies. Like the Reading newspaper, it uses older technology sold in the mid-1980s. "We use Tandy portable terminals when reporters go into the field on assignment," stated Managing Editor Park Burroughs (personal communication, December 27, 1993). "Then we transmit by phone direct to the front-end system."

At the Lawrence, MA, *Eagle-Tribune,* Brad Goldstein, special projects reporter, said his newpaper's reporters are equipped in the field according to the beat each one is assigned to cover. "It all depends on the beat," Goldstein (personal communication, December 21, 1993) stated. "For example, our police reporter uses a laptop."

Typically, newspapers and magazines maintain portable computers, cellular telephones, and beepers through a desk such as metro, state, or sports. It is rare to find portable systems assigned to individual reporters unless the reporter travels excessively. "We use a couple of Tandy notebook-style PCs, mainly in sports," stated Rex Rhoades (personal communication, January 2, 1994), managing editor of the *Sandusky Register,* a 25,000-circulation daily in Ohio. "We also have three bureaus online to inexpensive Radio Shack PCs. But we do not do much else with computers in the field. Our reporters are equipped with a pen and notebook."

What type of equipment was in place for remote reporting in 1994? Respondents to the Miami study revealed that among newspapers using portable computers, older technology remains popular. Numerous newspapers, such as the *Rochester Democrat and Chronicle / Times Union, Buffalo News,* and *Pittsburgh Post-Gazette,* still used Tandy 100s and 200s with their limited capabilities and built-in modems in 1994. Those systems require users to use built-in word processing and communications software. These systems offer no other computing power.

NEC, Toshiba, IBM, Dell, Everex, Compaq, Epson, and Macintosh are popular portable computer manufacturers among newspapers that have gone to more advanced systems and full communications links. *The Plain Dealer* in Cleveland has equipped its road reporters with powerful 486-based portables and several other newspapers report using high-caliber 386 systems, but the majority of those responding about their remote reporting hardware said they are using ancient technology that limits computing power for reporters.

Some journalists are considering use of personal digital assistants (PDAs), but their first year of sales during 1993–1994 was weak. Whether the technology will catch on remains to be seen, but the use of these devices is clearly helpful to traveling journalists who are not interested in using larger laptops, notebooks, or even subnotebooks. PDAs are compact devices that allow users to "hand write" on the electronic pad instead of typing information. Users can use the device to transmit information to other computer systems as well. Most PDAs offer calendars and address programs, or other forms of personal information managers.

The technology will continue to improve, but early versions of the PDAs are not really suitable for taking notes in the field, as reporters with a PDA may want to do (Casey, 1993b). These are the size of a paperback book and, like any newly introduced technology, the units will evolve rapidly over the next several years. New features and capabilities will be added in response to market needs. Until such PDA features as handwriting recognition improves, laptops, notebooks, subnotebooks, and palmtops may be the preferred alternatives.

Software for Travelers

A bonus for reporters and editors who travel often is the transition of travel information from printed to digital form. Reporters—and all other travelers, too—can learn from their portable PCs how to get "there" from "here," but also where to eat, sleep, and what airlines or ground transportation to use. There are several categories of travel software, including such tools as maps and atlases, restaurant and hotel listings, airline schedules, and online versions of traditional travel guides. These programs are available both on floppy disks and compact discs.

Atlas-type mapping software, products that permit planning and recommend the best, fastest, or most direct routes for trips, have been introduced. One example is Automap Road Atlas. It offers routing directions, distances, road information, extensive detail, and gives users the ability to plan trips to more than 20,000 U.S. locations. A European edition is also marketed. Street Atlas USA is similar but offers more local street detail. It is available on CD-ROM, which may make using it on the road difficult. Still, the program would be quite helpful in planning a trip before leaving the newsroom. With these programs, and others like them, reporters on the road can obtain information about travel distance, drive time, and recommended routing. Some of them even calculate mileage and cost of gasoline.

Another program is DeLorme Global Explorer, a compact disc product that offers full-color city maps of major cities, country profiles, air routes, indexed references to more than 120,000 places, and other general historical and cultural information. Most of these types of travel computer programs also offer on-screen maps as well as tables of driving instructions. Installation of this software will help reporters in unfamiliar territory who need to move from place to place. DeLorme also produces MapExpert.

Another software category that is helpful to traveling journalists is travel information. Electronic book publishing is a growing industry and some of the software can be useful for quickly finding traditional travel guide information such as hotel or other lodging listings and ratings, public and private transportation, historical background, geographic descriptions and maps, restaurant listings, shopping, and other various support service lists. News Electronic Data's Taxi, which has built-in information from Zagat city guides, is one example of this type of electronic "travelware" that focuses on major business locations. Computing power helps "digital travelers" locate the information faster with the built-in search and find functions (Langstaff, 1993; Seideman, 1994).

Still another option is to use travel-oriented information accessible through online services such as CompuServe, America Online, and Prodigy. The international access to these services makes this type of information particularly helpful to journalists on the road. One online category that cannot be placed on disk or CD is current weather conditions. Online services are superior for providing instant, up-to-date official weather reports when preparing for U.S. travel. There are also numerous traveler-oriented BBSs that can be contacted from just about anywhere. Bed and Breakfast Guide Online, which lists 20,000 locations, is just one example. Local Expert is a digital travel guide with maps, sightseeing, shopping, hotels, restaurants, and similar information. Personal Travel Guide offers another collection of travel-related information about specific cities (R. Goldberg, 1994).

Foreign language software may be helpful to reporters heading overseas. Software that translates from one language to another is one type, but a second variety is software that lists survival phrases in multiple languages and graphics. One example of this is Passport's World Travel Translator.

Some travel guide programs and databases are large enough to require special formats. For example, Fodor's Travel Manager for Top U.S. Cities is available on a PCMCIA card, which functions much like a hard drive. Because many new portable PCs can access these "hot" cards, there is no drain on hard drive space.

Online Services on the Road

With the computer technology available in the mid-1990s, reporters, graphic artists, photographers, and editors have the ability to go online for research while they are on the road. Few news organizations and reporters were actually doing this type of reporting in 1994, but the number seems to be growing. Reporters who use portable PCs to link up with their home newsroom computers can also use the same services they use in the newsroom or that their news researchers use in the library. They can; but few do. Why? It is unclear, except that some news organizations restrict access to control online spending and others simply do not have traveling reporters and editors who know how to use the services or have the time to learn them.

Jim Leusner, a veteran reporter for *The Orlando Sentinel,* often finds himself covering major breaking news events on the road. He is one example of a reporter who strongly believes in using online services on the road. Equipped in 1995 with a Toshiba 3300 portable PC with a modem, he had the tools to go online anywhere, any time. And he does. Leusner has been assigned to cover numerous major murder cases and trials in Florida, the Challenger shuttle disaster, and other stories that required special on-the-road command-post-type preparation to cover. "It is invaluable to have a laptop with access to driver's licenses [databases], Lexis/Nexis, CompuServe, and so forth, during major news events," Leusner (personal communication, February 13 & 16, 1994) stated.

Over several years, Leusner covered the investigation, arrest, admission of guilt, and sentencing trial of a man who killed five students in a short period of time near the University of Florida in Gainesville. Leusner had also been there during the initial investigations of the crimes:

> During the Gainesville murder trial for example, I used my Toshiba 3300. I have access to Autotrak [a Florida-based public records database], CompuServe (and the DMVHS computer), America Online and, of course, *The Sentinel* library to aid in my research while away from the newsroom. For example [had there been a trial as officials originally scheduled], I would have used Autotrak to identify witnesses, where they are from, ages, and so forth. I was using CompuServe to do research on DNA, which would have been a key element in testimony during the trial.

> What an example of CAR that case turned out to be. Danny Rolling entered a surprise plea in Gainesville. Many papers, including St. Pete and Miami, didn't plan to cover the first day of jury selection. They were going to wait until a jury was selected. Well, were they in for a surprise! The stuff hit CNN mid-morning and they scrambled to get people here, as did Jacksonville and other papers. They got to Gainesville and had not been up here earlier, like I had, to test telephone lines in the press room at the courthouse. It was specially equipped for the media, at our cost.

I was up there [the week before] to do some scouting around and some equipment tests, although the phones hadn't been installed at the courthouse. I then came up [the day before the scheduled trial date] and ran many computer tests. I brought a data phone and it didn't work, but thank God I had a spare analog phone. I carry two of everything on the road: two modems, two phones, two sets of phone cords, adapters, male-female connectors, phone splitters, sets of batteries, boxes of disks, everything. I'm a double-pack rat. My van is packed to the gills. I also have backup methods of transmitting stories over CompuServe, AOL, and even via Procomm in case my *Sentinel* SendFetch or the long-distance lines go on the fritz.

St. Pete got here late (mid-afternoon) and thought there were phones in the pressroom. The phones were wrong. The [Florida] *Times-Union* and other newspapers had archaic computers and did not have proper telephone equipment or adapters. They ended up typing stories on the computer and *dictating* from the pay phone in the hallway. What a waste of time. Along with AP and *The* [University of Florida *Independent] Alligator,* we breezed through the story.

We also got *real time* transcripts of Rolling's plea hearing from the court administrator-court reporter's office on a 3.5-inch diskette. I downloaded it to Orlando in a flash and my editors used it. I also have the 4,200 investigative reports on my laptop that I keyword-search in the Magellan sorting program. It's real handy. See, I'm slowly building my own command post.

HIGH-TECH RISKS AT AIRPORTS
AND OTHER PLACES

Just about every journalist who has used a portable computer has wondered about the unfavorable effects of taking it on the road. Can portables be checked like luggage? Are the computers themselves as sturdy as the manufacturers say they will be? How much bumping and banging can the PC take before it rebels? Do the airport's metal detectors damage disks, hard drives, RAM, or other magnetic storage? What happens if there are software troubles? Are electrical systems compatible with PCs outside the United States?

The answers to these questions are not as simple and straightforward as most journalists would prefer. The more that is known about transporting computers and using them in unfamiliar locations, the better. Problems that waste valuable time can be avoided and technical emergencies that could require expensive repairs will be kept at a minimum with the right preparation.

Simple movement of a portable personal computer opens it to the risk of damage. Transporting can make the unit vulnerable to being dropped from 4 to 6 feet and bounced off a hard surface. Most portable PCs are mostly plastic and are not well insulated against bumps. Yet, computers are better built and the individual parts are sturdier than earlier generations of hardware. Floppy disk drives and hard drives are less susceptible to read–write damage from sudden movement or jarring contact, for instance. It still makes sense to handle portable computing equipment, portable printers, and cellular telephones with care. In other words, common sense applies when working with portable electronic equipment. For instance, although some PCs can take a beating, dropping a PC or spilling coffee on the keyboard is not going to help it work its best. It follows, of course, that portable computers *should not* be included in checked baggage for a flight, a train ride, or any other trip because baggage handlers are not known for their soft hands and agility. Similarly, electronic equipment does not respond well to common road consumables such as food, drink, or cigarettes. Take care of the PC and it will take care of the user when it is needed the most.

Reporters and editors should make computers and peripherals part of their carry-on luggage. Packing the computer in an impact-absorbing shoulder bag or case is a common method. Soft-sided cases are sometimes vulnerable to severe bumps and kicks, so hard-sided cases are preferred. A soft case to cover a computer that is placed inside a hard case will offer even better protection in transit. The case should not be too large to prevent it from fitting in the overhead bin or under the seat.

For moving larger than conventional portable notebook and laptop computers, such as desktops, it is best to use the original carton and packing materials for each component. This is sensible, although some newsrooms simply do not have the space to store empty boxes over long periods of time. One solution might be to store one or two of the original cartons to use when the occasion arises. Some computer stores will offer replacement packaging, but the originals offer the best protection against damage.

Some experts, such as Russ Walter (1993), author of *The Secret Guide to Computers,* say it is smart to ask airport security officials to hand-inspect portable computers and diskettes instead of passing them through metal detectors and X-ray devices. "Do not carry the computer and disks in your hands as you go through the metal detector, since the magnetic field might erase your disks," Walter wrote (p. 554). "For best results, just tell the guards you have a computer and disks; instead of running the computer and disks through the detection equipment, the guards will inspect your stuff personally."

Experienced laptop and notebook travelers find the hand inspection strategy to be the safest, although it always takes longer. Airports, even just those in the United States, use different detection equipment made by different companies. The same equipment used in different airports is often set at different detection levels. Furthermore, airport security policies change frequently. This means there is really no certainty about the degree of risk when putting disks and computers through detection systems.

A hand inspection takes a few extra minutes, especially in a busy airport, and requires that a bag or case be opened and checked. This more conservative approach completely reduces the chance of lost data. A concern is battery power because almost all airport security officials require portable computer carriers to turn the unit on during a hand inspection. Dead batteries will not help establish that the system works. An alternative is to place the AC adapter in carry-on luggage for use if it is needed during an inspection.

Airlines are regularly revising their inflight rules about use of computing equipment. For a period of time in the late 1980s, airlines did not prohibit computer use during any portion of flights. Then evidence suggested portable electronic equipment that emitted certain signals may interfere with takeoff and landing systems of certain aircraft. Most airlines then restricted use of PCs during takeoff and landing, but continued to permit their use after the plane had reached its cruising altitude—typically a quarter hour or so into the flight until about a quarter hour before landing.

Telephone systems around the world create a different set of communication barriers. There are still telephone systems that are difficult, if not impossible, to use with portable computers. This is especially problematic for international travel. Numerous Third World nations utilize antiquated telephone technologies, including precomputer era analog systems. These systems are so difficult to work with that some high-tech journalists prefer to dictate stories to their newsrooms. Yet, there are some Western nations that are not much better in pure communication technology terms. In Germany, for example, reporters often find the analog dial telephone system as frustrating to use as they do systems in less developed parts of the world (Auerbach & Fisher, 1992).

Most important, these portable computers of small size and high value are easy theft targets when taken on the road. Thefts from careless individuals can occur at any stage of a trip, but they frequently happen while in transit, some experts have stated, if PCs are left unattended in cars or in airport concourse waiting areas and lounges. However, thefts may occur at "home" bases, too, if the usual safeguards are not taken (Bray, 1992).

It makes sense to consider service contracts or other extended protection arrangements against damage or failure because most systems have only a 1-year warranty. It also makes sense to take out separate theft insurance on expensive portable systems that are not covered by personal, business, or other general office computer theft policies.

Another form of protection involves backing up data against hard drive failure. Good file management habits include backing up valuable files daily or even more often. Software and data files loaded on the PC should also be stored on diskettes in a safe place as well.

LINKING UP WITH THE NEWSROOM

Most portable computer-using journalists seem to have their own hotel room "war stories" to tell about how a room that was not computer friendly was converted with some midnight rewiring under a table or bed headboard—much to the hotel manager's dismay. Rooms in older hotels are perhaps one of the major barriers to on-the-road communications. Public telephone booths are another. But this is changing. Many hotels provide telephones with standard RJ-11 connection jacks that no longer require users to disconnect wall wiring or unplug the telephones themselves. The same is occurring at pay phones in airport terminals throughout the United States. The transition is slow and journalists may still find smaller motels and hotels or resorts and many public telephones not up to date technologically. The main reason these shifts are occurring is that hotels and telephone companies want the growing business of "wired executives" regularly on the road (Bylinsky, 1991). Journalists with the same portable technological needs involving information as many executives are taking advantage as well.

The frustration leads some journalists to carry tool kits to rig connections when necessary. These include screwdrivers, pliers, wire, and even small soldering guns. Some innovative electronics companies sell ready-made kits for high-tech travelers. Because not all traveling journalists are electronics geniuses able to rewire their rooms, it may be worthwhile to request a "data-ready" room when reservations are being made, as a hotel or motel may have at least one or two rooms wired even if others are not.

Other locations may require much more creative solutions. Some establishments without proper guest room telephone line wiring may have more modern wiring in the lobby area or wherever pay telephones are located. Typically, pay telephone installations are more regularly checked, updated, and rewired than some hotels change their room configurations.

PRINTERS: A NECESSARY ROAD EVIL?

Although most journalists do not need printing capabilities while on the road, some find it necessary. The obvious option is to carry a printer. That may also mean carrying ribbons, cables, and paper. Unless travel is by automobile, transportation of the extra gear may be overwhelming. There are some options. First, a number of companies are manufacturing lightweight portable printers. Some are as small as laptop computers and can also fit into a briefcase or computer carrying case. Even some of the inexpensive standard size dot-matrix printers are reasonably small enough to carry if absolutely necessary.

These units may not be very sensible options for reporters traveling by air and moving frequently from place to place on some assignments. As an alternative, consider use of commercial printing businesses that will "lease" access to computers and printers by the hour. Some of these businesses are open all night—especially those located near university or college campuses or in metropolitan areas. Finding such a location would eliminate the need for anything but a portable PC to get printed output.

There are still other options to carting a bulky and heavy printer around. Printer use may be temporarily "borrowed." This means taking the portable PC to the location of someone else's printer and hooking it up using a printer cable. It makes sense to take a cable, although it may not always be needed. The downside to this approach is being certain the right printer software drivers are installed in the portable PC. The proper drivers will not always be available unless users travel with a disk containing as many drivers as possible or unless a PC user simply installs an entire set of drivers on the PC's hard drive.

Some computer and electronics manufacturers, such as Canon, have developed high-powered portable computer systems that have built-in printing capabilities. These one-stop office systems not only print copies of documents produced by the computer and its installed software, but they also double as copiers. With a fax modem PCMCIA card, the system also functions as a full-function fax machine with printed output.

Without such built-in printing potential, some enterprising journalists who need to produce a paper copy of a document, a spreadsheet, or some other file in their portable computer have discovered a neat trick: They send a fax to themselves. This is done by connecting the portable PC—it has to be equipped with a fax/modem—to the hotel room telephone line. The next step is to dial the same hotel's fax machine number. A hotel guest-accessible fax machine may be kept near the front desk. After the transmission is complete, obtaining the hard copy is as simple as going to the front desk and requesting it. Many hotels have fax machines for use by guests, but if there is not one available, local print shops and airport terminals often offer them for public use as well. This alternative may involve a service charge assessed by the business, but the cost is better than the alternative in some cases when hard copies are needed right away.

SOFTWARE FOR USE OUT OF THE NEWSROOM

In addition to the disk operating system, there are two basic types of software that need to be installed on every portable computer for remote reporting. The first type is a word processor. Without it, writing stories would be more difficult, if not impossible. The second type is a communications package. This software works in conjunction with an installed modem and permits journalists to transmit stories or other files to and from their home base, check their electronic mail, and access their online news research services. There are a handful of other types of software that could also be used on a traveling journalist's personal portable computer, but none of these can be classified as essential to road reporting.

Word processors are simply a user's preference. Reporters are no longer forced to use the built-in proprietary systems that came with older portable technology. The major word processors in the mid-1990s offer many of the same features, so selection is often a personal decision by the user. Most news organizations have front-end systems that can receive ASCII text generated from any recent version of a major word processor's file conversion utility. However, some reporters and their editors prefer to use word processing software that is the same as that used on the home front-end reporting and editing system to eliminate the need to convert files. For reporters seeking simplicity, the most basic form of word processors offers limited editing functions and works with straight ASCII file text. More sophisticated portable PCs permit reporters to do much more, but the power and range of capability of the word processor will depend on the mass storage and RAM size of the portable. Most reporters will not need elaborate, full-function GUI word processors on the road. The additional functions these programs offer are always useful, of course, but a fully installed program can eat up valuable hard drive storage space. The most recent DOS and Windows editions of the "big three" word processors—AmiPro, Microsoft Word, and WordPerfect—are very large when fully installed. Therefore, these packages offer portable, or minimal size, installations for portable computers with limited hard drives, but certain features such as online help or writing utilities such as grammar checkers are sacrificed to save space. Most major programs offer custom installation options also, that enable reporters to install only the features of the big programs that they will use.

Communications packages are usually not a major storage problem, although these products do offer different features. It makes sense to compare them before selecting one. For journalists on the road, select a communications package that has automatic log-on capability plus a wide range of protocols with which to transmit and receive files.

Fax software packages are one of many optional products. For newer model portables with fax-capable modems or PCMCIA cards, this software enables a reporter on the road to send and receive faxes from sources and from the newsroom. The convenience is a remarkable time saver. Fax capability at any location means much to reporters who have it. Like much new technology, until a reporter has tried it, he or she may not completely understand its significance in getting assignments completed.

Spreadsheet packages are clearly not necessary for traveling reporters, but the convenience of a spreadsheet for data analysis and even more practical tasks, such as compiling expense reports, is self-evident.

Similarly, database packages are not a road necessity. However, reporters with powerful enough computers can then perform analyses of newly acquired databases before returning to the newsroom if they have such a program installed on their portable PC.

Personal information managers (PIMs) may be more practical than database packages if a journalist is looking beyond just a word processor and a communications package. PIMs are a good way for journalists on the road to remain organized. These programs are often set up much like bound and printed personal organizer notebooks sold in bookstores or office supply stores. These programs enable reporters to keep lists; compile source directories of names, telephone numbers, and addresses; list activities and appointments by date and time; and make long-term planning charts. Some will even dial telephone numbers from address directories.

Furthermore, a utility package will come in handy during times of file and database trouble. These utilities provide features such as virus checking, file "undeleting," damaged file reconstruction, and similar file management tasks. These tools are not always a part of the basic operating system set-up of a portable PC, so it makes sense to include them for those deadline moments late at night when a local computer store is not available to solve data problems.

Any comprehensive collection of current roadworthy software and hardware is not the least useful if the newsroom management does not find time to teach road reporters how to use the tools. If use cannot be self-taught or internally taught, then an investment in external training classes is prudent. These are often offered by computer stores, local colleges and high schools, and private services. Some mail-order videotapes may be helpful, also. The best place to start is to read the documentation that comes with the hardware and the software. These reference books are getting more understandable. Despite age-old criticisms of their difficulty to be understood, these tools are part of the package and should be tried, at least, before they find their way into a file cabinet or bookshelf, rarely opened again. If self-teaching fails, organized training is the alternative.

FILING NEWS STORIES ON THE ROAD

Reporters file stories from just about any imaginable remote location. Sometimes, a reporter can file from newsrooms operated by sister news organizations that offer all the technological trappings of home. This is a luxury. Most of the time, the amenities of home are not so readily available. Stories have to be filed from hotel rooms, airports, convention halls, arenas, and other tech-unfriendly confines.

This is changing at some levels. A few hotel chains are beginning to offer rooms set up with telephones that have modular plugs that fit computer modems or telephones with "dataline" ports. Quality hotels are more frequently offering facilities compatible with office needs such as photocopying, fax machines, computers for guests, other office equipment, travel agent and secretarial services, and translation and courier services (Shea, 1992). More and more, these services are being offered at extended hours—even 24 hours a day, 7 days a week, in some major hotels. If these services will be needed as part of covering an extended assignment, it makes sense to "shop" for prices and availability because the facilities may enhance use of sophisticated reporting tools away from home.

One minor problem with using online services and electronic mail systems on the road is the constant need to change local contact numbers each time a user changes cities. For some reporters, such as those covering political candidates, these changes could occur several times a day. Usually, to make easy contact with online services, it requires remembering to check for the local access telephone numbers online *before* going to the new city. It would make sense, perhaps, to download entire lists of access numbers for a particular service and keep the file in the communications software directory on the hard drive for reference. Otherwise, finding the local node number—the local connecting station telephone number—could take more time and trouble than it should and perhaps even discourage use.

SETTING UP A REMOTE COMMAND POST

When the big news story occurs, such as the O.J. Simpson trial in California, journalists must quickly organize their remote reporting tools and get to the scene of the story. The effort to cover major stories is lengthy and often resource intensive, requiring considerable amounts of portable computing, graphics, and photographic equipment, transmission equipment, and the newsroom people who can efficiently use those tools. Most news organizations quickly set up "command posts" as central locations for communication and for news-related work. Often no more than hotel rooms or hotel meeting rooms, sometimes leased recreational vehicles, sometimes just a rental car, these command posts permit reporters, photographers, graphic artists, and editors to gather to direct and produce the day's coverage.

Most news organizations develop a "disaster" or "big event" reporting plan. In doing so, editors plan use of resources available to them. This includes news space, people, computer and other electronic equipment, and supplies. Most plans include access to additional news space, budgets, access to large sums of cash for situations when it is required, and ways to continue routine coverage when resources are thinned out.

Commonly used equipment for command posts at the sites of major breaking news stories includes portable computers, portable lighting, cellular telephones, backup telephone communication systems, electric power generators, beepers, two-way radios, printers, fax machines or fax modems, police radio frequency scanners, tape recorders, and flatbed scanners. Photographers will need portable darkrooms, in essence, including space and equipment to process film and print photographs. Photographers and newsrooms using digital cameras and electronic darkrooms will find these systems much easier to work with on the road.

Supplies to get the remote command post job done will also need to be a part of the plan. In preparing for command post set-up, editors and reporters must consider the need for an assortment of general office supplies such as reporter's notebooks, printer paper, and pens, but also more critical high-tech supplies such as batteries. There are different types of batteries, obviously, including both rechargeable nicad batteries for computers, cellular telephones, two-way radios, tape recorders, and other high tech electronic equipment, and regular dry cell batteries for tape recorders, cameras, and other more common electronic equipment.

More routine assignments—such as those that can be scheduled and anticipated like big court cases, major sports events, or festivals—also require the same sort of planning and resources. News organizations that regularly cover major scheduled events should periodically assess their plans for those events and the resources used to cover them. Included in this would be high-tech upgrades from time to time to reflect newly introduced technologies as well as replacement of older equipment as it fails.

Computer hardware and software needs are a major part of this planning review. New portable computing tools are a major expense, for certain, but the need is frequently there. Older computers still do the job, there is no question, but the capabilities of newer versions of portable PCs demand consideration of upgrades because the newer tools will not only make journalists working on the road more efficient, but will also widen the range of productivity of these "road warriors." Many journalists, such as *The Washington Post's* CAR Director, William Casey (1993c), have often remarked that they are not susceptible to technological fads. If a new hardware or software product does the job better and offers useful new tools, as Casey argued, then it should be acquired. But if it does not, chances are good that it can be bypassed. For some news organizations, the time has come for upgrades to enhance the ability to cover not only the major breaking story on the road but the routine day-to-day local stories as well.

The *Orlando Sentinel's* Leusner (personal communication, February 13 & 16, 1994) recalled how his newspaper set up a mobile command post on one major breaking assignment he was given in Central Florida:

> When William Cruse went on a murder spree, killing six people and shooting up a shopping center near Melbourne in 1987, we sent a bunch

of reporters to work out of our small bureau there. At my suggestion, I convinced editors to let me stay in Orlando so I could avoid getting trapped in the pack-journalism crowd—reporters from all media outlets were trampling on one another. My police sources gave me leads for our reporters in the field to run down and reporters called me with automobile tag numbers of witnesses and just names (no other identifiers) of people we heard knew of Cruse and his past. I spent hours doing basic DMVHS [Department of Motor Vehicles and Highway Safety] and public records checks from Orlando for our people in the field. We had a small two-person bureau in Melbourne at the time, as I recall, and it was not set up to handle all of our people.

If we had had a so-called "command post" computer in Melbourne, we would have saved a lot of time, long-distance calls and certainly would have sped up the reporting process. The same principle would have worked for tracking down witnesses/workers involved in the shuttle Challenger stories or any natural disaster, for that matter.

Access is everything and he who has the fastest access wins the information race. On the Cruse story, I did the first big stories on him and tracked him back to Kentucky through public records and newspaper libraries. We were able to gather an incredible amount of stuff on this guy in a day or two. With the advent of wireless and cellular communications, reporters in the field have instant access to databases and the like, and what a time saver these "mobile command posts" would be. I hope to be one of the reporters with that capability.

For remote command post situations such as Leusner describes, there are a few other computer-related equipment needs to consider. For instance, what basic capabilities are needed? Do command post set-ups need to mirror newsroom set-ups in all ways? It is clear that general capabilities must include word processing, communications links to the newsroom news-editorial computer system, fax machines or fax modems, and access to newsroom or other electronic mail systems. More sophisticated set-ups might also include remote online news research access and database building with spreadsheets and even a relational database package.

REPORTING AND WRITING
FROM HOME "NEWSROOMS"

Knight-Ridder News Service writer Rory J. O'Connor (1991) feels the personal computer has changed the nature of most office jobs, including those in newsrooms, forever. "The evolution of the white-collar job begun by the personal computer a decade ago will continue at an astonishing rate in the next 10 years," he wrote (p. 27BM). "Advances in computer technology will overcome the barriers of time and space and—in what some see as an ominous development—blur the distinction between work and private life."

The 1994 earthquake in Southern California did sufficient damage to the transportation system that the state that led the nation in home office workers found even more people working at home, linked to the office with a personal computer and a modem—a phenomenon known as *telecommuting*. About 12.2 million persons run full-time businesses from home and an estimated 41.1 million Americans—one third of the workforce—work from home at least some of the time. Estimates range from about 3.2 million to 7 million workers telecommuting to work in 1993–1994. By 2000, one computer magazine estimate predicted, there will be 25 million telecommuting workers. Figure 8.1 describes how personal computer use at home has changed from a device used by hobbyists in the late 1970s to a primary home office tool in the mid-1990s. Figure 8.2 shows that PCs are critical tools in several home-based businesses in the 1990s.

More and more people are working at home in the mid-1990s, with or without the transportation problems that Southern Californians endured from the 1994 earthquake. For journalists, the practical value of telecommuting is obvious. Reporters can work closer to stories, for instance. They spend less time commuting to work. This, of course, contributes to reducing pollution when commutes are over long distances and on crowded highways. The downside is less interaction with other reporters and editors in a direct personal manner. Some experts call this "out of sight, out of mind." The reduction in newsroom networking may be a toll that is too high to pay for some editors and reporters (Fasbinder, 1994; Levin, 1994; Resnick, 1993b).

News reporting is particularly well suited to the telecommuting lifestyle. Since the first desktop "dumb" terminals and acoustic couplers debuted in the late 1970s, reporters and editors have had the technological capability to work from home. Just like remote bureaus are set up, home "newsrooms" can be set up. The cost, regardless of whether it is paid by the employer or employee, is minimal to start up. A home office requires a little additional space and little more than an old door propped on a pair of saw horses to serve as a desk. Reporters, informational graphic artists, and columnists can write, draw, and transmit as easily from home as from other locations.

Remote reporting means writing and transmitting news stories from many locations, including journalists' homes. Many reporters and writers in the mid-1990s are conducting online research, writing columns and news stories, and transmitting them from home to the newsroom's front-end computer system. Some software on the market gives a personal computer user in a remote location, such as home, the opportunity to "control" a distant computer. One example is ReachOut Remote, which permits a user at home to dial into an office network system,

PERSONAL COMPUTER USE AT HOME

Personal computer sales to households will reach five million for the first time ever this year. Researchers say the way PCs are used in the home can be divided into five 'eras.'

■ **Late 1970s:** Hobbyists curious about the machines bought kits and early models such as the Apple II. **Chief use:** programming.

■ **1981-1983:** Children push parents into limited-use machines by Commodore, Atari and Texas Instruments. **Chief use:** games.

■ **1984-1987:** Children seek more powerful machines and adults find Apple Macintosh simplest for more sophisticated purposes. **Chief use:** education.

■ **1988-1992:** Adults, led by those who work at home, snap up IBM PCs and clones, particularly after Windows software eases use. **Chief use:** personal finance, word processing.

■ **1993-:** Desires of adults and children align in machines with multiple functions such as phone answering, fax. Machines combine data processing, video and sound. **Chief use:** communications, multimedia programs.

BZ:AUG26   AP and HIRAM HENRIQUEZ / Miami Herald Staff

FIG. 8.1.   The changing face of personal home computer use.

or the remote network system serving the office (in the case of a newsroom bureau), and use it as if the user was logged into the system in the office (Fasbinder, 1994).

A basic hardware and software set up for a home "newsroom" should include:

- A personal computer, keyboard, and monitor.
- Word processor, communications software.
- Internal or external modem.
- Dot-matrix printer.
- A telephone line, answering machine, or telephone answering software for PC.

A more sophisticated system, in addition to these items, would also include:

- A CD-ROM drive.
- Spreadsheet, database package, personal information manager, statistical package.
- Fax modem or fax machine.
- Laser or higher quality printer (e.g., color).
- Dedicated telephone line for computer fax/modem and fax machine.

- Home office photocopier.
- Cordless telephone or headset.
- Telephone service with call waiting, call return, two-line telephone with hold or other features.

As the computer hardware market focus shifted from business to home systems in the mid-1990s, this meant more hardware capabilities, preloaded software, and more features for home systems for less cost. Home systems offer not only use by journalists, but other features of interest to other family members such as multimedia tools.

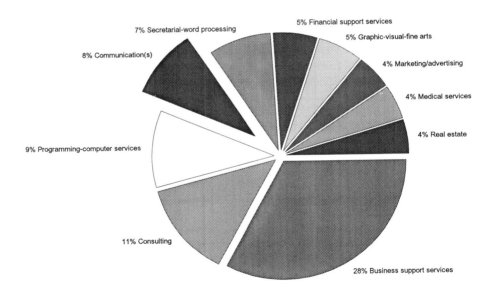

FIG. 8.2. Home-based businesses in the 1990s.

III Elementary Information Management

9 News Researchers: The Online Newsroom Specialists

Lisa P. Van Asch, one of five staff members who conduct online searches in the News Research Department of the Raleigh, NC, *News & Observer,* knows firsthand how online research completed by a news researcher can turn an ordinary news story into something special. "On-line research can make a good story great," the youthful Van Asch (1993, p. 2) told the audience at a recent Investigative Reporters and Editors national conference on computer-assisted reporting. "The information gleaned from databases can add depth and color to a story and give your paper the competitive edge, even on a tight deadline and a tight budget—*any* story, not just long-range investigative projects. The information you find might even turn out to *be* the story."

Van Asch described just how helpful news researchers can be in reporting a story that started when a reporter was routinely listening to the police scanner at about 7 p.m. on a Thursday:

A *News & Observer* reporter was working on a late brief about a local business owner charged with sexually assaulting a female employee. The man's name (John Stuart) sounded familiar, so the reporter came back to News Research and asked us to do a little digging. We used the phone book to get our subject's home address, then checked his business address in the county property records (available to us on-line) and found that the building was owned by Nancy Helms Stuart. We pulled her record in the voter registration files and found that she lived at the same address as our subject. We ran her name through the *N&O's* electronic files and discovered she was the daughter of Jesse Helms, North Carolina's infamous senator. We even had a picture of Mr. and Mrs. Stuart together. Good thing we checked, huh?

As Van Asch told her audience, that example is not "ground-shaking, law-changing journalism." But it shows, she stated, "that a little research can really make a difference." And she was not understating use of the word "little." Van Asch said the entire effort took about 15 minutes, but the effort occurred after business hours when government offices were closed. "This was not a big story. In fact, the charges were eventually dropped and it didn't amount to anything. But we had no way of knowing that on that first Thursday night. We had a few sketchy facts to go on, and we were on a very tight deadline, and we managed to put together that brief and feel confident that our facts/associations were correct," Van Asch (personal communication, March 8, 1994) recalled.

She warns that although such deadline research with databases can result in successes, it must be done with an element of care. Databases sometimes contain errors. It is standard procedure at the *N&O* to double and triple check spellings in other sources, she added: "My name is spelled wrong all the time in [Wake County, NC] databases I have searched," Van Asch (1993). "You really have to be careful about that. That's where you really have to be observant. We try to verify everything we find."

The same applies even on deadline. The computer resources in the research department are frequently used to check facts on deadline. She added:

> For deadline situations, we usually use computers to verify facts or fill in the blanks. It's usually a quick and dirty kind of thing—fifteen minutes to check on an age in voter registration [records], or what kind of property someone owns [in] property tax records, what kind of car they drive, or who drives the car with the license plate # xxxxxx [in] DMV records. Or if reporters hear on the police scanner about someone being shot, they try to identify sources (neighbors or family) to call, and that can be easily done with cross-reference directories and the county database records.

Van Asch and the four other members of the News Research Department at the *News & Observer* make up the staff of the prototypical mid-1990s daily newspaper "library." This high-tech staff deals directly with reporters each day. Van Asch (personal communication, March 8, 1994) estimates that News Research contributes information to about three quarters of all staff-written articles that are published. Further, about half of those contributions are computer based in some form.

Although all daily newspapers and major magazines have some form of a news library, their forms, functions, and levels of technical sophistication do vary (McCargar, 1993; Trimble, 1993). The 1950s and 1960s-style "morgue" is, appropriately, dead (Jacobson & Ullman, 1989). It left this world, with its clip files and dust, at some point in the 1980s or early 1990s, depending on the locale. News libraries, most of which have a mission to *share* information, are becoming increasingly high tech. "Computers are now an essential part of almost any library. They are used in cataloging, circulation, acquisitions, management, compiling lists, word processing, desktop publishing, electronic communications, etc.," wrote library science professor emerita Jean Key Gates (1994, p. 140).

NEWS RESEARCHERS IN ACTION

At North Carolina's Raleigh *News & Observer,* computerization of the newsroom and research departments has occurred at a level that serves as an industry model. News researcher Lisa Van Asch (personal communication, March 8, 1994) described four examples of situations in which use of computer-based news research enhanced her newspaper's reporting:

> The TV critic recently did a column about Roseanne Arnold and the controversy surrounding the *Roseanne* episode where her character kisses a character played by Mariel Hemingway. He asked for a list of everything Roseanne has done that has drawn criticism or caused a stir. I went online to Nexis, and had a two-page list ready for him in about an hour. Roseanne, as you can imagine, has done lots of controversial things!

> The senior government reporter had a list of out-of-state contributors who gave lots of money to our current governor, Jim Hunt. He had no idea who any of the people were, just a list of their names and addresses, obtained from campaign reports. I spent several days researching the names in databases like Nexis and Dialog, and found some interesting trends. It turned into a front page story.

> Our investigative reporter, Pat Stith, and the senior government reporter got a tip a couple of years ago about the chairman of the state Republican Party's relationship to an advertising agency called Capitol Hill Advertising. Pat has coined this phrase (and I love it when I hear it): "Get me the book on this guy." That's when it gets fun! I looked *everywhere*—county databases, Nexis, clip files, North Carolina databases, made phone calls, and so forth. I was able to provide the reporters with lots of little details—when the advertising agency was closed, who owned it, where the owner lived, the owner's relationship to the GOP chairman, and info about the chair's son (his age, job title, and so forth). The reporters did a *great* job—they had lots of their own information, and my stuff filled in blanks or verified what they had been told.

> Often we just go online to help the reporter do his (or her) "homework"—find past profiles and any recent antics of a person a reporter's about to interview, find statistics for a story about crime, find experts for the reporter to talk to, get an annual report on a company about to move to the Research Triangle Park area.

It is not inconceivable that one day early in the 21st century any library, particularly a specialized one like those that serve newsrooms, will become completely multimedia computer-based (Young, 1989). Such a library will not necessarily be confined to a single building (Qindlen, 1992). The technology is available; the transition from the traditional library to the high-tech version may take several generations, however, for attitudes to change and existing equipment to be replaced.

CONTEMPORARY NEWS LIBRARIES
AND RESEARCHERS

Some researchers have characterized news libraries as former "invisible empires" where information was cornered and stowed away. No longer. Beginning in the mid-1980s, and corresponding with the computer-based information revolution, news libraries have professionalized, modernized, and become "increasingly significant in the production of news" (Ward, Hansen, & McLeod, 1988a, p. 143).

"The continued existence and development of many special libraries and information centers may depend upon our response to technology," wrote librarians Norman Howden and John Dillard (1991, p. 288). "Online searching is a major component of our advance into new areas of technology. . . . Libraries may also be using computerized catalogs, telefacsimile, and local area networks. The rapid thrust of microcomputer technology into every nook and cranny of the library has inspired many people to make utopian predictions."

Such things as paperless societies may not become reality for a long time, but libraries are changing (Crowley, 1993). The way people use them is also changing. Traditionally, news libraries have been organized like larger general-purpose libraries. The two major organizational forms are open and closed stacks. *Open* areas permit use by anyone and materials may be removed on an honor system. Other libraries are *closed* and can be used only with the assistance of a library staff member and materials can be taken only when signed out (Crowley, 1993; Hansen, Ward, & McLeod, 1987).

Some people have argued that the growing cost of computer technology is a barrier to moving old-fashioned paper-based newsroom libraries into the new age. Others, such as most news librarians, disagree. Dolores Jenkins (personal communication, February 28, 1994), a journalism professor and librarian at the University of Florida, is one expert who does not support the cost argument:

Yes, it's worth it. No newspaper has the staff to maintain anything past a small reference collection, placing magazine subscriptions, filing, binding, checking out, or tracing missing books or overdues. Online resources on an "on-need" basis is *very* cost-effective, no matter what your budget. Of course, the news library manager does have to work up some sort of budget and typically has to serve as intermediary because not too many papers negotiate for flat fee access. Since we're all trapped by money/budgets, we look to the likes of the Internet to get us to free/cheap/accurate resources, not just Nexis or Dialog. [Groups such as the] Society of Environmental Journalists and Robert Logan's Science Journalism Center's databases [University of Missouri] are excellent examples of alternative sources for information.

Cost and other modernization problems aside, one thing is clear regarding electronic newsroom libraries, information centers, and research departments: Because of new information storage and retrieval procedures, the nature of news reporting and editing is changing (Howden & Dillard, 1991; Ward, Hansen & McLeod, 1988a, 1988b).

News research has changed. It will never be the same.

University of Minnesota researchers Jean Ward, Kathleen Hansen, and Douglas McLeod concluded there are several ways that newsmaking "protocols" were changed by electronic libraries. Once an assumed step in the news reporting process, checking clips is not as automatic as it once may have been, the three researchers believe. They determined, in a 1987 study, that some journalists were slow to adapt to the new technology. This, unfortunately, is a conclusion that has not changed nearly a decade later. The University of Miami CAR study found numerous daily newspapers still reporting the same problem. Whereas the Minnesota study found this problem at larger daily newspapers, the Miami study observed it is also a problem at smaller dailies that have begun to use electronic databases for news research only in the past several years.

Information professionals, a relatively new term given to librarians, are positioned to become very important players in many business settings, not just news organizations. Their role is growing daily at newspapers and magazines, as well as broadcast and cable stations. Lawrence S. Guthrie (1992), a librarian at the National Law Center at George Washington University, feels librarians of the last half of the 1990s will be one of two types: "commando" types, who are assertive and apply their expertise to manage information for an organization, and "nonassertive" types, who abdicate their chance at new organizational power by allowing others to control the information flow. Richard Withey, editorial services manager for News International, publisher of *The Times* of London, also feels news librarians, as other specialized librarians, must change with the technology or be displaced. Withey believes news researchers need to become information counselors and quality controllers who direct the input of a wide range of information sources. Withey even feels the need for news researchers as information retrievers may disappear completely not far into the next century as end users such as reporters become more skilled (Adair, 1992).

WHO'S IN CHARGE HERE?

Although the emerging struggle for who controls research resources such as information has yet to manifest itself in many newsrooms, numerous hints of turf wars are appearing as librarians begin to work side by side with reporters and editors who have less knowledge of the process needed to locate and retrieve information. One way the two groups have begun to show their sense of territory is in control of access to online services in some newsrooms. Some news organizations have placed that control in the hands of news researchers, whereas other newsrooms have left it to reporters, editors, news researchers, or anyone else needing access to the information.

What seems to be occurring in many newsrooms is that two movements are simultaneously transpiring: News librarians are becoming more like reporters in their duties and some reporters, those at the forefront of the computer age, are becoming more like news librarians (Ward & Hansen, 1991). "[C]omputerization of the newsroom and information-gathering functions is instrumental in showing us the collective nature of news reporting," concluded University of Minnesota researchers Jean Ward and Kathleen Hansen (1991, p. 497) after a national study of 105 major daily newspapers in 1990. "The merger of journalist and librarian roles illustrates this trend toward collective news work."

Ward and Hansen (1991), two leading authorities on newsroom research, identify two major roles shared by reporters and news researchers in daily newspapers. The first is information searching. Information searching uses the traditional and electronic news libraries to find needed facts. The second role is story framing. In this role, both reporters and librarians select information from the world of available material and, in doing so, informally set the parameters of news stories.

Reporters tend to use computers for public records database analysis, but few librarians are involved in such work. A second distinctive reporter role is in the responsibility for the final product. Reporters are given bylines, but librarians seldom receive published credit in any form. Librarians, however, have three roles that are clearly theirs. Ward and Hansen (1991) said librarians continue to dominate searching commercial databases, training journalists in using the electronic library, and managing revenue and use of the resources.

Some news organizations—particularly those with small and medium-size publications—still take a do-it-yourself approach to online news research. But even some larger dailies are trying this approach in some cases. The St. Petersburg Times, for instance, requires reporters to do their own electronic library searching unless they are on the road (Wolfe, personal communication, March 9, 1994). Although these news organizations have librarians or news researchers who perform other duties and, perhaps, even online research, reporters and editors are often found to be doing their own news research. Although it is often best to learn to "search-it-yourself," most news organizations prefer that librarians or a newsroom computer "guru" do the searches to control costs involved in using some of the most expensive database services.

The ultimate evolutionary path has yet to reveal itself, but it appears that the intermediate stop, at least, includes more and more news researchers in the newsroom and more and more reporters with their own research skills sharing that space. There will come a time, perhaps not in this decade but soon enough, when libraries as they are known in the mid-1990s will disappear, become research centers, if anything, and simply become another part of the newsroom just like a universal copy desk. Ultimately, one scenario could forecast, reporters become news researchers and news researchers become reporters, both winding up with the old-fashioned low-tech title of "journalist." It is apparent that computers and other high technology are a major reason for walls coming down in news organizations.

AN INTRODUCTION: NEWS LIBRARIANS AND RESEARCHERS

Elisabeth Donovan is a *Miami Herald* news researcher who did background research for Bob Woodward and Carl Bernstein during the height of the Watergate investigation when she was at *The Washington Post.* Donovan clipped stories from major daily newspapers for Woodward and Bernstein and helped them work on their book, *All the President's Men,* in the precomputer era of news research. She did her job the old-fashioned way: with scissors, file folders, rubber date stamps, glue and tape, and other low-tech tools. Donovan continues to conduct news research, but she does not work in the news library any longer. She works at a sophisticated personal computer station located in the newsroom, near the city desk, as the director of news research. She has witnessed the unpredictable, incredible changes that have occurred in news research. "In less than twenty years news libraries have helped to change the face of American journalism," said Donovan (1992, p. 90). "They have gone from clipping and photo repositories to database producers and centers for online research, electronic image archiving, and database analyses. Many reporters, as well, have become proficient at database searching."

Most mid-1990s news librarians consider themselves journalists. They are part of the information gathering process. "A news library's primary mission is to provide accurate, comprehensive information for the news staff in a timely fashion," wrote Susan E. McCargar (1993, p. 131), director of the El Paso County Library and former librarian at the *El Paso Herald-Post* in Texas. "This includes more than fact checking; it involves going beyond ready reference toward broader and deeper research services."

There is a growing role of news researchers in the newsroom and some, if not most, reporters and editors are accepting them as journalists. Titles are changing and the transition from old-fashioned librarian to news researcher and reporter is well underway. "The research needs of the reporters are their first priority," Raleigh *News & Observer* News Researcher Teresa Leonard (1992, p. 62) wrote in *Online*. Leonard made a strong case for including the news library or research department in any computer-assisted reporting program:

- News librarians have *expertise* in working with bibliographic and full-text databases.
- News librarians offer *stability* in the newsroom, a usually transient part of any news organization. They work with a wide range of reporters and are aware of the resources they are using, and they offer institutional knowledge useful in maintaining a CAR program.
- News librarians have no intention of usurping the research role of traditional reporters, only to *facilitate* it.

As El Paso's McCargar noted, news researchers do much more than work on files and access online morgues for their newsroom requesters. Debbie Wolfe, a former news researcher who became director of newsroom training at the *St. Petersburg Times,* calls herself an "information pit bull" (Wolfe, 1993). "It is our job to make sense out of the strange things in the news," she says. "We work with the obscure, the technical, the unwieldy, the questionable, and the bizarre."

It is typical for Wolfe to respond in minutes to requests. Wolfe (personal communication, May 16, 1994) recalled one such deadline-rushed occasion that required both online research and a cellular telephone:

> Police reporter Karen Datko's electronic library check via cellular phone was done en route to the address of a juvenile arrested for a crime. This reporter would often call me from the police-beat car phone. . . . This was one of her nuttier requests. While I had her on open hold, I checked the electronic library for information in one of her previous bylines. She needed background on a juvenile that was in trouble again. Just before I started to read her the answer, she asked me to pause while she sped down the off ramp of the interstate onto a city street.

Use of online services and other electronic sources of information by news researchers is becoming a growing part of the work in newsrooms. Online services and BBSs are helpful in developing story ideas, finding sources, verifying information, and developing supplementary information for a package, among other purposes. "The use of online databases and bulletin board services in newsrooms, sometimes referred to as computer-assisted research, can be valuable in all stages of news story development," stated the Poynter Institute's Nora Paul (1993c, p. 317). "This type of research is at the core of computer-assisted journalism."

Wolfe, Paul, and just about any other news researcher can offer a long list of responsibilities that are part of their work. For example, Wolfe lists 15 news-gathering-oriented roles she plays as a news researcher for a major daily newspaper:

- Summarize broad amounts of data.
- Locate nut "grafs."
- Select key stories.
- Highlight important areas.
- Locate and interview sources.
- Compile data.
- Write chronologies.
- Teach how to use online databases for searching.
- Teach other types of research techniques.
- Alert others to legal and ethical issues.
- Trade information with other news organizations.
- Investigate use of new information technologies.
- Write trade publication articles.
- Program and design software.
- Track ongoing topics and generate story ideas.

News researchers work closely with reporters and editors and, as Wolfe noted, begin to learn their strengths and weaknesses just as a teacher might experience with a group of students. The key, she says, is sharing. "Newspapers are moving toward *team* reporting," Wolfe (1993) emphasized. "Credit is being given to researchers as well as reporters. Bylines and other acknowledgments are more common. On a lot of stories, it is just too much now for one person to handle. This means a more proactive role for librarians."

Two growing skills used by news researchers are determining and applying proper search strategies for stories. Some reporters and editors have problems determining the focus of a story or, perhaps, the focus of a search for a story about a topic. "Reporters sometimes ask dumb questions: 'I want to know about Africa,' one of our reporters once said to me. What he really meant was that he wanted *issues* about the whole continent of Africa. This gets at search strategies. You have to construct your own and use your own search terms," Wolfe (1993) explained.

ROLES OF NEWS RESEARCHERS

Many libraries have become computerized in a number of areas during the past decade or so (Metcalf, 1993; Semonche, 1993). News librarians would not be considered a part of computer-assisted reporting discussions only a few years ago because, University of North Carolina journalism professor Barbara Semonche (1993, p. 265) says, "news research was perceived narrowly." She explained: "Historically, investigative reporting has been the singular province of a relatively small number of journalists, usually working on their own with comparatively little support from news editors, news researchers, or data-processing staffers. . . . The advent of increasingly sophisticated computerized information search, retrieval and analysis programs changed journalists' investigative methods. The 'lone-wolf' investigative journalist has given way to a newer concept of 'team journalism.'"

This change has occurred dramatically in less than a decade, greatly affecting the role of news librarians in the newsroom. Specialized librarians, such as those at newspapers and magazines, have wondered aloud whether their fate will be different in the computer age. Will their jobs be eliminated? Will they become the most important information managers of the entire news organization? Or will something in between those extremes evolve?

Some libraries, particularly those outside the news business, are thriving and growing in the computer age. Others, however, have had to experience staffing cutbacks and budget reductions. The situation is not limited to general libraries. Some specialized libraries have had similar experiences. Life is not just status quo. "I have heard of special libraries that have been temporarily or permanently closed with the stroke of a budget-conscious executive's pen," wrote Arlene Farber Sirkin (1992, p. 1), a Washington-based management consultant. Sirkin argues that special libraries—such as those at news organizations—must reposition themselves in their organizations by realizing that the traditional role of the institutional library has changed during the 1990s computer-based information revolution. At some companies, librarians are growing in stature and responsibilities through computerization. New titles such as chief information officer are appearing within some corporations. If nothing else, these "information czars" are becoming more important by serving as the points of consolidation of all information gathering, storage, and retrieval for the business. It is, as Sirkin suggests, an era of change for libraries.

Some news librarians are building original databases for their newspapers. Creating and using in-house databases seems to be the future for many news libraries. *Newsday* has made the move in this direction, write Elizabeth Whisnant, former library manager, and Mary Ann Skinner, director of the editorial library at the Long Island newspaper. "*Newsday* librarians wanted to make frequently requested information that is often generated by local organizations or the paper itself available via a reporter's terminal," they explained (Whisnant & Skinner, 1992, p. 24). "To accomplish this goal, 10 in-house databases have been created in the past six years." Databases include the newspaper's own news story files and various public databases such as those obtained from voter registration office data tapes for Nassau and Suffolk counties.

Because of the work at *Newsday* and other newspapers with databases and other forms of information, an information professional is emerging. Whether news librarians are known as news researchers, information professionals, reporters, or "journalists" seems to point to a single fact: News librarians are no longer passive supporters of the news-gathering process. In an age of computer-assisted reporting, these information experts have moved slowly into the newsroom, been given credits and occasional bylines, and viewed more and more as full-fledged contributors to the news process. They are no longer in the background. Titles often do not mean much, but in this case, the new titles reflect these changes in responsibilities in the news reporting process. The mid-1990s news researcher takes on a wider range of duties, including:

- *Summarizing and compiling data.* Often it is not enough for a news researcher to compile information from on- and offline sources. Increasingly, reporters and editors are looking to their news researchers to review and summarize that information before they see it.
- *Locating information and facts.* Historically, librarians have found information for reporters using reference works and clip files. This function has not changed, but expanded.
- *Locating sources.* Using online and published sources, news researchers have become even more useful to editors and reporters by offering skills at finding expert and eyewitness sources as well as other types of sources for stories, especially under deadline circumstances when time is valuable.
- *Writing event chronologies.* In breaking major stories, one of the copy desk/editing functions that has shifted to news researchers is compilation of event chronologies for background for reporters and, if space permits, for readers as well.
- *Teaching others online research techniques.* With computer-based research technology has come a rather steep learning curve for some old-fashioned newsroom veterans. News researchers in the library have often taken the lead in learning and teaching the tools to others in the news organization.
- *Generating story ideas and giving existing stories greater focus.* Another function of computer-based information storage and retrieval has been greater ease in generating story ideas and offering more focus to a story idea. News researchers can determine what has and has not been done on a subject by competing news organizations or by anyone else for that matter. Certainly a by-product of this is the ability to give a nebular or general story idea much more direction by determining new angles or dimensions to a story or, by simple elimination, what does not need to be done again.

- *Paying attention to information services marketplace.* Cost effectiveness is important to any business, even a news enterprise. The duty of finding the best information bargains has fallen to news libraries and their staffs. New products and the best buy for the budget dollar have become high priorities in management of newsroom libraries.

News researchers and librarians have one other important role to play. They must be models of responsibility and moderation. In doing so, news researchers must remind their newsroom colleagues that such fast and comprehensive tools for information gathering as online services and databases are only starting points. Online and other forms of database research done by news librarians or by reporters and editors is a first step, Poynter Institute Library Director Nora Paul (1993b) said. "This is computer kick-starting and it's not computer completion. I think that is the most critical thing that you should learn. . . . You have got to still go out and use every single one of the traditional reporter's skills," she said.

There is the chance of doing too much also. When she was library director at *The Miami Herald* through the 1980s, Paul said, the newsroom was just becoming accustomed to using online research and occasionally overdid it in stories:

Just because you have it, don't throw it into the story. It may not have any relevance to the story. When we first got real excited about all of this stuff and started getting all of these data sources, there was a murder–suicide in Broward County. This guy killed his girlfriend and then himself. This guy was all over the place [in state and local public records]. . . . We found out a lot about him and we even address-searched our own database and found about other cases, such as one involving child pornography and a police standoff that had occurred down the street. We threw all this into the story and it was the worst murder–suicide story that I have ever read. At the time, I thought it was wonderful—it was so cool, all this stuff we had found. But, in fact, none of it was relevant. Who cares how many square feet are in the condo? Just because you can do it, should you? And if you do do it, how do you do it right? I think you need to keep that in mind.

The University of Florida's Dolores Jenkins (personal communication, February 28, 1994) feels there are other dangers. One is the risk of thinking computer libraries can do it all:

For new users there is always the seductive impression that this technology is sexier and more efficient than manual methods. Also, many users or potential users suffer from the notion that computers in general access the mind of God—which they most certainly do not. Nexis, for example, only provides access to 5,000 or so publications. That's only a small library;

only certain types of publications and research are represented; same thing with Dialog, or BRS, or Internet services. You can only extract what has been entered and you can also only extract as efficiently as the quality of the retrieval software and your own thought processes. That certainly makes for the possibility of a few glitches. Couple these aspects with the pressure of deadlines and you don't always have a well-researched story.

There is also the problem of attribution. J-students have never been well schooled in citations, bibliography, crediting sources, and the nature of plagiarism—a real slippery slope here a la electronic sources.

Jenkins also raises the problem of confirming information gleaned from the information highway. Much of it will be tough to nail down in a deadline crush, even if these systems communicate information faster than conventional news services. She explained:

I have been intrigued with the parallel information dissemination [during the 1994] earthquake in California: The Internet versus CNN, CBS, NBC, and so forth. The information may have been microlevel, but it still was faster than commercial news services and was true mass media. Reporters with Internet access could track those three California sub-Internet networks and get more interesting stuff than off the classic wires. We'll have a jolly time of it verifying stories now; electronic rumor mills, and so forth, but that's a problem with the participants, not necessarily the system.

A LOOK AT A NEWS RESEARCHER
AND HIS/HER WORK

Tish Wells (personal communication, February 25, 1994) is one of the reference librarians at *USA Today* in Arlington, VA. Her job is a hectic one with a lot of pressure to produce the right information at a moment's notice. She keeps "busy," as she explained, in her specialization as an online services researcher. She admits she is one of the "heaviest users of the online systems in the library in doing searches."

Wells loves to use online services for *USA Today*'s deadline reporting:

[It is] helpful to have a computer when things break. For example, the Pan Am crash in Lockerbie. Reading the wires, we knew that the first stories they [the editors overseeing coverage] would need were any other major plane crashes with high body tolls. Then there was the terrorism angle; then we checked the type of plane and whether it had been in other types of plane crashes. Using our book collection and searching the major newspapers, we pulled together packages that could be given to all the different sections that would be working on the project. This applies to every "disaster"—plane crashes, deaths in Somalia, earthquakes, and so forth.

For some deadline stories, online services are not the best answer, she cautions:

> We don't count on the online systems in some cases—for example, when the Sioux Falls crash happened, we did the online papers file, but got very little because the papers in the area weren't online and the computerized papers weren't that helpful. At that point, we called Gannett's paper in the area for help. Sometimes going straight to the local paper is far faster than hitting the systems, especially if you are doing obituaries.

Library work for nondeadline and project reporting is somewhat different, she explained:

> We had a reporter in Somalia who needed a couple of stories on Aideed downloaded to his portable PC since there were no fax machines or any other way to get it there except to read it to him. I was able to download the stories and send them in message form so that he could get them in Somalia. Time? Oh, it was a half-hour after I found the stories. The difficulty in finding them was the many spellings of Aideed—Aidid or Aideed.

Two of Wells' favorite news research examples that involved some of the special projects work regularly assigned to her department are the *USA Today* staff's collaborative 1991 book, *Desert Warriors: The Men and Women Who Won the Gulf War,* and the newspaper's series of articles about child deaths from shootings. She explained:

> They [the editors] wanted to do profiles of each person who died in the Persian Gulf complex. This is where the online papers showed their strengths and weaknesses. First, having the list of dead and their hometowns was helpful, but most of the hometown papers were (and still are) too small to have anything online or they ran the Associated Press pieces. I was able to get about half the stories from the online systems, but the rest were from calling the papers or going through our papers and finding the articles ourselves. In the end, we got everyone except one man from South America (and I'm still looking).

> The child shootings request was simple: find a gun incident for every week from September 1992 to May 1993—the school year. This was done with a variety of techniques. First, I got a weekly calendar, then I did some basic searches in the "Major Papers" files to get a feel for the difficulty of the project. Fortunately, it wasn't that difficult to find. The problem lay in finding diversity of location as well as incidents. I ended up taking the ones from the "Major Papers" files, checking off the weeks, then going into regionals and finding some, checking them off the calendars, then going into the wires for the missing weeks. The wires would bring up the incidents in areas that didn't have papers online. At the end we found

difficulty in only two weeks—Christmas break and Easter break. The systems used were Dialog, DataTimes, and Nexis.

Wells said her news research department staff uses a wide range of online sources for the needs of the newspaper's editors and reporters. "We end up using a great many systems in this library: Periscope for military equipment, Baseline for entertainment issues (the only place to get *Variety)*, FedWorld for press conferences, as well as the big systems—Nexis, DataTimes, Dialog. When we get requests for international stuff, we go for the international databases; when we want local stories we try smaller papers or the wires."

USING ELECTRONIC NEWS LIBRARIES

Most major U.S. daily newspapers, many major magazines, NBC News, ABC News, CBS News, National Public Radio, and Financial News Network have gone electronic for internal and for public consumption. These sources of information have created electronic news libraries for reporters, among other users. In 1980, access such as this was only a dream. But the dream came true at a majority of major newspapers and broadcast news operations a decade later. "New predictions [in 1990] abound that soon reporters and editors will have unlimited access to commercial and public records databases via their PC-equipped workstations," wrote Minnesota's Ward and Hansen (1990, p. 34).

SEARCHING ONLINE IN NEWSROOMS

One of the computer-age concerns in newsrooms is the cost of online searching. It can be very expensive, depending on time used and the cost of the database, and some news managers are still deciding whether to assign the duty to anyone with the skill, the reporter on the story, the supervising editor or a designated editor, or news librarians or researchers. The 1994 University of Miami CAR study found a wide range of often-overlapping approaches, but of daily newspapers ($n = 208$) conducting online searches for news stories, the majority use either librarians or reporters themselves:

Circulation	"Anyone"	Reporters	Editors	Librarians	No Searches
Under 50,000	12.5% (2)	27.1% (13)	50.0% (6)	3.5% (2)	75.3% (64)
50,000–100,000	43.8 (7)	35.4 (17)	33.3 (4)	24.6 (14)	18.8 (16)
100,001–250,000	31.3 (5)	22.9 (11)	16.7 (2)	35.1 (20)	4.7 (4)
250,001–500,000	6.3 (1)	10.4 (5)	0.0 (0)	24.6 (14)	1.2 (1)
Over 500,000	6.3 (1)	4.2 (2)	0.0 (0)	12.3 (7)	0.0 (0)
Totals	100.0% (16)	100.0% (48)	100.0% (12)	100.0% (57)	100% (85)

Note: Percentages are for columns. Frequencies are in parentheses.

With these developments, the size of the newsroom library may be shrinking. Although it is still a large room stocked with books, file cabinets, and computers, it need only be the size of a personal computer and desk. Another major advantage is that electronic news libraries never, or seldom, close. Reporters are no longer restricted to normal business hours for their news research. One study found that reporters use electronic libraries for good reasons. Among them were to develop compilations and lists of information for crime story investigations, business stories, political stories, local government stories, trend stories, and stories about public figures (Splichal, 1991).

The proficiency of use issue is reminiscent of some fears expressed when computers used for writing and editing first arrived in newsrooms in the mid-1970s. Some veteran journalists, as well as beginners, have fears about using computers for something besides writing. Some newspapers even prohibit it until after users are trained to control costs (Ward & Hansen, 1990).

Some journalists ignore computer-based research because, *St. Petersburg Times'* Wolfe (1989a, 1990) said, the access procedures are too cumbersome, they lack the time to learn how to do it, computer searches actually increase research time, computer searches decrease the local perspective on a story, searches discourage original work, and searches increase errors (see also Jacobson & Ullman, 1989). Some reporters prefer someone else to search databases for them, if they use them at all, Wolfe (1989a) concluded.

The most difficult problems in computer searching are selecting the best database and deciding on the most appropriate key words that the computer uses to make its search. Since many index or full-text databases are bibliographic—that is, they contain bibliographic information such author, title, and subject—users have to have an idea about who the authors are or what specific words might appear in titles.

SEARCHING FREQUENCY IN NEWSROOMS

The 1994 University of Miami national CAR study ($n = 208$) found a wide range of frequencies of use of online database searching among those daily newspapers conducting searches for story background or other purposes:

Circulation	Daily	Weekly or Greater	Monthly or Greater	Monthly or Less	Other	None/ Missing
Under 50,000	3.6% (2)	30.0% (6)	11.1% (1)	87.5% (7)	30.3% (10)	70.7% (58)
50,000–100,000	23.2 (13)	30.0 (6)	55.6 (5)	12.5 (1)	36.7 (12)	22.0 (18)
100,001–250,000	32.1 (18)	35.0 (7)	33.3 (3)	0.0 (0)	27.3 (9)	6.1 (5)
250,001–500,000	26.8 (15)	5.0 (1)	0.0 (0)	0.0 (0)	6.1 (2)	1.2 (1)
Over 500,000	14.3 (8)	0.0 (0)	0.0 (0)	0.0 (0)	0.0 (0)	0.0 (0)
Totals	100.0% (56)	100.0% (20)	100.0% (9)	100.0% (8)	100.0% (33)	100.0% (82)

Note: Percentages are for columns. Frequencies are in parentheses.

Local beat reporters tend to use electronic news libraries more than other reporters, research shows. Beat reporters use database information for background before starting on a story, to find names for interviews or contacts, to verify information, and for general education about specialized subjects. The most obvious advantages to using electronic libraries are greater perspective, more detail, time savings, identification of new sources, wider geographic coverage, and increased accuracy (Jacobson & Ullman, 1989; Wolfe, 1989b).

INFORMATION PROFESSIONALS
IN THE MID-1990s

There is a growing industry of companies and individuals who will research information online for a requester-client. No, these are not necessarily news librarians or news researchers. There is a strong similarity in the two jobs, however, and some information brokers are also librarians or former librarians. "At the highest level, information retrieval is an art calling for a great depth of knowledge, a bubbling spring of imagination, and an ability to make creative leaps and connections," says online communications expert Alfred Glossbrenner (1990, p. 189). "Fortunately, for those who are unwilling or unable to do their own online searching, there are 'information brokers.' The term is not at all descriptive; 'professional searcher' or 'information professional' would be more to the point."

Information brokers are independent entrepreneurs who know their way around computers and online information services well enough to sell their services to individuals or organizations that do not have the time or the expertise to do it themselves. Information brokers say they do not sell information; they sell their ability to find information in the most cost-effective manner and then communicate it to a client in a professional manner (Rugge, 1993). Some news organizations may find information brokers useful from time to time on important projects, but these individuals are rarely used in the news business because many news organizations have professionals on staff on a full-time basis to do the information brokering.

The range of information brokering runs from the "sleazy character who uses illegal and unethical means to obtain and sell information" (Burwell, 1992, p. 6) to someone who can access confidential public or private databases to librarians looking for a second career to computer-savvy individuals who know how to use their modems to find information. Helen Burwell (1992), an information broker based in Houston, says information professionals fit into all of these categories.

There is, however, a possible problem with ethics and the level that some individuals will go to find online information. Some persons will bribe officials, "hack" their way into supposedly secure private databases, use fraud and misrepresentation, invade privacy, and even break computer security laws to locate information and pass it along to a client. The small number of individuals with this ability have endangered access for everyone who uses online tools in legitimate ways, leading some citizen groups and some government officials to seek more ways to restrict use of what is currently public information. The Seattle area's infamous Al Schweitzer is one example of this sort of information agent. He was convicted of illegally using federal databases with his information hunting. Some government officials have said individuals who readily break society's rules in their zeal to find information are singularly responsible for the nation's privacy crisis (Snepp & Kalbacker, 1993).

Legitimate information professionals who will hunt for data for anyone who will pay for the service have developed their own set of ethical standards, and many belong to such organizations as the Association of Independent Information Professionals and the News Division of the Special Libraries Association. Most information professionals have a library science background, and most are women, but this profile seems to be changing. Other individuals, educated in fields other than library science, have entered the industry. There are many more men who work as "information sleuths" than the number of a decade ago. All of these shifts in what used to be a rather small and quiet industry have led some professionals to call for an accrediting process (Mintz, 1991; Rugge, 1993).

Many information "professionals," as some prefer to be labeled, are particularly adept at locating private information that has been made public. This is an important distinction. Certain information is not found in public records. One example is a social security number. Often, an individual volunteers information such as a social security number and that information becomes part of other databases that are public records (Hill, 1993).

Corporate-level information brokers are emerging. When some individuals are successful in locating and presenting information to clients, companies are created and grow. This is how Atlanta's Information America began in 1981. Founders Mary Madden and Burton Goldstein saw the need for information at the Fulton County courthouse and began providing a service to the local legal community. A few months later, Information America began. The growth of the company, after more than a decade of business, shows how the demand for information can expand rapidly in this generation of computers and databases. Not only do journalists need information often provided by their own resourcefulness or news researchers, but information is needed by businesses willing to pay for the convenience and time savings. Often this is enough, but for some clients it is not. Information brokers also offer refinements such as organized presentations of the information, distillations of the data if large amounts are involved, and combinations and mergers of databases that might not have been possible using the original documents and records. Some business experts feel the demand for information through services such as information brokers will only increase through the rest of this decade (Marsh, 1992).

The point has been made earlier, but it is important to recall that most government databases are accessed through vendors. Private databases operate the same way. Either the owner of the database, or an organization that has leased use of it, provides access to the database. CompuServe is an example of a third-party information provider. These providers are best when using "static" data, Koch (1991) wrote. Static data are files that are not frequently updated (such as driver's license or bibliographic information). More and more, these database services are less static than in years before. There were something like 4,000 such databases in 1990, Koch wrote. Some databases are exclusive and not widely available (e.g., *The New York Times*). Some are available in numerous systems.

NEWS RESEARCH ETHICS

Some organizations and individuals have begun to develop guidelines for proper professional conduct when searching for information in a news context (Mintz, 1991; Shaver, Hewison, & Wykoff, 1985). "Since editorial decisions aren't made in a vacuum, but are relative to situations, guidelines may be of use," wrote Anne P. Mintz (1991), director of Information Services at *Forbes*. "I consider certain behaviors which are unethical also to be 'information malpractice,' since we should know better than engage in them" (p. 8).

Information professionals, such as Mintz (1991) and Shaver, Hewison, and Wykoff (1985), believe there is a substantial list of ethical concerns:

- Obligation to be prepared and possess skills to do the job.
- Elimination of bias and preconception.
- Use of misrepresentation to get information.
- Use of misrepresentation of the ability or the access to resources to complete a certain research task.
- Incomplete or sloppy research.
- Presentation of "half-baked" research.
- Disclosure of problems or errors in searches.
- Avoidance of industrial espionage.
- Violation of any law (e.g., copyright).
- Intentional presentation of false information.

- Breaching confidentiality.
- Acceptance of "kickbacks" from vendors or service providers.

News researchers and librarians need professional-caliber education as well, Mintz (1991) suggests. This includes formal education, continuing exposure to the literature of the field, and interaction with vendors to remain current in their field. "If our behavior is professional, cautious, based on a high base of education and training, is honest and demonstrates due diligence, we will continue to set a standard for information provision which will help to keep our organizations out of court on our behalfs [sic]," she concluded (p. 10).

10 Word Processors and Personal Information Managers in Reporting

The first computer-based word processors began appearing in newsrooms in the early to mid-1970s and news writing, reporting, and editing were changed forever. However, word processing is a computerized version of the work journalists had been doing with typewriters for more than 100 years and, for many more centuries before the typewriter came along, with just a pen and paper. Journalists have always had some sort of word processing tools with which to ply their craft, but the contemporary versions are so advanced that many journalists just do not realize the potential of these information management tools to do much more than text writing and editing.

Word processors have rapidly become reporting tools as well as writing tools. Alongside these complex and powerful writing packages are newer products called *personal information managers* that offer superior resource management capabilities for reporters, photographers, graphics specialists, and editors.

FEATURES THAT ENHANCE NEWS REPORTING

How can these word processing programs be used by reporters and editors to enhance their information-gathering abilities? Just ask Chris Feola, director of systems, new media, and computer-assisted reporting for the Waterbury, CT, *Republican-American*. "Database journalism requires a powerful word processor," Feola (1993c) stated. "And before Electric Pencil folks write in to tell me how they can do anything on their 8K Altairs: No you can't. We're not talking about copy editing here, we're talking about power macro programming. And unless your word processor has a language that can handle 'IfThen,' 'IfFor' and 'UponNotFound' conditional loops and the like, you need to switch."

Feola's newsroom uses WordPerfect because of the power of its macro language. Feola says he likes the 1,000 or so verbs available for programming macro files. For most people around newsrooms, the use of

203

word processing for writing is obvious, but these programs have powerful tools such as macros that make a word processor an analytical tool as well. Macros are not much more than a set of keystrokes or instructions recorded for a particular purpose. For word processors that include macro language, such as WordPerfect and Word, the language responds to certain words such as some verbs, and users can control the outcome of a procedure by asking the macro to do different things under different conditions (Woodcock, 1991).

In addition to the programming potential in macros, organizing tools are available. Those tools are ideal for reporters and editors to use in their daily work. They include:

- Outlining.
- Advanced searching.
- Indexing.
- Creating tables of contents.
- Cross-referencing.
- Sorting.

Outlining features are offered in many database-oriented programs but are also part of many advanced word processing packages. Some programs, such as Microsoft Word versions for Windows and Macintosh, offer an "outline view" option that permits journalists to take a different look at the information on the screen. Outlining offers users a chance to create hierarchies of information, ranking and ordering the information. This tool makes visualizing the information going into a story easier for some writers. The indention levels permit writers to find relationships between the topics contained in the notes on the screen. Outlines should be somehow related to the document that will be eventually created to be most effective. For journalists, this means the outline should become the skeleton for the article or series to be written from the notes in the document. In Word, for example, the outline *is* the document. Another related feature in some programs is the ability to work in both the outline view and full-text view on the same screen. Working outlines can be printed to serve as guides in final story or document preparation.

Another simple function of word processors that can benefit journalists is advanced searching tools for finding information in large documents. Apart from the obvious search-and-replace application commonly used for changing the spelling of a name or other word during the writing process, a journalist armed with a sophisticated word processor on a fast PC can use the search function to find key words in a large text database without use of a database manager or other software. These search, or find, functions are particularly effective on deadline when a journalist needs to locate references to a particular place, person, or object in a long document. More sophisticated word processors permit use of common advanced logical search operators such as the Boolean "and" and "or," which means these programs can even be used to combine unrelated terms. Furthermore, searching includes search expressions using "wildcard" strategies such as "?" and "*" symbols combined with partial, or truncated, words.

Indexing functions are also useful word processing tools for newsrooms. Reporters or editors seeking to better organize their notes or parts of articles they are writing or editing will find indexing to be quite a powerful tool. Indexes are created by linking the "indexer" to selected or typed entries in the text and selecting a format for the index. This feature will be of vast assistance to reporters and editors who keep notes, such as those from telephone interviews or typed into a file from their reporter's notebooks, for example, on their word processors. Some indexing utilities include automatic creation of index entries. Naturally, software that indexes also permits updates and editing of the index as well. If users want to be very elaborate with their notes or other documents, most high-end word processors also offer automatic table of contents functions that may be useful with larger manuscripts, documents, or notes files.

Table functions in word processors may be helpful utilities for reporters and editors, such as those on sports and business desks who must frequently work with tabular databases. Tables are simply lists of numbers or letters with tabs. Word processors that have table features offer a systematic and automatic approach to preparing such information in more readable formats. Tables help journalists "visualize" information in a more orderly form and some programs offer the ability to easily create and manipulate tables. This should be encouragement to journalists who have avoided using tables in the past. Table functions are not much more than automatic formatting and tabbing, but they are certainly time savers for anyone needing them.

Many top-of-the-line word processors also offer a feature known as cross-referencing. For reporters or news researchers, this is a highly useful tool for organizing story research and interview notes, manuscripts in progress such as longer stories, or groups of stories that might be part of a major project requiring several weeks or months to prepare. Cross-referencing permits a document user to locate additional information in the same document or in a completely different document used by the word processor. Cross-references can be used for subheads, footnotes and endnotes, captions, and other unique or specially marked sections of the text.

Sorting enormous amounts of information can be useful to reporters and editors facing analysis of large text files. Journalists can use search functions to identify passages of interest, capture those passages and move them around—to other files or to different locations in the original file.

Other features of word processors can make a reporter, news researcher, or editor's work easier or less time consuming. For example, mail-merge features can simplify and speed creation of multiple information requests (such as those commonly made through freedom of information laws) or other types of mass mailings. Many word processors can use mail-merge tools with external databases within other programs. Form letter and memorandum templates can make correspondence tasks easier.

THE LEADING WORD PROCESSORS

PC Magazine contributing editor Edward Mendelson (1993) wrote:

> Suddenly, no word processor is an island. Word processors have always been the central focus for most users; they are about to become even more central in a new era of mutual cooperation and integration among applications. Programs that once let you do little more than type and format unadorned text now serve as automated clearinghouses for spreadsheets, graphics, and databases, as well as workgroup comments and revisions. Even if you still use a word processor to work only with words, you'll find that the same technical prowess that now lets programs integrate disparate kinds of data into a single document can also automate and simplify the traditional tasks of writing and editing. (p. 108)

Given the observation that there are fewer major general-use word processing products on the market in the mid-1990s than there were 5 or 10 years earlier, there seem to be several major roles played by word processing packages:

- First, there are products such as WordPerfect, which seem to provide everything a user would want in a single package. They are a form of one-stop shopping.
- The second approach is a complete word processor that is designed to work individually or with other programs in a set or "suite" installation. This is exemplified by Microsoft Word in "Office" or Lotus' AmiPro in "SmartSuite."
- The third type of word processor is the more traditional 1980s product that has moved into this decade without too many new bells and whistles, but still offers the basics in a reliable form. Typical of these products are XyWrite, the favorite of many newsrooms, and WordStar (Castagna, 1994).

There are still other developments. More and more word processing products offer object linking and embedding (OLE), a process that allows a word processor to use information from other applications such as spreadsheets, tables, or graphics. There is increasing attention given by word processor producers to dynamic data exchange (DDE) also, another form of information sharing across applications. DDE enhances Windows' cross-program data sharing; it permits very different programs to set up ways to communicate and transfer information back and forth in a format each program can understand (Prosise, 1994). More DOS-based word processors are working with graphics and pointing devices such as a mouse. There is also growth in OS/2-oriented word processors. Most new products permit some sort of programming capabilities for companion applications through macro files.

There are dozens of word processors sold for every imaginable operating system and platform, available in many of the major written languages worldwide. In the United States, several programs have emerged as the most popular in newsrooms, and in the business and corporate worlds.

USING PERSONAL INFORMATION MANAGERS

Some experts have called word processing *the* software of the 1980s and have described personal information managers as *the* software product of the 1990s. Whether that turns out to be the case, it remains clear that the advantages of personal information managers have yet to find their

---

WORD PROCESSORS IN NEWSROOMS

The 1994 University of Miami national CAR study found a large majority of newspapers were using a general-purpose word processor instead of earlier generation dedicated front-end reporting and editing word processors. A wide range of brands of word processors is in use as well in newsrooms (*n* = 208). Although some newspapers continue to use dedicated word processing systems that operate on mainframe or minicomputers, those using PCs systems to prepare stories or for other functions most often use XyWrite, WordPerfect, and Microsoft Word:

Circulation	XyWrite	Word	WordPerfect	Other[a]	None
Under 50,000	23.1% (12)	20.0% (5)	19.2% (5)	39.1% (27)	58.2% (53)
50,000–100,000	21.2 (11)	28.0 (7)	30.8 (8)	20.3 (14)	23.1 (21)
100,001–250,000	26.9 (14)	40.0 (10)	30.8 (8)	24.6 (17)	14.3 (13)
250,001–500,000	17.3 (9)	4.0 (1)	11.5 (3)	8.7 (6)	4.4 (4)
Over 500,000	11.5 (6)	8.0 (2)	7.7 (2)	7.2 (5)	0.0 (0)
Totals	100.0% (52)	100.0% (25)	100.0% (26)	100.0% (69)	100.0% (91)

Note: Percentages are for columns. Frequencies are in parentheses.

[a]For these newsrooms, "other" includes proprietary or dedicated word processing software as well as all nonspecific responses. Some newsrooms reported using more than one kind of word processor.

way into newsrooms. But this could change because these specialized programs, designed to help individuals keep track of personal information, are growing in popularity in other business sectors and will probably wind up creeping into news departments as well in the next several years.

PIMs permit a user to organize a range of personal or business information previously kept in several different places—in appointment books, address books, planner books, and "to-do list" ringed notebooks. Over the past decade or so, some individuals upgraded their collection of these separate books to elaborate printed spiral-bound or three-ring bound and tabbed personal organizer systems. PIMs are the digital versions of these more sophisticated bound systems. Some PIMs even use the ringed binder metaphor in their basic screen designs and database views. Lotus Organizer, for example, resembles a colorful sectioned on-screen binder. PIMs permit users to become better organized when it comes to business or home information of an individual nature. As a result, PIMs are growing in scope and number. There were three dozen or more different products on the market in 1995.

PIMs are individualized software, moreso than other programs that help journalists do their work. "Anyone who has searched endlessly for the perfect PIM knows that what makes a PIM work for one person can be the very thing that makes it unsuitable for someone else. Matching style and work habits to an interface and a card file is not easy," wrote *PC Magazine* computer consultant and reviewer Hillary Rettig (1994, p. 211).

News organizations, oddly, have been slow to adopt PIMs. It may be because most newsrooms have not moved into GUI environments and most PIMs are at their best in a GUI form. Use so far seems to be very isolated, entirely on individual levels, in most newsrooms. For many newsrooms, use of PIMs on a widespread level is not yet possible because PCs have not yet made appearances on desks of all reporters and editors. The personal nature of the software also makes it less appealing in a LAN, perhaps.

The *Knoxville News-Sentinel* is typical of newspapers with newsroom computer systems that cannot run PIMs. Metro Editor Jail Lail, one of the advocates of sophisticated computing in reporting in his newsroom, says PIMs are gradually catching on, but cannot move in because of the hardware limitations in the newsroom. "I use askSam, which is often considered a PIM, for phone lists and scheduling [on my PC], but most of our reporters don't. Those in the newsroom don't have PCs on the desktop (we have an Atex system)," Lail (personal communication, March 14, 1994) explained. "We do have PCs in our bureaus. The only PIM-type products installed on those machines are the calendar and cardfile programs that come with Windows. But even there, we're only running three Windows machines in our bureaus right now."

Barton Gellman, a 33-year-old *Washington Post* editor who runs the newspaper's Jerusalem bureau in the Middle East and who formerly covered the U.S. Department of Defense for his newspaper works on a Macintosh and likes to use MORE from Symantec to organize his work. "I use MORE . . . to keep several daily outlines going," Gellman (personal communication, March 19, 1994) explained. "I have a story to-do list, a calls list, my main Rolodex, and often a detailed outline on a specific story or subject."

Gellman, who joined his newspaper in 1988 and also has experience covering local courts, further explained how he had things set up in mid-1994 when he covered the Department of Defense:

> My Rolodex is an outline called "phone lists." It has probably 2,000 phone numbers, organized by the structure of the defense department (my beat) and by subject. The first level headings are: OSD, JCS, Unified Commands, Ongoing Operations and Joint Task Forces, Defense Agencies, Army, Navy, Air Force, Marines, Coast Guard, Reserve Component, White House/NSC/OMB, Intelligence Agencies, State Department, Congress, Diplomats/Attaches, United Nations, Experts/Subjects, Think Tanks/Issue Groups, Defense Reporters, Industry—and a few others. There are as many as eight or ten subordinate levels to the outline, so that beneath OSD (Office of the Secretary of Defense), for example, there is a path to Undersecretary for Policy [to] Assistant Secretary for Nuclear Security [to] Deputy Assistant Secretary for Russia and Ukraine, and so forth.

> I will become Jerusalem bureau chief at the end of the calendar year [1994], so I am preparing. I have a Jerusalem outline with suggestions on things to read, people to contact here and there, and so on.

Gellman, who earned an A.B. in international affairs at Princeton University and a masters in political philosophy at Oxford, not only uses the outliner for organizing his sources and story ideas, he uses it to prepare stories as well. But he is not a computer-obsessed journalist. "I just kind of like computers," he admitted. Gellman discussed one example of how he uses the program to help his writing: "I'm working on a magazine piece on one Army battalion commander. The outline for that has his chain of command and contactables, scenes I intend to write in the piece, examples of Army jargon I'll explain, and so on."

Most reporters and editors, like Lail and Gellman, have discovered the advantages to using PIMs but are forced to use them on their own PCs at home or to install them on portables. Once available to reporters, the organizational benefits of PIMs are instantly noticeable and quite obvious. These programs may be the most personal, yet practical, software that can be of immediate use for journalists. It can be used for personal and professional purposes.

Most PIM packages can accommodate more than one set of data very easily, making it simple to separate personal information from office information if needed. This feature also makes it possible to keep separate databases for different beats or purposes as needed. Because these programs are so personal in their service to the user, some experts recommend that users be very comfortable in using them and be encouraged to use them often (Bray, 1993).

"Information anxiety is the scourge of the 1990s, but it's nothing that a trip to the software doctor can't cure. The prescription isn't pills; it is PIMs—personal information managers," wrote computer book author and business consultant Rosalind Resnick (1992, p. 76).

Another appealing application of PIMs is in a network instead of the individual PC set up. Many products have network capabilities. In a LAN or a WAN, a networked organizer would permit reporters, editors, and others in the newsroom to share most commonly used source names, to schedule meetings, to plan coverage and use of resources, and to schedule other coverage-related activities. "Link the personal organisers [sic] on a network, and you have a group organiser that lets colleagues share contacts, schedule meetings, and send memos and documents," wrote software reviewer Paul Bray (1993, p. 79). "Add more personal details, sophisticated call logging and a data archive, and the package can be used to manage . . . time more effectively." Some PIMs specialize in scheduling. An entire market of scheduling software has emerged in recent years. Several PIMs and scheduling programs are particularly effective in LAN environments, including OnTime, Time and Place, Organizer, Schedule+, CalANdar, Meeting Maker, and Network Scheduler.

PIMs are much like word processors in that their designs offer a set of basic functions and then their designers go in different directions for other features. Most PIMs permit a wide range of customization across the major features and they also offer integration. Perhaps the key element of quality PIMs in the mid-1990s is integration of elements within the program and integration of elements from other programs as well. Thus, journalists looking for PIMs may want to select software that offers the ability to combine and link features as well as data. This is an even more appealing feature when such a PIM is placed on a newsroom personal computer network for different levels of information sharing. Some data can remain secure and private for some users, but other data can be offered to the entire newsroom.

Among the basic functions and features of quality PIMs are:

- Calendar management through individual appointment scheduling, repeat appointment scheduling, and reminder sound- and/or on-screen alarms.
- Time tracking (and billing associated with time).

- Names, addresses, and telephone numbers data storage.
- Task management, or "to-do" list building, that can appear on a daily calendar.
- Notetaking and note storage (and importing from other sources).
- Long-range or annual project planning (one calendar year at a time).
- Data importing and exporting utilities.
- Event anniversaries that carry forward to each year.
- Information search and retrieval capabilities.
- Business-source and personal contact management.
- Password security levels for full or partial access by other individuals.
- Data sharing and integration.
- Output design and format options for files and for printing.
- Expansion and deletion of sections.

More sophisticated versions offer even more. Some of the elements of the advanced PIMs include:

- Data exchange (DDE) and object linking (OLE with other software): Integration of data and features from other programs and from different storage areas of the PIM.
- Notetaking in free format.
- Group meeting scheduling.
- Phone number dialing.
- Time billing options (handy for consultants and other professionals).
- Networking and database sharing.
- Program start-ups from individual calendar entries.
- Wide-ranging flexibility, extensibility, and portability.

Many people spurned the idea of using PIM tools in the mid-1980s when the first ones appeared (e.g., Borland's original "Sidekick" and "Traveling Sidekick") because computing was not as portable as the information kept in PIM databases needed to be. The early PIMs, and their predecessors, were clearly designed for desktop systems and were portable only if output was specially formatted for printing and placed in small binders for portability. The desktop manager programs were little more than a collection of smaller programs with separate functions and little, if any, flexibility.

With the growth in computing power and the shrinkage in size and weight of portable PCs, PIMs are growing in use in the business world especially, and in other applications. These programs are now quite sophisticated in their data processing range. As more and more journalists move to smaller portable PCs, it seems inevitable that PIMs will grow in popularity and in use as reporting tools. Perhaps the best use of PIMs for reporters is to keep track of appointments with sources and to organize information about regularly used sources. Editors can use them to keep appointments, but also to list staff information and information about sources as well.

One category of PIMs that has recently appeared on the software market is so-called "SuperPIMs." These PIMs are designed to provide additional power and features. Two examples are ECCO's Simplicity and ECCO's Professional. SuperPIMs offer even greater flexibility and power in building and manipulating personal information databases. These programs offer additional ways to link, view, and recombine information in the personal database. For example, outlining is one function not found in many other PIMs but is common in "SuperPIM" class programs.

Selecting the right PIM for the job is important. Some are designed to better serve attorneys or salespersons than reporters. These programs, like others used by journalists, have their strengths and weaknesses. But Rosalind Resnick (1992), a free-lance business journalist, reminds potential users: "It's also important to remember that whichever PIM you buy, it's only as useful as the data you put into it" (p. 76).

This is a potential problem for any PIM user, especially busy individuals such as reporters and editors. To have truly effective reporting and organizing tools, PIM users must be willing to set aside some time each day to enter personal information such as appointments, tasks, and new sources. It should be done with a high level of regularity and completeness to be most useful. The best process, some experienced users feel, is to make the PIM a habit and development of the PIM databases an ongoing process. As things happen, the database should be updated. In a short period of time, a surprisingly useful and large database will develop. As Resnick (1992) suggested, the program alone is not going to make a disorganized person suddenly become organized. "But a little organizational effort goes a lot further when a PIM is involved" (p. 76).

Some PIMs are sold as regular DOS programs; others are memory-resident "pop-up" DOS programs, and still others operate in Windows or OS/2. The versatility of a PIM that is immediately available is important for journalists who need to switch from a word processor or other program to their PIM at the ring of a telephone or the call of an emergency on a police radio. The need to switch or multitask seems to be fundamental for the needs of journalists at their computers in newsrooms or on the road.

USING CONTACT MANAGERS TO TRACK
NEWS SOURCES

Consider this scenario: A business beat reporter working at her computer is called by an executive from the leading corporate employer in

PERSONAL INFORMATION MANAGERS IN NEWSROOMS

The 1994 University of Miami national CAR study found very few personal information managers or contact managers in use in U.S. daily newspaper newsrooms ($n = 208$). A very large majority of newspapers report no use of these products yet. Some responding editors were completely unfamiliar with this category of software. Of those products in use, askSam, the free-form information management and database program, is the most popular:

Circulation	askSam	Act!	Organizer	Other	None
Under 50,000	0.0% (0)	0.0% (0)	0.0% (0)	15.8% (3)	44.0% (85)
50,000–100,000	0.0 (0)	0.0 (0)	100.0 (1)	15.8 (3)	25.9 (50)
100,001–250,000	80.0 (4)	0.0 (0)	0.0 (0)	47.4 (9)	18.7 (36)
250,001–500,000	20.0 (1)	0.0 (0)	0.0 (0)	10.5 (2)	8.3 (16)
Over 500,000	0.0 (0)	100.0 (1)	0.0 (0)	10.5 (2)	3.1 (6)
Totals	100.0% (5)	100.0% (1)	100.0% (1)	100.0% (19)	100.0% (193)

Note: Percentages are for columns. Frequencies are in parentheses. Some newspapers reported using more than one PIM.

town to discuss pending layoffs. Even though she was working on a different story, she quickly switches from her Windows word processor to the contact manager software on her hard drive and finds the source's name and background information on her screen in just a few seconds. In trying to build a stronger personal relationship with the source, she is able to ask the executive about the source's family by using names listed on her screen and she even reminds him of their last conversation by date and subject (Yakal, 1993).

The example describes a successfully organized reporter who uses a "contact manager" program. Contact managers are specialized forms of PIMs that can be highly useful to reporters (Yakal, 1993). These are usually found in the hands of salespersons, social workers, and others who deal with people on a regular basis. There are numerous characteristics of contact managers that are useful to people-oriented reporters and editors as well. Instead of clients and customers, news story sources can be plugged into the program. "While there is a core of commonality between contact managers and PIMs . . . we see a clear difference in emphasis. PIMs focus on a series of activities, usually loosely tied to a schedule or address database. Contact managers, on the other hand, primarily address people, associations, and history," writes veteran computer industry journalist Kathy Yakal (1993, p. 272).

These programs aim at managing information about people outside the newsroom. "Key features [of contact managers] include the ability to store detailed information on your contacts (such as the name of their secretary or their taste in restaurants), the production of tailored and mailshot letters, and a complete history of when you spoke to people and what they said. You should expect to be able to customize the software to suit the way you work," said Bray (1993, p. 79).

Contact managers should offer a number of basic features that include contact (source) interaction histories, meeting histories, follow-up reminders, contact search and retrieval capabilities, free-form notetaking fields, automatic telephone call logging capabilities, word processing or links to external word processors, mail merging, task listing, appointment calendars, data sharing, task switching, and a variety of printed and file output formats. Like other mid-1990s software, the more sophisticated the contact manager, the more features and usually, the higher the price.

Some of the most popular contact managers include Act!, GoldMine, Action+Plus—the Executive Power Tool, Commence, Contact Plus Professional, and In-Control. These programs are in the same price range as many top-flight word processors, relational databases, and spreadsheets that are list priced from $249 to $495. Network versions for newsrooms are also available (Yakal, 1993).

IV Advanced Database Reporting Strategies

11

Data Processing and Analysis for News Stories

Tom Foster, projects editor and *ex officio* director of computer-assisted reporting for the 90,000-daily circulation *Syracuse Post-Standard,* seems to thoroughly enjoy his work. He directs CAR projects, manages his newspaper's databases on the newsroom LAN, and oversees hardware and software purchasing. His efforts have made the *Post-Standard* a stronger information provider for its region of upstate New York. "Better availability of sources equals better stories," Foster (personal communication, March 1, 1994) said in summarizing his philosophy about CAR.

However, Foster feels CAR is off to a less-than-ideal start in some news organizations. Making a presentation at the Investigative Reporters and Editors CAR conference at Raleigh in 1993, Foster said CAR should not be considered a special projects tool but should be used as a daily reporting strategy:

> Computer-assisted reporting often becomes the domain of a few reporters and editors who work on projects. That's unfortunate. Ideally, newspapers should be able to use computers to assist investigations AND improve stories reporters write on a daily basis. At the *Post-Standard* in Syracuse, we've made a special effort to make databases easy to use and widely available. For the most part, this involves helping reporters on deadline locate sources, check facts and add detail. A reporter scrambling to cover a late-night fatal fire, for example, can count on being able to quickly find a list of neighbors to call, identify the building's owner, obtain the structure's assessed value, and review a demographic profile of the neighborhood's housing values, rents, and income levels from census data. (p. 2)

"The bottom line is," Foster argued, "if data is easy to obtain, reporters will use it." The *Post-Standard,* like many newspapers that have made, or are making, the transition to using computers in routine reporting, has a wide range of online services and databases in house for use in daily spot reporting. Other databases are purchased from often-costly vendors. Some databases fit a type somewhere in between those extremes. "Reporters don't care how flashy the software is; all they want is something accessible and relevant," Foster (1993, p. 2) observed. His newspaper regularly keeps databases containing practical information about city hall, the police department, local courts, the county courthouse, the environment, local, state, and national politics, regional businesses, and local and regional sports.

Reporters and editors at the *Syracuse Post-Standard* use up-to-date hardware and software for their CAR environment. They work on networked DEC 486 desktop PCs that run at 33 MHz. The DOS system is loaded with Windows and can be customized to each person's particular needs. With Windows, reporters and editors can write in a word processor at the same time they are checking information in a database or looking up usages in the computerized Associated Press stylebook. Recent CAR news projects at Syracuse include analysis of election participation and turnout among younger voters, unfair home property tax assessments, leap year birthdays, tax breaks given land developers, and poor quality of medical treatment given to New York state prisoners.

This type of newsroom computer configuration is the epitome of computer-assisted database reporting in this decade. "As far as I'm concerned, we're at the beginning of the road," said Elliot Jaspin (1994, p. 14), the Cox News Service Systems Editor in Washington and a pioneer in database reporting:

> [T]here's scores of newsrooms at this point using computer-assisted reporting but not hundreds. As time goes by, I'm sure that number is going to grow. . . . A couple of things are going to happen. The power and sophistication and ease of using a computer is going to increase geometrically. . . . It will mean two things: it will be far easier to use computers and what computers will be able to do will be far more extensive.

Steve Ross, another leading CAR proponent who teaches in the School of Journalism at Columbia University, feels journalists just got off to a slow start with computers. "The power of the computer can help reporters in many ways: word processing, data retrieval, data analysis, and information dissemination and storage," Ross (1992, p. 1) stated. "Yet except for word processing, journalists have been slow to take advantage of computer technology. And where computers have played a part in reporting, that part has usually been in the creation of massive 'investigative' stories, at major-market media outlets," Ross believes.

COMPUTER-BASED REPORTING STRATEGIES

Advanced reporting techniques take basic reporting skills to a higher level. Journalists have an introductory knowledge of observing, interviewing, and using documents as news-gathering tools. Advanced reporting techniques use these traditional tools and combine them with even more rigorous and systematic information collecting tools originally developed and used by social scientists, computer scientists, and others in the academic world.

Advanced reporting methods often go beyond events (McCombs, Shaw, & Grey, 1976). To do this faster and more accurately, many of the advanced reporting tools in use in the mid-1990s are computer based. "The tougher assignments increasingly are being tackled by today's journalists, at least the ones fortunate enough to work for media that have gone beyond just covering news events as defined by other people. . . . These journalists are trying to make their own definitions of what is news," noted advanced reporting authorities Gerry Keir, Maxwell McCombs, and Donald L. Shaw (1991, p. 7).

Database-oriented reporting is slowly catching on. It began at larger newspapers and is gradually spreading to all levels of daily newspapers, wire services, and news magazines. CAR is beginning to appear as the foundation for some network and affiliate television news journalism as well. One example of an average-size news organization doing this is the 42,000-circulation Lewiston, ME, *Sun Journal*. Craig Doremus (personal communication, February 2, 1994), Sunday staff writer and an investigative reporter for the newspaper, explained how his newspaper uses CAR:

> We are a small newspaper, but very hardware advanced. For about a year and a half, we have been fully paginating our newspaper using PCs and Macs. Every reporter has a PC on his or her desk (usually a 386). Editors sit in front of 486s. We are currently switching over from Mac pagination to PC pagination using Quark Xpress. However, despite my enthusiasm for computer-assisted reporting, editors here are reluctant to jump into this brave new world of journalism. It all boils down to time and money. Like at all small newspapers, both of them are at a premium at our paper. Those constraints have made most of my efforts at computer-assisted reporting modest compared to what the big papers do. There are, however, valid ways of using computers to analyze issues.
>
> In fact, many big newspapers are still reluctant to get into CAR, not knowing what they'll get in return for a lot of investment in hardware, software, data and on-line time. But most newspapers will be switching to pagination in the next few years, so there will be some powerful PCs ending up on the desks of many small and large newspaper journalists. So it is important . . . to give them a hint of the potential of CAR.

Doremus (personal communication, February 2, 1994) said he has found that many public offices in Maine offer their databases at no cost or for a nominal fee in the area of $50. "Emphasize databases and spreadsheets," Doremus stated. "I think they are of value to most reporters and editors. You don't have to be a big newspaper to do this type of reporting. I'm sure there's a lot of PCs hanging around newsrooms that can be used for computer-assisted reporting."

Despite Doremus' enthusiasm, some news organizations are less quick to adapt and have chosen to make the transition in stages. One such group is in Fort Wayne, IN. "We have used basic online text searches for several years, but only in the last two years have we expanded into true CAR programs," said *Fort Wayne Journal-Gazette* investigative reporter Glenn Hall (personal communication, February 21, 1994). "Last year, we purchased dedicated hardware and software for the [CAR] program, and I am pioneering the use of the equipment and trying to show others what can be done. There is a lot of interest, but I have been surprised at how little my colleagues know about computers!"

This type of database-oriented information gathering has been given a number of names: *Number crunching, database journalism,* CAJ, and CAR are the most common. Whatever it is called, the approach has moved well above the horizon in U.S. journalism. The database era has arrived.

SOCIAL SCIENCE TRADITIONS IN JOURNALISM

Sociologists study human behavior in social relationships, social institutions, social problems, social development, and social organization. Psychologists study individual human behavior by focusing on the mind and mental processes. Anthropologists study the social relationships, behavior, and customs of humanity. Similarly, economists, historians, and political scientists are social scientists. All social scientists study human behavior, and so do journalists. There is a little of all of these social scientists in most journalists, whose duties include observing the many forms and results of human behavior.

Journalists have a strong behavioral science heritage. Most journalism schools in the United States are rooted in one or more of the social sciences. Journalists usually study human behavior in one or two persons at a time, but they also study human behavior in aggregate form. Journalists often study human behavior in manners similar to those of their colleagues in the academy. Social science research techniques have been considered a part of reporting for several generations of journalists, but they have been used broadly only in the past two decades, paralleling the growth in use of the computer in the newsroom. It is only in the past three decades that reporters have begun to use the research tools—both quantitative and qualitative—of social scientists in their reporting on more complicated stories.

Journalists gather news by observing, interviewing, and studying documents. For a moment, think about how sociologists, psychologists, and even anthropologists work. They observe. They interview. They study documents (and other artifacts of human life). The groups' goals are very much the same, too: Reporters and social scientists want to know what has occurred and why it happened. One difference, of course, is that social scientists often wish to construct theories to explain human behavior. Reporters often generalize, too, but seldom develop formal theories with which to do it.

DEVELOPMENT OF "PRECISION JOURNALISM"

For more than 30 years, journalists have tried to merge reporting with the power of computers. In the mid-1960s, however, the only computers available were massive mainframe systems that were difficult to learn to use and even more difficult to access. Only the most die-hard devotees to the precursor form of computer-assisted reporting of that era actually started and completed projects. One of them was Philip Meyer, who was a reporter for the *Detroit Free Press* when he began using computers to analyze public opinion in the Detroit metropolitan area. Meyer later worked for *The Miami Herald* and Knight-Ridder, Inc. In 1967, Meyer led a team of journalists from the *Free Press* that analyzed public opinion in the newspaper's region following the urban rioting that occurred that summer in Detroit. Other pioneers included *Philadelphia Inquirer* reporters James B. Steele and Donald L. Barlett, who used computers in the early 1970s to investigate bias in the justice system and inequities in the federal income tax system. With their traditions of street reporting and an interest in using the latest computing technology, Meyer, Steele, and Barlett took different routes to rise to the top of their profession. After moving from Detroit to Knight-Ridder's Washington bureau, Meyer went to Miami. He eventually left the newsroom of *The Miami Herald,* but remained in Miami to direct research for its parent corporation, Knight-Ridder. Eventually, Meyer moved to the University of North Carolina to teach journalism and to write. Barlett and Steele have remained at *The Inquirer* and have won two Pulitzer Prizes and countless other national awards for massive investigative reporting projects that utilized their computer analysis abilities, document searching and finding knowledge, and other equally productive information gathering skills.

Philip Meyer Defines "Precision Journalism"

While still working as a reporter, Meyer took the school year during 1966–1967 to study at Harvard University on a Nieman Fellowship. It occurred to him at the time that reporters could also use many of the social science research tools about which he was learning. Meyer soon began writing a book—he took a year during 1969–1970 at the Russell Sage Foundation in New York—that would change the way many reporters looked at information gathering. Meyer demonstrated in the original edition of his book, *Precision Journalism* (1973), that social science research methods can and should be used in gathering news. Focusing mainly on survey research, but also looking at experimental and observational tools such as content analysis, the book and its two subsequent versions have affected more than a generation of journalists.

Meyer is widely acknowledged as the "father" of computer-assisted reporting because of his pioneering work in precision journalism. He is simply a journalist and teacher who has been far ahead of his time. He is widely acknowledged for drawing the attention of journalists world-wide to the techniques of an approach to reporting he labeled, with the help of communication scholar Everette Dennis, *precision journalism.* Precision journalism, the code word for a generation of computer-oriented journalism, may be giving way to the term computer-assisted reporting, but the two terms essentially describe the same quantitative approaches to news reporting.

Precision journalism, as Meyer uses the term, is a *methodology* for collecting information. CAR is similar, of course, but the term more appropriately describes a range of computer-based information-gathering *tools,* not so much a research philosophy, that include precision journalism approaches utilizing computers. It is, perhaps, possible to use techniques described by Meyer without the assistance of mainframe or even personal computers, but such reporting is really impracticable because most precision journalism is often highly quantitative. In the second edition of *Precision Journalism,* Meyer (1979) said journalists would be wrong less often, to be less likely to make impressionistic mistakes, "if we adapted to our own use some of the research tools of the social scientists" (p. 3). Meyer's latest treatment of the subject, the third, is entitled *The New Precision Journalism* (1991).

Meyer focuses on use of scientific method and the research techniques of the social sciences that journalists can apply to story development. Measurement of public opinion through polls and surveys is one subject synonymous with precision journalism and now a part of the duties of many CAR desks. There are other forms of precision journalism, including field experimentation and systematic content analysis of records and documents, which remain at the edge or even out of the scope of most CAR activities.

CAR AT A REGIONAL LEVEL

Like the *Syracuse Post-Standard,* the *Raleigh News & Observer* has built a reputation as an innovator in the area of computerized reporting.

Over the last decade, this regional newspaper has moved ahead of most other newspapers in use of computers to gather information on projects, to cover breaking stories, and for day-to-day routine news. Lisa Van Asch (personal communication, March 8, 1994), a news researcher for four years at the *News & Observer,* says the transition of her newspaper has been dramatic:

> We have gone from basic "information storage" (clips, photos, books) to information retrieval (commercial databases, county and state databases), to information generators. We have hired Dan Woods as database editor, and Jon Schmid as assistant database editor, and they— along with Pat Stith, who started all this years ago—have brought a new dimension to this [research] department.

> Dan, Jon, and Pat (and several reporters they've converted) have acquired, loaded and analyzed hundreds of government databases—most on nine-track tape—including the state medical examiner's database, state personnel records, DMV records, OSHA records, and marriage license records. As of this date [March 1994], the *N&O* has published 211 computer-assisted stories—"computer-assisted" meaning that the story was based on in-house analysis (usually the reporter working with Dan or Jon) of a database. Dan and Jon have taken it a step further, and have started to copy the databases to CD-ROM format, making them easily accessible to everyone in the newsroom. So now I (or anyone) can sit down at our public terminal (which has a CD-ROM player), put in a CD of the state DMV records and, using the FoxPro software, search on a license plate number or a name. We don't have to reload the tape or save the data on our network, which used to fill up our hard drives and network. Now, instead of asking, "Do you have a book on . . . ?" reporters ask us, "Do you have a database on . . . ?"

These changes meant growth. The *News & Observer* decided to enlarge its news research department. "We have gotten a lot bigger. We have added several researchers, another assistant database editor (Donna Seese, a reporter who moved over to News Research in 1994), and several people with expertise in developing computer applications. . . . These applications allow us to do things like convert Fahrenheit to Celsius, or compare figures in the consumer price index (quickly see what $5,000 in 1946 equals today), or create our own databases (researchers spend a minute typing in each research request), and at the end of the month we're able to run reports on what we've done. We've also developed databases of football and basketball statistics, a local restaurant guide, and so forth," said Van Asch (personal communication, March 8, 1994).

The effect has been nothing less than dramatic in Raleigh. The level of expertise in computer use has increased exponentially. The newsroom staff has become computer savvy, Van Asch (personal communication, March 8, 1994) stated. "We are all fairly computer literate now. We use

Lotus 1-2-3 to do our budgets (even our staff phone list!), type our memos in AmiPro, retrieve our 'clips' from a database (DataTimes, currently). It is frustrating sometimes, because things change so fast. We have learned to be good adapters."

CAR AT THE NATIONAL LEVEL

USA Today is located in the perfect place for computer-assisted reporting at the national level. Its news and editorial offices are situated in suburban Washington, DC, just across the Potomac River from the nation's capital. The location makes it relatively easy for the newspaper's reporters and editors to access federal government databases. Perhaps easier, but the data analysis task at this newspaper is unique and probably more complex. Many newspapers and other publications that use databases in reporting news focus on their own regions and communities. Things are different for Gannett Company's flagship newspaper, now in its second decade. The 1 million-plus circulation newspaper has a "community" of 50 states and millions of potential readers. It is, like the *Wall Street Journal* and the handful of other nationally oriented publications, a newspaper read by individuals in all parts of the country and, in fact, in a number of foreign countries.

"We have to do our database projects with a national twist. We have to leverage national news stories from government data," explained Larry K. Sanders (personal communication, January 9, 1994), special projects editor at *USA Today* since 1989.

Sanders heads a unit at *USA Today* that researches a wide range of stories with a national perspective. His team of three other database editors works behind the scenes with staff reporters who prepare the stories. Sanders, a journalist for 25 years and former editor of the *Santa Fe New Mexican* and managing editor of the *El Paso Times,* founded the unit in 1988.

He likes to point to a 1990 project on dangerous interstate highways as an example of what his group of number crunchers can do:

Most newspapers would look at only those in their communities or their state. We had to have a national perspective. The roads project involved analysis of the FARS data (Federal Accident Reporting System) from the National Highway Traffic Safety Administration [NHTSA] which is a part of the DOT [Department of Transportation]. We were the first to use the FARS to pin down the country's most deadly section of interstate highway. We had to analyze millions of records of data from the NHTSA and the Federal Highway Administration.

The story began because, Sanders recalled, some 16th-floor staffers began to believe that the most dangerous highway in the country had to be the interstate highway system that rings the District of Columbia. "We thought it would be the Beltway, but we were surprised to find out it was a stretch of interstate highway in southeastern Idaho."

Sanders explained that his staff compiled a traffic fatality index by combining a database of fatal traffic accidents with a database of traffic volume for each highway, resulting in an equalizing statistic that enabled highways with widely different traffic volume to be compared. That is how I-84 in Idaho could outrank I-5 in San Diego or I-95 along the East coast as the most dangerous road.

The study focused on the impact of traffic factors such as seat belt use, speeding, and use of alcohol. A three-part series resulted, including cover story status for the first 2 days. That project, Sanders said, is typical of the way CAR projects work at one of the nation's largest newspapers: An idea is developed into a story. Databases are obtained and analyzed. A preliminary report is prepared for the reporters and editors involved. The reporter sits down with the database editor and goes over the analyses. "The reporter may let us tell him or her what we think is most interesting or ask us some questions to answer with the database that we did not think to ask," Sanders explained.

The CAR project office's space includes a dozen or so desks with computers for the editors and their assistants. There are a total of eight persons in the database section of the special projects area and two or so more news researchers in the library who also work on the projects when needed. Editors use 486 IBM personal computers with 16 to 24 MB of RAM and from 600 to 800 MB of storage on hard drives. The desk has several CD-ROM drives and an optical drive. Sanders has also tied one powerful PC with the Gannett Company's mainframe computer a few miles away in Maryland with a microwave link and, he said, a user could never tell it was not the PC being used. The mainframe link is used for very large databases, containing millions of records.

"When you use databases that we have to use for national stories, they tend to be very large files with millions of records," Sanders noted. "That's why we need the mainframe."

Sanders prefers to use SAS (Statistical Analysis System) on the mainframe. On the IBM PCs, the software of choice includes Word-Perfect and XyWrite for word processing, Quattro Pro for spreadsheet analysis, Paradox for DOS for relational database analysis, and Atlas GIS for database mapping.

"We'd like to spend more time with the Internet," Sanders said in describing the growth and advancement directions he planned for 1994 and 1995. His desk has enjoyed some considerable reporting successes, he admits. "We were the first to analyze the financial issues involving the savings and loans, the first to analyze TRIS [Toxic Release Inventory System] from the EPA. This is the database that has all the emissions by chemical factories of toxic chemicals. We got it on nine-track tape about six months before it was available on compact disk. Now, it's available through EPA online," he said. "Our biggest failure, though, has been our inability to get more reporters directly involved in doing CAR."

REPORTING ABOUT SOCIAL TRENDS

Social trends often make news. Trend stories earn the status of covers of national news magazines and front pages of Sunday newspapers on a regular basis. It is often difficult to see or hear a trend, of course, but it may be newsworthy once it is detected. For journalists, newsworthy trends are general tendencies found in collective human behavior or a series of events. Trends, unlike event-oriented stories that occur in just a short period of time, develop over a longer period of time.

How do reporters determine trends? There are various ways, but many begin with simple personal observation. Then advanced reporting methods can be used to check for developing trends, to confirm or refute the observation, in the social order of a community or region. For example, public opinion polls and surveys can be used to determine trends in behavior and, perhaps more important, the major reasons behind those trends. It is one aspect of newsworthiness to determine a significant trend is developing; it is yet another matter to explain the major reasons behind the trend.

Another method is to monitor social indicators contained in public databases. These are statistics kept by a community, a regional government, or the federal government on a variety of social characteristics such as population, housing, transportation, banking, consumer purchasing, employment, illnesses, deaths, and births. For example, a reporter may determine, by checking real estate records or census data, that a significant segment of the community's population is moving back into the center city. By combining content analysis of these sales records with census population statistics and with interviews from a public opinion poll of those moving back into the city, a comprehensive look at the trend will result. The best part, of course, is not only telling readers that the trend is occurring, but also telling them why it is occurring.

Polls and surveys are one relatively easy way to detect social trends and they do not always concern political campaigns and the leading candidates for office. Some of the most meaningful polls and surveys focus on community or regional issues and concerns, revealing behavioral tendencies that perhaps readers did not know were occurring in their own communities and regions.

Social scientists also use *trend design* in their research. It is one of several forms of long-term, or longitudinal, research. Trend designs used by social scientists involve measuring and evaluating changes in a defined population over a period of time. This is perhaps the most widely used type of long-term research in the social sciences (Demers & Nichols, 1987).

The University of Texas' McCombs suggests trend analysis can also be achieved with surveys and polls simply by linking a series of surveys over time to determine trends (McCombs, Shaw, & Grey, 1976). This is called *secondary analysis* because it involves use of data that have already been analyzed by another researcher or journalist. *Primary analysis,* in contrast, is original data collection and analysis. The advantage to the journalist, of course, is that someone else has already collected the data (and paid for the effort). McCombs also suggested merging old data with new data in determining some trends. For example, a reporter can conduct a new poll and also use data from an older poll as a baseline for comparison—if the two polls are methodologically similar.

Research design is a "map" for information gathering strategy, so it can be quite helpful. Journalists are not too different from social scientists in this way, too. When journalists study trends, they often use many of the same indicators and database analysis methods that social scientists use.

Nonevent reporting is a somewhat hazy area of journalism that is difficult to define. Nonevent journalism includes stories about investigations, social trends, and overviews of situations (McCombs, Shaw, & Grey, 1976). Nonevent advanced reporting is much more structured. "When we begin systematically to assess our communities and their situations, we typically are going to obtain a mixture of the good and bad, of bright areas and problem areas," McCombs wrote (McCombs, Shaw, & Grey, 1976, p. 8).

Trend reporting is illustrated by the work of Steve Doig, *The Miami Herald's* associate research editor. Doig has completed dozens of database-oriented reporting projects. In one example, he studied population integration by using both 1990 and 1980 U.S. census databases. Doig and Knight-Ridder colleagues from the *Detroit Free Press* and *Charlotte Observer* found "only marginal gains" in urban racial integration. Doig's reporting was not based on a single event, but on a series of events that, when analyzed in aggregate form, revealed a tendency of slow racial integration in urban neighborhoods across the United States. "Census data, crime statistics, and other similar information are a useful way of describing human behavior," said Doig (personal communication, May 20, 1991). "When you deal with mass human behavior, statistics are the way to do so. Most reporters deal with anecdotal information. This goes beyond the anecdotal to describe trends," he explained.

COMPUTERS IN INVESTIGATIVE REPORTING

Investigative reporting is the most popular advanced information gathering approach. Reporters have been conducting their own investigations for generations, but they are using much more sophisticated computer-based investigative tools in the mid-1990s. Reporters use computers to systematically research background information in investigations and to find links of previously unrelated separate events where they may have not been known to exist. Reporters also use computers to analyze data to gain new insights and understanding of their communities.

"Investigative reporting doesn't have to mean large staffs, huge risks and high costs. It can mean, for instance, checking no-bid contracts, seeing if specifications for a building or a police car are tailored to fit one supplier, learning whether your town's ambulance response time is significantly longer than average," wrote *Publisher's Auxiliary* reporter Bill Kirtz (1991, p. 12). "Investigative reporting tests how the system— for which our readers pay, on which they depend—works, or doesn't work."

Investigative Reporters and Editors, Inc. (IRE) has devoted itself to refining methods of investigative journalism and has taken a leadership role in incorporating CAR tools into mainstream reporting. John Ullman, former investigative projects editor for the *Minneapolis Star and Tribune* and former executive director of IRE, explained the nature of investigative reporting:

> We like to say among ourselves that "investigative reporting" is redundant, that all good reporters are investigators by definition. But clearly and, at the very least, there is a great difference in the quality of all these "investigative" reports. One of the reasons why daily journalism is criticized for being shallow is that the skills common to most investigative reporters—the ability to locate, understand and ultimately use a vast number of records and documents in order to determine the real story— are unknown to many journalists. (Ullman & Colbert, 1991, p. 1)

Keir, McCombs, and Shaw (1991) emphasize that nonevent journalism such as investigative reporting requires a different mind set. It also requires a change in allocation of time and energy. These characteristics also describe precision journalism. Literally, precision journalism means reporting with the fine-tuned precision of the social scientist. Journalists must think of themselves as social scientists. These changes have a price. Most newsrooms may have to expand. This means, at a minimum, possibly more people and resources. It can be done without growing, but some aspect of coverage must be sacrificed.

Computer-assisted reporting analyzes original data obtained—usually purchased—from a public or private source. Some CAR is simple enough to do in the newsroom without the help of number crunchers, the people who program and analyze data with computers. Elliot Jaspin, an editor at Cox Newspapers, and David Burnham, a Syracuse University journalism professor and former *New York Times* reporter, have developed reputations as two of the leading experts in computer-assisted reporting. Jaspin, while a fellow at the Freedom Forum Center for Media Studies in New York, developed techniques to link nine-track computer tape drives with advanced personal computers to analyze government information. Jaspin authored a program known as "NineTrack Express" that makes it easier to transfer data from a nine-track tape drive connected to a reasonably powerful personal computer. He was the founder of what became the National Institute for Computer-Assisted Reporting (NICAR).

The one premise is that the information reporters wish to analyze will be available to the public on computer tape, CD-ROM, or other digital format. Despite increased computerization of records in this decade, government agencies do not always file records in electronic form. James Stewart and Andrew Alexander, Cox Newspapers national correspondents based in Washington, DC, once experienced this problem. They eventually had to build their own database of assault weapons used in crime from the original paper records compiled by the federal Bureau of Alcohol, Tobacco and Firearms (ATF) in Washington, DC, to develop their series.

In addition to NICAR, another center is the National Institute for Advanced Reporting at Indiana University's Indianapolis campus. The institute offers seminars and special programs on advanced reporting techniques. IRE, based alongside NICAR at the University of Missouri, is also a leading resource. At Syracuse University, the Transactional Records Access Clearinghouse helps reporters gather and analyze computerized government records.

The Miami Herald's Doig strongly recommends that journalists learn to use personal computers for data analysis. There are at least two applications that Doig feels reporters should take time to learn: spreadsheets and database programs. "Spreadsheets help you to learn more about budgets and elections, for example. You can analyze them yourself," Doig (personal communication, May 20, 1991) said. "If you take a course to learn about these programs in college, then you will have an idea of what they can do to help you as a reporter."

REPORTING STORIES USING STATISTICS

Journalists traditionally have had little affinity for numbers. Audiences feel generally the same, usually avoiding stories heavy with statistics. This will eventually change. Statistics are becoming as much a part of journalism in the mid-1990s as press conferences and speeches. Reporters and their editors must become comfortable dealing with statistics. Stories with numbers are not limited to business or sports beats. They are found in just about all fields and an ability to understand and interpret statistics is an essential advanced reporting skill.

The other side of the coin is translating the meaning of statistics to readers. Stories laden with numbers—such as those about the economy, businesses, elections, budgets, and public finances—are particularly tough assignments for some reporters. Miami's Doig, however, is comfortable writing stories dealing with statistics. "I'm a black box for the newsroom where things can be put and, a few hours or days later, an answer emerges. If I can understand it, we can make it understandable for readers," Doig (personal communication, May 20, 1991) explained. Doig's census-based state and regional population trend stories, written just after the first releases of data from the 1990 census and as Congressional reapportionment was occurring, demonstrate how reporters can make complicated demographic data understandable.

Translating statistical information into understandable narrative often means defining and explaining complicated statistical or other sophisticated research terms for readers. It means providing space to define and explain at the expense of other potentially important information. It also means explaining statistical information with which readers can identify. What do the statistics mean to average citizens in the community? How will the essence of this information impact their lives? Yet, although journalists must answer these questions, they cannot do so at the expense of accuracy or objectivity. In other words, they must use the same news values in precision journalism they would use with any other reporting tool.

"You, first of all, have to know which of the tools which you have used which you cannot put into the story. For example, I never write about standard deviations. I write about range instead. I don't write about means. I write about averages instead," Doig (personal communication, May 20, 1991) explained. "Keep it simple. You have to keep it as simple as the first chapter of a statistics book."

Another reporting and writing method Doig uses that is helpful to readers is interviewing experts who speak in understandable scientific terms. Although this is not always necessary or always possible, it helps. Journalists must also know the meaning of these complex terms for their audiences. Clearly, reporters can become experts when it comes to originating database-oriented stories. Even so, independent authorities can lend greater credibility and objectivity to interpretations.

"There are different ways of being a reporter. Using a computer to analyze information and produce a story about human behavior is only one way. It is a new way of doing something we have always done as reporters," Doig (personal communication, May 20, 1991) said. "But before we had computers, the work took much more time to do—using index cards. Now we can do stories such as this one in a few days when it might have taken years to do before."

USING THE CAR PROCESS

Executing a CAR project using a database does not have to be difficult. The trick is to conduct the project by completing one step at a time. One expert, Wendell Cochran (1993) of Gannett News Service in Washington, DC, suggests nine steps in Fig. 11.1.

Sharon Parker Warden has extensive experience in planning and executing computer-based research for news stories. She works in the survey research unit of *The Washington Post*. "Most of your problems will be with systems inside your own newspaper," Warden advised journalists (1992, p. 2). "You will have to be persistent, resourceful and resilient as you work your way through the steps needed." After being a part of dozens of such newsroom projects, Warden concluded that there are 16 distinct steps in the process of completing a project. "Not all steps will be accomplished in the order listed. The project, newspaper and reporter will determine the order of training compared to acquiring data, for example, because in some instances training will take place at each step. The first few steps . . . are common to all stories," she explained (p. 2). Warden's steps to completing a CAR project, with explanation added, are:

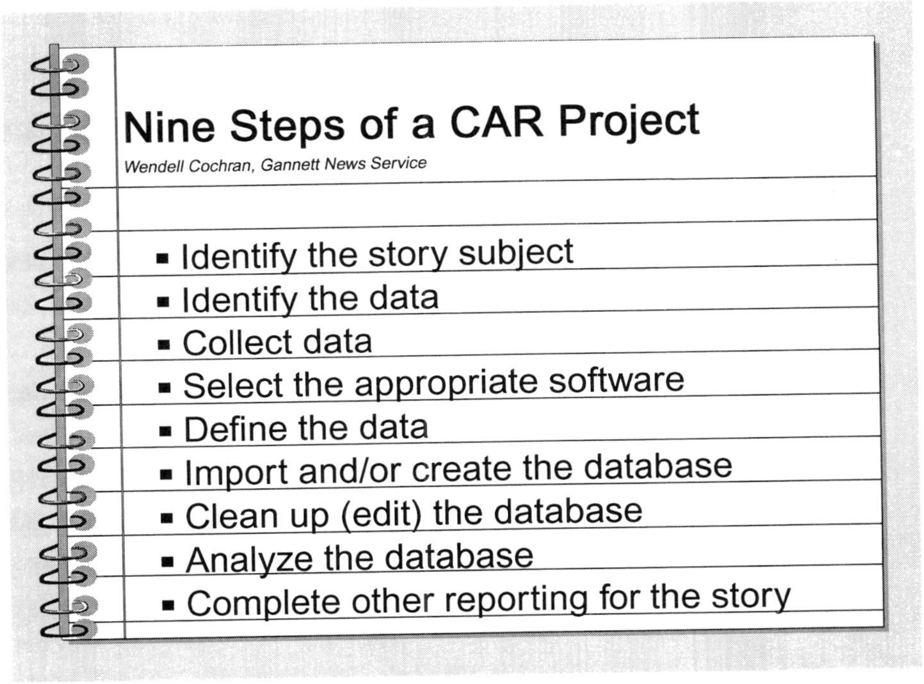

Nine Steps of a CAR Project
Wendell Cochran, Gannett News Service

- Identify the story subject
- Identify the data
- Collect data
- Select the appropriate software
- Define the data
- Import and/or create the database
- Clean up (edit) the database
- Analyze the database
- Complete other reporting for the story

FIG. 11.1. Suggested steps for a CAR project.

• *Story idea generation.* Every news story begins with an idea. CAR projects are no different. CAR project ideas can come from any number of places, including other news stories, other news organizations, and even sources.

• *Selling the story to an editor.* Once an idea takes root, it needs an editor's support to get going. The editor must free up the time, however much it might be, for the reporter, for a small project. The step is more critical for very large projects, because a larger group of reporters, photographers, graphic artists, news researchers, database editors, and copy editors is often involved.

• *Interviewing and exploring story ideas.* An idea needs nurturing. A reporter with an approved idea must next refine that idea. Some polish comes from preliminary interviewing, observation, and other ways of exploring. This could shift the nature of the idea a little or a lot, depending on what is learned during this stage.

• *Getting commitment of resources.* An editor may approve a reporter's time needed to work on a CAR story, but this in itself might not be enough. Other resources are often needed. Is available support, such as typists or clerks, in place for the project? If not, where can it be obtained? What other resources are needed (i.e., travel funds, telephone toll funds, a dedicated telephone line, databases, time on the mainframe or CD-ROM drive, etc.). If any cash expenses are involved, these must be approved, as well, at this stage.

• *Getting computer hardware and software.* If appropriate computer hardware and software are not in place, the project can be stopped in its tracks. Assessment of what is needed must be done at this stage and then acquisition of those tools must occur.

• *Acquiring data.* With resources under control, the necessary database or databases are located and accessed. This could involve simply duplicating data at no cost, but it could also involve a complicated negotiation process—what will be released and for what price—with a public agency before it is available.

• *Getting training.* Training is a part of most CAR projects. Often operation of new hardware must be learned. It is assumed there will be new tricks to learn involving software, even if the project and database involve familiar analytical tools. An experienced CAR project planner will include time for learning, perhaps as Warden said, for just about every step of the project process.

• *Loading data.* This can be one of the most complicated or one of the easiest steps in the process. At the point that a database has been acquired for use, it has to be "loaded" into a computer system with appropriate software. This process involves putting the database into some sort of readable form. As Warden discussed, this step can be quite complicated and the degree of difficulty often depends on the source organization providing the database.

- *Running data.* This step involves setting up and "crunching" the database. The act of getting data into a computer can be easy if it involves a PC, but can be more complicated when time sharing on a company or another institution's mainframe is involved. Very large databases require more powerful minicomputer or mainframe computers. This could make running a database a very difficult step to take.
- *Checking data for accuracy.* Checking accuracy is an editing process. Once the data run, problems with the database are likely to surface. These problems can include data fields, or variables, that cannot be read, codes that cannot be understood, keypunching errors, and more. This process of database editing is as critical to data processing as copy editing is to the story.
- *Analyzing data and interpreting results.* After the database has been cleaned up, it can be analyzed and interpreted for meaning. Although Warden (1992) calls this "pretty easy and straightforward" (p. 12), it is this single moment of discovery that is perhaps the most exciting for many CAR journalists. This is the point in the project when the database reveals what is and what is not there. When the facts have been organized and sorted, this stage requires some derivation of meaning.
- *Fact checking and reality checking.* The purpose of this stage might be self-evident in the label Warden gives it, but this step is the chance to make certain of what has been learned so far in the project. Are the facts right? How do they compare to other similar situations? How do they compare to reality as the reporters and editors working on the project know it?
- *Interviewing and follow-up.* By now, certain things will be clear to those working on the project. There is *new* knowledge, new information gathered. An important stage in the development of a CAR project is to find out what experts feel about the new information. Authorities can offer more independent interpretations and a different level of understanding. Interviews with officials of the organization that provided the database, if there was one, are also appropriate, of course.
- *Writing the story.* For some reporters, this is an easy step. However, as Warden (1992) explained, "writing the story and including data analysis will be a new challenge (or hurdle) for some reporters" (p. 14). Writing a story with numbers requires a certain finesse and a reporter must be careful to only use the numbers and not permit the numbers to dominate the story. It is also important to remember that not everything "crunched" has to be used. There may be a compulsion to use it all, even if it is not all that interesting and useful to the story. Most CAR projects will be edited, rewritten, edited again, and revised on several occasions before they are finished.
- *Creating graphics.* Graphics are tools that help make quantitative stories easier to follow. Charts, tables, graphs, and maps will supple-

ment and make explanation of the story much easier for the reporters writing the story, the editors editing it, and, most of all, the newspaper's readers. Photographs cannot be overlooked either. On some occasions, photographs and photo illustrations are major aids to telling the highly quantitative story, too.

• *Negotiating for story and graphics space.* The newly written stories, perhaps longer than originally assigned and complete with the visual package, are ready for publication. The final step in many projects is finding editors to push for the story in news meetings to get proper play in the newspaper.

Warden said there are three optional steps to the process:

• *Maintaining (and updating) the database.* Once a database is acquired, it makes no sense to put it on a shelf and forget about it. It should be retained in an accessible location for reuse. It may be possible to update the database within the newsroom. Decisions must be made as to whether this is worthwhile or not, and one argument to do it might be that additional stories could come from the database in the future.

• *Making the database available to others.* Many newspapers are placing databases on local area network file servers to permit wider access. Another way of looking at access includes public availability through BBSs or sale of the entire database or parts of it on CD-ROM.

• *Revisiting the database.* There may be later uses of some databases, including different analyses or combinations of the database with other yet-to-be-acquired databases.

The ultimate keys to making it through the entire process, Warden (1992) said, are newsroom teamwork and project leadership. "The solution to the liturgy of obstacles to computer-assisted journalism . . . is a project strategy that includes teamwork and that the team is led by someone with *authority* in the newsroom," she stated (p. 15).

WORKING WITH VARIABLES AND THEIR MEASUREMENT

Anyone working with a database will begin to think about that information in terms of its units—called fields, columns, or variables. For the most part, these three terms refer to the same thing. Users will quickly learn that some computer programmers have different names for these items in the research process. For simplicity, they will be discussed in the social scientific usage, *variable.* Database journalists work with variables and measurement of those variables on a daily basis. A collection of different variables creates a *case* or *record.* For continuity, they will be referred to as cases.

Journalists may be more accustomed to working with a limited number of cases when preparing a story. In more traditional terms, a case might be the equivalent to a human source or a document. A person's set of responses to a questionnaire is the single collection of variables making up that individual record. Using a database forces a researcher to think about his or her set of variables and measurement of those variables at both the single case and complete database levels.

Types of Variables

Variables are supposed to *vary.* That is, variables represent phenomena or events that can vary, can be measured, and even manipulated. A variable is a logical collection of attributes that are simply characteristics of people or things. For example, the attributes for a variable called "publication frequency" might be daily, weekly, semiweekly, monthly, semimonthly, and so forth.

Researchers use variables in a wide range of ways. Some are manipulated to determine their effect on other variables. Manipulated variables are often called *independent variables,* and those variables observed and possibly affected by the intentional manipulation are known as *dependent variables.* In some research, this distinction is important in determining causality, or cause and effect.

Variables can assume other roles in a database or functions in a research project. Some predict, some control, and some serve as performance markers. Other names of variables reflect their type and how they are measured. *Continuous variables* can take on any value, including meaningful fractions, within a given range (e.g., age). *Discrete variables,* on the other hand, can be divided into a finite number of indivisible parts (e.g., the number of television stations in a community).

Levels and Types of Variable Measurement

Variable measurement is essential to building any database. Variables must be evaluated in terms of their attributes. Guidelines, or rules, for the evaluation must be established by the researcher. There are different levels of measurement that create different types of variables and the type determines how the variables can be used in the final analysis. It is important to remember that certain analytical tools have been created by statisticians based on assumptions about the characteristics of the variable and how it can be measured. To use the tools properly, researchers must understand the nature of the variables they are using. The four major levels of variable measurement are:

- *Nominal measurement.* The most basic level, this describes fundamental differences in attributes of a variable, but nothing else. Example: gender or political party affiliation of election campaign contributors.
- *Ordinal measurement.* Assumes differences in attributes, but also assigns ranking. Example: academic year status in college.
- *Interval measurement.* Assumes differences and order in attributes, but also assigns meaningful equal increments in the ranking. Example: daily high and low Fahrenheit temperatures.
- *Ratio measurement.* Assumes the variable's attributes have differences, order, and increments, but also has a meaningful zero point. Example: personal income or the age of a political campaign contributor.

DATABASE DESIGN AND DATA PROCESSING BASICS

Databases are an increasingly important part of daily journalism. Understanding the nature of databases and what they can and cannot do is essential to success in working with databases. It is even more fundamental to CAR to know how to create databases and how to manipulate them. As shown in Fig. 11.2, a database is an organized collection of information, or data, in a digital file. Databases and tables are terms that sometimes are interchangeably used. Some relational database program developers, such as the authors of Microsoft's FoxPro, however, consider databases to be collections of tables. These definitions are in a computing context, so it is helpful to remember that databases, much more broadly defined, can be any useful collection of information such as a telephone book or 3 × 5 card file. Sophisticated computer databases, of course, include the tools to manipulate the information, such as searching, sorting, or reorganizing software.

Databases that contain more than one table have been divided into subsets containing organized groups of information that pertain to the general subject at hand. Each subset should be logically interrelated. The different tables can be linked, but do not have to be, when analysis of the database occurs. They do, however, require some sort of linking variable that the two tables have in common (e.g., a case identification number or other unique "key" variable). Some databases, though, do not require more than a single table. These are commonly called *flatfile databases*. Most spreadsheet programs are considered flatfile programs because all data are entered into a single spreadsheet, or table. Tables have their own structure and design, of course. Tables are built on the general data matrix structure of columns and rows.

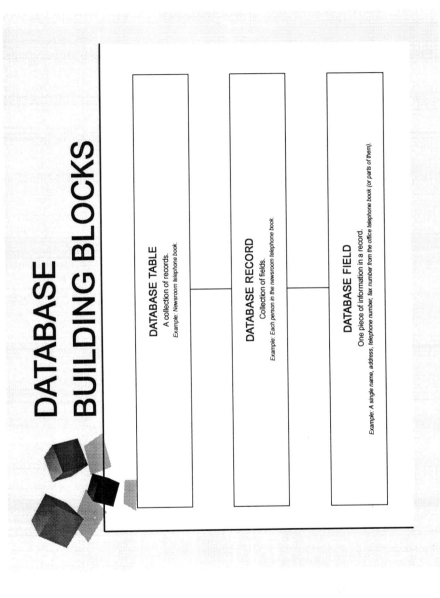

FIG.11.2. Keys to database design.

237

For information to be useful in a computer system, it must be put into a form that is understandable by both the computer program and the user. This transformation process is called *data processing*. This is a term most often associated with mainframe computer systems, but as personal computers and their software are becoming more powerful, the term is appearing more often in other contexts, such as personal computing. Data processing is an important part of computer-assisted reporting. Several major steps are involved in data processing. These include general database design, data matrix design, data coding, and data editing. Other aspects of the process are described in later chapters.

Designing a Database: Setting the Structure

When a new database is started, the creator must consider how the database will be organized. In what manner will the data be entered? Does the database design simply follow the documents being used? In what ways will output be reported? Often, these decisions are easy to make, but in some cases, they are not so easy. When dealing with databases created by external sources, many of the database design issues are decided by those who created the database or downloaded the parts of a larger database that are being used for the news story. These decisions can sometimes be undone, but doing so often requires additional time-consuming work.

"Designing a database is a lot like packing for a long trip," said Waterbury, CT, *Republican-American* CAR director Chris Feola (1993c). "You'll have a lot better idea of what you need after you get there, but it will be way too late by then to go back and get anything you've overlooked."

Poor database design can cause nightmarish problems, perhaps even resulting in starting over or causing hours of repair work to the design. Most database design has a logical, common-sense, structure. Sal Ricciardi (1994b), a contributing editor for *PC Magazine* and author of two books about Microsoft FoxPro, recommends five steps in database design:

- Write down the purpose of the database.
- Gather the information required to be stored in the database.
- Divide the information into tables, if more than one table is needed. Choose the major entities, or subjects, from the information listed in the second step. Write down the purpose of each table.
- Convert the information items in Step 3 into columns.
- Refine the design. This includes adding variables that may have been overlooked or adding tables to set up desired relationships between the tables.

It is important to know certain characteristics of the database, too. There are two critical characteristics called the type of information and the ranges of the information. *Type* refers to whether the data are characters, numbers, dates, graphics, or various combinations of them. *Range* refers to the minimum and maximum values, shortest or longest field lengths, and so forth. Most database programs treat the types of information differently, a fact that has subsequent data analysis implications, so this is an important consideration in planning a database.

Superior database design meets the goal of removing data redundancy. This reduces work and ultimately saves time. It does not make sense to enter the same information in several different places or tables. "To accomplish this goal, you divide your information into many narrowly defined tables so that each is represented only once," advised Ricciardi (1994a, p. 285).

DATABASES: GETTING STARTED AT A LOW COST

Steve Segal (personal communication, April 26, 1994), information graphics specialist and database editor for the Greensburg, PA, *Tribune-Review,* offers one way to get into databases and computer-assisted reporting even if local governments do not have their own records in electronic form and even if a news organization cannot create its own public opinion databases with its own interviewing:

> I have been told by many people that since their local government system is not electronic yet, they cannot do any CAR. However, there is so much federal data available on so many subjects, you would be surprised what you can get. But, how do you deal with those nine-track type tapes the government will give you the data on?

> One trick I have used several times is to find someone—typically at a university—who is working with the data. They will usually sell you the data you want for a nominal fee.

> Numerous universities and colleges have public opinion research centers that sell data to other academic organizations. Often these data would also be current enough and suitable for a news organization.

> On one project I am working on, I could buy ONE year from the federal government for $170. Then, I would need to get it translated to PC format. Then, extract the data I needed. All this from a "monster-size" file.

> With some digging, I found a university that specialized in these data. They sold me 3½ years of Pennsylvania for $200. They mailed it in fixed-length ASCII fields on a few diskettes and included the documentation.

> What a deal.

Some data are best placed in a single-table, flatfile, design. Databases that are not large or complicated do not need more than one table. A census database, for example, may require only one table to list data about a county or city over a period of time. A database of traffic tickets issued by the state police may be set up into several tables serving different purposes such as officers, violations, and incidents. Multiple table design is not possible with some database software (e.g. "flatfile" software such as spreadsheets and some database programs), so it is important to understand the range of features of the database program to be used when planning and designing a new database or when planning to analyze an existing database from another source.

Building the Data Matrix

A *data matrix* consists of two dimensions, called *columns* and *rows,* of information contained in vertical and horizontal planes. Most often—although it is not necessary—a data matrix is designed with columns representing variables such as income, political party affiliation, or daily newspaper circulation. Rows are used for the units or entities of measurement, the cases, such as people, arrests, property addresses, businesses, or institutions.

A sample data matrix (table) design could be as easy as this simple address listing data matrix for a spreadsheet:

ID	Name	Address	Telephone	Fax
Person A	xxxxx	xxxxx	xxxxx	xxxxx
Person B	xxxxx	xxxxx	xxxxx	xxxxx
Person C	xxxxx	xxxxx	xxxxx	xxxxx

This whole process of placing information into a table and tables into a file leads to the next step known as data reduction. It might be easy to read individual information in a table that is three records by five variables, but consider the information in a table containing 300 variables for 5,000 cases. Because reading a table that size is out of the question, computing collapses this into more understandable form by finding relationships and by grouping the information.

For a relational database system with more than one table, the procedure remains the same. The second table can take a similar design, but will include many different variables. There needs to be at least one *key variable* or *key field,* such as an ID number, that relates to both of the tables, however. In many cases, the key variable is a name or an address. This could be a second table to accompany the first one in the example:

ID	Age	Nickname	Occupation	Marital Status
Person A	xxxxx	xxxxx	xxxxx	xxxxx
Person B	xxxxx	xxxxx	xxxxx	xxxxx
Person C	xxxxx	xxxxx	xxxxx	xxxxx

"This [linking tables] is the beauty of database reporting, computer-assisted reporting—the relational database. Elegant in its simplicity," said Andy Scott (1993a), former executive director of the Investigative Reporters and Editors. "This is what allows you do to stories like Elliot Jaspin did a couple of years ago linking a table of school bus drivers with a table of drunk driving convictions. This is what allowed George Landau of the *St. Louis Post-Dispatch* to take two databases, two tables, of voter registration records and death records and find out how many people were crawling out of their graves to go vote. Great stories. That's the excitement of computer-assisted reporting."

Coding Data

One of the first steps to take in data reduction is translation of responses to a questionnaire, information from an application, or other data from a document, into a form that can be read and manipulated by the computer and its software. Obviously, computers are strongest when

---

REAL-WORLD ADVICE: SETTING UP A DATABASE

"I would say I create about 50 percent of my databases from scratch," explained Steve Segal (personal communication, April 26, 1994), who works with databases and is an information graphics specialist for the Greensburg, PA, *Tribune-Review*.

"The key to a successful database is in the setup. When I do use existing data, I make major changes in the structure so I can get the information that I want. The most important tip I can give on setting up a database is to make sure each record has a unique, identification field. I call mine 'ID' and it is a unique number for each field."

Segal offers three "important reasons" for using an ID field:

1. If you make a mistake, you can go to your backup and you are sure you are looking at the correct record.

2. Some programs like Paradox (for DOS), treat records that are completely identical as the same record—in certain conditions. A unique ID field avoids this.

3. Records are usually in some kind of order when you get them (maybe the date they happened—but the date is not noted). By sorting them in ascending order by the ID field, you can put them back in the original order—assuming you put the IDs in before you did any sorting.

dealing with numbers, so when the term *coding* is considered, it usually means numeric coding. However, alpha and alphanumeric coding are useful in some circumstances as well. Coding is the process of applying a standardized symbol such as a number or character to represent information being counted or otherwise analyzed. In developing a database, these are decisions that remain with the journalist to be made. When working with a database obtained from an external source, the codes have already been determined and some sort of codebook is needed for interpretation.

Variable coding is somewhat arbitrary and should be simple. It should be logical and consistent, too. For a variable such as "state of residence," one coding scheme would assign a unique number from 1 to 50 representing each state, plus a separate number to represent the District of Columbia and U.S. territories if these are included. Not all coding is that clear cut and simple. Some coding, such as open-ended answers on survey questionnaires, police report incident descriptions, or other documents, may require considerable discretion. In these cases, for consistency and reliability, it is best to define codes in writing and to have second or third opinions about coding decisions.

Cleaning Up "Dirty" Databases

Data, whether they have been entered in-house or from other sources, must be edited. A critical step in the CAR process is to check the database, when in processed form, for errors. This stage, called *data cleaning,* must take place before any analysis occurs. Most researchers know from experience that, regardless of the level of care used in entering data, some errors occur. The point of cleaning data is to eliminate as many of those errors as possible.

There should be serious concerns about databases generated by external sources. Time should be built into the analyses to clean all databases, but the situation is even more acute when involving databases of uncertain quality. Local and federal government databases are notorious for their frequent keypunching errors. Just as a reporter must check out raw information in other forms provided by sources, so he or she must check databases once they are in house. Bob Port (1993), a computer-assisted reporting editor for the Associated Press, agrees that there is a "dirty" nature to many public databases. Dirty databases can contain keypunching mistakes. Other errors originate from machine sources, such as misread pencil markings in optically scanned data forms. More subtle errors can occur as well. These include measurement errors and data coding inconsistencies. Port said journalists should consider at least three factors involving any database:

- Where did the database come from?

- What was the original purpose of the database?
- How is the database being used (it could be different from the original purpose)?

Database cleaning is simply common sense. All the work that went into collecting and assembling the information is lost if an undetected error occurs in data processing. Furthermore, an accumulation of "minor" errors ultimately leads to larger errors and misinterpretation of what the database actually represents.

Managing Database Costs

Database journalism can be expensive, make no mistake about it. Yet, it does not have to be. There is an art to negotiating the price of databases from most public sources, especially those public databases not often in demand. There may also be some leverage in setting prices from private commercial database vendors, but costs are less flexible. Even creation of original databases can carry a high budgetable cost in terms of labor and equipment.

Initial costs of databases can be sobering for news organizations just beginning their CAR work. Prices vary wildly from government agency to government agency and database to database. Pricing structures vary also. Some databases are purchased at a per-record rate, whereas others are a flat price. Some fees include the cost of data technicians' time to duplicate the database and the cost of disks, discs, or tape reels.

Recycling databases makes the per-story cost drop if more than one story or project can be derived from a database. Sharing databases with sister news organizations or groups of news companies will also reduce initial cost but might lessen exclusivity. Database editors of some news organizations, after finishing projects, have decided that larger databases have a marketability and have begun selling databases in enhanced or value-added form on disks and CD-ROMs or online through a BBS or other online service. It is an ideal way to recover some or all of the initial costs of acquiring the database, and perhaps even some of the time costs for those working on the project.

12

Using Data in Spreadsheets and Statistical Packages

William Casey, director of computer-assisted reporting for *The Washington Post,* says spreadsheets are an essential part of his work. It is his role in the newsroom to provide database support and instruction about use of databases and software for reporters and editors. Casey is a spreadsheet advocate. He runs Microsoft Excel on *both* a Macintosh and a Windows-based PC and he says spreadsheets permit users to "see" the data—including the worksheet, notes, and graphics—all at once. Another advantage is what Casey (1993a) calls "very powerful formatting capabilities, great non-programming power through formulas, [a] rich supply of functions, easier and visible cross-checks, formatting and printability/readability, documentation through in-cell notes, [and] programmability if needed. Most people do not know that a spreadsheet can do the kinds of things I'm describing" (p. 2).

Casey has used the power of spreadsheets to help *Post* reporters develop several major metro desk stories. In 1993, he supervised data research for a project analyzing 2 years (n = 1,286) of homicides in the District of Columbia. One of the purposes of the homicides project was to determine whether the killers were ever brought to justice for their crimes. About a year earlier, Casey worked with another Metro Desk reporter to analyze a homemade Excel database of 8 months (n = 245) of carjackings—cases in which cars were taken from drivers by individuals using force. The resulting story, which told readers what types of cars were most often selected and where the incidents occurred, was highly popular with readers. But the importance of the numbers in both projects was not overwhelming and that approach appeals to Casey:

> I like this [the carjacking project] because . . . the role that the numbers and the quantitative part of this project played—and this was just a small project, hardly a project—was small. Look through the piece and you will find specific areas where Debbi Wilgoren, the reporter, used some of the numbers we came up with . . . . So, the idea is that these stories really need to be story- and reporter-based. We're using this tool [the

spreadsheet] to, in some way, enhance and to allow her to go down avenues of inquiry that with other tools she may not be able to do.

The records for the carjacking database were pulled from three different jurisdictions and entered into an Excel worksheet. Columns of the worksheet served as the point for entering different information about each incident. The 245 individual incidents became rows in Casey's data matrix.

Casey, a former geographer and teacher at the University of Minnesota, joined *The Post* staff in 1992. He has extensive experience working with databases such as those created by the U.S. Bureau of the Census. Casey says he likes to use spreadsheets because of the way these programs display information. Spreadsheets, he believes, reduce data volume and are easy to understand, especially for reporters and others who have to work with the data:

> It seems that when it comes to personal computers and personal computing tools, people tend to get pretty exercised about what's the right way to do things and what's the wrong way to do things. To me, seeing the data in the simplest, clearest, and the tersest possible form [is most important]. The less space it takes up, the easier it is for myself and a group of reporters and editors to sit down and talk about it. . . . My ideal is to get every project reduced to a single piece of paper. You have a tremendous ability to do that with the formatting capability in 1-2-3, Quattro [Pro], and in Excel. (Casey, 1993a)

Casey's background is a bit different from most CAR editors. He is a veteran computer user who came late to journalism. His career of working with computers began over two decades ago when he worked for a mainframe database business. It was the early 1980s when he discovered spreadsheets, he recalled. "I started using a PC in 1982 and, when I got my first one, one of my friends in New York said I could use an electronic spreadsheet. 'What's a spreadsheet?' I asked. 'You know, one of those sheets you put things on for budget purposes,' he said. . . . I had no feeling that it would do anything for me or make anything easier that I was trying to do." Casey said it was only a few months later that he bought the then-new Lotus 1-2-3 Version 1A and he worked with it for the next 5 or so years. He said he used to think there could be nothing better than that first version of 1-2-3. "So I guess all of our perceptions about these tools and products have really changed," he added.

Casey does not feel spreadsheets are the only solution to working with databases. He also uses the FoxPro and Paradox relational database systems, but he admits that some computer users are happier with some products more than they are with others, mostly because of their design. "We all are probably born with certain inclinations to use certain kinds of products and there are certain metaphors that some of us find easier to use or make more sense to us than other people and other products," he said.

There is a group of six database researchers who work for different desks in *The Post* newsroom, Casey said. "They receive a lot of training from me, particularly in spreadsheets—but also in FoxPro—to manipulate, import data, and to do the analysis," Casey explained. He works with reporters but rarely writes news stories himself. However, he does write a regular column about computing. Most of his work, he says, is part of a team effort.

Spreadsheets are one of several major categories of software products that enable journalists to build databases and manipulate the databases for greater understanding of the information contained in them. Among the others are statistical packages, free-form database programs, relational database packages, and geographic information systems for analytical mapping. This chapter focuses on two of those categories, spreadsheets and statistical analysis packages.

Spreadsheets are a major part of PC business software lore. When the first PCs were being developed in the late 1970s and early 1980s, programmers were also seeking to develop business applications. Programs such as VisiCalc and Lotus 1-2-3 emerged. Lotus' name actually refers to spreadsheets, databases, and chart graphics, the three original functions of that program. One of the earliest business products for the PC was the spreadsheet—intended to permit business users to develop financial databases and applications such as accounting and trend modeling.

Over the past decade and a half, spreadsheets have gradually become essential to computer-assisted reporting. Rich Gordon (1993a), newsroom technology editor at *The Miami Herald,* has described spreadsheets as "the fundamental building block of computer-assisted journalism" (p. 143). Gordon advocates access to a spreadsheet for every reporter in the newsroom and says each reporter should know how to use one. "Why? Because it's an inexpensive tool that will run on any computer and make your life easier almost any time you're presented with numerical information." Steve Ross (1992), who teaches computer-assisted reporting at Columbia University, agrees. "I am convinced that students will better understand the function of specialized database software if they first use a spreadsheet to sort through data," Ross stated (p. 3). "That's because in a spreadsheet, each row is a database record and each column is a data field—just as would be the case in a printed data table."

Brant Houston (1994), managing director of the National Institute for Computer-Assisted Reporting, believes spreadsheets are an easy tool for all local government reporters to use:

City budgets are the most typical thing that spreadsheets can be used for. Every reporter covering city hall in America should be getting the city hall budget on a little diskette, slapping it into their laptop when the budget comes out, immediately rearranging the figures. Once you've imported the information, a simple calculation such as percent change from one year to the next, takes about five seconds to do. And there's the lead story for the next day's newspaper.

Like Gordon and Ross, John E. Mollwitz (personal communication, May 8, 1994), a long-time reporter and senior national editor at *The Milwaukee Journal,* feels spreadsheets open up the world of databases to journalists:

Spreadsheets are the building blocks to understanding the creation of any database. Once one learns what kind of information can be obtained sorting mere columns and rows, free form databases take on a whole new meaning. Spreadsheets also often help translating data from one format to another that appears seemingly incompatible. File created by Program A can't be read by Program B, but can be read in Program C, which can then save it as a file that Program B can read and eventually save in a more efficient format for Program B. Comma delimited files are great learning tools.

Statistical packages are less commonly used by newsrooms—so far. Originally designed for use by academics and certain business applications on mainframe computers in the 1960s, these programs were rewritten for personal computers in the early 1980s when PCs became powerful enough and grew larger in storage capability. In the mid-1990s, only the largest of databases—ones with hundreds of thousands of records and bigger—cannot be handled by a statistical package on a portable or desktop personal computer. Although some of these programs are expensive, like the most advanced spreadsheets, there are less expensive spreadsheets and statistical packages available. Statistical packages do what the name suggests: They offer more powerful and broadly ranging multivariate statistical analysis than most spreadsheet and database programs can offer. The programs also offer statistical significance testing tools that may be needed for some types of computer-assisted reporting.

USING SPREADSHEETS FOR BUILDING DATABASES

Spreadsheets are sometimes described as *flatfile* programs. This means spreadsheets are files that consist of records of a single type and there is no embedded structure information governing the relationships of the records. There is another way of looking at it: Flatfile programs work with only one table of columns and rows at a time. Any cross-referencing of multiple tables must be completed manually (Hartmann, 1994; Woodcock, 1991).

Relational database programs, on the other hand, offer more powerful analytical features. Relational database programs permit users to create links between the different tables of one or more databases. The tables are linked with a common variable.

For journalists just getting started with databases, confusion often exists over whether to use a spreadsheet or a relational database program. Because of their simplicity in database design and use, spreadsheets might be the best software choice, however, when first learning CAR techniques. There are various ways to make the choice, but it is ultimately best to use both types of programs because some projects will require one type and other projects will call for the other type. Spreadsheets have strengths for certain kinds of database work and relational database systems have advantages for still other purposes.

For journalists on a budget, there is no doubt that an inexpensive spreadsheet can be a relatively painless way to begin database reporting. Then, if some successes are gained from using the spreadsheet, it makes sense to begin looking around for a relational database system with which to expand. Simply described, spreadsheets work best for smaller databases that require less sophisticated types of analysis and manipulation. Databases, on the other hand, have greater scope and customizability in database design.

There are two main levels of spreadsheet programs in the marketplace. First are the "premier" packages, those that offer just about every feature currently available. These include Lotus 1-2-3, Microsoft Excel, and Novell's Quattro Pro. The "big three" spreadsheets are commonly available on major platforms. Lotus 1-2-3 and Excel are available in DOS and Windows, Macintosh, and OS/2 versions. Quattro Pro is available in DOS and Windows. Macintosh systems run Excel, 1-2-3, and Claris.

The second layer of programs is less expensive and offers fewer features. These programs often do not have the wide range of time-saving tools, basic computing power, or speed of the leading products, but they offer the advantage of substantial cost savings and still offer the basic tools of spreadsheet database building. These could be the smartest place for beginners on a budget.

Spreadsheet Terms to Know

Like many other major categories of PC software, spreadsheets have a certain language common to most products. To help understand how the software works, some brief definitions are offered:

SPREADSHEETS OR DATABASE PROGRAMS?

Ed Hartmann (1994), a database consultant and author of a book about Microsoft's Access database system, says deciding whether to use a spreadsheet or a database program is "usually easy" (p. 176). Hartmann produced comparisons to help database builders:

Use a Spreadsheet:	*Use a Database:*
Data consist of just one table.	Your data are stored in several related tables that need to be cross- referenced.
You need to produce only one or two reports similar to data table.	You need to produce many different reports in several formats.
You need to store a mixture of data types in each column of table.	Your data have uniform structure: Each column is one type of data.
Calculations are based on values scattered throughout the table	Calculations are based on values appearing uniformly in the table, such as columns or rows.
Summary calculations are based on entire table or a few subgroups of the table, and the number of subgroups remains constant.	Summary calculations are based on many subgroups within data and number of subgroups can vary a lot over time.
Graphs are the preferred format for output and you need a wide variety of graph formats.	Most of the output is in the form of text reports.

- *Cells* (addresses). Cells are locations in the worksheet where data are entered, the intersections of columns and rows. Worksheets can be very large. Excel, for example, permits as many as 256 columns and from 8,192 to 16,384 rows. Most worksheets use the same system of identifying cell addresses. Columns are lettered and rows are numbered. Thus, the top left cell would be A1.

- *Charts.* Data in a worksheet can be transformed into visual presentations through use of charting capabilities. Commonly used charts are two- and three-dimensional pie, bar, line, area, column, radar, scatter, and various combinations of these main types.

- *Formulas.* Formulas combine data in cells with mathematical operators to produce a new value. A simple formula might require a worksheet to look at two different values in two different cells and compute a percentage of change from one year to another.

- *Functions.* Many spreadsheet programs have built-in arithmetic functions and formulas that save time. Functions perform standard worksheet and macro calculations. These functions are literally formula-entry shortcuts that replace commonly used formulas, such as adding a column of numbers. A basic one might be "@SUM," in which a range of numbers is identified and added by using the function command instead of repeatedly using the "+" symbol.

- *Labels.* Labels are alphanumeric text that can be entered at any location to describe a set of numbers. Typically, labels are entered at the far left of a row or top of a column. These can be used anywhere and help users to understand the numerical information entered. Labels also explain a chart function by identifying information taken from a worksheet and used in a graphic.

- *Macros*. Macros are another automatic feature of spreadsheets that permit repetitive tasks to be completed by executing a "program" within the program. Macros permit high levels of customization and give the ability to complete specialized tasks that may not be provided by the basic program package.

- *Number formatting*. Number formatting automatically converts numerical information into a particular style such as percentages, currency, fractions, decimals, or even date and time. When a number is typed, the format setting will convert it to the designated form.

- *Ranges*. A range is a series of cells in a column or row. Identifying and calculating with formulas using information in a range is one of the many shortcuts offered by spreadsheet programs.

- *Spreadsheets*. Spreadsheet is another commonly used term for worksheet. Some users refer to spreadsheet as the entire program and worksheet as the data file portion of the program.

- *Templates*. Templates are a type of worksheet that contains pre-designed worksheets, charts, and macros assembled for a particular purpose. They can be copied over and over to be used whenever a new application comes along. Templates typically include formulas, formatting, text, and other automatic settings, and all that users need to do is enter data. Some programs come with templates, but experienced users also set up their own templates. An example might include a city budget template, a voting records template, or a crime report template that can be used to set up numerous separate worksheets without starting from scratch each time.

- *Worksheets*. Worksheets are the primary "view" of a spreadsheet program. Worksheets are on-screen areas that permit users to store data, modify them, and perform calculations.

Major Spreadsheet Features

Although all spreadsheet publishers would like users to believe their products are quite distinct from others, spreadsheets have many common elements and features. In fact, most spreadsheet veterans would argue there are few substantial differences in what each of the major products can do. The difference is most likely in how the task is completed.

As one personal computer magazine writer said in 1994, spreadsheets are getting smarter (Stone, 1994). Like their word processing counterparts that do much more than process words, the most sophisticated spreadsheets are much more than just worksheets for compiling and analyzing data. Many of these are fundamental to the purpose of a spreadsheet. The basic spreadsheet features include:

- Worksheets for storage and manipulation (editing) of data.
- In-cell editing (calculation and analysis capabilities for data).
- Printing of entire or partial worksheets, charts, and other documents.
- Database sorting and searching.
- Charting and graphing.
- Data formatting.
- Data recoding and transformation.
- File importing and exporting of limited formats.
- Basic application templates for business.
- Cutting and pasting or moving data ranges.
- Predefined function formatting through specially defined keys.
- Computation of basic descriptive statistics.

More sophisticated packages also include other user features to make work still easier. Many, it could be argued, are not necessary and would seldom be used by average users. These bells and whistles are offered, though, in the competitive marketplace and such features can be helpful in some ways. They include:

- Creation and editing of presentation- and publication-quality graphics based on the database.
- Drawing tools and an even greater range of chart and table types and presentation formats.
- Editing tools such as spell-checking.
- Auditing features for checking formulas, keystrokes, and circular references.
- Presentation templates and output type formatting for printing.
- Increased range in file importing and exporting formats including comma delimited, tab delimited, and user-defined delimited files.
- Macro file language for task simplification, calculation, and customization.
- Ability to produce multiple worksheets for a single file (called "3-D" "tabbed" or "notebook" structure).
- Ability to open and work with more than one worksheet or more than one file at a time (linking).
- Object linking and embedding (OLE).
- Dynamic data exchange (DDE).
- Network–workgroup database sharing.
- Version tracking.
- Powerful analysis, model building, and forecasting tools.
- Sophisticated bivariate and multivariate statistical tools such as crosstabulations, regression analysis, and analysis of variance.

- Horizontal and vertical split-screen ability to view different parts of the same spreadsheet or of a different spreadsheet.
- Multiple windows views of a single worksheet (in Windows, OS/2, and Macintosh versions).
- Database program-type capabilities such as searching and querying.

Choosing the right spreadsheet is another one of those computing decisions that will perplex a beginner. The decision can be as simple as going with a gut reaction (e.g., "I like the way that basic worksheet screen looks") or working with the same product a friend at another newspaper uses or the one the guy down the street uses. Another determining factor may be the product used by the government agency that will probably provide the most data in the next year or two. City hall budgets, election office statistics, or police department crime incident data may be recorded on 1-2-3, Excel, or Quattro Pro. It should not take much effort to check.

M. David Stone (1994), a contributing editor to *Windows Sources* magazine and author of books about PC software, offers three questions that spreadsheet shoppers should ask when deciding on a product to use:

- How strong must the program's graphing features be?
- How much do you rely on spreadsheets to maintain data as a database?
- How important is it for the program to be able to read, analyze, and manipulate data stored in an external database format? (p. 200)

Stone also lists availability of macro features, data importing and exporting, function categories, and function creativity as important in the decision-making process.

With so many programs and so many features, the decision about what spreadsheet to use may be difficult for some journalists. Rich Gordon (1993b), newsroom technology editor for *The Miami Herald,* says selecting spreadsheet software should not be difficult if new users follow three basic rules:

- Buy the same spreadsheet that someone else you know is using so that person can be a tutor during the learning period.
- Never pay the full price for software because there are discounts and upgrade offers that save large amounts of money.
- Try another program if the one in use does not seem to be doing the job. The switch to a second program might be easier than the experience of learning the first one.

"Entering the world of computer software can be bewildering. Everyone has a favorite database or spreadsheet program, and will argue forever about why it's better than the competition," Gordon (1993b, p. 1) said. "But here's the dirty little secret: *these programs all do the same things.* The main differences between different kinds of spreadsheets, or different kinds of database managers, lie in which keys you push to accomplish certain things. Once you press those keys, they operate very similarly. . . . The main differences are in ease of use."

Setting Up a Worksheet

Most newsroom spreadsheet projects begin with a blank worksheet. One of the first steps in using a spreadsheet is to develop a general design for data entry into the worksheet. Basic decisions include determining what information goes into the columns and what information is placed in the rows. Most often, columns are characteristics of what is being measured, such as the specific information or characteristics about a series of criminal incidents. Each row, in this example, represents a each single criminal incident.

Column headings and row labels should be decided and entered in the appropriate locations in the worksheet—usually the top row and first column to the left. Order of columns, from left to right, should be decided in a logical manner to make use and data entry easiest. The order of the columns can be determined by the position of information within the documents being used for data entry. Or the order can be set by chronological factors or other legitimate reasons determined by the user. Although each row has its own identification number given by the worksheet as part of its address, it is sensible to assign a separate and unique case ID number and use it in each row of the first column. For most worksheets, row order may not be meaningful. For some, however, it could be very important—for example, if a spreadsheet is divided into sections such as a set of census data or different types of crime statistics.

Another one of the early steps in building a database in a worksheet is number formatting for the columns (or rows). Insertion of formulas into the required cells should also take place during spreadsheet design. Macro files for special customization of the data analysis, if there are any, should be written because they save time. Finally, any charts that may be needed should be designed.

Data entry can occur at any time after the initial design is completed since the frame of the worksheet has to be in place prior to entering any data. For especially complicated or very large spreadsheets, "dummy" data should be entered to test formulas, number formatting, and macros. Another step to consider, before beginning to enter data, is to determine whether a copy of the final, but so far dataless, worksheet should be saved for later use as a template. When data entry begins, some errors are likely to occur. Entries can be edited during the entry process or after a worksheet has been completed.

Spreadsheet Uses for Journalists

As spreadsheets have become popular in newsrooms, there are thousands of examples of their daily uses as well as project uses for building news stories. Some reporters use worksheets for source telephone lists. On a more analytical level, agency budget analysis is an ideal type of application. Crime statistics, population trends from census data, and sports statistics work well with the quantitative tools of spreadsheets, also.

The Washington Post's Casey (1993a) feels there are certain basic uses of spreadsheets for everyday reporting that may be the best starting places for beginners. "The kinds of analysis and kinds of operations . . . putting data on a spreadsheet, showing percent change, sorting data in order, doing other kinds of arithmetic operations on some collection of records—budget records, people who have been appointed to judges— that is something that is basic use of a spreadsheet," he explained.

In the past 5 years or so, hundreds if not thousands of news stories using data in spreadsheet files have been developed. Many have been used in major investigative projects:

- The *Columbus Dispatch* used Excel to study theft in office by state officials.
- The *Waterbury, CT, Republican-American* used Quattro Pro for Windows for analysis of a homemade worksheet database for a 1992 presidential campaign series called "The Tax on Living," that focused on what Connecticut residents were paying in taxes, what they were getting for their money, and what public officials said about the spending.
- *The San Jose Mercury News* used Quattro Pro to create a homemade worksheet database of disability retirements of individuals in 1,700 state and local agencies to determine abuse of the pension system in California by those making bogus claims.
- The *South Bend Tribune* in Indiana used 1-2-3 to build and analyze a worksheet database of car thefts in the region.
- The *Lewiston Sunday Sun-Journal* in Maine used Excel on a Macintosh to analyze a homemade worksheet database of information about the state's welfare recipients and overpayments made by the state system.
- The *Key West Citizen* used 1-2-3 to analyze 1980 and 1990 census data to study population and housing trends in the city and in surrounding Monroe County, FL.

USING ADVANCED STATISTICAL PACKAGES

Why bother with statistical packages if spreadsheets and relational database programs are so powerful? Statistical packages do some tasks

SPREADSHEETS IN NEWSROOMS

The 1994 University of Miami national study of computers and newsrooms found spreadsheet packages widely in use in U.S. daily newspaper newsrooms ($n = 208$). Of those in use, the "big three"—Excel, 1-2-3, and Quattro Pro—are the most popular, but the number of newspapers using each one shows no single product to be dominant. In fact, some newspapers reported using more than one of the major products in the same newsroom. This suggests spreadsheet choice, in some cases, may be a personal matter at newspapers with the resources to provide reporters and editors or individuals at separate locations such as bureaus with their spreadsheet of choice. The study findings:

Circulation	Excel	1-2-3	Quattro Pro	Other	None
Under 50,000	25.6% (11)	12.5% (5)	8.6% (3)	26.7% (4)	63.4% (64)
50,000–100,000	25.6 (11)	32.5 (13)	28.6 (10)	46.7 (7)	21.8 (22)
100,001–250,000	30.2 (13)	37.5 (15)	37.1 (13)	13.3 (2)	9.9 (10)
250,001–500,000	11.6 (5)	10.0 (4)	14.3 (5)	6.7 (1)	5.0 (5)
Over 500,000	7.0 (3)	7.5 (3)	11.4% (4)	6.7 (1)	0.0 (0)
Totals	100.0% (43)	100.0% (40)	100.0% (35)	100.0% (15)	100.0% (101)

Note: Percentages are for columns. Frequencies are in parentheses. Some responding newspapers reported using more than one type of spreadsheet.

with a database that cannot be done at all, or as well, with other database-oriented programs. Some complicated research questions require more analytical power; it is that simple. Statistical packages do not require users to work within worksheet cells when designing the data management and analysis strategies. This category of database-oriented programs has its strength in the raw power and speed of statistical analyses they can do. These programs also offer flexibility in output reporting and graphics or chart creation.

Three programs are most often mentioned when statistical packages are discussed. These are the Statistical Package for the Social Sciences (SPSS), the Statistical Analysis System (SAS), and the Biomedical Data Processing system (BMDP; also called "Biomed"). SPSS came from a group of scholars based at the University of Chicago, BMDP was developed at UCLA, and SAS was developed out of Duke University and North Carolina State University. Each had its beginnings long ago on mainframe computer systems and each was originally used in mostly academic or institutional research environments. MINITAB, a program first developed in 1972 at Penn State University, was introduced a decade or so later, but also became popular for its interactivity. Early mainframe versions of the "big three"—SAS, BMDP, and SPSS—originally were not interactive.

Nonacademic researchers quickly learned of the value of these programs for certain types of projects. When PCs grew in power and storage capability in the 1980s, the major mainframe products were transported into PC editions. But something else happened: A large number of other PC-designed statistical packages, some very inexpensive, came onto the market to help entice researchers away from their mainframes. These early PC versions operated with command lines and database size capacities much less than mainframes. The major difference in the two approaches is that mainframes required "batch" data entry, which meant the entire job had to be submitted at one time. Processing occurred and the user then viewed the output on screen or on a printout.

PCs, on the other hand, permit data entry on screen and complete editing and manipulation during full and partial views of the database before any processing occurs. PCs also allow users to obtain output in on-screen, printed, graphic, and other user-defined reporting formats. Perhaps the most persuasive argument about PC-based statistical packages is the elimination of mainframe costs and access problems. With a PC, there are no connect time costs, time-sharing, or access scheduling problems.

Basic Software Set Up for PCs

To use a statistical package on a PC, there is a need to understand database design. Most statistical packages work in a cell-like worksheet structure of spreadsheets or in a database structure of simple columns and rows. Most use either command line or menu selections to give the programs instructions for analysis of the database. Most statistical packages, such as SPSS, will import ASCII text data matrices developed in word processors and will import files directly from major spreadsheet programs and database managers. Some beginning users feel this approach is easier. The major steps in the data preparation process are the following:

- The first step in statistical analysis with a PC is to design the database. This involves setting the order of variables and cases.
- The second step is to decide which analytical approaches—within the scope of the software being used—will be necessary to answer the questions posed about the database.
- The third step is entering and editing (or cleaning) the data set. This step may involve using a conversion utility if the data set originates from a file created in a different program.
- The next steps are often optional. For most statistical packages, variable labels, or identification names, and value labels (for each of the possible replies for each variable) will have to be added, although they are not always necessary. Most programs offer a standardized output format, but if variations of that output report format are required, these need to be designed and programmed also.

- The last step is running the data. Decisions must be made about the appropriate statistical tools to use on the database.

There may be other decisions to make and more steps to take, but these are the basics. For a well-designed but small database of a few hundred cases and only several dozen variables, these steps can be completed in just a few hours by an experienced data processor using a PC. With the power of laptop, notebook, and subnotebook PCs, data can be entered from remote locations directly into the statistical package. This would save time and perhaps even document duplication costs.

Regardless of which PC statistical package is used, there are numerous features offered by the major software publishers. Most users look for the range of analytical tools, statistical detail provided in output, ease in creating and editing databases, graphics, compatibility with other data formats, case and variable limitations, flexibility, and customizability. For beginners who do not know what to look for, a statistical package should include the following:

- Database and data matrix building and editing.
- Command line editing.
- Logical command line language.
- Data recoding and data transformations (computations on variables).
- Data storage and retrieval.
- Variable and value labeling.
- Variable frequencies and descriptives (univariate analysis).
- Crosstabs (contingency tables).
- Other bivariate analysis such as measures of association (correlation).
- Multivariate analysis such as analysis of variance, regression, cluster analysis, and factor analysis.
- Basic parametric and non-parametric statistical tests.
- Data importing and exporting utilities.
- Output report customizing.
- Data charting, graphing, and plotting.
- Statistical probability testing.
- Understandable error messages and online help.
- Macros for customizing and preserving repeated data processing and analytical actions.
- Programming language for creating statistical routines.

Major Uses for Journalists

Regardless of whether a statistical package user is working on a mainframe, a minicomputer, or a PC, there is a wide range of applications of

STATISTICAL PACKAGES IN NEWSROOMS

The 1994 University of Miami CAR study found that few newspapers use statistical packages. Only a few statistical software packages are in use in newsrooms (n = 208), but of those, the Statistical Package for the Social Sciences (SPSS), in its variety of mainframe and PC user versions and operating systems, is the most popular.

Circulation	SPSS	SAS	Other	None
Under 50,000	5.9% (1)	0.0% (0)	20.0% (2)	45.3% (82)
50,000–100,000	23.5 (4)	0.0 (0)	20.0 (2)	27.1 (49)
100,001–250,000	29.4 (5)	25.0 (1)	20.0 (2)	20.4 (37)
250,001–500,000	23.5 (4)	25.0 (1)	10.0 (1)	6.6 (12)
Over 500,000	17.6 (3)	50.0 (2)	30.0 (3)	0.6 (1)
Totals	100.0% (17)	100.0% (4)	100.0% (10)	100.0% (181)

Note: Percentages are for columns. Frequencies are in parentheses.

these programs. Some projects are so large that they require mainframes to drive the statistical package with the databases involved. Some require statistical packages on reasonably fast and powerful desktop systems. Others, small enough, can be handled on portable PCs.

Survey data are a time-tested newsroom application of statistical packages. Survey researchers have traditionally used social science-oriented mainframe statistical programs for their work and moved, as did their software, to PCs in the past decade. Few surveys are large enough, in terms of variables and cases, to require use of a mainframe. Most, with respondent n sizes of 400 to 1,500 or 1,600 and the number of variables ranging from two to five or six dozen, can be easily handled by a desktop PC. Surveys, originally limited in their journalistic context to elections, have a wide range of public opinion measurement uses. No matter what the subject, it seems that surveys are best suited of all computer-assisted reporting approaches for using statistical packages.

Census data is another traditional category of databases that are analyzed using statistical packages on mainframe systems. One of the reasons for this, until recently, was that the only way census data could be obtained was on nine-track tape for use on a mainframe. Census data are now available in a number of magnetic media formats, including CD-ROM and floppy diskettes, permitting wider use. There are many other examples in recent years. Here are a few examples offered from IRE files (Scott, 1993b):

• *Miami Herald* reporters used a mainframe system and SAS to analyze several very large databases in the wake of Hurricane Andrew to determine how well the local construction codes had protected structures. In a second project, reporters also used the same set-up to analyze

10 years of criminal court cases containing 500,000 individual files to investigate bill padding and fraud by private attorneys appointed by judges to represent the poor.

- *U.S. News & World Report* reporters used their PCs and SPSS/PC+ (and other database programs) to analyze the Food and Drug Administration's database of reported failures and injuries caused by using various medical devices.
- *USA Today* and Gannett News Service combined to study how the U.S. House of Representatives spent $700 million on itself in a single year. Using a mainframe system and SAS, as well as other database programs and PCs, the reporting team showed poor accounting of the funds, among other things.
- The *Birmingham Post-Herald* used a PC and SPSS to analyze the nation's air safety system. Using a national database obtained from the National Transportation Safety Board, the newspaper analyzed the search time involved in finding small planes involved in crashes in the 1980s.
- The *Minneapolis Star Tribune* analyzed patterns of predatory sex criminals who had served prison sentences by creating a database from several state crime sources. After building the database, the newspaper's reporters analyzed the 20 MB data file on a mainframe using SAS and other database programs.

WRITING STATISTICS-BASED NEWS STORIES

One reason some reporters may shy away from database-oriented reporting is their aversion to anything involving numbers. This is especially true if the numbers are so small or so large most people cannot comprehend them. Readers often have the same aversion to statistics. Articles burdened with statistics chase away certain readers. It is up to reporters and their editors to judge the right amount of quantitative information in their articles. Often, this means finding ways to "sugar coat" the statistical medicine for readers. The information may be critical to the story and it must be used. Being creative helps retain readers. There are some tips to beat the numbers game:

1. Use *informational graphics* to tell the story visually.
2. *Simplify numbers* by rounding off or shortening the detail of certain numbers. Although this cannot be done to all statistics, it can be done to very large or small numbers.
3. Put numbers in a *meaningful context* for readers with examples. If statistics represent an entire state or country, reduce them to a level that makes more sense.
4. *Interpret unusual statistics.* Tell readers what they mean. Is a statistic good or bad? High or low? (Garrison, 1992a).

When a reporter sits down to write a database-oriented story, the usual rules for good writing and organization always apply, but because of the unusual nature of the material involved, a little extra effort will make a difference. Regardless of the organizational plan for the story or project, if the writer accomplishes these four goals in the story, it will probably succeed:

1. *Get the reader's attention.* Draw the reader into the story. Make the reader want to read what is written. Create drama. Use tension. Regardless of what is done, do not lose potential readers with a slow, unimaginative start.

2. *Get readers personally involved.* After gaining the reader's attention, show how this subject affects him or her. What does it mean to the reader? Can the way the story is written help readers identify with the subject? Has the story been written in such a personal way that it appeals on an individual level? How can readers benefit from the story's content?

3. *Illustrate main points.* If the story achieves this goal, the writer is showing the "what" element. Give examples and case studies. Writers should try to provide situations that can be understood at the level of the local reader—whether the general public or the sophisticated specialist.

4. *Explain the meaning.* Tell readers what these data mean. Do not leave a reader with the feeling, "So what?" when he or she puts down the story. This is the major point of the story, so be certain the writing has made this assessment at some point. Many reporters recommend the answer to "so what?" be placed in a conclusion.

VISUAL HELP FOR THE DATABASE STORY

Visual communication tools, such as informational graphics, help to tell the database-oriented news story that contains complicated statistics, numbers, or other quantitative information. That is only one important use of graphics and illustrations in computer-assisted reporting. Newspapers and news magazines have found new artistic and computational means to create visual tools to explain complex issues. These illustrations combine factual information with visual devices such as graphs, charts, maps, or "exploded" diagrams to tell the numbers-oriented story. With more and more publications using color throughout their pages, the value of these visual packages is growing. Because computers and photocopies are aiding in the rapid preparation of these images as well, they can be prepared more easily on shorter notice by art departments. Specially prepared images can also illustrate critical points in complex stories.

At times, photography can be the answer. For some situations, posed photographs labeled as illustrations will make the point. Original art such as drawings, maps, and charts can show the interrelationships of parts, procedures, and plans to clearly explain things for audiences. In many cases, it is appropriate and necessary for the reporter to take the lead in suggesting such visual applications for a news story.

These techniques are particularly helpful for computer-assisted reporters. The principle is no different from certain types of service feature articles, such as the "how-to" story. To make information more understandable, illustrations are necessary to report the story. Relationships between and among variables, proportion, and even descriptive text can be clearer and more concisely presented with information graphics. Legible and accurate graphics have no substitute in words. They simply add a valuable dimension to any project series or individual story.

The Elements of Quality Graphics

Certain decisions have to be made once it has been determined that graphics are needed to enhance a CAR story. Among the most critical decisions are those about content, order of data presentation, the number of charts that are needed, the images that will strengthen the graphic, and the content of the introduction to the graphic.

Simplicity is the rule. Most information graphics experts recommend it. The point is to give the reader a fast summary of information and relationships. As a CAR project develops, there will be some point in the work where the individuals involved begin thinking about graphics. This stage, when it is reached, requires two levels of thought: Analyze the audience and the information to present and decide how best to display it, then develop the graphic. Larger newspapers and magazines have art departments that specialize in visual presentation. As more smaller publications get involved in CAR projects and apply CAR to daily news coverage, the graphics work may also fall to reporters or editors. With database programs such as spreadsheets offering somewhat sophisticated publication-quality charting tools, creating graphics is not out of the range of possibilities. Graphics such as charts must communicate. There are four purposes of informational graphics:

- Show change over time.
- Compare items at one point in time.
- Compare parts of the whole.
- Compare data by geographic location. (Langham, 1993)

Reporters and editors should discuss the main point of their story or project and then determine the point of each graphic. "What do I want the readers to understand when they are finished with the chart?" asks

Steve Segal (1993, p. 1), information graphics specialist for the Greensburg, PA, *Tribune-Review*. Segal says he uses five major types of charts with computer-assisted reporting projects:

- *Text (table) charts.* Numbers and/or words arranged in columns and rows.
- *Bar charts.* Bar heights represent quantities.
- *Fever (line) charts.* Plotting data over time.
- *Pie charts.* Division of a circle into slices that total 100%.
- *Wild cards.* Other forms of graphics such as maps, flowcharts, time lines, and supergraphics that combine two or more of the major types.

13

Database Management, Mapping, and Nine-Track Systems

Violent crime in Gary and other communities in northwest Indiana reached a dangerous record level in late 1993. That year, even 2 months before it ended, was more dangerous than all of 1992, when Gary's homicide rate ranked fifth in the nation. Residents were becoming concerned about that serious social problem. The 70,000-daily circulation *Times* in Munster, IN, located about 11 miles southwest of Gary and just south of Hammond, used the tragedy of a 10-year-old boy who was murdered while he slept to introduce a major in-house analysis of the violent crime problem in the metropolitan area. Focusing on regional cities such as Gary, Merrillville, and Hammond in addition to Munster, *The Times* staff collected crime statistics from the Gary police department, county coroner's office, county prosecutor's office, and the county crime lab. A four-part series was published, including the opening Sunday installment, written by reporter Cindy Eberting, that focused on Gary and its "killing zone."

Eberting, with the assistance of *The Times'* CAR coordinator Carol Napolitano, used a popular relational database management system, dBase, installed on the newspaper's Sun (UNIX) operating system, to compile the database for analysis. The package offered a profile of the area's violent crime. Eberting studied the 90 homicides in Gary and total of 107 cases in Lake County. The analysis looked at crime characteristics such as time, date, place, motive, weapons used, and official cause of death. It also studied the victims in terms of their races, ages, and places of residence. Defendants were analyzed as well, with such data as criminal records and ages.

The Sunday package included a full-color double-truck graphic about the violence in Gary. *The Times* used an analytical mapping software package, MapInfo, to create several "killing zone" maps. The program merged the homicides database with mapping database power to locate each incident by address and by motive. MapInfo, like other geographic information system programs, placed the "geocoded" addresses of locations of the Gary homicides on a city map. The resulting maps of the locations of the homicides presented a very clear portrait of the crime pattern—drugs were the leading motive (about one third of all incidents in Gary) in a concentrated area of the city near downtown.

"Our editors are extremely supportive and understand the need for time and the special needs of CAR, like statistical accuracy and bad data," Napolitano (personal communication, December 22, 1993) stated. She said she wants every reporter at the newspaper to have access to databases within the next 2 years. "I am currently developing a formal CAR training program that will encompass relational databases, online, Internet, and statistics." Napolitano also said the newspaper had five reporters and editors working on CAR projects at the time the "killing zone" project was finished. "By mid-1994, we hope to have at least 12 to 15 reporters, editors, and other news personnel involved."

Medium-size newspapers, such as *The Times* in Munster, are discovering that advanced computer-assisted reporting tools such as relational database management systems and sophisticated analytical mapping programs are not just the investigative territory of major dailies. The advent of less expensive—compared to mainframe, at least—computing has made much of this type of original analytical journalism possible for reporters in the past decade. Personal computers, first desktop and more recently powerful portables, offer convenience, increased speed with each new model introduced, and much simpler operation, in addition to the lower cost to get started.

Even a few small dailies are beginning to look beyond the most basic levels of computer database analysis. As discussed previously, more and more newspapers are discovering the benefits of online research each day. Database tools such as spreadsheets and statistical packages are gaining broader acceptance as analytical tools of reporters. The most powerful and versatile of the quantitative approaches used by computer-oriented reporters, relational database management systems, analytical mapping software, and nine-track tape drive PC database systems, are the focus of this chapter.

BASICS OF DATABASE MANAGEMENT SOFTWARE

Chris Feola, news systems editor in charge of computer-assisted reporting for the *Waterbury Republican-American* in Connecticut, has likened database-oriented reporting to that of a regular exercise program. "Databases have always been a lot like professional body building—it looks easy when Arnold Schwarzenegger does it," Feola (1993, February 28) told Journalism Forum members on CompuServe:

> Then you find out how he does it: He just lifts weights three hours every morning. And three hours every night. Six days a week. Every week since

he turned 19. Right about that point most people decide that's just more trouble than it's worth. That's pretty much been the deal with databases. They're great—if you don't mind devoting your entire life to one. But here's the bottom line: You need a database, no matter how much trouble they are. Only a database has the power to do what we now call database journalism. The power to extract essential knowledge from mounds of raw data.

Feola may be exaggerating a little about the amount of work required for database work. But it does take time and the right tools. Steven Segal (personal communication, April, 1994), database journalist and information graphics specialist for the Greensburg, PA, *Tribune-Review,* says the value of relational database programs for his newspaper has been immense:

> With the power of a personal computer database program—I use Paradox 4.5 for DOS—and a scanner we can tackle projects that only large newspapers could do in the past. I use our art department scanner and OmniPagePro—an optical character recognition program that can "read" text. . . . At first, it is difficult to grasp just how much power you have at the tip of your fingers. Analyzing thousands and thousands of records in a few seconds is quite a feeling.

Assuming the right hardware configuration is already in the newsroom, there are two types of database software packages commonly used by journalists that must be considered for database-oriented reporting. The first type, *flatfile database programs,* is represented by spreadsheets. Flatfile programs can manipulate only one data table at a time. Any cross-referencing or merging of information in more than one flatfile table at a time must be done manually. The second type of software, *relational database management systems* (RDBMSs), is more sophisticated and enables the user to work with two or more tables in the same database or in different database files at the same time. Users are able to develop links between the tables using common elements, or variables, in the tables (Ricciardi, 1993). Examples of flatfile database programs, in addition to spreadsheets, include personal information managers, contact managers, and free-form text database search programs. RDBMSs include widely used programs such as Paradox, FoxPro, Access, and dBase.

"Flatfile databases are related to relational databases about the same way that toy trucks are related to Mack trucks," Feola (1993b) observed. "Flat databases are good for keeping lists: A library card catalogue, for example. It will sort and group things for you: All the books written by people named Smith, for example. Relational databases can do all that and more. But the more powerful things these complex programs can do is to compare multiple databases—each containing thousands or millions of pieces of data—to look for relationships."

Understanding the Key Terms

There are several important terms frequently used when working with database programs. These include the following:

- *Attribute, field, variable.* Each of these terms refers to the intersection of a row and column and a characteristic of the base unit of analysis. In some literature about database software, this is a single "piece" of data.
- *Case, record.* A row of information or the collection of attributes, fields, and variables about the unit of analysis. These are commonly people or incidents.
- *Crosstab.* The intersection of a table row and column resulting in a cell. In some database programs, such as Paradox, this refers to the conversion of data in records and fields to a spreadsheet-type format. In statistical terms, a crosstab is also known as a contingency table, in which individual value frequencies of two variables are counted and analyzed for their intersections.
- *Element.* A data element is the smallest piece of data. An address is not usually considered an element, but a zip code, street name, or block address number might be an element, depending on the database design.
- *Form.* A customized screen view offered by some programs, such as Paradox, of a single case or record.
- *Join.* This term refers to the process of merging two or more tables to create a new table that represents the common elements of the original tables. It is sometimes used as a noun also.
- *Key.* A key or a key field is the unit that is used to join, merge, or relate two different tables of data.
- *Query.* A question posed of a database to retrieve information in a particular order or form. Queries select from tables, they combine tables, they can insert or delete data, they can change values in tables, and they can define data groupings on which calculations are executed.
- *Report.* A customizable arrangement of output in printed or file form that does not follow the original structure of the data table. Database programs can directly print tables created from queries but often the need for presentation or publishable quality output calls for customized reports.
- *RQBE and QBE.* These acronyms refer to "relational query by example" and "query by example." RQBE and QBE represent one of the two major ways of retrieving information from a database.
- *SQL.* Structured query language. This is the second of the two major ways of retrieving information from a database.
- *Table.* An arrangement or collection of data using a matrix format of rows (cases or records) and columns (attributes, fields, or variables).

The Basic Features of Relational Database Programs

The most basic elements of relational database programs are:

- Sample databases and tutorials for learning the program.
- Database viewing and browsing options.
- Database entry form customization.
- Database building and editing.
- Adding and deleting cases/records.
- Text editing.
- Case/record modification and manipulation.
- Database file importing and exporting conversion utilities.
- Various record search and retrieval approaches and commands.
- Field type customization.
- Network or group use capability.
- Indexing.
- Mathematical computations on records in the database.
- Creation of crosstabulations.
- Database structure modification (adding and deleting fields and changing the type of fields) after the database has been created.
- Database "slicing and dicing" (splitting up a database into parts).
- Basic querying; selecting groups of records that meet defined criteria.
- Advanced querying; using calculations and operators on groups of records.
- Query report design and customization.
- Graphing and charting.
- Output in printed, file, or on-screen form.
- Tools for file, table, and data management, copying.
- Table modification and restructuring.
- Online and documented help.
- Scripting language for database application development.
- Object linking and embedding (OLE).
- Dynamic data exchange (DDE).
- Data integrity checking tools.
- Database security features.

USING DATABASE MANAGERS

At first look, a relational database package can be quite intimidating. The documentation is often massive and complicated. Programming language guides are as thick as some telephone books. Installation of the packages is usually easy enough, but after working through the "quick start" directions and initial tutorial lesson in the user's guide, some people may be seriously challenged to stick with it. Once the initial shock of learning a database management system (DBMS) program wears off, the utility and power of the software may begin to manifest itself. There are six categories of DBMS skills that should be learned for working with databases:

- *Building and editing the database.* For beginners, designing the database and entering original data should be the first skills to master. In addition to typing in data case by case and field by field, some news organizations use optical scanners to enter large amounts of text. But scanners, efficient time-savers that they are, can have data-reading error problems that will require considerable effort to clean.
- *Importing and cleaning external databases.* Once a database has been designed, data collected from other sources can be imported into the data table, as a new table, and then cleaned up where errors exist.
- *Querying databases using query language.* When the data are completely entered and clean, inquiries about the data can be made. This is the "getting the answers" stage of the project. In the query process, the user asks a question of the database to find out which cases or records meet the criteria of the question.
- *Reporting the data queries.* After queries are defined, the "answers" can be printed out, sent to a file for storage, or viewed on screen.
- *Designing custom input screens and report forms.* For sophisticated input and output, most DBMSs allow users to customize their input screens and output reports for presentation purposes. For newsroom applications, this may not be an important part of the process, although reports with the right design could be camera ready for use by news organizations with limited art departments or those under extreme deadline circumstances.
- *Developing customized applications using the database programming language.* The most sophisticated users can advance to customizing and writing new applications for use with the database. This is the highest level of DBMS expertise. These tools permit users to go beyond the range of the software itself to solve special database management and use problems.

Querying and Structured Query Language (SQL)

Querying is the process of asking questions of a database. There are a number of ways to retrieve information from a database once it has been created or imported into a DBMS. Querying permits data to be selected from a table, data from two or more tables to be combined, data to be statistically analyzed, data to be inserted into a table or deleted from a table, and data to be converted into a table. A query can be as simple as: "Which trucking companies are the most likely to be involved in an accident on a particular highway?" or "Which family contributes the most money or most often to a particular political action committee?" These queries can be answered from the right databases. The process involves identifying the field or fields (e.g., company name and highway name or family name and PAC name) containing the information and determining the proper operation (e.g., listing names alphabetically or sorting frequencies from highest to lowest) that should be completed.

The two major tools of querying are *structured query language* (SQL) and *query by example* (QBE) or *relational query by example* (RQBE). SQL and QBE/RQBE are powerful tools. They are probably the most important feature of a database management system.

SQL is a standardized language designed to pull information from databases, commonly found in the major database packages such as Paradox and FoxPro. Although a query might not be needed for small databases, even some large flatfile programs need an SQL to speed finding and ordering information. SQL is one of the most necessary elements in RDBMSs. SQL is a fast and the most direct way to query using a command line of a DBMS. The standard SQL approach works with a command line and instructions that define the fields and tables to be used as well as the relationships of those fields and tables.

Instead of using a query language, often an intimidating element of DBMSs for new users, queries can be asked by using examples. This is particularly useful for beginners who have not learned the basics of the program's query language. Some DBMSs, such as FoxPro and Paradox, offer the option to create queries by giving examples. In doing so, the user selects fields or variables and uses operators or qualifiers to learn something from the database. An example might be: How many licensed bus drivers (Field 1, Table 1) in a particular county (Field 2, Table 1) have been convicted of driving under the influence of alcohol (name is Field 1 and conviction is Field 2 of Table 2) or drugs (Field 3, Table 2). A program using RQBE will allow the user to select the query by selecting from menus of fields and tables as well as menus of operators and other instructions.

Some users believe querying is difficult and patience-testing, especially in DOS versions of the most popular programs. But for individuals who learn those programs, there are none better. For new users, Windows, OS/2, and Macintosh versions may be easier to learn because of the dialog box, pull-down menu, and other graphical user interface features.

CONVERTING DATABASES TO USEFUL FORM

Why do database files have to be converted? It is simply because not everyone speaks the same language, database-wise. Some people like to compare converting databases to going from one country to another where there is a different native language. There will be common elements in both languages, but not enough to always make sense. Database files are much the same. When using different database creation and analysis programs, the "languages" may be different. Most full-service DBMSs have utilities that permit conversions, however. Think of them as interpreters. Somehow, however, the data have to be put into readable form.

What exactly is readable form? This term can mean several things. First and most important, it means *machine readable*. Machine-readable data are in a form that can be interpreted by a computer and used as input. All data, to be useful, have to be put into machine-readable form. The data might be machine readable, but that status is not valuable to a user if the data cannot be read by the DBMS being used. A second meaning of readable form relates to software. Because not all DBMS software reads all formats for databases, this can become a problem. It is a major concern for anyone obtaining external databases and converting them into something useful for analysis.

Do-it-yourself data entry is the safest way to be sure of the accuracy of the database. This is also the most expensive way to enter data—in terms of time, if not money. Some editors and reporters simply cannot afford the time to enter hundreds, thousands, or even more cases involving what seem like countless fields of information. It is, however, the most certain method of properly entering data. For sensitive projects, for complicated data, or for limited-resource situations, doing it yourself is the only answer. But a word to the wise: Be prepared to spend some time and have someone check the work for typing errors or other problems. Self-entry of databases is often smart, but think of building a database in the same way as writing a news story. A second set of eyes is the only way to do it right. The reward is a clean and ready-to-go database.

Commercial data conversion services exist to help convert databases. Many specialize in converting nine-track tapes from mainframe systems into PC-readable formats. But they also work with CD-ROM and diskette databases. One example is Interface Systems in Gaithersburg, MD, which offers to convert at least nine different types of data media for clients. Some businesses also lease nine-track drives for temporary use, usually in 3-month increments. Lease arrangements are good ways to check out the territory before investing. Commercial data entry services also exist, but these are most helpful when it comes to converting paper-based data into digital form. These options may be less expensive than longer term investments in hardware and software, not to mention training time.

Importing Files Into Database Management Systems

Importing is the process of bringing data from one database system into another. The process allows the internal structure of the original database to be maintained while the file is converted into usable form by a second program or computer system. Most DBMSs import, but they have some limits. For example, Paradox for Windows only allows importing data files, not applications or forms. For most journalists, these types of restrictions are not a problem, however.

Advanced software packages, such as the most recent versions of DBMSs, offer conversion utilities to ease the process of importing and exporting data. For competitive reasons, if none other, most of the major relational database programs and spreadsheet programs support conversions to and from their competitors.

One of the most common conversions involves using tab or comma delimited files. Files that have been produced in ASCII form are often in *delimited* form. Delimiters separate information in fields or records. The most common delimiters are commas, quotation marks, or tabs. Collectively, such forms are called .CSV files for *comma separated values*. Most conversion utilities recognize any user-defined unique identifying character or symbol. Some databases require *parsing,* the process of separating information that has not been delimited to the level required by the user.

Database Programming Languages

Most major database packages, such as FoxPro, Access, dBase, and Paradox, offer programming languages that enable advanced users to develop their own applications of databases built with the database program. FoxPro, for instance, comes with a 1,200-plus-page language reference manual. With programming languages, users can issue a series of commands instead of one instruction at a time. This saves time over manually entering the commands. The programs can be used over and over for repetitive uses of a changing database. The programs can run other programs also.

Shawn McIntosh (1993), computer-assisted reporting editor at the *Dallas Morning News,* developed a Paradox programming language program when she was at *USA Today* that allowed editors and reporters to press one key at a desktop computer to get the latest campaign contributions to a particular candidate from an Federal Elections Commission database. She explained how it worked:

Paradox has an underlying programming language. It basically allows you to script anything that you do repeatedly. I wrote a program for *USA Today.* A clerk comes in and selects from a menu [on the screen] which says "What do you want to do?" The clerk says, "I want to get campaign contributions for presidential candidates." The clerk hits that button and walks away. The computer dials up the Federal Election Commission. It asks for the candidates running for president and it downloads every campaign contribution given to them. Because the FEC does not offer an update, the program then compares those to the ones we already have in Paradox and it updates the tables with the new contributions that are not in Paradox. So, it basically imports those into Paradox and updates them. It then does links. It links all the tables from four years ago. . . . It prints out about 10 to 15 reports and it takes about nine hours. So you take one keystroke from a clerk and get all that. It was not easy to write and I would not recommend it be something that you do on your first time out.

THE MOST POPULAR DBMSs

Several software products have evolved as the favorites among news organization database managers. The leaders among relational database management systems are Access, Approach, dBase, FoxPro, Paradox, and XDB. The favorites among text database manager programs are askSam and Magellan. There seems to be less difference in the major products than there was 5 to 10 years ago, says *Newsday's* Russ Buettner (1993):

A couple of years ago, FoxPro and Paradox were real different. FoxPro was mostly SQL based. Paradox mostly used this point and click thing, which is called relational query by example. FoxPro was considered to be a lot faster, but you had to know a lot more. Paradox was considered easier to use, but slower, so it was a trade off. Since the big companies have gotten involved and bought the small companies that originally developed those programs, there's not much difference in speed any more. . . . The point is that you are not going to go wrong with either one of these programs. It is just two different ways to get to the same point.

DATABASE MANAGERS IN NEWSROOMS

The 1994 University of Miami national CAR study found a wide range of database managers in use in U.S. daily newspaper newsrooms ($n = 208$), but of those in use, Paradox (both DOS and Windows versions) and FoxPro (both DOS and Windows versions) are by far the most popular. However, dBase is also popular and XDB seems to be growing in use:

Circulation	Paradox	FoxPro	dBase	Other[a]	None
Under 50,000	13.7% (7)	5.7% (2)	6.7% (1)	14.6% (6)	67.0% (71)
50,000–100,000	27.5 (14)	34.3 (12)	33.3 (5)	24.4 (10)	22.6 (24)
100,001–250,000	37.3 (19)	31.4 (11)	26.7 (4)	26.8 (11)	8.5 (9)
250,001–500,000	13.7 (7)	17.1 (6)	26.7 (4)	22.0 (9)	1.9 (2)
Over 500,000	7.8 (4)	11.4 (4)	6.7 (1)	12.2 (5)	0.0 (0)
Totals	100.0% (51)	100.0% (35)	100.0% (15)	100.0% (41)	100.0% (106)

Note: Percentages are for columns. Frequencies are in parentheses. Some newspapers reported using more than one database program.

[a]The leading "other" DBMS product used was XDB ($n = 12$).

DATABASES AND MAPPING SYSTEMS

News organizations have had a century-long history of using maps to enhance their news coverage. Many are informative, some just offer visual impact, and others offer both advantages. One of the most common uses has been "locator" maps. In recent years, corresponding with the growth of personal computing, computerized mapping software has become a significant tool in reporting news. Analytical mapping software, a tool that permits merging databases, was part of a market estimated at $380 million in 1992 and growing at about 20% annually, according to an estimate by Daratech, Inc., in Cambridge, MA (Strategic Mapping, 1993, p. 1).

"Words structure information linearly, in one dimension, whereas maps structure information graphically, in two dimensions," wrote Syracuse University geographer Mark Monmonier (1989, p. 1). "Readers and viewers seem more at home with words than with maps, and journalism uses many more paragraphs. . . . But 'Where?' is a question of journalistic concern because some news has an important geographic component, most non-local news at least has a dateline, and many persons have an only rudimentary knowledge of their own city."

Monmonier (1989) also says journalism is "ideally equipped to demonstrate still further the integration of text and graphics" with the improvements in hardware and mapping software. "Technology can compensate for much of the journalist's probable lack of drawing skill, and an artistically talented editor might easily make needed refinements." he wrote (pp. 246–247).

There are two distinctly different categories of mapping programs. The more basic and less expensive category, *navigational mapping* software, offers use of existing databases for plotting trips, measuring distances, and simply doing what a printed atlas does for a journalist. These programs have a high degree of utility and function in any newsroom. The second and more sophisticated category, *analytical mapping* software, is known as geographic information systems (GIS) software. GIS programs—Atlas GIS and MapInfo among the most popular of them in newsrooms—permit users to combine a database table from a different source with the mapping power of a software "atlas" to produce highly accurate and analytically powerful research and reporting tools. Strategic Mapping (1993), makers of Atlas GIS, estimates that at least 75% of database files in existence contain some type of geographic fields such as addresses or zip codes that would be needed for mapping without modification of those databases. MapInfo estimates that 85% of databases from state and local government agencies have geographic identifiers such as addresses, census tracts, zip codes, or latitude and longitude coordinates (MapInfo, 1993).

Mapping programs are popular among government agencies for planning and zoning, law enforcement, and emergency response. New communities, expanded developments, shopping center projects, school districts, health and social services offices, economic development offices, public works departments, environmental and natural resource management agencies, and elections offices are often dependent on databases that include mapping data or, at least, mapable data. Numerous law enforcement agencies use mapping software to monitor crime patterns and traffic movement and to enhance emergency response time. As more government organizations use mapping, access to those databases will be enhanced with mapping software available in the newsroom in a manner similar to the way some reporters use spreadsheet or relational database system files directly from agencies. And, of course, reporters can use analytical mapping tools for their own analyses of community planning and public safety data.

These tools offer a wide variety of graphic output quality that makes selection of the program important to news organizations hoping to publish the output of the program, especially as camera ready. Because publication quality is a goal for almost all newsroom users, this is a serious matter to consider. Graphic artists will want a program that can generate camera-ready maps or, at least, produce graphic files that can be fine tuned in a drawing program such as Aldus Freehand or Adobe Illustrator. Such fine tuning includes adjusting line weights, selecting text fonts, and adding other graphics (Gaughan, 1993).

"The arrival of desktop publishing and mapping tools a few years ago was welcomed as a significant development in mapmaking," wrote Timothy Gaughan (1993, p. 50), a marketing research analyst. "Since then, however, a conflict between art and science has emerged over just what the software should be capable of." Publishers and designers want high-caliber graphics and cartographers want analysis and precision, he stated. And, it seems, journalists need both.

Navigational Mapping Tools

Navigational mapping software is quite inexpensive, often priced at less than $100 for a basic program and even a metropolitan area or county street map set. But analytical mapping tools are quite pricey—from $500 to $5,000 or more per package. Pricing also indicates, like most software, the quality of the mapping. The less expensive programs offer fewer features, less customization, and less refined and often less than publication-quality mapping. "Perhaps because maps provide the world's most intuitive graphical interface, businesses seem to be warming to mapping software without the skepticism that usually greets a new application genre," wrote *PC World* freelance writer Laura Lang (1993, p. 185).

Navigational programs can contain a great deal of useful information. These programs not only provide street maps, but offer databases containing restaurants, hotels, and other information of particular value to travelers. In essence, navigational programs are the best of an atlas combined with a tourist's guide book for a city, county, or region.

Analytical Mapping Tools

Analytical mapping tools are quite different from navigational tools. The analytical mapping programs also offer maps, of course, but basic maps are about all the two types of mapping programs have in common. GIS software is the offspring of mainframe mapping, evolving over the past decade in much the same manner as the sophisticated statistical packages. "Maps lift you above normal perception and show you how to get from one place to another. Computers enable you to analyze and manipulate vast quantities of data. Put maps and computers together, and you have a supremely intuitive tool for visualizing information," Lang wrote (p. 182).

Analytical mapping works in a logical manner. Putting data onto a map involves several steps. First, the user must develop or provide an existing database with some type of geographic information, such as an address field. The mapping programs on the market offer database editing and cleaning tools. The program then does the next step: assigning "x" and "y" coordinates to each geographic location for each record (such as the address). This table of coordinates can come with the mapping program or it may have to be purchased as an additional database. Once the process of geocoding is complete, the user can check addresses that have not been automatically coded and manually change the addresses or database fields to complete the coding. The final step is to design the map by placing layers together on the screen through varying layer control commands.

There is no doubt about the power of mapping to permit readers to visualize a trend, to understand patterns in data that are difficult to see in a table or other type of graphic, and to identify new patterns and relationships among variables. Journalism professor and computing consultant Tom Johnson aptly describes what the newest and most powerful analytical mapping programs can do. "GIS is as old as maps, but off-the-shelf software like MapInfo and Atlas Pro can give a journalist with a PC unparalleled power to analyze social, economic, and political circumstances," Johnson (1994b, p. 14) wrote.

Lang said one of the obvious strengths is the presentation power of the software. "Integrating data with maps is an efficient and convincing way to present information as well as analyze it," she stated (pp. 187–188). "[I]t won't be long before software-based maps become a common way of viewing business information."

GIS software is becoming so important to newsrooms that Johnson (1994b) says they "are becoming the fifth tool in a suite of fundamental utilities for journalists" (p. 14) in addition to word processing, communications, spreadsheets, and databases. The new analytical boost given reporters by computers has allowed more than just the graphic power of mapping to make this an important device for describing and explaining news events. Mapping software in the mid-1990s adds the dimension of taking databases and plotting information from those databases onto maps.

With their power, analytical mapping programs can be enormous and require systems with considerable processor speed and memory. Many require a minimum of 640 KB to run on a 80386 or better processor, but some require as much as 4 MB of RAM. In reality, they run better with a 486 processor and a minimum of 8 MB or more and it helps to have a high-quality color monitor with additional graphics card memory as well. In terms of storage space, the demand is great also. Most mapping programs come with basic installations of some substantial size, but after adding databases for streets, population, and other purposes, the installed size can be staggering. Minimal installations are about 2 MB of hard disk space, but some programs are easily in the 10 to 15 MB range. Basic Tactician and PC Arc-Info each require a humbling 40 MB of hard drive space for full installation. GISPlus needs 22 MB of space and Streets on a Disk needs up to 20 MB.

Basic Mapping Software Features

If hard drive space needs can be met, users can expect certain basic elements and features of mapping programs. These include most if not all of the following features:

- Library of general use color maps (e.g., United States and Canada) with subdivision boundaries.
- Search capabilities by geographic designations (e.g., place name, address, intersections, area codes, and zip codes).
- Area fill maps and thematic mapping with user-provided or user-originated databases.
- Accurate street maps using most commonly known names of streets with more than one name.
- Ability to edit, such as renaming and adding streets, points of interest, and so forth.
- Dot-density maps.
- Boundary and tract maps.
- Point-of-interest databases or maps.
- Ability to use customized and homemade maps.
- Symbol size proportioning according to database.
- Geocoding (address matching and mapping).
- Projection customization.
- Trip routing and calculations (navigational systems).
- Zooming in and out for varying map views.

- Addition and deletion of layers (also called "overlays") of data to maps and other layer controls.
- Charting and graphing capabilities.
- Built-in database management system (for originating data tables).
- Interactivity with databases from other programs (object linking and embedding and dynamic data exchange).
- Database querying.
- Thematic data representation using percentiles.
- Spatial database querying (finding data in a geographic context).
- Flexible database import range including delimited ASCII files and the most common database programs (e.g., dBase, FoxPro, Paradox, 1-2-3, Quattro Pro, and Excel).
- Flexible database export range including delimited ASCII files and the most common database programs.
- Printing and file output customization.
- U.S. cities database.
- U.S. counties database.
- U.S. 1990 census population databases.
- Network usability.
- Optional foreign maps with boundaries and major features from publisher.
- Optional databases for county and city streets from publisher.

There is a big three in analytical mapping emerging. These are Atlas GIS, published by Strategic Mapping in Santa Clara, CA; MapInfo, published by MapInfo Corp., in Troy, NY; and PC Arc-Info, published by Environmental Systems Research Institute (ESRI), in Redlands, CA. Figure 13.1 shows a typical MapInfo street map and Fig. 13.2 shows a MapInfo national "shade by value" map.

MAPPING SOFTWARE USE IN NEWSROOMS

The 1994 University of Miami national CAR study found only a few geographic information systems or other mapping software in use in U.S. daily newspaper newsrooms ($n = 208$). Atlas GIS and MapInfo are the most popular:

Circulation	Atlas GIS	MapInfo	Other	None
Under 50,000	0.0% (0)	0.0% (0)	30.0 (3)	47.1% (81)
50,000–100,000	0.0 (0)	27.3 (3)	20.0 (2)	28.5 (49)
100,001–250,000	40.0 (6)	45.4 (5)	20.0 (2)	18.0 (31)
250,001–500,000	26.7 (4)	27.3 (3)	20.0 (2)	5.2 (9)
Over 500,000	33.3 (5)	0.0 (0)	10.0 (1)	1.2 (2)
Totals	100.0% (15)	100.0% (11)	100.0% (10)	100.0% (172)

Note: Percentages are for columns. Frequencies are in parentheses.

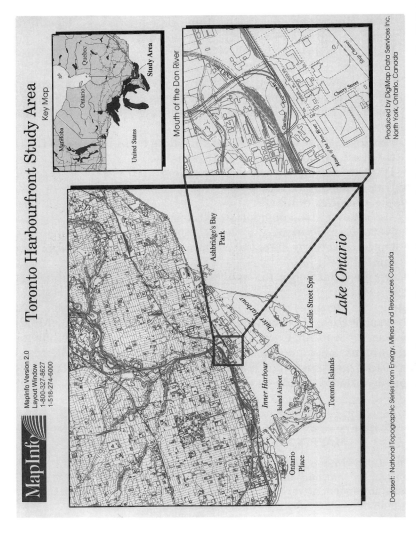

FIG. 13.1. Street maps are one leading use of analytical mapping tools. In this MapInfo example, Toronto's downtown streets are displayed in three different views using a street database. (Courtesy of MapInfo Corp.)

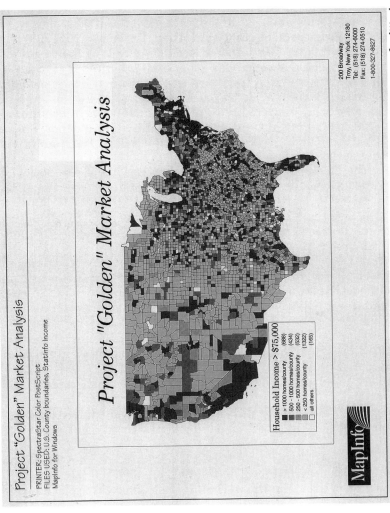

FIG. 13.2. One of the most common uses of analytical mapping software is to create maps of political or other areas shaded by values. In this example, all counties in the continental United States are shaded according to household income levels. Each color variation represents the number of households in a county with income greater than $75,000. (Courtesy of MapInfo Corp.)

279

Producing Stories With Mapping Software

Scott Anderson, a longtime investigative and enterprise reporter, is the newsroom computer resources manager for the Fort Lauderdale *Sun-Sentinel*. He wound up working with computers and databases by writing census stories when the first databases of the 1990 census were released. Anderson (personal communication, December 20, 1993) has been using MapInfo for Windows for several years to enhance stories that his newspaper's newsroom has generated. "MapInfo is just fun to play with," Anderson stated (personal communication, December 20, 1993). For his CAR work, Anderson uses a Compaq 486 PC that runs at 66 MHz, a nine-track reader, 12 MB of RAM, a 150 MB internal hard drive, a 700 MB external hard drive, a 14400 baud modem, and a CD-ROM reader. His PC system is also connected to the mainframe system that serves the *Sun-Sentinel*.

Among the stories Anderson uses as illustrations of the power of MapInfo and geographic information system mapping software include:

- Traffic ticketing patterns of 2.4 million tickets given to 1.9 million drivers, in Broward County, FL, where the *Sun-Sentinel* is published, broken down by racial groups.
- "What-if" scenarios based on 1992's Hurricane Andrew striking in parts of Broward County instead of 60 miles further south in southeastern Dade County.
- Commuting habits of Fort Lauderdale area residents based on census data.
- Campaign contribution patterns for Broward County based on Federal Election Commission data crosstabulated by zip codes for the county.
- Underground gasoline storage tanks and leakage reports and inspections.
- Hospitalization and health care patterns involving reasons, patient demographics, costs, and billpayer by county and zip code.

Other examples? *The Arizona Republic* in Phoenix used Atlas Pro to create maps at the precinct level for the 1992 presidential campaign and for an abortion project. *The Miami Herald* used Atlas GIS to plot damage to housing in the aftermath of Hurricane Andrew.

The Cost of Analytical Mapping

Mapping software is an expensive proposition that will remain outside the boundaries of many news organization budgets for much of the rest of this decade unless software prices drop further, less expensive versions of programs are developed, or newsroom software budgets grow.

But prices began to drop in late 1994, giving the tool promise just the same. The base cost of the software is higher than most of the CAR tools in use and the cost can become even higher because of the need for add-on products such as street map databases. "When you purchase a mapping system, keep in mind that the basic system may not meet all your needs," said NICAR's Jennifer LaFleur (1993). "For example, with Atlas GIS, you probably will need to buy boundary files for your area (ZIPs, census tracts, and so forth). Many data files are also an additional charge. When checking prices, check for your 'whole' package, not just the basics."

As LaFleur points out, there may be costs for certain compatible utilities such as programming language, database file conversion utilities, and street map databases. Other databases to be used may be expensive, also, depending on the jurisdictions involved and their public fees.

Editors and reporters who feel mapping is a required tool for some of their reporting projects, but who have limited resources, have alternatives. There is the possibility of sharing mapping resources with other units within the company—such as the art, marketing, promotion, circulation, and advertising departments. There is also the possibility of working with other news organizations within the ownership group or ones with a common interest in the subject that are willing to share costs. A third alternative would be to work with area universities and colleges where some individuals in journalism, geography, or other social science programs may be using mapping software. For example, The *Newport News Daily Press,* a daily of 105,000 circulation in Virginia, uses GIS Plus at a local college when it needs access to analytical mapping.

USING NINE-TRACK TAPE DATABASES

Nine-track tape is a storage medium used mostly on mainframe computer systems. The format of nine-track tape places data on nine distinct tracks that are parallel on a reel of ½-inch-wide magnetic tape. The format gets its name because the information on the tape is recorded in groups of eight bits (one byte) at a time with the addition of a ninth bit track for parity. A typical nine-track tape stores about 200 MB of data.

Magnetic tape storage is fundamentally different from disc or disk storage. Nine-track tape requires two reels, just as a reel-to-reel audiotape or videotape recorder would work. As the tape moves from one reel to the other, the tape passes over a "read" and "write" head that reads the data from the tape or writes data to it. Tape is also different in that it is a continuous magnetic surface in which the read and write head does not have continuous access to all areas of the tape at the same time.

Because the head cannot move randomly to any location on the surface without the tape moving, as a read and write head can do with a hard drive, floppy disk, or compact disc, the data must be read and written sequentially.

For several decades, nine-track tape has been the primary storage and data transfer medium for major electronic databases kept by government agencies. To help access these databases available on mainframe computers, some reporters at larger daily newspapers bought the entire tapes and loaded the databases on their own company's mainframe systems or they invested in devices commonly called nine-track tape drives, or readers, and found a way to connect them to smaller computing systems.

Nine-track tape readers remain relatively expensive tools, running about $5,000 per unit in 1994, but these mechanical readers enabled reporters without access to mainframes, or those with limited access to them, to use database tapes with a reasonably powerful PC. As desktop systems became more powerful and the availability and cost of nine-track readers dropped, more news organizations became involved in in-house analysis of nine-track tape databases in the past decade.

Mainframe systems are rapidly falling into disfavor in many business environments. News organizations are gradually eliminating them as leases expire or as hardware needs replacement. Although powerful, mainframe systems are quite costly to purchase or lease and often equally expensive to maintain and operate. But because many public agencies require the data processing storage power of mainframes, nine-track tapes remain a necessity of database journalism. PC-based systems, the heart of most computer-assisted reporting, are connected to the mainframe world through mainframe-to-PC data interchange systems.

"There are 35,000 mainframe computers that the federal government has, but it's also an old technology," said journalist Andy Scott (1993a), former executive director of IRE. "It's inefficient and they are moving away from it. But you also know how quickly the federal government moves. Nine-track tapes are going to be around for a long time. And even if they start putting the new data on newer technology, the old data is still going to be on nine-track tapes."

For news organizations interested in serious original database work, work with nine-track data is nearly a daily activity. A nine-track reading and writing device is part of the hardware set-up of many daily newspaper CAR desks. Some newspapers even maintain portable nine-track systems to enhance their ability to copy tapes from public agencies.

Chris Feola, systems, new media, and CAR director at the *Waterbury Republican-American,* believes nine-track readers can be a major newsroom asset. "We have a nine-track reader and they are enormously useful. We survived for years without one, however, and so can you,"

Feola (1993c) stated. "Universities can often be persuaded to run your nine-tracks for you. There are also companies who will do it for a fee. If you can afford your own nine-track, there are programs such as NineTrack Express that will interface the tape drive with your PC."

Understanding Nine-Track Language

There are several important terms frequently used when working with databases on nine-track tapes:

- *Blocking.* When storing data on tape, this is the process of splitting up the records into fixed-size blocks. Records are usually blocked to save space on a tape.
- *Coding.* The two most common binary codes for nine-track tape are the American Standard Code for Information Interchange (ASCII) and Extended Binary Coded Decimal Interchange Code (EBCDIC). Some nine-track tapes from major mainframe systems use EBCDIC and these need to be converted to ASCII for use on PCs. ASCII is the standard for PCs. Coding translation is usually a simple act.
- *Labeling.* A label is important in data storage. Many nine-track tapes offer a label that describes information about block size and record length. Some database editors who work with nine-track tapes call these labels "indexes" to the information on the tape.
- *Parsing.* This is the act of breaking data into smaller pieces so it be can more easily and precisely analyzed. DBMSs and spreadsheets often offer utilities for parsing data. Some data are stored in ASCII form, delimited by spaces, commas, tabs, or some other unique character. There are two types, generally: record and field delimiters.
- *Record layout.* This is the "road map" to the database. Acquiring the layout is probably the first step to take when obtaining data from a public agency. This can be obtained long before the database itself is purchased. The layout tells users how the data are arranged and lists the fields or variables and their types. This is necessary for importing any data to a PC from a mainframe. Not only does the layout tell whether the database can be useful, but it also tells what fields are and are not included.
- *Tape density.* The density of a tape reflects the number of bits per inch (BPI). The more dense, of course, the more data capacity on the tape. Most nine-track tapes use a 6,250 BPI density but some are less dense.

Waterbury and Raleigh: Two Case Studies

Chris Feola is in charge of his newspaper's computer journalism department, the state capital bureau, pagination, and newsroom computer systems. Before coming to his Waterbury post, he worked at six other papers in 18 states and five countries on two continents, including a 2-year stint covering Asia as a foreign correspondent for *Stars & Stripes*. One major CAR project he supervised, "Lost in America," showed that the incidence of urban violence and decay does not track directly with poverty or race, but does correlate with neighborhood stability. In "The Tax on Living," Feola said, "More than half of their [Connecticut residents'] income went to taxes while their elected officials stuffed budgets with billions of dollars in perks, pork, and favors." Feola also supervises an annual analysis of Connecticut's budget and an annual report card on local schools that includes a decade's worth of standardized test scores.

Feola, a member of the National Institute for Advanced Reporting Steering Committee and Investigative Reporters and Editor's CAR Committee, discussed one of his projects using a nine-track tape:

> The most recent nine-track work we did involved the release in late winter of the new "grand" list, a record that shows the owner and value of every building and piece of land in the city. The original record was a 34 meg tape file in a print-file format. We downloaded it onto our Novell network, then pulled it into my desktop with askSam. We tend to like databases that can be used over and over. In this case, askSam gives us an invaluable resource that we search constantly. We can look up the owners of buildings involved in fires, property involved in zone changes—the uses are endless.

> The tape was completely unlabeled. We've even had trouble getting the field names explained. Never take for granted that a field name means what it says. Names—which are usually set up when the database is first created—often bear no resemblance to the actual use of a field. The data were a mess. It took us a while to figure out, for example, that street address searches often turned up erroneous results. When property is sold in a block, all parcels are listed under the first address. We figured this out when we couldn't find a known address that was something like 417—but turned up a half-dozen different properties under the address 403.

> Our nine-track [drive tape reader] has a piece of software we use to mount the tapes and copy them over to the Netware server. We prefer to get it on the server before attacking it. Of course, I've got gigs of space to play with, so I have that luxury. This particular database was designed to be used over and over. We didn't want to spend tons of time parsing it, especially since this is primarily a search database where we sort and look for things, as opposed to a database we'll want to combine with other databases. Therefore, we put it in askSam. We can specify ranges, tell askSam to search, and it outputs answer files. We never leave home without it.

The database has been used for a reference source for many stories: stories on slumlords, problem housing, buildings involved in municipal dealings, etcetera.

In Raleigh, NC, investigative reporter Pat Stith works with databases for the news department of the *News & Observer.* He has helped his newsroom gather more than 100 databases in recent years from various agencies in Wake County and throughout the state of North Carolina. Most of the databases that the newspaper obtaines and uses come to the newsroom on nine-track tape. His experience has been a good teacher, he said.

"When you decide to ask the government for an electronic database, or you're trying to make up your mind, the first thing you should do is ask for a copy of the record layout," Stith (1993) recommended. "Sometimes, after looking at the record layout, you find that the database does not contain the information you want. And you may decide not to get it. After you have the record layout, the agency will not be able to delete fields without your knowledge."

Stith, like other database editors who work with nine-track tapes from public agencies, is concerned about cost. Governments try to overcharge at every opportunity, he says, and his newspaper tries not to pay for data. He is also concerned about quality of the data he obtains. "Agencies are great collectors of information, but poor processors," Stith (1993) stated at a recent IRE CAR conference. "They fail to use data that they've collected even to improve their own operation."

Stith told the audience at his presentation about using vehicle inspection records. The state of North Carolina, like many other states, requires vehicle inspections and the state also keeps records of those inspections. The *News & Observer* asked for the state's database on nine-track tape. "When we analyzed the car inspection records, we found that the failure rate for tires was highest at stations that sold tires. It was highest for mufflers at places that sold mufflers," Stith stated. "We found that some stations failed few vehicles—one had a failure rate of less than five percent. A number of stations failed more than half. One guy failed more than 80 percent. When you see those extremes, you know something is not clean in the milk."

14 Polls and Surveys as Reporting Tools

One of the nation's leading news media polling and survey research units is housed at *The Washington Post*. For several decades, reporters and editors at *The Post* have conducted original polls to take the pulse of U.S. public opinion on national, regional, and local issues. Despite the national leadership reputation that *The Post* enjoys in measuring public opinion with polls, it manages its high-caliber work with only two full-time editors, Richard Morin and Sharon Parker Warden.

Morin was the survey and research editor at *The Miami Herald* for 5 years before moving to Washington in 1987. He is *The Post's* director of polling and also serves as a staff writer and columnist. Warden is the newspaper's senior polling analyst. Instead of maintaining a large in-house staff, the newspaper works with other news organizations to contract out much of the labor involved in survey research. For national polls, such as those involving major political races or social issues, the newspaper has worked for a number of years with ABC News. Morin is responsible for all local and national news polling, including those jointly conducted by his newspaper and ABC News.

Like most news organizations involved in original polling, *The Post* uses telephone interviewing for its information gathering and uses computers for data processing and analysis, Morin (personal communication, January 10, 1994) explained. Morin said that a project director from Chilton Research in Philadelphia is assigned to work exclusively on *Post*-ABC projects.

"About two out of each three projects we initiate and suggest to people in the newsroom," said Morin, who earned a B.A. from the University of Redlands in California and an M.A. from the University of Missouri journalism school. "We have very informal relationships with reporters and editors, so it's just a question of sitting at someone's desk and talking about a number of things and then an idea happens."

Morin and Warden work with editors and reporters—a "collaborative effort," Morin says—to produce the poll questionnaire after the idea is approved. The final questionnaire is then sent to Chilton for field interviewing via one or more of the company's three Pennsylvania telephone centers. After the field interviews are conducted by professionally trained interviewers, Chilton's project director sends a raw data file and a Statistical Package for the Social Sciences (SPSS) control file to *The Post* by modem, ready to be checked and then analyzed on *Post* computers by Morin and Warden.

Part of the basic analysis provided by Chilton is descriptive, simple frequency counts and percentages for each question, Morin said. This may be enough for some reporters and editors, but there is need from time to time for more analysis. Morin explained that *The Post* will usually interview about 1,500 respondents for a national survey. But such efforts, although thorough, are not inexpensive. "Fifteen hundred interviews, say 20 to 22 minutes in length, will cost between $35,000 and $40,000," he said.

There are no individual departmental budgets for surveys, Morin stated. His department has a budget to serve the entire *Post* newsroom. "I think we try to be more responsive to people who come in with ideas, even if it means asking a couple of questions ['piggy-backed' on a particular survey already being planned] that we might not use, that we might have questions about. We try to encourage that sort of through-the-door traffic and often times it works out. But let's face it, a lot of times we get results back and they can be disappointing to the reporters, also."

Morin, unlike some CAR "number crunchers" working at major daily newspapers, writes stories and receives frequent byline credit for his work. A 1980 finalist for the Pulitzer Prize in investigative reporting, he writes a syndicated weekly column about public opinion and polls that appears in the *Washington Post National Weekly*. He also writes a biweekly Sunday column about social science research. Warden is often credited in print for her work as well. Morin explained: "Essentially, I get the data and sit down and write based on the numbers. If I'm working with someone else, that person will be writing specific elements of the story or, more than likely, calling people for reaction. During an election year, I do the inside numbers stuff and political reporters do the outside contacts and reaction."

Morin said he, along with many other editors at the newspaper, is concerned about "horse-race" approaches to polling, and his newspaper actually has killed off projects with that sole purpose. He said he hopes his newspaper's polls will offer deeper meaning and insight into public opinion about candidates or issues.

The *Post* is also endeavoring to conduct more local polls. "That's the one area of the budget which has increased the most since I have been here," Morin said. "The publisher of *The Post* wants us to be a really strong local newspaper, and that has translated, quite frankly for me, into increases come budget request time. I know requests for national polling really have to be justified, but they look very favorably upon requests for local polling."

Morin and Warden said they list projects they want to do each year and then request enough funds for them. "We don't just ask for money and then go think up ways to spend it," Morin said.

News polling has become a major trend-tracking tool for larger newspapers over the past two decades and is gradually moving into use at medium-size daily newspaper newsrooms, as well as some news-oriented magazines. *The Columbus Dispatch* in Ohio, with a daily circulation of 264,000, has been conducting news polls in one form or another since the beginning of the century. It has produced statewide polls since 1970. The effort requires more of a team approach, involving the editors and reporters, but also involving the news library staff for the past decade and a half. "The polling service has, in fact, become a vital library product for the newspaper and the community it serves," stated James Hunter (1993, pp. 346–347), library director. "Polling is a serious business, becoming more so with each election."

There are many similarities in opinion polling and more typical forms of news reporting. Polls are information gathering tools. Polling and journalism have had a symbiotic relationship that has evolved over nearly a century. Ohio State University politicial scientist Herbert Asher argues convincingly that the news media's function in the measurement of public opinion is an essential one in a democracy. "The media's role in public opinion polling is twofold: to inform the public of poll results and to sponsor polls," Asher (1992, p. 77) stated. "[T]he fact that the media make a substantial investment in developing their capacity for public opinion polling may result in a tendency to use that capability even when it is not appropriate to the topic at hand."

News organizations have been measuring and reporting public opinion for most of this century, but mainframe computers forever changed polling methods in the 1950s and 1960s and personal computers have changed the tool once again in the past 10 years. The proliferation of computing tools in newsrooms has given polling a fast-growing popularity as a news-gathering resource in both political and nonpolitical contexts. The PC has changed how news organizations conduct polls in the past decade because the process is easier and more streamlined than ever before. PCs and specially designed software have made polling almost a one-stop effort for journalists of the mid-1990s.

POLLING: THE ORIGINAL CAR TOOL

The oldest form of computer-assisted reporting is survey research. Crude man-on-the-street polls were conducted by a few news organizations even before World War I, but the so-called "modern" era of polling began in the mid 1930s. This was when George Gallup, Sr.—once a professor at the University of Iowa—formed the American Institute of Public Opinion and began conducting polls. It is also when Elmo Roper and Paul Cherington conducted polls for *Fortune* magazine and Archibald Crossley supervised polls for Hearst Newspapers (Cantril, 1991; Meyer, 1979).

"Modern polling made its debut in the 1936 election by predicting FDR's election to a second term," wrote public opinion authority Albert Cantril (1991, p. 5). "In the more than 50 years since, public opinion research has seen three generations of practitioners. It has taken hold in the academic disciplines of political science, psychology, sociology, economics, statistics and even history."

Cantril, like anyone else who has studied polls as news-gathering tools, acknowledges the symbiotic relationship of polling and journalism. Polls, like other types of interviewing, are mass information gathering tools. Polls, politics, and the news media interact with reciprocal effects, Cantril observed. "There is much in the relationship between polling and journalism that benefits both enterprises," he stated (p. 33). "But polling and journalism also play to one another's vulnerabilities."

With increased power from more sophisticated tools such as mainframe computers and telephone systems, surveys and polls became the original and most visible form of computer-assisted reporting. University of North Carolina Professor Philip Meyer popularized use of polls with his ground-breaking books about precision journalism and discussions of some of the polls he was conducting in the late 1960s in Detroit. In the 1960s and 1970s, polling and surveys were tools of only the largest of news organizations, ones that could pay large fees for outside professional polling organizations to conduct the polls at national and regional levels. Few local polls were conducted by newspapers or other news organizations themselves because of the cost or the lack of opinion polling skills.

A TOOL FOR REPORTING COMMUNITY TRENDS

Of all the advanced computer-based reporting tools, polls are the best known. Polls are in increasingly wide use in the mid-1990s, especially in a political context. But it is important to remember that polls have become important as reporting tools in nonpolitical contexts as well. Journalists have used polls as public opinion trend gauges in the political arena for many decades, but the application of polling in other areas is not as well established. Yet, wider use of polls for noncampaign trend stories seems to be on the horizon.

Journalists presently use polls for news in two ways. First, outside sources conduct polls and provide the results to reporters and editors for news stories. Second, reporters design and conduct their own polls about an increasingly wide range of subjects. Reporters and news organizations have conducted their own polls in growing numbers in recent years. This type of advanced reporting can be accomplished in two ways.

On one hand, an enterprising reporter can learn survey research methods to supervise and conduct an original poll that may lead to a news story or series of stories. On the other hand, a reporter can work with an independent commercial polling organization, a local college class or faculty member, or a research institute to originate a poll. The approaches cost money, but probably less than using a commercial enterprise for much or all of the work. Like other computer-assisted reporting tools, polling is not inexpensive. Other CAR approaches require hardware and software, but many do not require much labor. Polling, however, requires the computer tools but is also labor intensive during the interviewing stages. This requires substantial financial support by the news organization.

Polls were once rarely used to measure public opinion about subjects other than politics and the leading political candidates' popularity in a major campaign. But contemporary journalists use polls to assess many different subjects, including social trends and changing lifestyles of residents of their communities and public opinion about major public issues such as abortion, taxes, recreation, capital improvement projects, foreign policy, and gun control. Polls can even be done just for fun to see, for example, what readers think about sports teams, entertainers, pets, vacations, and other less serious matters.

Telephones are the primary polling tools of news media researchers in the mid-1990s. Almost all serious news polls are conducted by telephone (Cantril, 1991). Until the 1980s in many rural and some urban areas of the United States, household saturation by local telephone service was not high enough to justify this approach. Door-to-door contact was the interviewing method of choice because it was more methodologically sound. At that time, there was just too much risk of bias against low-income households that did not have telephone service, researchers believed. However, by the 1990s, most communities have saturation percentages sufficiently high enough to lessen the risk of inherent socioeconomic biases. Furthermore, many polling and survey firms have found it is simply too dangerous for employees to conduct in-person interviews in some urban areas.

Computer-Assisted Telephone Interviewing

Most professional polling organizations and a few do-it-yourself news organizations employ a state-of-the-art polling method commonly known as *computer-assisted telephone interviewing* (CATI). CATI systems integrate telephones and personal computers into either a local area network (LAN) or in a group of stand-alone interviewing stations instead of using telephones with a printed questionnaire, pencil, and answer sheet. The effect of using a CATI system is more efficient field work because the computers form and control the sampling pool, prompt interviewers with the poll "protocol," display the questionnaire, can be programmed to skip specified questions depending on previous replies, code and record responses, and tabulate results (Lavrakas, 1993). These software systems permit professional interviewers to work with headsets and use their PCs for the rest of the work. PCs can be also be programmed to randomly select telephone numbers to dial. CATI software also tabulates the database being built in whatever manner the project director has determined.

"The overall flow and logic of the interview are controlled by a computer program," explained Ohio State University professor Herbert Asher (1992, p. 70). "Among other things, the program makes sure that the questions are asked in the correct sequence and that the responses are consistent with the question(s) being asked. Running totals are easily generated with CATI, so that survey results are available almost instantaneously. CATI systems are becoming more sophisticated, so that investigators can save money by using CATI, particularly as sample size grows larger."

There are variations in CATI systems, of course, but most software will provide telephone number sampling, questionnaire development, data entry, data analysis, and report writing. A number of private companies have begun CATI services for news and other departments of the mass media. Companies such as Chilton, used by *The Washington Post,* will do as much or as little of the project as the newsroom requires. Some universities and colleges have established their own polling organizations that work with the news media from time to time.

Moving Toward In-House News Polls?

The ideal situation for most news organizations, with a CAR desk or some other level of CAR effort, is to develop a program of regular in-house polling. The more control over the polling effort, the better, and in-house units provide the maximum controls. But this sort of enterprise is costly and time consuming, making it out of reach of many medium-size and small news organizations.

Some news organizations are making the move in stages. The transition includes completing different stages of the work in-house. Gradually, more and more steps can be brought into the newsroom. The model typically involves beginning with questionnaire development in-house. A second transitional step brings analysis into the newsroom. The third step involves developing an on-call group of part-time interviewers, planning field work, and supervising the actual field work. A fourth step would be to move to full-time operation of the unit and to include other news research projects, such as readership studies, and other company research, such as market and advertising research.

The decision to bring the polling project completely into the newsroom is not an easy one. There are practical matters. For example, where will interviews be done? Can interviews be completed in the evenings without interfering with the normal flow of activity in the newsroom? Is it cost-effective? To answer these questions, each news organization has to try a project itself to determine what works best, but a gradual transition may be the least traumatic way of building a home-grown polling unit.

STAGES OF THE POLLING PROCESS

Even if a news organization with a CAR program cannot conduct its own polls, the need to understand the procedures and approaches to polling is necessary for almost all reporters. The act of judging the newsworthiness of a poll conducted by an outside organization is a fundamental one for political reporters, editors, and CAR desk staffers. It is helpful for any reporter to have a working knowledge of the polling process. The following sections briefly describe the basic stages for conducting an in-house computer-assisted, telephone-based poll.

Choosing the Poll Topic

Some beginners, given the responsibility of overseeing a poll project, decide to do the poll before they even know the focus of the project. But the "Hey, let's do some kind of a poll" approach is not the way to do serious newsroom reporting and research. Social scientists first decide there is a problem to investigate, then choose the proper method for finding answers or solving the problem. This rule applies to newsroom polls, too. It is logical. A decision must be made about the nature of the project before any decisions about the method can be discussed. If the problem involves evaluating the opinion trends of voters, residents, or other groups in a community, then a poll may be the appropriate approach. But a focus group may also get the job done. Reporting about and analysis of some issues are not always best handled by a poll.

There are seemingly countless social issues that lend themselves to public opinion measurement. Political activity involving leadership, such as a key regional or local election, remains the standard application of news polls. But other political concerns, such as controversial issues and long-term policymaking, are also appropriate for news polling. Gambling, abortion, international affairs, major trials, and public health care programs, each a hot topic in the 1990s, have been examples of subjects ripe for public opinion measurement.

For maximum newsworthiness, poll topics must be timely for a news organization. There needs to be an awareness level on the part of the community, also. Some of the best topics are ones that involve local controversy and opposing positions.

Creating Focus With Research Questions

Social scientists typically develop research hypotheses or general research questions as ways to give their research focus for an academic survey. In the applied world of news polling, hypotheses and research questions are not so important, although their value in offering direction, focus, and organization remain significant to the overall opinion measurement process. Often this step is skipped in the newsroom because it does no damage to the credibility of the poll, but research questions do help to formalize project goals. Researchers in the academy often use an outline, a list of priorities, a written statement of purpose, a list of research questions, or a few testable hypotheses to determine the scope of the actual questions asked and types of responses to be gathered. In taking this step, ask: What is the point of the poll? What opinions are being measured? What issues or events are most important? What do I need to know about the respondents? What findings are expected? These are the framework for developing research questions or hypotheses for a poll.

Formulating the Overall Design

Once the subject and the focus of the study have been determined, the project must be designed. This means the individual or individuals supervising the project must plan its execution. These steps include:

- Determine whether this will be a "one-shot cross-sectional" study or whether it will require several a panel design of several measurement points (meaning several different polls over time).
- Design the questioning: Make general decisions about the topical focus of the poll.
- Decide when the study will be conducted.
- Plan study logistics such as where and how interviewing will be done.
- Establish a budget and confirm financial support for the study with an editor.

These are the more practical aspects of the project. These take on added importance if the poll is conducted in-house. Each decision, it should be noted, impacts on others in the complete process, so the decision and its effects should be weighed carefully and discussed with others involved in the project.

Determining the Sample Design

Polls rarely include every member of a population. Thus it is important to select a subdivision, or sample, from the population. Thus, *sample design* is still another important step in the polling process. It is essential, if a poll is to be considered "scientific" in its method, for each member of a defined population to have an equal chance of being selected in a sample. The requirement exists because of assumptions made in estimating sampling error and for other statistical reasons. There are numerous ways to select samples within this "equal chance" rule. The different ways a sample can be taken from a population are called sampling designs.

Probability sampling design is the preferred means of drawing a sample because it enables the user to avoid certain design biases in nonprobability sampling. The designs discussed in this section are examples of probability sample design. Probability samples are based on certain randomness assumptions, not the least important being equal chance of selection. This principle requires all members, or elements, of the population to have the same chance of being selected for the sample, regardless of whether selection was or was not made.

Most polls use a form of *simple random sampling* to select respondents from the defined population. The most common variations of random sampling that involve telephones are known as *random digit dialing* (RDD). In its most primitive form, RDD simply involves random generation of the final four numbers for a particular area code and telephone number prefix or exchange. Usually, the random generation of the final four numbers can be done either by using a table of random numbers or using a simple computer program. However, randomness is never perfect. RDD cannot reach individuals without telephone service, for example.

RDD computer programs can be written in an easy-to-learn language such as BASIC to generate the last four numbers and print them out—even with the predetermined area code and prefix or exchange (Frey, 1989; Lavrakas, 1993). Professor Paul Lavrakas offers an elaborate four-step program for use within the Statistical Package for the Social Sciences (SPSS) for generating RDD sample pools in his book about telephone survey research methods. For those seeking even easier solutions, Professor Philip Meyer (1991, p. 108) provides an elegantly simple BASIC program to generate 99 four-digit random numbers that can be matched with prefixes for RDD. It can be modified to produce any number of random sets by replacing the 99 in line 10 with the desired number of sets. This is Meyer's program:

```
10 FOR I = 1 to 99
20 PRINT INT(RND*10000)
30 NEXT
```

There are numerous methodological reasons to use RDD. The main advantage to RDD is that it reaches unlisted, unpublished, and newly assigned numbers (Frey, 1989). Disadvantages include the prospect of reaching unassigned, nonworking numbers in addition to working numbers serving businesses, computers, car phones, answering systems, and fax machines. Because of this problem, the completion rate is often lower than other designs. There may be ways to reduce the number of bad contacts, if, for example, the local telephone company lists the entire exchanges or number series typically assigned for exclusive use by mobile phones or other specialized purposes. The more a poll director can learn about the telephone systems being used, the more effective RDD can be. But telephone companies are both difficult and inconsistent with regard to revealing information about assigned numbers and patterns of number assignment, although it is likely that some information, such as public prefixes or exchanges, can be found out easily.

There are other less commonly used forms of random sampling in telephone news polling. These include stratified sampling, interval (or systematic) sampling, and multi-stage (or cluster sampling):

- *Stratified sampling* can reduce variation in the sample by randomly selecting respondents based on known characteristics of the population. For example, if it is known that the population consists of certain percentages of gender or age groupings, then respondents can be randomly selected from membership in the defined subgroups, or strata. If a news organization seeks to compare certain groups within a region, such as Blacks and Whites, it must stratify with equal size samples of each group. Generally, though, if a population is large enough and the sample design is well executed, the stratification approach will not be necessary because a simple random sample design will provide large enough samples for each stratum.
- *Interval sampling* or *systematic sampling* is based on availability of a list of all elements or members of the population. Unfortunately, finding or obtaining such a list for the general population is often impossible. They rarely exist for public use or carry very high price tags. Telephone directories can work, but only if the proportion of unlisted and unpublished numbers is tolerable. Some researchers use telephone directories but adjust numbers using a "one-digit up" or "one digit down" procedure to reach unlisted numbers. This means simply increasing or decreasing the last digit of a number selected in a telephone directory. Another example of such a list is a *directory* of members of an organization. If the group contains 30,000 members, such as the full-time enrollment at a major university, an interval is set to draw a subset of that group. For a sample of 1,000 persons, every 30th person on the roster will be selected after a random starting point is determined.
- *Multistage sampling* or *cluster sampling* involves selecting respondents from a population in several stages. It is possibly the most complex sampling design, but it also reduces "misses" in sampling. For example, this design is often used in national polls. Although the stages vary, depending on the designer, the first level could involve selection of a specified number of counties from a list of all counties in all states. The

next stage involves selecting certain zip codes (or census block areas or some other subdivision) within the specified counties. The third stage involves selecting a group of households within the selected zip code. The fourth, and final, stage selects a respondent from within a given household because there is usually more than one person per household. Thus, multistaging or clustering selects a small group of respondents from the same area, such as a neighborhood. It is economical, particularly for in-person or door-to-door polling, but the procedure also works with telephone polls.

Determining the Sample Size

Sample size is another sampling decision to be made. Most national polls draw samples resulting in about 1,500 *completed interviews*. Keep in mind that to get 1,500 completed interviews, the original sample that was drawn must be larger. There will be refusals, unsuccessful callbacks, nonworking numbers, and incomplete and unusable interviews. Using a conservative refusal factor of about one third, a sample of 1,500 completed interviews would require about 2,250 selected telephone numbers. Similarly, a desired set of 400 completed interviews would require an original sample of about 600 telephone numbers. Some local and regional polls use 1,500 completed interviews as the target *n* size, because it produces a more accurate margin of error of plus or minus 2.5%. The minimally acceptable number of completed interviews for a scientific poll is around 370, because this provides an error range of plus or minus 5%. Polls with fewer than 370 completed interviews carry larger error and are not usually considered suitable by professionals. The difference in cost for completing 400 interviews and 1,500 interviews is considerable, so the price of accuracy is a very practical matter.

Sampling error, also called margin of error, is another important factor related to both sample design and sample size. Because a sample is only part of the population, there is always going to be some sort of error resulting from the difference in the true population value and the sample value. Statisticians have determined how to estimate this error. In probability sample-based polling, error is tied to sample size. Generally, the larger the sample, the lower the error. But the curve that results when error rate is plotted against sample size begins to level off at a point around 750 to 1,500 interviews, making it less cost-effective to do more interviews in the interest of reducing error for accuracy.

Most polling organizations seek margin of error ranges from +/– 2.5% to +/– 5.0%. Error can be easily calculated using a formula with a pocket-size calculator with a square root key:

- Enter 0.25.
- Divide by the number of persons in the sample (*n* size).

- Press the square root key without clearing the value.
- Multiply the resulting value by 1.96.
- Optional step for a percentage format: Multiply final total by 100.

The value that is displayed is the estimate of the margin of error. For an $n = 500$, for example, the value would be 0.043826932359, or, if the percentage step was taken and the number rounded off, +/– 4.4%. The margin of error is a range of values. If it is *plus or minus* 4.4%, then a particular candidate's support measured at 45.5% in a poll would actually range from 41.1% to 49.9%.

Some news organizations develop and draw their own sample designs and others use consultants for that task. Often this decision is determined by the size of the budget for the project because some of these companies can be quite expensive for the quality and range of services rendered.

Designing the Questionnaire

Another important step is creation of the interview questionnaire. The act of designing and developing the data collection instrument, often called a *protocol* because it serves as a "script" for telephone interviewers, requires several steps of its own:

- Decide what to ask by drafting questions and possible response sets. Decide whether open-ended or closed-ended questions are better suited for the subject. Remember that open-ended items are more difficult to code and analyze.
- Place the list of questions and response alternatives into a script format by developing the questionnaire's format (or overall design). Add the introduction and other instructions for interviewers.
- Pretest the first draft of the completed questionnaire with one to two dozen persons similar to those in the population to determine whether the questions are clear and measure what they are supposed to measure and whether anything has been omitted.
- Train interviewers on interviewing skills.
- Brief and orient interviewers about the questionnaire.

There are software packages designed for telephone surveys that include the questionnaire development stage. CATI systems include questionnaire development modules.

A example of a telephone survey questionnaire, developed for a national study of journalism ethics and privacy issues that was conducted at the University of Miami, is contained in Appendix D. This questionnaire was designed for use in hard-copy form with separate answer sheets used by interviewers to record responses. Because the respondents were senior-level newsroom managers, there was no RDD involved. Instead, numbers were selected from a directory and newspapers were chosen using an interval sampling procedure. A CATI system, although desired, was not available and was not used.

Field Interviewing and Data Collection

The era of the door-to-door interviewer is long gone, mostly because of the amount of time required, the high labor cost, and potential danger to urban interviewers. Because it has been established that responses to questions and sampling of populations by telephone are as valid and reliable as in-person interviewing, most polling organizations have switched to telephone-based polling. Telephones also offer greater speed in interviewing and control over interviews. This, of course, is a major factor, if not the only one, for journalists.

Because journalists usually do not want to recruit and train interviewers, some news organizations turn over the interviewing stage to commercial firms that specialize in field polling services. Like the cost of sample design consulting services, commercial interviewing consultants can also be quite costly. The services include RDD sample designs, targeted sampling, and business and industry sampling and may be worth the cost, if a news organization can afford it. The American Association for Public Opinion Research's (1994) *The Blue Book, 1994 / 1995* lists several hundred agencies and organizations in 31 states and 34 nations engaged in public opinion research, market research, or other types of social research.

No matter who does the interviewing, quality field interviews are critical to the success of a poll. They must be done in a professional and thorough manner. To achieve this, interviewers must be experienced and, if they are not, they must be trained and oriented to the work to be done. Interviewer training should include rehearsing the process. The key is consistency. Each interview should be conducted as much like the others as possible. "Unless one has participated in a public opinion survey, it is difficult to appreciate the critical role that the interviewer plays in measuring public opinion," wrote Herbert Asher (1992, p. 67). "[A]s someone who agrees to be a respondent . . . I have been surprised by the obvious disparities in the training and competence of the interviewers."

Control and supervision of interviewing are part of the field interviewing stage. Interviewers must first be familiarized with the poll, its purpose, instructions, and the content of the questionnaire or protocol, including anticipated responses. If computers or other automated polling systems are involved, interviewers must be trained in the proper use of the CATI system. Inexperienced interviewers must also be trained in the art of survey interviewing as well. It is often best to provide a list of contingencies, for unexpected situations, for interviewers to use during an interview.

When the interviewing is underway, there is need to supervise and troubleshoot because problems may arise. It is preferred that as little time be spent in the field as possible to reduce the chance of intervening events influencing the outcome. As interviewing is completed, the poll director or assistants need to begin verifying interviewing, or spot checking, interviews for accuracy and completeness. This is done through call-back procedures in most cases, but it is not necessary for all completed calls; only a selected random number from each interviewer as needed to establish confidence in the accuracy of the work.

There are still other concerns in the interviewing process. Records should be kept that indicate the amount of respondent refusals to be interviewed as well as other nonresponses (e.g., nonworking telephone numbers). Refusals can account for as much as one fifth to one third of all contacts, and refusal rates have been slowly increasing for the past four decades (Cantril, 1991). Response rates can be computed in different ways, depending on what type of response is being measured, but, most important, the response rate records help determine whether problems—such as patterns of systematic bias or larger than usual proportions of incomplete interviews—exist in the set of respondents not participating.

Coding and Processing Poll Data

Once interviewing is satisfactorily completed, data processing begins. The sole purpose is *data reduction,* the act of reducing thousands of answers into understandable data to obtain useful information for a news story. The first step is to code the questionnaire responses for computer keypunching or edit the data for optical scanning. After codes are assigned to the responses, the data are keypunched. If a CATI system was used, these steps have been effectively bypassed because they were combined into the interviewing process.

Following data entry, the poll director and assistants must check the resulting data matrix for errors. Response patterns must be checked for range and accuracy errors and for missing data. Problems in the data matrix should be checked against the original answer sheets or questionnaires and resolved.

Analyzing Poll Data

A clean database is ready for analysis. A statistical program should be used, but less powerful programs such as spreadsheets and relational databases can also do a minimal statistical job. The best software for the job depends on the degree of sophistication needed for analysis. For purely univariate analyses, or if there is no budget to acquire the statistical software, spreadsheets can be used to calculate basic descriptive statistics such as the mean, mode, median, range, variance, and standard deviation. For more advanced work, such as bivariate cross-tabulation or correlation, other programs are better suited and perhaps even easier to use. But for journalists with limited resources, the job can be done with spreadsheets or other database packages. After all, most poll data matrices are nothing more than flatfile data tables.

Common analysis procedures used for news media polls include descriptive statistics and frequency counts computed on individual variables, crosstabulations computed on two different but related variables, and correlational analyses computed on two associated variables. Advanced procedures include multivariate approaches such as regression analysis. Software packages, such as the Statistical Package for the Social Sciences (SPSS) and the Statistical Analysis System (SAS), are popular among many newspaper poll directors. A 1993 University of Miami journalism ethics study, used as an example of questionnaire development in an earlier section of this chapter, was analyzed using a recent DOS version of SPSS. Appendix E shows how the processing job was set up. The file in Appendix E includes the variables identifications, data formatting instructions, variable labels, the 283-variable data matrix, and analysis commands.

A sample set of processed output is shown in Appendix F. This output is the initial analysis of the data from the ethics study questionnaire and SPSS job discussed already. There are dozens of options for such an analysis, but the initial run in the appendix is typical of the first-level review needed of a dataset. The output provides the datalist, variable recode instructions, summary listing of variable labels, summary listing of value labels for each variable, frequency counts, histograms, and descriptive statistics.

Interpreting Poll Results

One of the toughest jobs for reporters and editors directing a poll is to interpret the results. Interpretation is derivation of meaning from the numbers. Once analysis is completed, the difficult job of making sense out of the findings occurs. This can take place at two levels.

- *Newsroom experts.* First, the poll director will have educated ideas. So will the beat reporters who have an interest in the subject of the poll. Editors responsible for the project will offer perspectives, also.
- *Outside experts.* Specialists from outside the newsroom can also be helpful. These sources are often consultants, professors, activists, organizational leaders, and nonteaching social scientists at research institutes.

Interpretation requires looking at findings individually and collectively. Individual interpretation considers an item alone. Collective interpretation looks at an item (e.g., a question or variable) in relation to one or more other variables on the questionnaire. Part of collective interpretation is using one variable to help explain another. For example, in interpreting support for a candidate in a campaign poll, use of certain demographic variables such as party affiliation or income will assist in understanding the patterns of support or nonsupport. Interpretation also means reviewing findings in comparison and contrast to earlier similar projects, if they are available.

Reporting Poll Results as a News Story or Series

The main point of conducting a news poll is to produce a story or a series of stories. Most news organizations collect so much information in their polls that they can generate a lengthy series of stories from the single project. Some editors choose to publish the findings in a series over a few days or weeks, depending on the nature and timeliness of the new information.

Writing the story can be an act filled with uncertain steps. To avoid being tripped up, Associated Press advises its editors and reporters to pay "close attention" to four particular areas when writing (Goldstein, 1994):

- Do not exaggerate the poll results.
- Comparisons with other polls are often newsworthy, but be careful when comparing polls from different organizations because different techniques can cause different results.
- Sampling error is not the only means of error in poll findings—watch out for problems with question wording, interviewer quality, and computer analysis.
- Polls do not say a candidate will win an election. Polls can be wrong and people do change their minds.

Most news organizations publish the results of a major poll project in a package. The elements of the package include the major story itself. They also include a sidebar or two focusing on one or two particular elements of the main story. Informational graphics, such as bar graphs, pie charts, or an illustrated table containing the most important questions and the complete results for those items, are included to illustrate the major findings. Finally, some publications also include a short separate story focusing on the technical or "how-to" information about the poll's methodology. Part of the poll planning process also includes budgeting for additional news hole, if it is needed. This way editors and managers of other departments of the newspaper are not caught by surprise and be unable to provide the needed space or other publication resources.

A poll conducted by another organization will probably not get such royal treatment by most publications. Typically, these polls generate news coverage consisting of a single-story approach or even become part of a news roundup. Some publications will produce an informational graphic or use an existing one from a news service if space permits. And, if the news hole is tight, methodological details are integrated into the main story or used as a "footnote" within the graphic.

PROBLEMS WITH NONSCIENTIFIC POLLS

Polls and surveys are the primary reporting means for measuring public opinion of large groups of people. News-oriented polling has become synonymous with precision journalism. Magazines and newspapers originated use of polls as reporting tools more than a half century ago, and broadcast news organizations also use polling frequently. Many news organizations at the national and regional levels, both print and broadcast, have joined resources to do original opinion polls, in fact.

Two major areas of concern to journalists conducting their own polls, and especially those using polls from external sources, are reliability and validity of the opinion measures used. *Reliability* refers to the consistency of the opinion measures, and *validity* refers to the appropriateness of the measures used. Does the poll measure what it purports to measure? Measurement can be reliable, but not valid.

A growing number of news organizations are conducting their own polls and an even larger number are running the results of polls conducted by other news organizations, nonnews organizations, and special interest groups. Combine this with the ease in conducting polls through advances in telephone and computer technology already discussed: There has been an unfortunate proliferation of poorly designed and nonscientific polls in recent years. Despite advancements in the past two decades, surprisingly few editors and reporters are aware of the proper procedures to conduct a poll and often overlook serious methodological problems with polls that others have conducted.

Some local television stations, newspapers, and magazines, for example, routinely broadcast and publish stories based on nonscientific call-in polls "for fun," but they treat the results with more than a casual manner. Even with a disclaimer that the poll "is not scientific," the poll results go on the air or into a publication. The fact that the results have been broadcast or published gives them legitimacy in the minds of audience members who do not note methodological concerns but think only about the findings. Too often, readers or audiences cannot distinguish between a serious scientific poll and a less-than-serious one because the news organization's editors and reporters cannot make the distinction either. Therefore, nonscientific polls can be extremely troubling. They cheapen the value of legitimate polls.

Journalists must be concerned about how polls are published or broadcast, how the results are reported, and how the research itself is conducted. Several red-flag areas in polling exist. Among them are "horse race" style results reporting, exit polling, instant polling, and "900" number polling:

Horse Race Poll Reporting

A poll or survey is a snapshot of public opinion taken at the time the field interviewing occurs. Too often, however, reporters misuse the predictive power of polls and surveys to forecast the outcome of an election. Often, public opinion on an issue is too volatile for predicting the outcome of voting. This creates a horse race atmosphere for the news that emerges from the results of a poll. Numerous critics have argued that this sort of journalism is creating news instead of reporting it. Journalists respond that "who's ahead" is newsworthy (Cantril, 1991). Some observers also believe reporting results can have either bandwagon or underdog effects, depending on whether readers support the leader or the nonleading candidates.

Exit Polls as News Reporting Tools

In the past two decades, some news organizations have begun to conduct exit polls. Exit polls interview respondents at the polling location after voters have voted on election day. The purpose of these polls is to find out the winner of an election before the final results are announced, to get the story before the competition does. Because of the nature of exit polling, it is popular with radio and television news organizations. Because exit polls are reported on the day of the election, it makes little sense for newspapers or magazines to use them because election returns themselves are counted and reported to the public within hours of poll closings in most parts of the nation. If they are done well, exit polls can be useful tools. But often these polls are troublesome because of flaws in sampling designs.

Radio and television networks are frequent users of exit polls. These are methodologically similar to other types of polls in most ways, but involve in-person interviewing at the voting precinct location. Precincts are randomly selected to represent the entire voting district. Morning and early afternoon interviews are completed using interval selection techniques. Respondents are asked to complete a short mock ballot and deposit into a box. Fast reporting to the election reporting center, such as a newsroom, and rapid tabulation enable broadcasters to predict or "call" the outcome of an election immediately after polls close (although they could do so sooner, if they so wished).

The biggest advantage to exit polling is that it enables journalists to study the "why" angle to election results more quickly and more accurately. Exit polls typically not only ask about voting decisions, but also gather certain voter demographic information such as party affiliation, age, gender, occupation, income level, and education level. Combining these variables enables journalists to understand the outcome of a vote more quickly than casually studying precinct-by-precinct voting patterns and matching them up with precinct population characteristics a day or two after an election.

Because of the sizes of the United States and Canada and their time zones, some critics feel exit polls have an undue influence on voting turnout and voting decisions themselves in western regions (Cantril, 1991). Another problem is connected to the high refusal rate in exit polling. Many people simply refuse to participate; at least one third according to some estimates (Meyer, 1991). There are administration and control problems, too. There are inconsistencies in the interviewing process involving time of day and individuals selected because there are few real controls because the work is done entirely in the field. The better trained and more experienced the interviewers, the less of this type of trouble, of course.

Problems With "Instant" Polls

With improved computing technology combining with almost complete telephone service saturation of households, some news organizations have begun to develop same-day and overnight measurement of public opinion. Often, use of this tool occurs after major news events and is used as sidebar coverage. When a presidential campaign debate takes place, or a major appointment is made, some news organizations plan and execute a poll to measure public reaction to the event immediately after it ends. On some occasions in recent years, network news broadcasters have reported results the same evening that an event occurred or major newspapers have published results of polls the next morning. Technological advances permit these immediate measures of public opinion, a phenomenon of unparalleled concern in the history of polling.

Some public opinion experts question the value of such instant polls. Concerns arise about methodological soundness and whether the public is truly being served by such journalism. Furthermore, opinions and attitudes take time to form. Asking a person how he or she feels about something right after it has happened may or may not garner the same reply that a poll a day or two later would obtain. Sampling problems also exist because call-back time is reduced or nonexistent. "[Q]uick measures are notoriously perishable," wrote public opinion and polling authority

Albert Cantril (1991, p. 47) in discussing the documented rapid changes of opinion that occur after major events. At best, some experts have stated, such rapid assessments of opinion can be dangerously misleading.

Problems With "900" Call-In Polls

Another problem that has crept into news polling in recent years is the growth of "900" number call-in polls (Rosenkrantz, 1991). These are methodological nightmares and should not be used for any news stories, even with a caveat that the poll is "non-scientific." This type of poll damages the credibility of all legitimate scientific polls.

The reason these polls are completely unscientific and misleading lies in flaws in their sampling design. The "900" number requires the participant to pay for the call. As a result, the polls are anchored in self-selection and economic bias. Furthermore, they typically take place in a short time span such as a few hours. Respondents decide whether to participate, whether to pay the cost of the call, and even how often to call because there are no limits to the number of "votes." As a result, the findings are not representative of the population represented by the sample. Biases frequently appear in the results. There are numerous documented cases in which well-funded special interest groups have flooded call-in polls with "votes" to sway the outcome in the desired direction.

Furthermore, "900" number polls may give the news organization a public relations black eye. They often make the news organization appear greedy, because these numbers require the caller to pay a fee of a few cents to several dollars per call. These types of call-in polls do not constitute legitimate polling methods and are not reliable as advanced reporting tools. Thus, they should not be used by any serious news organization.

MANAGING AND SHARING THE COSTS

News organizations on limited budgets that wish to conduct scientific news polls should try to work with other news organizations to share costs. At the community level, it is becoming commonplace for a local television news station to collaborate with a local newspaper to produce a poll and split costs. Or a regional poll can be cosponsored by noncompeting newspapers or television stations. Often, news organizations within the same corporation combine for poll sponsorship. This pattern has been well established at the national level for many years.

Another way to save money is to join forces with a local college group. If the reporter or editor directing the poll can find a professor in mass communication, journalism, political science, sociology, or business, for instance, who wants to use the poll as a class exercise or for research purposes, labor costs for all groups involved may be reduced or eliminated. Other expenses, such as keypunching or mainframe computer time, may also be saved. To save on costs, try these ideas:

- Involve college classes, preferably at the graduate level, to help with interviewing and even data processing and analysis. This way, labor costs may be reduced or eliminated.
- Design samples and questionnaires in-house.
- Use news organization telephones, such as those in the advertising or circulation departments, in the evenings when they are not needed for regular business.
- Learn to analyze data in-house.

METHOD DISCLOSURE IN NEWS STORIES

There will be times when reporters and editors must judge the quality of a poll or survey as part of a news story. Even though the poll may have been conducted by someone outside the news operation, its news value must be judged on two levels. Much of the news value decision, of course, is based on the findings of the poll. What do the findings say? But another significant part of judging the poll's news value is the quality of the poll itself. How was the poll conducted? Was it scientific? Nonscientific? The *Associated Press Stylebook and Libel Manual* (Goldstein, 1994) lists eight key questions to ask about a poll's methodology. Somewhere in the story, perhaps in a box accompanying the story, the information should be included. Answers to these questions will not only satisfy the journalist's need to judge the poll's quality, but they will help readers to do the same. These are AP's 1994 guidelines:

1. *Who conducted the poll?* This is the actual group that did the interviewing and other field work. But this does not necessarily mean the same people who paid for the project.
2. *How many people were interviewed? How were they selected?* AP cautions that only polls based on random samples are reliable. Be particularly suspect of polls using sampling procedures that involve self-selection by participants.
3. *Who was interviewed?* Describe both the sample and the population.
4. *How was the poll conducted—by telephone or in people's homes?* Method is very important because there are many ways to conduct interviews for a poll—some more reliable and valid than others. AP recommends that reporters should avoid polls conducted on street corners, malls, or by mail because they involve self-selection much of the time and are not random.

5. *When was the poll taken?* Opinion changes quickly and may be influenced by intervening events.

6. *Who paid for the poll?* Be careful with polls presented by sponsoring organizations that offer findings supporting their position on a controversial issue or support their candidate for office. This is the reason many interest groups arrange their poll work with credible polling firms.

7. *What are the sampling error margins for the poll and for any subgroups mentioned in the story?* Journalists can obtain this information from the sponsor or the organization that actually conducted the poll. Sampling error gives the possible range of the percentages of each answer to each question. There may be a problem if the error is higher than plus or minus 5 percentage points.

8. *What questions were asked and in what order?* Question wording can make a difference in the response, as all journalists know, so it is important to ask sponsors for a copy of the entire questionnaire, and, if this is not possible, copies of specific key questions, to determine question quality.

The American Association for Public Opinion Research (AAPOR) is one of the leaders in setting standards for disclosure of polls. Despite the efforts of AAPOR and other organizations, there are still numerous incomplete disclosures on a regular basis (Salwen, 1985). There has been some improvement in the late 1980s and early 1990s, but studies still show the inadequacies of how journalists report methodological issues involving polls and surveys. "[T]he level of reporting on methodology by the media remains lower than what some methodologists would like to see," wrote AAPOR's Jack Elinson (1992, p. 113). "For example, the media rarely report response rates."

The National Council on Public Polls (NCPP), another organization concerned about methodological disclosure in the news media, feels there are at least eight minimal elements of disclosure. These elements are sponsorship, interview dates, interviewing method, population description, sample size, subsample descriptions and sizes, relevant questions wording, and percentages on which conclusions are based (Cantril, 1991). NCPP has published a 12-page booklet, written by Sheldon Gawiser and G. Evans Witt (n.d.), cofounders of the Associated Press/NBC News Poll, that goes much farther than the eight minimal method elements of disclosure. It lists 20 questions journalists should ask about poll results. Single and bulk copies of the brochure can be purchased by contacting NCPP at (212) 986-8262.

V Computing Goals
for the Newsroom

15 Creating the Computer-Literate Journalist

This bytes. Terminal illness. Key-bored.

These are typical expressions of frustration sometimes found tacked onto newsroom bulletin boards or taped by reluctant users to their desktop personal computer monitors. The individuals posting these modern-day criticisms of computer-based journalism might be highly computer-literate newsroom staffers having a laugh at themselves or they could be more serious-minded and well-meaning journalists making calls for help in a changing world of cyber-communication.

Some journalists, like many other adults, simply dislike using computers. But others are afraid of them. Some experts have labeled the fear of computers and other forms of modern mass communication a "technophobia" (Donoho, 1994). Although this may seem amusing to those converted individuals in the newsroom, technophobia can be a time-consuming problem. There is no doubt that just about every newsroom has one or more technophobes wandering about, trying hard to get their assigned work completed with the least possible interaction with a computer, an online research service, E-mail, a fax machine, their voice mail, a VCR, or any other office or home electronic devices or services. A 1993 Dell Computers study found one third of adults interviewed were intimidated by computers and were afraid they could harm a computer system if they did the wrong thing when using it. Another national study found that more than one third of adults questioned who had PCs in their offices believed their computer skills to be inadequate (Donoho, 1994). The numbers in newsrooms may not be as high, but the levels of computer skills of many journalists remain not much higher than writing and editing with a word processor and keyboard or creating artwork with a graphics program and a mouse. Figure 15.1 displays the extent of technophobia among adults in the United States in 1994.

John E. Mollwitz (personal communication, May 8, 1994), senior national editor at *The Milwaukee Journal,* describes how frustrating life can be for both computer-literate and computer-illiterate newsroom personnel. "Just this week I received a pleading call from a staffer who

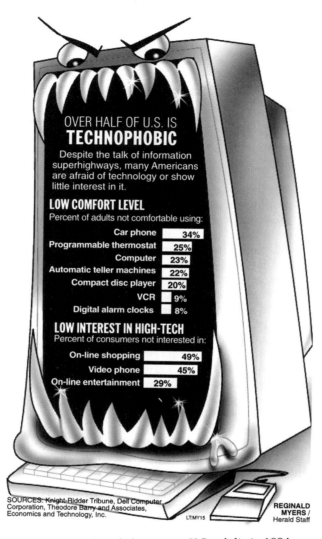

FIG. 15.1. Technophobia among U.S. adults in 1994.

couldn't get a story into the newsroom computer from home. Would I help? Of course," he recalled. "The problem: There was no cord connecting the modem to the telephone jack. 'But, you told me all I needed was a modem and communications software,' the co-worker protested. Laugh, yes, but not too hard. This type of problem is quite common. It need not be if we properly train not only our staffs, but ourselves."

Society and its work tools are changing. Journalists must change their habits as new tools are developed. "You can't walk into the newsroom of even the smallest operation and not find some sort of personal computer. How well it is used depends very much on the skills of the user. Even a small operation can use it to keep track of voting records of a municipal council," says Mollwitz (personal communication, May 8, 1994), a member of the Society of Professional Journalists' national committee on technology:

> My experience is that computer skills, as well as computer acceptance, are much greater on small operations, both print and broadcast. The bigger the operation, the more likely there will be someone in-house to install a modem and software, do online research, set up databases, sort out information and a myriad of other tasks. There is little incentive to learn anything about computers until a light bulb explodes and some says: "I'm 40, and I don't even know what a byte is. Somehow I'm going to have to learn this stuff." Meanwhile, the 40-year-old on a small weekly already knows.

Eric Schoch, a medical reporter for the *Indianapolis Star,* believes computer literacy is not a major matter in the mid-1990s, but it will gradually become more important. "On a day-to-day basis, many reporters still are getting along just fine without much personal computer literacy. Over time, it will get much harder to function effectively as a reporter (and editor) without a basic understanding of computerized and online information," Schoch (personal communication, May 11, 1994) stated. "For now, it's enough to understand the potential and have someone else do the database crunching for you—in five years, say, your average reporter will need to know how to do it herself."

The digital revolution is well underway (Johnson, 1993). For the journalists who have not yet discovered the personal computer as a reporting and information gathering tool, it is probably not a matter of technophobia. It is more likely a matter of not being given the chance to learn about their computers. Their newsrooms have not yet made the transition to PC-based systems or they have PCs but their newsrooms have not added software tools beyond word processing. These journalists are, in essence, technologically frozen by their companies.

There are other journalists, in newsroom situations where they could try new computer-assisted reporting approaches offered through their PCs, who just have not been aware of them or sufficiently motivated to learn. Some newsroom staffers have just been too busy with other editorial responsibilities to learn how to get a little bit more from their computing systems each day. They can learn, they want to learn, and they will learn . . . eventually.

DEVELOPING TECHNOLOGICALLY ADVANCED
NEWSROOMS

In the mid-1990s, news organizations fall into three distinct technology categories. Some news organizations are *technologically advanced.* Other news organizations are *somewhat advanced.* And some are *not technologically advanced.* Raleigh's *News & Observer,* Waterbury's *Republican-American,* and a handful of other news organizations discussed throughout this book are examples of *technologically advanced newsrooms,* or TANs. These news organizations have embraced personal computing for all it is worth and, as a result, have enhanced their community news coverage with the PC's retrieval and analytical power.

Most other news organizations, at least those aware of what could be called the recomputerization of newsrooms (the original effort occurred with mainframe front-end editorial systems in the 1970s), are hustling to catch up. A few other news organizations have choosen to ignore it all and are operating on their own technological terms.

Some businesses, particularly the very large ones, are slow to make changes in computing software and hardware. This is particularly true in the corporate world. Problems often arise from information systems administrative policies and priorities. The same can be true of news-oriented companies, regardless of their size. Houston computer consultant Cheryl Currid (1994) recommended several options for individuals in work environments that are technologically out of date or insufficient for current needs:

- Try to make peace with the information systems people.
- Spread the word around the company to make management aware of the need.
- Petition for "self-rule"—that is, not all users are the same and some company-wide computer policies are not always appropriate.
- Establish peer-level training.
- Offer your own time and talent to researching new tools, preparation of proposals, testing equipment, purchasing, and even set-up.
- When all else fails, bring in personally owned computer and software (this, Currid says, may embarrass management into doing something positive).

Technologically advanced newsrooms are not places loaded with pricey television sets with cable hook-ups, VCRs, fax machines, voice mail, satellite dishes, or other high-tech office tools. It would be a safe bet, though, that news organizations with TANs probably have, and use, those devices in addition to their personal computer system.

Instead, TANs are newsrooms that have moved beyond simple use of personal computers for word processing and typesetting. TANS have achieved a greater realization of the retrieval and analytical power of personal computing. The movement has begun, but not many newspapers and news magazines in the United States have achieved technologically advanced newsrooms. Very few television and radio stations have them in place, either. Without question, the 1994 University of Miami national CAR study establishes this fact. The changes have begun to occur, especially at larger newspapers, the wire services, a few news magazines, and at some levels at the networks, but the transition will probably require the rest of this decade to completely catch on, perhaps even longer. In essence, TAN simply reflects a state of operation and a state of mind about the practicality of computing as part of the information gathering and processing effort.

The Indianapolis Star's Eric Schoch (personal communication, May 11, 1994) believes journalists will have to continue their growth in using computers:

> Reporters and editors don't need to know how to program in C++, but they should have some basic understanding of operating systems, file structures, and so forth. They should also be comfortable with computers, have used them enough to be willing to experiment, to know that if you press F1, you're liable to get a help file, and so on. Right now a reporter or editor needs to know the potential—what sorts of databases are out there, how they can provide information that otherwise would be completely inaccessible, how a database program can be used to analyze them, what a spreadsheet program can do. For now, that's enough—if their newsroom has a CAR coordinator who can do the actual computer work for them. Computer databases are being used in a growing number of stories at *The Indianapolis Star,* and it's no longer considered unusual. But most of the actual computing work—from converting the nine-track tapes to performing the data analysis—is being done by the newsroom's CAR coordinator, who is an assistant city editor. He's only got so much time, so as demand grows, more people are going to have to learn how to do such work.

The state of being a technologically advanced newsroom is not an end accomplishment so much as it is a level of operation achieved on an ongoing basis. Lisa Van Asch (personal communication, March 8, 1994), a news research department staff member at the Raleigh *News & Observer,* believes newsroom technology will continue to evolve, as will her own role:

> News Research's role is going to change again soon—we're still information retrievers (and generators), but we're also evolving into information mentors. Reporters and editors are relying on us to teach them how to use this stuff. They want to be able to do some of their own research, they want to be able to use their computers at home, they want to explore the Internet, and they want to analyze their own data and create their own databases.

This scares lots of news librarians and researchers—they think we won't be necessary anymore if we train our "clients" to do the job themselves. I disagree. I think as teachers we will become more important, and we'll develop a better relationship with the newsroom along the way. Who better to teach them? Researchers and librarians have used computers for years, we're service-oriented, we know where the goods are, and we are fanatical about accuracy. And we're always here to answer questions.

I am, of course, not talking about giving reporters access to big-money commercial databases like Lexis/Nexis or Dialog. That's where the researcher's expertise comes in. But I think reporters should know how to access public records, how to navigate the Internet (how to send E-mail, join a newsgroup, find other libraries and databases), how to create a Lotus 1-2-3 spreadsheet and analyze data (like the county budget) on it, and how to search CDs and use our in-house databases to enhance their stories. The *N&O* has always stressed involvement and inclusion—we have held many classes for reporters and editors on computer-assisted reporting.

For a technologically resistant newspaper to move forward will require some coordinated and designed effort, perhaps starting at the top. The University of Miami CAR study determined that the problems do not always lie in the rank and file areas of the newsroom. They can, at times, exist in their most severe form at the very top.

IMPLICATIONS OF HIGH-TECH JOURNALISM

Becoming computer literate at the individual level and developing a technologically advanced newsroom bring with it more than academic-sounding labels. The transition brings a change in the way news reporting is approached and the types of information that are reported. Online research consultant and journalist Tom Koch (1991) has written that online services affect the narrative form of news writing. He argues that online information changes relations between writers and the subjects about which they write. He says the role of the news media in a democratic society is changing and how journalists use online services will have an impact on society, politics, and culture. How much is traditional contemporary news reporting limited by ordinary, more conventional sources and tools? Is CAR even more to journalism than what Philip Meyer called the same old journalism but with "new tools" (1979, p. 15)?

Indiana University researcher David H. Morrissey (1993) feels computers have produced mixed effects on journalism, some good and some not so good. On the positive side, Morrissey says computers help reporters gather more information, obtain that information more quickly, analyze and manipulate information not capable of analysis before, save time in examining public records, and access sources more easily. The less desirable effects of computer-based reporting, Morrissey said, are the cost, the reduction in privacy, the easy deletion of records and information, the ease of sabotage, elimination of old useful technology, and a public re-examination of the rights carried within the First Amendment.

THE IMPORTANCE OF COMPUTER EDUCATION

A national study of U.S. adults found that almost half of all respondents and a majority of those over 35 years of age feel the race for technological advancement has left them at the starting line. People feel that computers have made life easier and made work faster, but most feel they are not keeping up with the advances in computing, according to the study by ICR Survey Research Group of Media, PA (H. Goldberg, 1994).

The speed at which computerization is occurring in some segments of life, such as the communication industry and journalism education, is quite amazing. It is no wonder many people feel computer technology, as well as other electronic advances, is zooming past. The rapid recent changes occurring in use of the Internet, for example, are often mind boggling. Growth in computer education in public and private schools in some parts of the country is rapidly creating a generational gap in computer literacy. Children are much more comfortable with home computers than their parents—a phenomenon of much of the past decade. The gap is making it almost impossible to consider how different younger people in the same newsroom will be from their older colleagues in terms of their computing skills—in just a few more years, if not already. A severe haves and have-nots dichotomy in terms of computing skills has begun to emerge in newsrooms.

San Francisco State University Professor Tom Johnson, who teaches both computer-assisted and more traditional reporting techniques, cannot preach the message loud enough or fast enough. "I've been amazed this past year . . . how quickly the Internet snowball has picked up speed and size. And I continue to be even more amazed at our colleagues in the academy who can't seem to grasp the fact that third and fourth graders are putting out full-blown electronic newspapers, complete with animated art work, and putting them on LANs and the Internet," Johnson (personal communication, May 2, 1994) said. "In the meantime, I know college professors who have never even used E-mail and can only imagine that it would be a bore and a pain."

Training and education are essential to computer literacy in the newsroom. Yet at least one national study determined that most major U.S. schools and departments teaching journalism and mass communication do not plan to add CAR or other forms of computer-based information gathering instruction to their class requirements. Communication researchers Margaret H. DeFleur and Lucinda Davenport (1993) found that the idea had not caught on at many universities and colleges even though there was growing use of CAR techniques in newsrooms across the country. Times are no doubt slowly changing and this attitude will gradually evolve. Accordingly, DeFleur and Davenport concluded that "unless these plans change, their students will enter employment in news industries with significant gaps in their preparation. Specifically, they will not be able at the time of employment to access rich sources of information that are now routinely used in the newsroom to improve the depth and quality of stories that they will be assigned to cover," they wrote (p. 33). The two researchers also feel these ill-equipped beginning reporters will be passed over for investigative projects and will wonder why they were not educated in these essential tools.

Johnson (1994a) believes the shift to what he likes to call "analytic journalism" is already occurring. Schools and colleges with journalism programs can no longer afford to ignore computing. The shift in the debate has gone from whether computers should be taught to who, where, and how computers should be taught. In his CAR education model, Johnson advocates a "RRAW" process in which journalism students and journalists learn to use computing power for the *researching, reporting, analyzing,* and *writing* processes for each story. The transition to learning about the power computing gives journalism is beginning on some college campuses.

Indiana University's Morrissey (1993) says journalism schools must plan for the computer-based future. Morrissey offered 10 ways to educate journalists about technological change:

- Expect the electronic society.
- Totally immerse students in telecommunication.
- Anticipate an increase in the amount of information journalists will face.
- Journalism schools should begin their own database libraries.
- Realize that use of computers in the future will be significantly different from the present.
- Increase emphasis on how government works and the information it produces.
- Study government agencies, but also study democracy.
- Arrival of new technologies increases the value of teaching old ethics.
- Educational programs must avoid the lure of technology for technology's sake.
- Those learning about computers and communication should be challenged to define the undefined boundaries of the new electronic and information age.

Gerry Keir, editor of the *Honolulu Advertiser,* and University of Texas Professor Maxwell McCombs and University of North Carolina Professor Donald L. Shaw (1991) point to the core need for journalists to learn computing:

> If the mass media are to utilize the potential of computerized information files, reporters and editors must come to view the computerized file itself—not just its keepers—as a news source. To exploit this new freedom for creative reporting, you must be trained to use these new sources. This means learning the rudiments of electronic data processing and data analysis. [F]or creative reporters who want to exploit the advantages of these technological advances, the ability to properly and directly employ the computer becomes a necessary skill. (p. 175)

There are signs that the shift in training and education priorities is occurring in newsrooms, too, as newer generations of PC-based systems are installed to replace single-purpose front-end editorial systems. But the process is painfully slow, especially at smaller newspapers with little or no in-house training. "Our reporting staff tends to be computer-illiterate and resistant to trying online services, spreadsheets, and so forth," said Michael Walsh (personal communication, March 14, 1994), a legal affairs reporter for the *Muskegon Chronicle* in Michigan. "Some [of them] would utilize computer-assisted reporting if management would make training available and encourage it."

Some news organizations conduct in-house training after a core of knowledgeable CAR staff members develops. Usually, these trainers— who learned their skills somewhere else—conduct classes in the newsroom on a regular basis. Gail Hulden (1993), a trainer at *The Oregonian* in Portland, feels such a program can be highly successful, but she says in-house programs have to be flexible. "You need to see what options are available to you," she stated. "Appraise what is possible at your paper now. Start this while you are still 'pumped' . . . and preferrably before you update your résumé." She offers five tips to make an in-house program work:

- Take stock of exactly what computerization is already available.
- If you don't already have CD-ROM databases accessible to you, see if you can get a simple single CD reader attached to a PC in the research library, or at a nearby workstation.
- Cast a net of followers. Schedule an initial brown bag seminar. Let the excitement rub off on those who attend.
- Pass around publications that profile news stories that highlight CAR.
- Start a team of three to five people to supervise the growth of CAR.

The *Dayton Daily News* takes a slightly different tactic. Its editors brought in an expert. The *Daily News,* a Cox Newspaper, invited noted CAR authority Elliot Jaspin to serve as a CAR consultant to the newsroom for 3 days, explained the *Daily News'* Mike Casey (1993). Jaspin trained a selected group of reporters at the newspaper in three areas: loading nine-track tapes, arranging fields to enable the data to be read, and analysis of the database. Then those reporters became the trainers and they worked with others about ways to use their new skills for daily stories and projects. As a Cox staff member in Washington, Jaspin remains available to the newspaper through his newsroom "consulting" arrangement. "The decision to hire a consultant is going to have to come from the top," Casey (1993) noted. "I'd write up a proposal on the advantages you see. . . . Then take the proposal to the editor or publisher and see what happens. The secret is winning over someone who can make the hire and then they'll decide on who to hire."

At *U.S. News & World Report,* CAR training is an interdepartmental team effort involving a reporter, a news librarian, and a data processing staff member. Reporter Penny Loeb (1993) explained that the magazine conducts in-house sessions in small groups of three persons each for 3 days of 2-hour sessions. Class sizes are limited by the number of computers, she stated. The classes integrate material from the magazine and from a NICAR training seminar attended by staff members. The magazine does utilize extensive external training opportunities whenever they are available, Loeb explained.

Some individuals, news companies, and organizations recognize the value of advanced continuing education and training of those already on the job. A 37-page Freedom Forum report analyzed continuing education in the newsroom, concluding that journalists do not get the training that they want, although almost all journalists want professional-level training (Newton & Thien, 1993). Ethics and writing were the most often mentioned topics in the national survey conducted by the Freedom Forum, but CAR was also named as a leading topic. There was either high or moderate interest expressed in learning CAR among 66% of the respondents. Freedom Forum researchers also concluded that regular training does not reach most journalists and that the training gap is harmful to news organizations, causing reduction in quality, morale, and retention.

If CAR training is not available internally, some reporters and editors try to find it elsewhere—either on their own initiative or with newsroom and company support. Some training is occurring in special credit-earning journalism school, business school, and computer and information science department classes or through training seminars of national professional associations and organizations. Some of the degree-granting national programs with high visibility are located at the University of Missouri, Syracuse University, and Indiana University at Indianapolis. Short-term continuing-education type programs are offered by IRE, NIAR, the Poynter Institute, and NICAR.

NICAR and IRE have offered week-long training programs for small, but highly motivated, groups of reporters and editors—commonly called "boot camps"—in Columbia, MO. IRE and NICAR, for example, have offered training at recent conferences devoted to CAR. NICAR, beginning in 1994, initiated a traveling national training program that moved from region to region instead of requiring participants to go to the program site. A full-time training director has made this traveling curriculum possible (LaFleur, 1994).

Some news organizations want to hire individuals with the basic computer skills in place rather than have to train them in-house. Some larger news organizations want advanced computer literacy. "We're trying to find people who can do computer-assisted reporting. The academic world has to train these guys, too," offered Scott Anderson, newsroom computer resources manager of the *Sun-Sentinel* in Fort Lauderdale (personal communication, December 20, 1993). "My initial thought was that everybody would be jumping for joy for this, and when they sit down and try it, many of them can type their résumé into the word processor and that's the extent of their computer knowledge. It isn't easy. It's hard to learn this stuff. And it's frightening."

Anderson (personal communication, December 20, 1993) says reporters and editors need a minimum level of computer literacy to survive in the last half of this decade. But he is willing to be patient for even that much. Perhaps the first step, Anderson said, is awareness and the simplest level of just thinking about databases and how they can be used to enhance most stories:

> What we're trying to get them [beat and general assignment reporters] to do now is to get them to think to ask for data like they ask for records. Then teach them some basic spreadsheet skills, some database skills, so they understand what can be done. That's what we have to do to start. If we can do that with every single staffer here in the next year or two years, I'd be very happy. That's the big hurdle. They don't necessarily have to be able to use the spreadsheet now, but if they ask to get the data, then we're way ahead. . . . If we can get everybody on the street asking for these things [databases], it makes our staff aware, it makes the bureaucrats aware. A pattern starts to evolve. We're getting much better at it than a year ago.

> This is step one. To have select people to be able to actually do CAR is step two. And eventually everybody who needs to use a spreadsheet will learn it. Other programs [e.g., relational database systems and statistical packages] are side issues right now. These are a step in the future, a step ahead. It could help, too, if reporters learn how to use these tools when they are out of the office.

San Francisco's Johnson (1994a) feels computing education must occur at two levels. The first is what he calls "Chevy-sedan, manual-shift, analytic journalism." By that he means that students and journalists must learn the practical and "no frills" use of the tools of analytic journalism. These are fundamentals of operation of computers and software related to journalism. This approach is strictly utilitarian. Johnson's second level goes beyond basics to the "philosopher's cave of analytic journalism." This is the sophisticated level that has shifted focus from just skills to pondering questions such as "What's it all about?" Not only do journalists who have mastered the basics have to work at this level and think about what they are doing, they must continue to increase their skills and their critical thinking about use of those skills.

MOVING TOWARD THE COMPUTER-LITERATE NEWSROOM

The basic message keeps resurfacing: *Computers are the future of news reporting. The future is now.* Jules S. Tewlow (1993), former director of special projects for Lee Enterprises, points to the fast spread of computerization as the cause of changes in how journalists work. As the mainframe computer has already done, other forms of computing—in whatever form they take—are going to modify how journalists report and how their work is done. "The computer has ushered us into the digital age and the personal computer has hastened the spread of this technology to a far wider audience and at a faster pace than one could foresee a couple of decades ago," he stated (pp. 30–31). "Technology, socio-economic changes and societal needs are opening the door wide, but only a break with the traditional concepts of what a newspaper is will keep that door from slamming shut." Not only does Tewlow's sentiment apply to the form journalists use to disseminate news and information, but it also refers to the way journalists will gather and process that raw information.

John S. Makulowich (personal communication, May 8, 1994), vice president for Internet training for The Writer's Alliance in Maryland, agrees that computers will change the nature of journalism and how reporters do their work. One example he points to is the growing number of newsgroups on the Internet. Newsgroups are collections of news stories about specific subjects. "There's no newspaper that can compete with newsgroups," he explained. "To stay competitive, news organizations are going to have to become what is called distributed newsrooms—with distributed information processing. This is the newsroom of the future."

Literacy is normally a word used in the context of reading and writing, reflecting an individual's level of knowledge and education. It has been given to refer to other bodies of knowledge such as geographic literacy and computer literacy. There are many ways to define and classify literacy of all types and computer literacy is no exception. There are numerous ways to describe and achieve computer literacy. Perhaps the best is to use stages or levels to represent advancements in individual and institutional computer learning. To become computer skilled, journalists must experience each of the three levels of computer literacy. The levels include (a) individuals feeling at ease with a computer, (b) feeling confident with a computer, and (c) liking the computer (Loyd & Gressard, 1986).

Computer literacy has to become the highest priority for newsrooms for the remaining years of this decade. Newsroom management must take the lead for the entire company. The fact that the news industry does not always use the most advanced communication tools available is puzzling, even though to do so seems obvious.

Elliot Jaspin has led the effort to move computer use in newsrooms beyond word processing. He proposed five guidelines for newsrooms and editors:

- Make the program broad based, to get as many reporters and editors involved in the CAR effort as possible.
- Have clear lines of authority by putting someone in central control of the program's development and day-to-day story development.
- Remember that CAR is still reporting, or just ordinary reporting by other means.
- The newsroom needs to remain in control of information such as databases, so do not leave it with information systems or other departments outside the newsroom.
- Match resources to the task, so do not skimp or overspend. Staff adequately and do the same with hardware and software.

"Despite all the fancy equipment and high-tech jargon, success or failure is determined by leadership," Jaspin (1991, p. 8) stated.

Makulowich takes an interesting but somewhat different look at what he calls "electronic literacy." Instead of viewing electronic literacy as a set of developed skills in a workplace such as a newsroom, he proposes emphasis on the "cyberworker." Makulowich (1994) explains:

> Let's look at electronic literacy within the business setting, within the work force with distributed information and decision-making power, within the increasingly competitive global environment. The picture of electronic literacy that emerges is one which interweaves the roles of the knowledge worker, the learning organization, and quality management. It involves nothing less than the creation of the cyberworker—one attached to cyberspace as well as clientspace and workspace, one attuned to

principle as well as policy and practice, and one attentive to detail as well as design and decorum. In principle, the cyberworker will play a pivotal role in measurable improvements in productivity, the acceleration of technology transfer and product development, the enhancement of internal employee communication and education, and continuing external customer contact. (p. 1049)

Makulowich, who writes five regular columns about the Internet and online computing, is a former magazine and newspaper journalist who has been using various types of computer-assisted reporting since 1984. He distinguishes between computer literacy for online services and for data analysis for journalists. "The reporter of tomorrow, the next generation, will be deeply involved in computers. Reporters are going to need to know how to gather and retrieve information on a computer network," said Makulowich (personal communication, May 8, 1994), who spends much of his time teaching other professionals how to use the Internet. "The newsroom is now global. I found out the other day that there are now 69 countries on the Internet. The stories we do, such as one on the stock market, will have to take into account all markets around the world. The only way to do it is with computers. You can't do it by telephone."

Although Makulowich feels online use of computers is essential for all reporters, he does not think it is critical for all reporters to learn how to use PCs as analytical tools:

I don't think all reporters have to learn all sorts of different software. There will be a team approach instead. Bruce, John, Vic, Tom, and Mary will each bring something to the team's story. One will bring languages, one data processing, one foreign culture and travel, and so forth. There is just too much information now. This is a form of information overload. You cannot learn it all. I have been on the Net since 1989 and I feel deficient. There's always something new.

The Milwaukee Journal's Mollwitz (personal communication, May 8, 1994) feels a moderate level of computer learning is necessary, but not everyone needs to know it all:

It isn't necessary to be anything more than an intermediate level user. If you get right down to it, people who earn college degrees to learn how to program will be able to write any software much better someone without that training. With every new software application there's a learning curve. A few weeks back a vice president of a computer department of a major company here in Wisconsin told me at a PC user's group meeting that despite degrees in computer science and despite understanding UNIX, he had to buy *Internet for Dummies* when he first got on the Net. So one is always a "beginner" in some phase of computing, and that concept is hard for many big egos in this business to accept.

Mollwitz (personal communication, May 8, 1994) does feel that knowledge of the basics of personal computing will take journalists a long way in this computer information age:

> Journalists, however, should understand such concepts as bits, bytes, directories, directory trees, executables, terminal emulation, various communications protocols, as well as various media used to store data. The natural question, again, is: Why? The answer, once again, is that most of the information with which you will deal was not created by the journalist. That reporter/editor has to know how to access that data with the full understanding that someone will try to find a way to hide what they don't want you uncover even if they give you all of the data file. . . . [A] greater depth of understanding of how a computer works is needed if one is to "gather" the information that is needed.

Some computing experts feel leadership is the key to improving computer literacy in organizations. "Unfortunately, feelings of techno-inadequacy in a boss can lead to trouble for a whole company or association. An insecure CEO who feels surpassed in computer literacy may decide not to upgrade an organization's computer system, which leads to staff frustration and puts the company at a competitive disadvantage," concluded conventions and meetings industry magazine writer Ron Donoho (1994, p. 48).

Jaspin also believes that the rapid growth and increasing sophistication of computing tools will begin to include more and more journalists who, because they lacked levels of computer literacy, were shut out of CAR projects. "[I]t will be far easier to use computers and what computers will be able to do will be far more extensive [in the remaining half of this decade]," said Jaspin (1994, pp. 14–15). "Now that will mean reporters who have been locked out because they didn't understand DOS, or they had trouble remembering all the funny little commands, will be able to simply type on a screen, tell me how many friends of the mayor have gotten contracts, in a natural language type of way." The computer, he continues to explain, will do the rest of the job. "At that point, the only reason a reporter wouldn't do it is sheer laziness."

Dan Woods, a database editor for the Raleigh *News & Observer,* says there are certain goals for individuals to achieve in becoming competent computer-capable journalists. "Computer-assisted reporting won't blossom overnight. Even in the best of all possible worlds, changing the way reporters and editors work is a lengthy process that is easily stalled," Woods (1993, p. 1) said. "Newsrooms in which everybody—from publisher to reporter, editor, and news researcher—have the same goals in mind will have the best shot at success. What's success? Success is a newsroom in which computer literacy is so widespread that the adjective 'computer-assisted' falls into disuse because everyone reports with the best tools available, whatever they may be." Woods (1993) listed these basic goals for the computer-based newsroom:

- Graphical user interface (GUI) literacy.
- Spreadsheet literacy.
- Data cleaning and structured query language/report.
- Graphical user interface application development.
- Remote access skills. Journalists need to be masters of remote information access, including accessing their own desktop systems from out of the office as well as reaching other systems from their own when in the newsroom.

Debbie Wolfe, newsroom training director at the *St. Petersburg Times,* has developed a model for a computer-assisted newsroom. Her model, a mixture of her ideal world and the realities of budgets and other newsroom forces at the *St. Petersburg Times,* are gradually moving from mostly idealistic to mostly realistic, she explained (Wolfe, personal communication, May 16, 1994). Wolfe's team approach, depicted in Figs. 15.2, 15.3, and 15.4, demonstrate a need for a public records research network that is a combination of efforts headed by a news editor and an information editor. The result is a synergy of team journalism combining the best efforts of news reporters and news researchers. The efforts of these team members are best enhanced by the right tools. Wolfe prefers a three-step process of developing the best hardware and software tools. As the graphics demonstrate, she advises a basic start-up, followed by upgrades of equipment as stages of computer-assisted reporting are mastered.

A MODEL FOR ACHIEVING COMPUTER LITERACY

Woods (1993) and Johnson (1993) have given computer education and training of working journalists and student journalists a significant amount of thought. But even these leaders in CAR education are not completely in agreement about the best way to approach computer literacy in the newsroom. They do agree on the goal, however. What is it? Computer literacy for news gathering and news editing.

Any sort of computer literacy, individual or newsroom level, depends on development of a hierarchy of skills that build on one another. CAR is no different. Computer literacy for most journalists can be accomplished in five distinct stages that build on each other:

Stage 1: Basic Operational Mastery

Most newsroom people know how to power up a personal computer and a printer. Unfortunately for some, this is almost all they know about

GETTING STARTED

Equipment

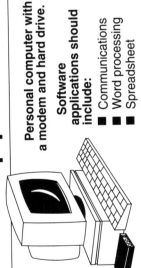

Personal computer with a modem and hard drive.

Software applications should include:

- Communications
- Word processing
- Spreadsheet

Note: The budget approach would be to use MS-DOS as an operating system with used hardware. Be sure the computer you buy, new or used, can be upgraded to accept more memory and/or add-on peripherals like a CD-ROM drive. The Windows operating environment is a must for multi-tasking, but may be too pricey as an initial purchase; if this is the case, save it for your upgrade list.

1ˢᵀ UPGRADE

What you can do/access

- Online databases
- Electronic mail
- Internet
- Bulletin Board Services (BBSs)
- University mainframe systems
- Create your own databases

Note: Allow for a realistic budget to cover monthly charges such as subscriptions and long-distance telephone calls. Some information providers charge per-hour access fees for certain files and may charge additional fees for printing or downloading.

PLUS

Concept by Debbie Wolfe, illustrations by Nelda Barlow, both of the *St. Petersburg Times*

FIG. 15.2.   Getting started on a research network.

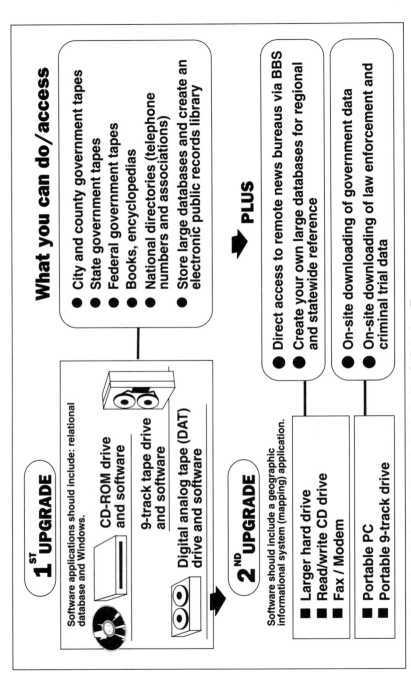

What you can do/access

- City and county government tapes
- State government tapes
- Federal government tapes
- Books, encyclopedias
- National directories (telephone numbers and associations)
- Store large databases and create an electronic public records library

➤ **PLUS**

- Direct access to remote news bureaus via BBS
- Create your own large databases for regional and statewide reference

- On-site downloading of government data
- On-site downloading of law enforcement and criminal trial data

1ST UPGRADE

Software applications should include: relational database and Windows.

- CD-ROM drive and software
- 9-track tape drive and software
- Digital analog tape (DAT) drive and software

2ND UPGRADE

Software should include a geographic informational system (mapping) application.

- Larger hard drive
- Read/write CD drive
- Fax / Modem

- Portable PC
- Portable 9-track drive

FIG. 15.3. Upgrading for a public records research network.

Concept by Debbie Wolfe, illustrations by Nelda Barlow, both of the *St. Petersburg Times*

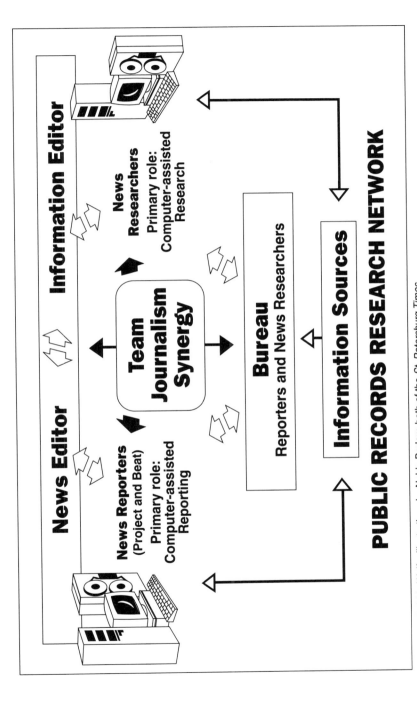

Information Editor

News Editor

News Reporters
(Project and Beat)
Primary role:
Computer-assisted
Reporting

Team Journalism Synergy

News Researchers
Primary role:
Computer-assisted
Research

Bureau
Reporters and News Researchers

Information Sources

PUBLIC RECORDS RESEARCH NETWORK

Concept by Debbie Wolfe, illustrations by Nelda Barlow, both of the *St. Petersburg Times*

FIG. 15.4. The team approach to a public records research effort.

their desktop computers. Another group, slightly further advanced than the first, uses the word processing software to write or edit. Some of these users feel they know enough, but these technologically innocent individuals just don't know what they don't know.

One of the most critical steps toward computer literacy in a newsroom is to learn the basics of operation of the existing hardware and software. This includes mastering the disk operating system, the basics of the operating environment, and a relatively simple application such as a word processor or desk organizer. For PCs and Macintoshes, this includes understanding the main features of DOS, OS/2, and the installed Macintosh system version. The first stage of personal computer mastery should include:

- *Fully understand the user's own PC hardware configuration, its general operation, and its functions.* This includes basic operation of the central processor, the monitor, keyboard, and if necessary, a printer. It includes knowing what hardware features are part of the set-up, such as RAM, hard-drive size, operating system, and CPU speed.
- *Basic ongoing maintenance.* This includes cleaning up around the system, the ability to handle minor problems such as monitor/display adjustments (e.g., brightness or contrast), and printer maintenance (e.g., replacing ribbons or cartridges and refilling paper supplies).
- *Develop troubleshooting skills.* This should include some fundamental knowledge about what do to when floppy or hard disk failure occurs, when a system "freezes," or when a program "bombs."
- *Learn to install and run existing software.* There are some users who do not know how to change the hardware or software configuration of their personal computer, whether it is part of a newsroom network system or not. To get the most of a newsroom PC, journalists must know how to fully customize their systems—within newsroom hardware and software policy—for maximum usage and efficiency. The most important function, perhaps, is simply installing and deinstalling various software tools. This, of course, includes changing settings of the software running on the system to fit the individual user needs. Many programs, such as ground-floor basics like graphical user interface environments and word processors, have numerous customization options. This stage includes installation of new upgrades of software when acquired.
- *Learn DOS or other appropriate operating system (e.g., Macintosh).* This step peels away the mysteries of DOS, OS/2, or whatever other operating system is in use in the newsroom. Learn how to make the PC do what it needs to do when a "housekeeping" task involving the PC arises.
- *Learn file and hard drive management.* One of the first things a user must learn is how to manipulate the disk operating system and how to manage files. This includes learning how to copy files, how to rename them, how to delete files, how to make backups, how to create

new ones within a given application, and how to check for viruses. This should also include hard drive space management and creation of directories and subdirectories for file storage organization.

• *Use the computer for writing and editing.* This is quite basic but needs to be part of the first stage. If a journalist is using a computer at all, it is likely to be used for writing and/or copy editing.

• *Use a computer application for more than writing and editing.* At first glance, this might include complete confidence in operation of the word processor used for writing and editing. But it means more. This includes a form of PC competency branching into another software application such as a spreadsheet or a personal information manager. Still other applications will be learned as literacy growth occurs at later stages.

• *Forego paper or "hard copy" dependency.* For many beginners with PCs or other computer systems, there is reluctance to give up hard copy. A perfect example of this is use of hard copy with the word processor, keeping the copy as "insurance" against accidental loss of the file or keeping a personal information manager at the same time a hard-copy organizer is kept. At some point of comfort with personal computing, a user will decide hard copies are no longer needed. At this point, a new stage of computer literacy is emerging.

Stage 2: Remote Access Capabilities

After mastering the basics of PC operation for the newsroom, journalists need to transfer their knowledge to remote reporting and editing situations. Of course, this is becoming easier because portable systems have recently become as fast and powerful as most desktop PC systems and adjustments to portable equipment shortcomings are less important than when first introduced. The second level of this stage is to learn to access and use the newsroom system from a remote location, including the individual desktop system. Remote literacy includes the following:

• *Learn basics for using the newsroom's preferred telecommunications software package and file transfer protocol.* For any type of remote computer-to-computer communication using telephone lines, users must learn use of a communications package. They should learn how to transfer files from a remote location to the newsroom editing system. This includes learning how to upload and download files from the newsroom computer system and from other services.

• *Learn basics of fax and modem operation and/or PCMCIA card settings and operation.* This includes learning to transmit files and the most basic functions of the modem (and how to set it up if the modem is not internal).

• *Learn procedures for connecting remote hardware and software to the newsroom system.* At times, connection may not be easy. Part of learning to communicate from remote locations includes the ability to overcome hardware incompatibility (e.g., phone line wiring and "jack" connections), calling from public telephone locations, and manual dialing when necessary.

• *Communicate with sources and with colleagues with E-mail.* At the point when hardware and software used in telecommunications are confidently mastered, so should use of the tools for accessing and transmitting electronic mail, sending and receiving faxes (if available), sending and receiving files within the E-mail system, and accessing and communicating within the newsroom memo or internal E-mail system.

• *Work with online commercial services such as CompuServe, Nexis/Lexis, or Dialog.* Journalists, as early in this second stage of development as possible, need to learn minimal levels of use of the most frequently needed newsroom online services, such as those used for searching and retrieving information. This includes learning the nuances of proprietary online services software in addition to the telecommunication software itself because each online system has its own access commands and procedures.

• *Conduct online news story research out of the newsroom.* Just as staff members should learn to use online services in the newsroom, they should acquire skills to use these services when out of the office—such as from bureaus, from home, or from hotel rooms. In reality, this skill is no different from use of the services in the newsroom unless there are communication software or hardware differences in portable PCs used.

• *Learn to set up automatic log-on script files.* To save time and increase efficiency, journalists should learn how to set up and modify script files for streamlined log-on to services and E-mail systems and for automatic file retrieval.

• *Explore and regularly use bulletin board services.* At the same time journalists are developing information retrieval skills for commercial services, they should become comfortable with private and public bulletin board services and their features.

• *Access and use the Internet.* When the newsroom gains universal access to the Internet, journalists should be encouraged to access the system and learn about its wide-ranging potential for all forms of information gathering. Because use of the Internet requires learning the network's interface, this becomes a significant part of the education process.

• *Create an online source network for reporting and editing specialties.* Combining the availability of resources on commercial online services, BBSs, and the Internet, journalists should develop a national and international network of online sources according to their reporting and editing specializations. Just as reporters develop newsroom card files, they should learn to use their online reporting power to develop international and national networks of expert sources.

Stage 3: Intermediate Personal Computer Skills

The third stage is an intermediate level of computer literacy. This is a stage where journalists are becoming more sophisticated in their use of computing tools and are beginning to branch out to more specialized applications and advanced tools. This stage includes the following:

- *Learn advanced use of a graphical user interface system such as Windows, OS/2, or the Macintosh system.* It is one thing to select an option from a menu, to point and click, or to command DOS to run a program. It is another to learn the capabilities of the user's operating system and environment for maximum benefit.
- *Work with a pointing device.* GUIs require some user familiarity with pointing devices. Many journalists who have learned to use computers on DOS systems or have little or no PC experience might find pointing devices such as a mouse, a trackball, or electronic pen uncomfortable to use at first. Although these are not necessary for basic computer use, more sophisticated programs are often designed to include pointing devices for faster and more convenient use. For example, it might be possible to run Windows or a word processor such as AmiPro without a mouse, but it is not nearly as easy.
- *Learn to transfer information between applications.* This includes importing and exporting files across applications and learning how to share information between applications, such as a word processor and personal information manager or word processor and spreadsheet.
- *Learn to use GUI programs to generate graphics for help in analysis of data for stories.* Many programs available in GUI environments are capable of information gathering functions, but also information processing ones such as creating graphs. Top-of-the-line word processors and spreadsheets can produce numerous types of tables and graphs. At the intermediate level, users must begin to make the most of the tools of their software.
- *Develop extended knowledge of spreadsheets.* Beyond the basics of entering information and primitive formulas into spreadsheets, users at this stage should advance their spreadsheet knowledge to include sorting, parsing, advanced computations, graphing, modeling, macro development, data sharing, using multidimensional spreadsheets, and importing and exporting files.
- *Use data and information stored on compact disc.* Just as online services and remote reporting tools are important, journalists should quickly become comfortable with use of data found on compact discs and with use of the software that is often needed to access the information stored on many CDs. Included in this learning process are mastery of the basics of operating a CD-ROM drive and other hardware associated

with multimedia systems including some minimal familiarity with sound and video.

Stage 4: Database Creation and Analysis Skills

The fourth stage of growth is in the areas of advanced database development, advanced statistical analysis, and geographic information systems database analysis. This stage includes the following abilities:

- *Learn minimal skills for free-form text database managers.* Reporters and editors must learn the elementary use of free-form text-oriented database programs such as askSam and Magellan.
- *Learn minimal skills for relational database management systems.* This step includes advancing to more sophisticated relational database programs such as Paradox, dBase, Access, Approach, and FoxPro.
- *Analyze databases from other data sources.* Countless databases are available in many different software applications and it is necessary to take files from one format and transfer them into the database programs used in the newsroom. This skill simply involves learning the conversion utility that is part of the database program.
- *Convert a database from a nine-track tape to a PC system.* Because many government agency databases remain on nine-track tape, this remains an essential step toward complete literacy. This step includes loading nine-track tape on PC-based tape drives and learning use of conversion software necessary for moving data to a PC hard drive file.
- *Create and analyze an original database within a newsroom DBMS.* At the same time journalists learn how to import databases, they should be developing skills in creating new databases in these same programs.
- *Master database editing and cleaning techniques.* Once a database is imported or created, it must be edited and cleaned for use. These skills should be developed at this stage of literacy growth.
- *Learn how to use database query languages and how to prepare customized database reports.* Journalists at this stage in their computer literacy development need to harness the power of structured query language (SQL) and/or query by example (QBE) features available in most major database programs.
- *Conduct advanced original statistical analysis using spreadsheets and statistical packages.* Parallel to developing database management system skills is basic understanding of data matrix design and use of statistical packages at minimal levels to permit descriptive statistical analysis as well as bivariate and ultimately, multivariate, statistical analysis.
- *Develop skills in using geographic information systems.* A third category of database analysis for this stage is acquisition and development of geographic information systems, or database mapping pro-

grams. Skills learned in database management software are easily transferred to GIS software for specific applications.

Stage 5: Developmental Computer Skills

By this point in the evolution of a journalist's computer literacy, most newsroom users will feel confident and have a wide range of highly useful computing skills. However, the ultimate stage in literacy includes addition of application development and programming capabilities. This stage includes the following user abilities:

- *Build minimal programming language skills.* A good place to start programming is using macro tools within word processors and spreadsheet programs. To do more, some programs, such as relational database management and geographic information systems, include more powerful programming languages for development of customized applications for databases.
- *Develop new applications for database analysis where they do not exist, using commercial programs for application development.* A major use of programming skills, within DBMS and GIS software, for example, is to create new applications for database manipulation. This is particularly helpful when commercially developed applications do not exist. This form of customized programming can be extraordinarily beneficial to newsrooms with particular information gathering and processing needs.
- *Learn BASIC.* BASIC is perhaps the simplest programming language that comes with DOS and Windows systems and is available to almost all computer users. For GUI-oriented individuals and newsrooms, this includes programming tools such as Visual BASIC.
- *Learn an advanced compiler programming language.* The final stage of computer literacy also includes growth beyond programming languages offered within commercial packages to use of general programming skills in development tools such as C and C++.

MOVING FORWARD: TAKE IT FAST OR SLOW?

Raleigh's Dan Woods (1993) once stated that newsroom computer literacy cannot occur overnight. In too many newsrooms in the mid-1990s, particularly at small daily newspapers across the United States, it has not even begun. Yes, many of these newsrooms have personal computer systems, but their usefulness does not often go beyond word processing or the creation of informational graphics.

For most news organizations, achievement of newsroom-wide computer literacy at any level is a matter of deciding what is important and what the newsroom needs to accomplish. Prioritization of skills must occur, perhaps even prioritization of departments within the newsroom. These decisions are in the hands of newsroom management but can be influenced from the bottom up. Perhaps the model proposed in this chapter will be helpful toward achieving computer literacy in newsrooms, perhaps not. Perhaps the stages of the model are out of reach for the average newsroom and journalist, for now, but they will not be for long. Goals such as these, for a large group of individuals of varying computer skills to begin with, will probably seem difficult or even impossible with current standards applied. It may take a generation of journalists or longer for some newsrooms to achieve any levels of literacy beyond the first or second stage. It could be accomplished at a faster rate, however, with the right motivation and learning environments.

There will be resistance. As with any work-related innovation, there will be some rejection of and opposition to the plan. Managers must get the status quo types involved. These types of technology-related transformations have occurred in newsrooms in the past. Newsrooms in the 1970s, for example, experienced problems when the first computer systems began to replace manual and electric typewriters with optical scanning systems and first-generation front-end systems with video display terminals and dedicated word processing software.

There will be expenses associated with developing more complete computer literacy among all newsroom newsgatherers. Advanced computer literacy for an entire newsroom is not cheap. Ask any educator in a public school system trying to educate hundreds of children. The same learning process in a newsroom means new costs in a number of budget categories, but these expenses can be anticipated and gradually covered. Education and training programs will be one of the big expenses, if not the largest. There will also be the hidden cost of regularly assigned time lost for training and education programs for many on-the-job news gatherers. Certainly expansion of hardware and software capabilities, both in-house and remote, will also be costly. Online services, as they increase in use, will be still another expense.

One successful way to manage the cost of extensive newsroom computer literacy is planning. A committee approach will involve staff members in a positive manner and may work effectively at several levels. Certainly in an extended literacy program such as that being proposed, there are a multiplicity of approaches and perspectives represented in the newsroom to be considered and debated. A group of newsroom managers and staff members is a proven effective method for determining overall long-term goals, short-term objectives, timetables, and budgets.

Throughout the process of developing newsroom-wide computer literacy, it is essential to remember the applications of it to daily local reporting. How does the computer fit in average assignments, as well as special projects? Computer literacy and computer-assisted reporting must become a part of the general philosophy of daily journalism in the newsroom.

CHOOSING THE ULTIMATE GOAL?

At several recent national journalism organization meetings, prominent computer-assisted reporters such as Raleigh's Dan Woods and The Associated Press' Bill Dedman have argued that there will be a day in the future when computer-assisted reporting will become ordinary daily reporting. After all, when was the last time someone said he or she was involved in a "telephone-assisted" or "fax-assisted" reporting project? Technology comes, is learned, and becomes part of the routine in newsrooms. Veterans of newsrooms can still remember when electric typewriters replaced manual typewriters and those were, in turn, replaced by the first computer terminals. The goal is simple: Make personal computing part of routine reporting.

Newspapers will undoubtedly undergo remarkable changes in the next decade. The newspaper of the early 21st century will probably not resemble the newspaper of the mid-1990s in many ways. It will be available in both electronic and printed versions as more and more households become computerized in one form or another. The technology for mass distribution of information is changing so quickly that forecasts of how and what will be the norms in a decade are outdated by the time they are published. John K. Hartman (1994), a journalism professor at Central Michigan University, believes the newspaper of 2003 "will be a combination of the ink-on-paper product of 1993 and the latest in communication technology, information delivered electronically to home computers and data storage and retrieval systems" (p. 1).

Such electronic systems will bring newspaper and magazine newsrooms to deadline and production situations more like those of the wire services or even broadcast stations. Updating and revising stories and information will be an around-the-clock effort. How reporters get this work done and how editors process it will also be changing.

With all this comes a word of caution. Dwight Morris, a *Los Angeles Times* editor who was one of the earliest advocates of CAR in newsrooms, warns that journalists must be careful not to let CAR get out of control. At the 1992 national conference on computer-assisted reporting hosted by the National Institute for Advanced Reporting, Morris called the idea of reporters going crazy over computing a "nightmare" and cautioned all reporters and editors to mix its use with traditional forms of reporting (Fitzgerald, 1992, p. 15).

Computers have already become an essential part of the newsroom culture. Computers are the best reporting tools of this generation and will be as basic to the journalism of the next two or three generations of journalists as telephones have been to the present generation. This is the threshold of a new world of reporting. The computer has given journalists unparalleled potential for information gathering and dissemination to the present generation. In the mid-1990s, to not know how to use a personal computer in reporting is equal to the experience of the library patron who discovered, after picking up a book, that he did not know how to read. Journalists so far have witnessed only the infancy of this new era. It is truly exciting to think about what can happen next for reporters. Is there a way to program a personal computer to peek into the future?

Appendix A: Leading Online News Research Databases and Commercial Database Services

A

ABI / Inform—Available on several major services, this database provides hundreds of thousands of citations and selected full text about business and management. 800-626-2823.

Accounting & Tax Database—Accountants and accounting firms are the focus of this database. Includes legislative information. 800-626-2823.

Ageline—Bibliographic database of the American Association of Retired Persons (AARP). 202-434-6231.

America Online—Library of numerous databases and other online services. Includes interactive services for *The New York Times, Time, Chicago Tribune,* CNN, *Omni* magazine, and full text of other databases, and other user features. 800-827-6364 (ext. 7477).

American Banker—Full text of the major content of the publication *American Banker.* Focus is on banking industry news. 800-356-4763.

APN Access—American Political Network lists files of APN electronic publications. 703-237-5130.

Autoadvantage Online—New and used car descriptions, prices, and service and repairs information. 800-843-7777.

B

Best–North America—Database of research projects and scientists at major U.S. universities. Good for source development. 800-BESTNA-1.

Biobusiness—Lists opportunities in life sciences such as engineering, pharmaceuticals, agriculture, and technology of food. 800-523-4806.

Birth Defects Encyclopedia—Full-text articles. 800-955-0906.

Books in Print—Online version of reliable reference books found in libraries and bookstores. 800-323-3288.

Boomer Report—Newsletter text database pertaining to the consumer and market habits of the baby boomer generation. 800-345-1301.

BRS—Wide range of libraries and databases including health and medicine. 800-289-4277.

Burrelle's Broadcast Database—Full-text transcripts of ABC, CBS, NBC News, and other network news division programs, Financial News Network, National Public Radio. 800-631-1160.

Business America Online—Mailing and marketing lists. 402-593-4593.

Business Dateline—Full-text stories about U.S. business from business periodicals. 800-626-2823.

Business Software Database—Business, industrial, and engineering applications. 800-433-6107.

Business Wire—Full texts of press releases from thousands of organizations on a daily basis. 212-575-8822.

C

Capcrime—Crime statistics. 800-876-6732.

Career Placement Registry—Résumés. 800-331-4955.

Club Metro—Travel, entertainment, and nightlife services. 212-969-8753.

CompuServe—General commercial interactive service including gateways to news such as full-text AP, UPI, some newspapers, numerous other commercial databases and other research services. 800-848-8199.

Computer Database / ASAP—Full text, abstracts, and indexes of computer industry publications. 800-321-6388.

Computerized AIDS Information Network (CAIN)—Abstracts and full-text articles about AIDS. 213-464-7400.

Congressional Quarterly (CQ)—Contains legislative records, bill tracking, campaign contributions data, and other information. 202-887-8500.

Corporate Jobs Outlook—Employer database based on newsletter. 512-755-8810.

Corptech Database—High tech corporations database. 617-932-3939.

D

Daily Report for Executives—Summary of legal decisions that affect businesses. 800-862-4636.

Data-Star—Wide range of more than 250 international libraries and databases includes business, industry, health, and medical information. 800-221-7754.

DataTimes—Full-text regional and international newspapers, magazines, wire services, newsletters, international databases. 800-642-2525.

Delphi—General online services including database libraries, financial information, encyclopedias, newswires, special interest areas, and complete access to Internet. 800-695-4005.

Dialog—Hundreds of bibliographic databases for thousands of publications and millions of references, including full-text newspapers, journals, and other periodicals, journals, and numerous specialized publications. 800-334-2564.

Disclosure Line—Corporate financial information. 800-843-7747.

Dow Jones News / Retrieval—Several major databases including Dow Jones Business and Financial Report database, Dow Jones Capital Markets report database, Dow Jones News (*Wall Street Journal*), and other Dow Jones data and information. 609-522-3567.

Drug—Information about alcohol and drug abuse. 800-289-4277.

Dun's Market Identifiers—Dun & Bradstreet's directory of business profiles. 800-624-5669.

E

Electronic White Pages—Residential, business, and government telephone listings. 404-512-5090.

Emerging Markets—Stock market financial statistics. 202-473-9550.

Employment & Policy Guide—Legal and other aspects of human resources management. 800-452-4132.

ERIC—Educational Resources Information Center lists bibliographic reference materials on many subjects. 800-424-1616.

E-Span—Employment advertising service. 800-682-2901.

Eventline—Massive listings in calendar form of conventions, conferences, exhibitions, trade fairs, sports events, and so forth. 800-334-2564.

Exceptional Child Education Resources—ECER focuses on education and development of people of all ages. 703-620-3660.

Executive System—Domestic and international economic information. 800-332-9332.

F

Fairbase—Calendar of trade shows, conferences, and exhibitions worldwide. 800-289-4277.

Fedix / Molis—Research funding and minority opportunities. 301-975-0103.

Findex—Market research study summaries. 800-843-7751.

Finis: Financial Industry Information Service—Abstracts on subjects of interest to banking and financial businesses. 800-433-9013.

Foundation Giving Watch—Newsletter that follows foundation activity. 800-345-1301.

4-Sights Network—Databases include an occupational information library, job listings, and technology for the blind or visually impaired. 313-272-3900.

Free Financial Network—Financial computing with information about stocks, mutual funds, markets, and more. 212-838-6324.

G

GEnie—General services database comprised of libraries, databases, news, information, and various other services. 800-638-9636.

Government bulletin board systems (BBSs)—Specific information from individual state and federal agencies such as announcements, statistics, press releases.

Grants Database—Funding sources. 800-334-2564.

Green Marketing Report—Newsletter about environmentally friendly products and packaging. 800-345-1301.

H

Handicapped Users—Articles about handicapped and disabled people. 800-848-8199.

Handsnet—Human services organizations network with summaries of articles about human services. 408-257-4500.

Haver Analytics International Service—Eight worldwide databases covering economic and financial information. 212-986-9300.

Healthnet Reference Library—Health information about diseases, drugs, and home treatments of health problems. 614-457-8600.

I

Information America—Real estate public records, easy to search for people. 800-235-4008.

Insider Trading Monitor—Securities Exchange Commission records of sales and other transactions. 305-384-1500.

Investext—Reports on thousands of companies prepared by investment analysts. 617-345-2000.

J

Japan Economic Newswire—Economic, political, and other news about the Pacific Rim region. 212-397-3723.

K

Kidsnet—Clearinghouse for information about TV, radio, and film/tape programs for children. 202-291-1400.

Knight-Ridder/Tribune Business News—News coverage and other information about small and medium-sized companies in addition to the major businesses. 202-383-6134.

Knowledge Index—Now accessible through CompuServe, this library contains hundreds of bibliographic databases including full-text daily newspapers. 800-334-2564.

L

Labor Arbitration Reports—Rulings by arbitrators on labor relations issues. 800-452-7773.

Legal Research Center—Seven databases containing referencing articles for hundreds of law journals and other periodicals. 800-848-8199.

Legis—Congressional bill tracking, voting records, campaign contributions. 800-227-4908.

Lexis / Nexis—Lexis is a significant collection of libraries of full-text legal/law databases; Nexis is a comprehensive set of full-text daily newspapers, magazines, wire services, newsletters, and numerous other databases. 800-227-4908.

M

Magazine Index—Indexes popular periodicals of a wide range of topics dating from 1959. 800-321-6388.

Marketing and Advertising References Services—New product information in abstracts and full-text form for marketing, advertising, and public relations users. 800-321-6388.

Media General Financial Services Common Stocks—Database of thousands of stocks containing information from SEC and company reports. 804-649-6736.

Medis—Medical databases. 800-227-4908.

MEDLARS—Major collection of health and medical databases from the National Library of Medicine. 800-638-8480.

Merck Index Online—Descriptions of chemicals, drugs, agricultural, and other products. 908-594-4890.

Metronet—Change-of-address database, other public records related to individuals and households. 800-927-2238.

Military & Veterans Forum—Files about MIAs/POWs and current military news. 800-848-8199.

N

National Newspaper Index—Index to *New York Times, Los Angeles Times, Wall Street Journal, Washington Post,* and *Christian Science Monitor.* 800-321-6388.

Network Earth Forum—Based on a television program, this is a BBS-type database including Sierra Club information. 800-827-9489.

Newsbytes News Network—Computer and telecommunications industry files from this daily news service. 612-430-1100.

Newsnet—More than 500 newsletters, news service full-text databases. 800-345-1301.

NewsNet—Business information through over 300 newsletter databases. 800-952-0122.

P

PAIS International—Public Affairs Information Service publications include indexes online. 800-288-7247.

PEP Database—Personal Employee Profiling provides background checking on individuals such as potential employees. 800-648-6261.

Philosophers Index—Index of books, articles, and other materials about philosophy. 800-444-2419.

PR Newswire—Press releases from the business and financial community. 800-832-5522.

PR On-Line—Free access to press releases for journalists from the day or release up to seven days following release. 410-363-0834.

Prentice Hall Online—Local public records from a wide range of categories in databases from each of the 50 states. 800-848-8199.

Prodigy—General interactive service containing libraries, databases, interactive activities of all sorts. News section includes AP. 800-776-3449.

Productscan—Information about new consumer products, press releases, and other news. 800-836-8710.

PROMT—Predicasts Overview of Marketing and Technology has over 2.5 million abstracts and full-text articles on companies, industries, technologies, and products. 800-321-6388.

PTS Newsletter Database—Full-text articles from business and industry news about companies, government regulation, and trends, at domestic and international levels. 800-321-6388.

Public Health Information Services—Information about the health care profession and public health problems and issues. Includes resources of the Centers for Disease Control Information Service. 202-898-5600.

R

Real Estate Buyers and Real Estate for Sale Directories—Listings of potential real estate buyers and their interests and listings of property available. 814-272-7602.

Real Estate Venture Funding Directory—Sources of real estate loans and venture capital. 814-274-7602.

S

Schoolmatch—Data about thousands of public and private schools. 614-890-1573.

Space/Astronomy—Launch reports, other NASA information, plus access to several online periodicals. 800-848-8199.

Standard & Poors Biographical Register—Biographical directory of American business executives. 212-208-8300.

Super Bureau Inc.—Request service that conducts searches about people and companies from public records databases and sends results to E-mail address. 800-541-6821.

T

Telescan—Data about thousands of publicly traded stocks, mutual funds, and more. 713-952-1060.

Trademarkscan Federal/State/United Kingdom—Over 1 million federal trademark registrations database, almost 1 million state registrations, and a half million in the United Kingdom. 800-692-8833.

Training Media—In-house training programs database for vocational, industrial, and professional levels. 505-265-3591.

21 CFR Online—Available on BRS or Data-Star, this database contains information about federal regulations for food and drug products. 301-881-2100.

U

U.S. Datalink—Public records data from all 50 states. 800-527-7930.

V

Vu/Text—Now part of Dialog and Knowledge Index, the service offers full text of more than 70 daily newspapers, newswires, magazines, and business publications. 800-334-2564.

W

Washington Alert—Full-text of legislation tracked through all steps of the lawmaking process. 800-432-2250.

W.D.I.A. Corp.—Personal background information about individuals based on their credit, criminal, financial, and other records. 800-374-1400.

Westlaw—Legal citations, full-text opinions of major courts, Congressional bill tracking. 800-432-2250.

Women's Online Network—Information about political and social activities designed to improve the status of women. 212-255-3939.

Source: Editors choice: The database directory. (1993, September). *Online Access, 8*(5), pp. 61–77.

Appendix B: Online Services in Use at Selected Daily Newspapers

The commercial online information services and databases that receive the most use, as reported by editors or reporters from the responding newspapers in the 1994 University of Miami national survey:

Newspaper	Most Often Used Databases and Services
Allentown Morning Call	PACER, Nexis
Anchorage Daily News	Vu/Text, Motznik (state records), CompuServe
Annapolis Capital	AP Graphics Net, Presslink
Arkansas Democrat-Gazette	PACER, Arkansas courts, local taxes-deeds
Asbury Park Press	Nexis, CompuServe, Internet
Asheville Citizen-Times	CompuServe
Atlanta Constitution	Dialog, Lexis/Nexis, DataTimes
Atlantic City Press	Lexis/Nexis, CompuServe, FedWorld
Austin American-Statesman	Local court files database, Internet, PACER
Battle Creek Enquirer	PACER
Beaumont Enterprise	Texas Controller's Office, Texas Employment Commission, various private BBSs
Belleville News-Democrat	Regional government BBS, State pollution BBS, NUDOCS (NRC)
Bend Bulletin	County tax records, Dialog, state road reports
Bloomington Pantagraph	DataTimes
Camden Courier-Post	CompuServe
Cape Cod Times	Dow Jones, CompuServe, PACER
Charleston Post & Courier	CompuServe, state BBSs
Charleston Gazette (WV)	In-house library, government databases
Chicago Tribune	In-house database, Nexis, DataTimes, Dialog
Cincinnati Enquirer	Tristate Online, Internet, CompuServe
Cleveland Plain Dealer	County auditor records, Information America, various other online government databases
Columbus Dispatch	Internet, Lexis/Nexis, FedWorld
Dallas Morning News	CompuServe, America Online, MetroNet
Dayton Daily News	County government, Prodigy, Nexis
Decatur Herald & Review	Dun & Bradstreet Market Identifier, Business DB Plus, Disclosure II
Des Moines Register	Iowa motor vehicles, Local property records, DataTimes (in-house)
Deseret News	DataTimes, CompuServe, Internet

Detroit Free Press	Lexis, Internet, PressLink
Detroit News	Lexis/Nexis, National Credit Data Network, local court records
Doylestown Intelligencer Record	CompuServe, Bell Atlantic Intelligate
Elmira Star-Gazette	Prodigy, CompuServe
Eugene Register-Guard	CompuServe financial databases, regional online public records services
Evansville Courier	Vu/Text, Fed World
Flint Journal	County court records, Dialog, DataTimes
Florida Times-Union	Lexis, Nexis
Florida Today	CompuServe
Fort Lauderdale *Sun-Sentinel*	In-house database, Dialog, local courts, Nexis
Fort Wayne Journal-Gazette	Vu-Text, DataTimes, Dialog
Gannett Suburban Newspapers, Westchester	Nexis, CompuServe, Internet
Greensboro News & Record	Dialog, Nexis, Dow Jones, DataTimes
Greensburg *Tribune-Review*	Federal Election Commission online, CompuServe, Nexis, Dialog
Harrisburg Patriot-News	DataTimes
Hartford Courant	CompuServe, local BBSs, Nexis
Houston Chronicle	Nexis, DataTimes, Dialog
Huntington Herald Dispatch	CompuServe
Huntsville Times	PACER
Indianapolis Star	DataTimes, Nexis, government databases
Kansas City Star	Nexis, DataTimes, Dialog
Knoxville News-Sentinel	CompuServe, East Tennessee Bankruptcy Court (PACER), Vu-Text
Lakeland Ledger	Internet, DataTimes, CompuServe
Lansing State Journal	America Online, Labor Market Info. Online
Long Beach Press-Telegram	DataQuick, Dialog
Lorain Morning Journal	Nexis/Lexis, Presslink
Louisville Courier-Journal	Dialog, DataTimes, Nexis
Memphis Commercial-Appeal	Dialog, Nexis, DataTimes
Miami Herald	CompuServe, Nexis/Lexis, Dialog
Milwaukee Journal	Wisconsin census data, FEC, Nexis
Mobile Press Register	Dow Jones, Alabama Legislative Reports (ALERT), America Online
Modesto Bee	Nexis, DataTimes, America Online, Internet
Munster Times	Dialog, NewsNet, CompuServe
Muskegon Chronicle	DataTimes, Internet, Dialog
Newport News Daily Press	Dialog, state database services
Newsday	In-house databases, Nexis, Dialog, Dow Jones
Orange County Register	Nexis, Prentice-Hall Online, Dataquick/Damar
Orlando Sentinel	Dialog, Nexis, America Online
Peoria Journal Star	DataTimes, CompuServe, PACER
Philadelphia Inquirer	Nexis, Dialog (Vu/Text), CENDATA
Pittsburgh Post-Gazette	Vu-Text (own library), Nexis, Prodigy
Poughkeepsie Journal	CompuServe, National Library of Medicine, New York state motor vehicle database
Quad City Times	CompuServe
Reading Eagle and Times	DataTimes

Raleigh *News & Observer*	Lexis/Nexis, NandO.net/Internet, Dialog, Wake County database
Richmond Times-Dispatch	Dialog, state employment and corporate records
Roanoke Times & World-News	Lexis/Nexis, DataTimes, state court records, Internet, ProfNet
Rochester Democrat and Chronicle/Times-Union	N.Y. Department of Motor Vehicles, ProfNet, Internet
Rocky Mountain News	Denver court records, Internet, DataTimes
Royal Oak Daily Tribune	CompuServe
St. Louis Post-Dispatch	CompuServe, Dialog, Dow Jones, Nexis
St. Petersburg Times	Nexis/Lexis, Dialog, DataTimes
San Jose Mercury News	Mercury Center (AOL), Internet
Santa Cruz County Sentinel	Dow Jones, Internet, various private BBSs
Santa Rosa Press Democrat	Dialog, Infotek, Nexis
Sarasota Herald-Tribune	Nexis, CompuServe, Dialog
Seattle Times	In-house, state courts, CompuServe
Spartanburg Herald-Journal	DataTimes, CompuServe, PACER
Syracuse Post-Standard	Nexis, Dialog, CompuServe
Tallahassee Democrat	Vu/Text, Dialog news, Dialog business databases
Tampa Tribune	CompuServe, Dialog, Delphi/Internet
The Buffalo News	DataTimes, Dialog, Nexis
The Daily Oklahoman	In-house, DataTimes, Commerce Department BBS
The Eagle-Tribune (Lawrence)	PACER, Federal Election Commission online
The Press Enterprise (Riverside)	DataTimes, Lexis/Nexis, Local courts files
The Washington Post	In-house database, Lexis/Nexis, DataTimes, Dialog
The Columbian (Vancouver)	DataTimes, Washington state judicial and public disclosure databases
Torrance Daily Breeze	DataTimes, Nexis, Dialog
Tri-City Herald	CompuServe
Tucson Citizen	CompuServe, PressLink
Virginian-Pilot and *Ledger-Star*	Internet, Dialog, Nexis/Lexis
Waterloo Courier	Dialog
Wichita Eagle	Dialog (Vu/Text), DataTimes, Nexis
Wisconsin State Journal	Nexis, CompuServe, Dialog

Appendix C: Major Federal Government Bulletin Board Systems

BBS Name	Source	2400 Baud	9600 Baud
Agriculture Forum Library	Agriculture	301-504-5496	
		301-504-6510	
Alternative Treatment Technology	Environmental Protection Agency	301-670-3808	301-670-3813
Astronomy	National Aeronautics and Space Administration	301-286-9000	
		301-286-9500	
Aviation Safety Exchange	Federal Aviation Administration	800-426-3814	
Biological Impact Assessment	Agriculture	703-231-3858	800-624-2723
Bureau of Mines	Interior		202-501-0373
Census	Commerce	301-763-7554	301-763-1568
Cite	Federal Court System	513-684-2842	
Civil Rights Division	Justice	202-514-6193	
CleanUp Information	Environmental Protection Agency		301-589-8366
Climate Dialup Service	Commerce	301-899-1173	301-899-1174
Coast Guard Global Position System Information Center	Transportation		703-313-5910
Congressional Budget Office	Congress	202-226-2818	
Consular Affairs	State		202-647-9225
Computer Security	Commerce	301-948-5717	301-948-5140
Customs	Customs		202-376-7100
Data Management Information Exchange	Commerce	301-948-2059 (1200 baud)	
Defense Communications Agency Acquisitions	Defense	618-256-8200	
Drinking Water Information	Environmental Protection Agency	800-229-3737	
		703-339-0420	
Economic	Commerce	202-482-3870	202-482-2584
Emergency Management Data Users Group	Federal Emergency Management Administration		202-646-2883
Environmental Protection Agency	Environmental Protection Agency		919-541-5742
EPA Research & Development	Environmental Protection Agency		800-258-9605
			513-569-7610
EPA Technology Transfer	Environmental Protection Agency	404-347-1767	
Export License Status Advisor	Defense	703-697-6109	
FCC Public Access Link	Federal Communications Commission	301-725-1072	

Service	Agency	Phone	Phone
FCC Industry Analysis	Federal Communications Commission	202-632-1361	
FedWorld	Commerce		703-321-8020
Federal Energy Agency Issuance Posting System	Energy	202-208-1397	
Federal Highway Electronic	Transportation	202-366-3764	
Federal Info Exchange	Education		800-783-3349 301-258-0953
Federal Jobs Board	Office of Personnel Management	313-226-4423 (1200 baud) 404-730-2370	215-580-2216
Federal Quality Institute	Office of Personnel Management	202-606-4800	
Federal Register (Electronic)	National Archives	202-275-1583	202-275-0920
Federal Reserve Board	Federal Reserve Board	214-922-5199	
Federal Reserve Economic Data	Federal Reserve Board		314-621-1824
Fire Research	Commerce	301-921-6302	
Food & Drug Administration	Food and Drug Administration		800-222-0185 301-227-6849
Fossil Energy Telenews	Energy	202-586-6496	
Global Seismology & Geomagnetism Online Info	Interior	800-358-2663 (1200 baud)	
Government Ethics Office	Executive Offices		202-523-1186
Government Printing Office	Government Printing Office		202-512-1387
Gulfline	National Oceanographic and Atmospheric Administration		800-258-9605 513-569-7610 708-972-3275
Hazardous Materials Information Exchange	Federal Emergency Management Agency		
Head Start Resource and Training Center	Education	301-985-7936	
Health and Human Services	Health and Human Services		202-690-5423
HUD News and Events	Housing and Urban Development	202-708-3562	
Information Reporting Project	Internal Revenue Service	304-263-2749	
Inventory Line	Treasury	202-874-6817 202-874-7034	
Jet Propulsion Laboratory	Jet Propulsion Laboratory	818-354-1333	
Kimberly	Federal Reserve Board		612-340-2489
Labor News	Labor	800-597-1221 202-219-4784	
Library Information Exchange	Library of Congress	202-707-4888	
Library of Congress Events	Library of Congress	202-707-3854	
Mechanicals & Materials Science	Food and Drug Administration		301-443-7496
Minority Impact	Energy	202-586-1561	
National Ecology Research Center	Interior		202-208-7119
National Education	Education	800-222-4972 202-219-2011	
Naval Computer and Telecommunication Station	Navy	202-433-8530	
Navinfonet	Defense		301-227-4424

Navy Justice School	Navy		401-841-3990
Navy Online Automation System	Navy		804-445-1121
NCJRS	Justice	301-738-8895	
Nutrition Databank	Agriculture	301-436-5078	
Offshore Oil and Gas Statistics	Interior	703-787-1181	
PerMaNet	State		703-715-9806
			703-715-9851
Pesticide Information Network	Environmental Protection Agency	703-305-5919	
Pollution BBSs	Environmental Protection Agency	703-506-1025	
Science and Technology Info	National Science Foundation		202-357-0359
Science Resource Studies	National Science Foundation	202-634-1764 (1200 baud)	
Small Businesses	Small Business Administration	800-859-INFO	800-697-INFO
Software Engineering Support Division	Army	703-285-9637	
Space Environmental Lab	National Oceanographic & Atmospheric Administration		303-497-5000
Spacelink	National Aeronautics & Space Administration		202-895-0028
Surety Bond Board	Treasury		202-874-7214
Tax filing (1040 BBS)	Internal Revenue Service	202-927-4180	
Wage Reporting	Internal Revenue Service		410-965-1133
Wastewater Treatment Info Exchange	Environmental Protection Agency	800-544-1936	
		304-293-3150	
Whistleblower Deficit Reduction Board	Congress	202-225-5527	

Source: Government BBS List. (1993, August). *Online Access, 8*(4), pp. 11–15.

Note: Some lines may be upgarded to 14400 and 28800 baud service. Dial 9600 number to check for updated service.

Appendix D: Sample Survey Research Questionnaire

In 1993, a national ethics study was conducted at the School of Communication of the University of Miami that focused on private lives and public officials. The survey was supervised by Professors Bruce Garrison and Sigman Splichal and data were collected by telephone. This is the questionnaire, or protocol, that was developed and used:

SURVEY RESEARCH PROJECT CENTER
JOURNALISM AND PHOTOGRAPHY PROGRAM
School of Communication
University of Miami
Coral Gables, FL 33124-2030

PUBLIC OFFICIALS AND PRIVATE LIVES SURVEY
QUESTIONNAIRE PROTOCOL

INTERVIEWERS: INSTRUCTIONS ARE WRITTEN IN ALL CAPS LIKE THIS. YOUR INTERVIEW "SCRIPT" FOLLOWS IN UPPER AND LOWER CASE LETTERS. DO NOT READ ANY INSTRUCTIONS ALOUD TO THE RESPONDENT. READ ONLY WHAT IS WRITTEN IN UPPER AND LOWER CASE IN THIS PROTOCOL TO A RESPONDENT. IF A QUESTION ARISES, ASK YOUR SUPERVISOR OR PROFESSOR.

BEFORE YOU GET A RESPONDENT ON THE LINE, ENTER THE FOLLOWING INFORMATION ON YOUR ANSWER SHEET. THE INFORMATION IS FOUND ON YOUR CALL LIST.

1. NEWSPAPER CIRCULATION (NUMBER)
2. OWNERSHIP (GROUP OR NON-GROUP)
3. STATE
4. REGION

AFTER YOU GET THE RESPONDENT ON THE LINE:
Good (morning, afternoon, evening). My name is _____
and I am calling from the School of Communication at the University of Miami. We are conducting a national telephone survey of newspapers that concerns journalism ethics, specifically upon public officials and their privacy. We will need only about ten minutes of your time. (IF RESPONDENT CANNOT COMPLETE INTERVIEW AT THIS TIME, ASK FOR AN APPOINTMENT FOR CALL BACK. GET PHONE NUMBER, DATE, AND TIME)
First, I need to gather information about you and your newspaper.

5. What is your present job title? (INTERVIEWER: SELECT RESPONSE WHICH BEST MATCHES THESE RESPONSES):
    (1) EDITOR OR EXECUTIVE EDITOR
    (2) MANAGING EDITOR OR ASSISTANT MANAGING EDITOR
    (3) STAFF ASSISTANT TO THE EDITOR OR MANAGING EDITOR
    (4) SECTION EDITOR
    (5) OTHER POSITION NOT LISTED ABOVE
    (8) REFUSED TO ANSWER
    (9) MISSING

6. Number of years as a journalist? _____

7. What is the number of newsroom employees at your newspaper? _____

8. INTERVIEWER, RECORD THE GENDER OF THE RESPONDENT ON YOUR ANSWER SHEET (IF YOU ARE NOT CERTAIN, CHECK THE PERSON'S NAME).
    (1) MALE
    (2) FEMALE
    (8) REFUSED TO ANSWER
    (9) MISSING

9. What is the <u>highest</u> level of education you received? Was it (READ RESPONSES):
    (1) High school degree or less
    (2) Some college, but no degree
    (3) College degree
    (4) Some graduate school, but no degree
    (5) Graduate degree
    (8) REFUSED TO ANSWER
    (9) MISSING

Now I would like to ask some questions about journalism ethics and privacy.

10. Does your newspaper have its own code of ethics? (DO NOT READ RESPONSES)
    (1) YES
    (2) NO
    (3) USES A CODE OF ETHICS OTHER THAN ITS OWN (e.g., SPJ)
    (4) DON'T KNOW
    (8) REFUSED TO ANSWER
    (9) MISSING

11. Does your newspaper have a formal policy regarding disclosure of intimate private information about public officials or public figures? (READ RESPONSES)
    (1) Yes (IF YES, GO TO QUESTION #12)
    (2) No (IF NO, GO TO QUESTION #13)
    (4) DON'T KNOW
    (8) REFUSED TO ANSWER
    (9) MISSING

12. Is this formal policy written? (DO NOT READ RESPONSES)
(1) YES
(2) NO
(4) DON'T KNOW
(8) REFUSED TO ANSWER
(9) MISSING

Now I would like to ask you a series of questions about the ethics of reporting about private lives of public figures. Answer these according to how you personally feel.

13. Should American voters be informed about the private lives of presidential candidates—including any extramarital affairs? (READ THE RESPONSES)
(1) Yes
(2) No
(3) DON'T KNOW
(8) REFUSED TO ANSWER
(9) MISSING

14. Does the press pay too much, the right amount, or too little attention to a candidate's personal life? (DO NOT READ RESPONSES)
(1) TOO MUCH
(2) RIGHT AMOUNT
(3) TOO LITTLE
(4) NOT SURE
(8) REFUSED TO ANSWER
(9) MISSING

15. If a competing medium reveals charges about a candidate's personal life, should an editor: (READ THE RESPONSES)
(1) Consider the charge to be news in itself and report it on that basis
(2) Check out the charge and do a story only if it can be independently verified
(3) Ignore the charge unless it seems clearly connected to the candidate's public duties
(4) DON'T KNOW
(8) REFUSED TO ANSWER
(9) MISSING

16. If your newspaper confirmed through routine reporting that a married candidate for a public office was having an affair, what would your newspaper do? I will read a series of options: (READ THE RESPONSES)
(1) We would definitely disclose
(2) Probably disclose
(3) Probably not disclose
(4) Definitely not disclose
(5) DON'T KNOW
(8) REFUSED TO ANSWER
(9) MISSING

17. If the married candidate having an affair made "family values" a political issue in his or her campaign? (READ THE RESPONSES)

(1) We would definitely disclose
(2) Probably disclose
(3) Probably not disclose
(4) Definitely not disclose
(5) DON'T KNOW
(8) REFUSED TO ANSWER
(9) MISSING

18. If you suspected a married political candidate was having an affair, which one of the following would you most likely do? (READ THE RESPONSES)

(1) Nothing at all
(2) Nothing, unless candidate or someone else made the issue public
(3) Ask the candidate and report only if he/she agrees to talk
(4) Seek sources with reliable knowledge of the affair
(5) Hire a private investigator to check it out
(6) Use reporters to put the candidate under surveillance
(8) REFUSED TO ANSWER
(9) MISSING

Now I have some questions about candidates for public office. Please describe how likely you would be to report information about a candidate for political office in the following situations:

19. If the candidate had a potentially debilitating disease, or had earlier suffered a serious heart attack, would your newspaper publish an article about it? (READ THE RESPONSES)

(1) Very likely
(2) Somewhat likely
(3) Not very likely
(4) Very unlikely
(5) DON'T KNOW
(8) REFUSED TO ANSWER
(9) MISSING

20. If the candidate had been accused of cheating in college, but the college never took formal action, would your newspaper publish an article about it? (READ THE RESPONSES)

(1) Very likely
(2) Somewhat likely
(3) Not very likely
(4) Very unlikely
(5) DON'T KNOW
(8) REFUSED TO ANSWER
(9) MISSING

21. If the candidate had been convicted of a crime, would your newspaper publish an article about it? (READ THE RESPONSES)
(1) Very likely
(2) Somewhat likely

(3) Not very likely
(4) Very unlikely
(5) DON'T KNOW
(8) REFUSED TO ANSWER
(9) MISSING

22. If the candidate had been accused of sexual harassment, but the charge proved inconclusive, would your newspaper publish an article about it? (READ THE RESPONSES)
(1) Very likely
(2) Somewhat likely
(3) Not very likely
(4) Very unlikely
(5) DON'T KNOW
(8) REFUSED TO ANSWER
(9) MISSING

23. If the candidate had undergone an abortion, or had a close family member who had done so, and then spoke publicly against abortion, would your newspaper publish an article about it? (READ THE RESPONSES)
(1) Very likely
(2) Somewhat likely
(3) Not very likely
(4) Very unlikely
(5) DON'T KNOW
(8) REFUSED TO ANSWER
(9) MISSING

24. If the candidate had been treated for substance abuse, would your newspaper publish an article about it? (READ THE RESPONSES)
(1) Very likely
(2) Somewhat likely
(3) Not very likely
(4) Very unlikely
(5) DON'T KNOW
(8) REFUSED TO ANSWER
(9) MISSING

25. If the candidate had been treated for a psychological disorder, such as depression, would your newspaper publish an article about it? (READ THE RESPONSES)
(1) Very likely
(2) Somewhat likely
(3) Not very likely
(4) Very unlikely
(5) DON'T KNOW
(8) REFUSED TO ANSWER
(9) MISSING

26. How would you rate *your readers'* interest in intimate details about public figures?

(1) Very interested
(2) Somewhat interested
(3) Not very interested
(4) Very uninterested
(5) DON'T KNOW
(8) REFUSED TO ANSWER
(9) MISSING

27. How much do you believe news media coverage of intimate private details about public figures hurts news media credibility?
    (1) Hurts very much
    (2) Hurts somewhat
    (3) Doesn't hurt very much
    (4) Doesn't hurt at all
    (5) DON'T KNOW
    (8) REFUSED TO ANSWER
    (9) MISSING

That concludes my questions. I want to thank you for your time and your responses. Good-bye.

INTERVIEWER: PLEASE REVIEW YOUR ANSWER SHEET CAREFULLY AT THE END OF THE INTERVIEW. CHECK FOR MISSING RESPONSES. IF YOU REMEMBER AN ANSWER MARK IT. IF NOT, ENTER A "9" ON THE SHEET.

Appendix E: Survey Database and SPSS Programming Example

The following sample program commands are written for the Statistical Package for the Social Sciences (SPSS/PC+) Studentware Plus. These are only basic examples of possible analytical approaches using descriptive and crosstabs procedures. The data were collected from the 1993 University of Miami ethics study questionnaire contained in Appendix D.

```
set printer on.
    data list /ID 1-3
    circulat 5-11
    owners 13
    state 15-16
    region 18
    jobtitle 20
    yearsexp 22-23
    staff 25-28
    sex 30
    educate 32
    code 34
    policy 36
    written 38
    affairs 40
    personal 42
    compete 44
    married 46
    family 48
    coverage 50
    health 52
    cheater 54
    crime 56
    sexual 58
    abortion 60
    drugs 62
    psycho 64
    intimate 66
    credible 68.
```

```
begin data
001 0005500 1 14 3 2 30 0007 1 2 2 1 2 1 1 1 3 1 2 1 2 1 2 2 1 2 2 1
002 0007800 1 14 3 2 18 0011 1 3 1 2 9 3 1 2 3 2 2 1 3 1 2 2 2 3 2 2
003 0035000 2 14 3 2 20 0044 1 3 1 2 9 3 1 8 5 2 8 2 8 1 1 5 2 5 2 2
004 0005500 1 14 3 4 30 0025 2 2 2 2 9 2 1 2 4 2 1 4 4 1 2 4 4 4 1 1
005 0031000 2 14 3 2 21 0030 1 3 2 2 9 3 1 2 3 2 2 2 3 1 2 3 2 3 2 2
006 0007200 2 14 3 2 35 0009 1 3 2 2 9 2 1 3 3 2 1 3 3 2 3 3 3 3 1 2
007 0032000 1 48 2 1 22 9999 1 3 2 2 9 1 1 2 3 2 4 1 4 2 4 3 2 5 2 2
008 0015800 2 48 2 4 07 0012 2 3 1 2 2 1 4 2 2 2 2 2 1 2 5 1 2 2 1 2
009 0020800 2 48 2 1 46 0026 1 5 1 2 9 1 2 2 2 1 4 1 5 2 2 1 1 1 2 4
010 0008500 1 48 2 1 10 0013 1 3 2 2 9 2 1 1 4 2 4 2 4 4 3 1 2 3 2 1
011 0033801 1 50 4 4 20 0021 1 3 1 1 2 3 2 3 5 2 2 1 3 5 3 2 2 1 2 5
012 0003800 2 50 4 2 21 0005 1 3 1 1 1 1 2 1 1 4 2 1 2 3 1 1 1 1 2
013 0004000 1 50 4 2 10 0006 1 1 2 2 9 1 1 2 1 1 4 1 1 2 3 1 1 1 1 1
014 0009500 1 13 3 2 19 0012 1 3 1 2 9 1 2 2 2 2 4 1 2 1 3 1 1 1 2 2
015 0005800 2 13 3 2 30 0007 1 1 1 1 2 9 1 1 2 5 2 2 2 3 1 2 5 3 5 2 2
016 0007000 1 13 3 1 22 0040 1 3 3 2 9 1 4 1 2 1 4 1 4 1 4 2 3 3 3 2
017 0015000 1 13 3 1 20 0085 1 3 2 2 9 1 2 2 2 1 4 2 3 1 2 1 2 3 2 3
018 0005000 1 13 3 2 25 0004 1 1 1 2 9 1 2 2 5 1 4 4 3 1 3 3 2 2 1 2
019 0030000 2 09 2 2 12 0030 1 3 2 2 2 1 2 2 2 2 4 1 1 1 3 3 1 3 2 2
020 0011000 2 10 2 1 19 0010 1 3 2 2 2 1 2 8 3 8 2 2 4 8 4 4 3 4 2 4
021 0029000 1 10 2 1 26 0032 1 3 2 2 2 1 2 2 2 1 3 2 3 2 3 1 2 2 1 3
022 0006000 1 10 2 1 16 0006 1 3 2 2 2 1 2 1 3 3 2 1 4 1 1 1 8 8 1 4
023 0022000 1 09 2 1 12 0026 1 5 3 1 4 1 2 3 4 8 8 8 8 8 8 1 8 8 2 8
024 0012000 2 07 1 1 24 0016 1 3 2 2 2 2 1 2 3 2 2 2 3 2 3 2 3 3 1 2
025 0005000 1 09 2 4 35 0003 1 3 1 1 2 1 1 2 2 1 4 1 3 1 3 1 2 3 2 2
026 0043000 2 42 2 1 51 0050 1 3 1 1 1 1 2 2 1 1 3 1 4 1 4 2 2 2 1 3
027 0127000 1 42 2 2 27 0112 2 4 2 2 9 2 1 2 8 2 3 1 8 1 8 1 2 3 3 1
028 0007400 1 43 2 2 09 0027 2 1 3 2 2 2 1 2 3 3 2 2 4 1 3 4 2 3 2 2
029 0023000 1 43 2 2 28 0025 2 4 1 2 9 1 1 2 3 2 4 3 4 1 3 2 2 4 2 1
030 0003400 1 43 2 1 20 0008 2 1 1 2 9 2 1 3 4 4 1 4 4 3 4 4 4 4 1 1
031 0017000 2 43 2 2 19 0020 1 4 1 2 9 1 2 2 2 1 3 1 2 1 2 2 2 2 2 2
032 0180000 1 09 2 1 21 0238 1 5 1 2 2 2 2 8 3 1 4 1 3 2 3 1 3 2 1 3
033 0125000 1 09 2 5 20 0090 2 2 1 2 2 1 1 2 3 2 2 2 2 1 2 1 3 3 1 2
034 0014000 1 09 2 1 27 0009 1 2 1 2 2 1 1 3 3 2 3 1 4 1 4 3 2 2 2 1
035 0017506 2 48 1 2 24 0022 1 3 1 2 2 2 1 3 3 3 2 1 4 1 2 1 1 1 2 1
036 0007500 2 49 3 1 25 0025 1 3 1 2 9 1 1 2 1 1 4 5 4 2 3 1 1 1 1 3
037 0022000 1 49 3 5 04 0020 2 3 4 2 4 1 1 2 1 1 4 1 2 1 2 1 1 1 1 1 1
038 0088000 1 49 3 5 01 0035 1 3 1 4 1 1 1 2 2 1 4 1 4 1 4 1 1 1 1 2 2
039 0280000 2 49 3 2 01 0060 2 2 4 4 4 3 2 2 2 1 4 3 4 2 2 1 3 5 2 2
040 0025000 1 33 2 1 14 0045 1 2 2 2 9 2 1 2 2 2 1 3 2 2 1 3 2 2 2
041 0002500 1 33 2 2 07 0020 1 5 2 2 9 1 1 2 2 1 3 3 3 2 2 1 3 3 1 2
042 0045000 2 32 1 2 15 0150 1 5 1 2 9 1 1 3 3 1 2 1 8 1 8 8 8 8 2 2
043 0088000 1 32 1 2 17 0550 1 4 2 2 9 3 1 4 3 2 2 1 3 1 3 5 2 2 1 1
044 0003000 1 32 1 1 05 0025 1 5 2 2 9 1 1 4 3 3 2 2 2 2 4 2 2 2 1 2
```

```
045 0005700 1 32 1 1 08 0045 1 3 2 2 9 1 1 2 2 2 6 2 4 4 4 2 2 4 2 2
046 0010000 1 32 1 1 08 0070 1 3 1 2 9 3 2 2 2 2 2 2 2 2 1 3 2 2 2
047 0007000 1 32 1 2 15 0100 1 3 2 2 9 3 2 4 5 2 2 2 3 1 1 5 2 3 1 3
048 0120000 2 32 1 2 15 0025 1 1 1 1 2 2 4 3 2 1 2 2 1 2 2 5 2 5 2 2
049 0005000 1 32 1 1 22 0030 2 1 1 2 9 3 2 2 3 2 2 2 3 2 3 5 2 3 2 1
050 0018500 1 32 1 5 36 0125 1 3 1 1 1 1 3 1 1 2 1 3 1 3 3 1 3 2 2
051 0020000 1 32 1 1 12 0100 1 3 2 2 9 1 1 2 3 1 2 2 3 1 3 1 3 3 3 2
052 0016000 2 32 1 2 20 0050 1 3 2 2 9 3 2 2 5 3 1 2 2 1 2 4 2 4 3 2
053 0005000 1 22 3 1 03 0004 1 3 1 2 9 1 1 2 3 1 2 1 4 5 4 5 4 4 2 5
054 0006000 1 22 3 1 03 0007 1 4 2 1 9 1 1 2 2 1 2 2 3 1 2 1 3 4 2 2
055 0074000 1 22 3 2 21 0064 1 4 1 2 9 1 1 2 3 2 1 2 4 1 3 2 3 3 2 2
056 0026568 1 22 3 1 15 0034 1 5 1 2 9 1 2 3 3 1 2 2 3 2 2 1 3 4 2 2
057 0078000 1 13 3 2 17 0075 1 3 1 2 9 1 2 2 5 2 4 1 5 1 5 5 2 5 2 2
058 0005000 1 13 3 1 23 0005 1 3 2 2 9 3 2 2 3 2 2 1 4 2 3 4 4 5 2 2
059 0010000 2 29 1 4 06 0085 1 3 2 2 9 1 1 2 2 2 3 2 3 2 3 1 2 3 1 2
060 0016000 2 29 1 1 27 0085 1 4 1 1 1 3 1 2 3 1 4 2 4 1 2 1 2 3 1 2
061 0030000 1 29 1 1 30 0100 2 4 2 1 2 1 2 2 3 2 4 2 3 1 2 1 1 2 1 2
062 0012000 1 30 1 1 17 0018 2 3 2 1 2 1 1 2 3 1 6 1 3 1 1 2 4 3 1 2
063 0050000 2 30 1 1 30 0250 1 5 2 1 9 3 2 4 3 2 2 2 3 5 5 5 5 3 2 3
064 0015000 1 31 4 1 12 0060 2 5 1 2 9 1 2 2 2 2 2 2 1 2 2 2 4 2 2
065 0010000 1 31 4 1 35 0048 1 1 2 2 9 1 1 2 1 1 3 1 4 1 4 1 1 1 1 2
066 0003000 1 31 4 1 43 0013 2 3 2 4 9 1 8 2 3 2 3 8 8 8 8 8 8 8 1 2
067 0020000 1 30 1 1 34 0080 1 4 2 2 9 8 2 3 3 3 2 2 3 1 1 2 1 3 1 4
068 0067000 1 30 1 2 17 0055 1 3 1 2 9 1 2 2 2 4 1 2 1 1 1 1 1 2 3
069 0008000 2 14 2 1 24 0008 1 3 2 2 9 1 2 2 3 2 4 2 4 1 4 4 3 4 2 2
070 0021000 1 14 2 2 32 0025 1 2 1 2 9 1 1 2 3 2 4 2 2 1 3 4 3 3 2 1
071 0007000 1 14 2 2 10 0007 1 3 1 2 9 1 2 2 3 2 1 3 2 2 5 2 3 2 2
072 0006500 1 14 2 1 21 0007 1 3 2 2 9 1 1 2 3 2 4 2 3 2 3 3 2 2 1 2
073 0014000 1 14 2 2 20 0017 1 3 1 1 2 3 2 2 5 2 8 2 5 1 3 5 2 3 1 2
074 0012560 1 36 2 2 26 0014 1 2 1 1 2 1 2 2 2 1 4 1 3 1 3 2 2 2 2
075 0012000 1 14 3 1 35 0010 1 3 2 1 2 2 1 3 2 2 3 1 2 1 2 2 3 3 1 2
076 0032356 1 20 2 2 25 0028 1 2 2 2 9 1 2 2 5 1 8 1 4 1 4 2 2 4 2 4
077 0041000 1 21 1 4 13 0048 1 3 2 2 9 2 1 2 4 4 2 2 3 1 4 3 3 3 2 2
078 0004300 1 21 1 2 10 0006 2 3 2 2 9 1 1 3 2 1 2 3 3 1 3 3 3 3 1 1
079 0013000 1 18 2 1 18 0009 1 3 2 2 9 3 2 2 3 1 2 2 3 1 4 3 3 3 2 3
080 0015000 2 21 1 2 20 0015 1 3 2 2 9 2 1 3 3 2 2 2 3 1 5 1 3 3 1 1
081 0014500 1 19 1 2 18 0026 1 3 2 2 9 3 2 3 3 1 1 1 2 5 4 1 4 4 1 3
082 0020000 1 18 2 2 16 0010 1 3 2 2 9 2 1 2 3 2 2 3 3 1 4 3 3 3 1 1
083 0022500 1 20 2 1 17 0035 1 3 2 2 9 2 1 3 3 3 4 2 4 1 3 3 2 3 1 2
084 0048500 1 18 2 1 31 0047 1 4 2 2 9 1 1 2 3 2 2 1 3 1 2 2 1 2 1 2
085 0020000 2 20 2 2 20 0050 1 2 2 1 2 1 1 2 3 2 2 2 3 1 3 2 2 2 2 2
086 0025000 1 19 1 1 25 0035 1 5 2 2 9 1 1 2 3 2 2 2 3 2 3 1 4 4 2 2
087 0120000 2 21 1 1 15 0115 2 3 1 2 9 1 2 3 3 2 2 3 4 3 3 3 3 3 2 2
088 0022000 2 21 1 1 25 0044 1 3 2 2 9 1 2 2 2 2 2 4 2 4 2 2 2 2 2
089 0025500 1 38 1 2 20 0039 1 3 1 2 9 1 2 2 3 2 1 1 3 2 2 2 2 2 1 2
```

```
090 0015000 1 40 2 2 13 0021 1 4 2 2 1 2 1 2 3 2 1 2 3 1 3 1 2 2 2 2
091 0016200 1 40 2 9 13 0021 1 4 2 2 9 2 1 2 3 2 1 2 3 1 3 1 2 2 2 2
092 0035000 1 38 1 1 25 0038 1 5 2 2 2 1 1 2 3 5 1 1 3 2 1 2 2 5 2 2
093 0003700 1 36 2 4 03 0005 1 3 1 2 9 1 1 2 2 1 2 2 3 2 3 2 2 3 2 2
094 0008100 2 35 3 1 05 0005 2 2 1 1 2 1 1 2 3 2 4 2 4 1 3 3 2 2 1 2
095 0007220 1 35 3 1 10 0007 1 3 2 2 9 1 2 2 2 1 2 3 3 2 3 2 3 4 2 3
096 0023000 1 35 3 2 10 0021 1 3 2 2 9 1 1 1 3 2 1 1 4 1 2 2 2 1 4 2
097 0005300 1 36 2 4 03 0007 1 3 1 1 1 1 2 2 2 2 4 2 3 1 1 3 1 2 2 2
098 0030000 1 16 3 2 22 0036 1 5 1 2 9 1 1 3 3 3 2 2 4 1 3 2 2 2 2 2
099 0142150 1 46 2 9 15 0130 1 3 2 2 9 1 2 2 2 2 2 1 1 1 3 2 2 2 1 2
100 0030165 1 47 4 2 19 0015 1 3 1 4 9 1 2 3 2 1 3 2 3 1 4 2 4 3 1 2
101 0008800 2 46 2 2 22 0016 1 3 1 2 9 1 1 2 2 2 4 1 4 1 2 2 3 3 1 2
102 0011200 1 46 2 2 21 0013 1 5 1 2 9 1 2 1 1 1 5 1 1 1 1 1 1 2 1 4
103 1325500 1 46 2 9 17 0160 1 3 8 4 9 1 1 3 2 1 2 2 4 2 4 2 3 4 1 2
104 0010000 1 45 1 2 16 0014 1 5 2 2 9 1 1 1 2 1 2 2 2 1 3 1 4 3 1 2
105 0023500 1 46 2 1 27 0034 1 3 1 1 1 1 4 2 9 2 2 1 3 3 3 2 3 3 2 3
106 0013391 2 35 3 1 26 0012 1 3 2 2 9 1 1 2 3 2 2 1 3 1 3 1 2 3 1 2
107 0007400 1 35 3 1 13 0005 1 3 2 2 2 9 1 3 4 2 2 2 3 1 2 1 1 2 2 3
108 0057280 1 35 3 3 18 0060 1 3 2 1 2 1 1 9 2 1 4 1 3 1 3 1 1 4 1 2
109 0009696 1 35 3 4 07 0013 2 3 1 1 1 3 1 3 2 2 2 1 2 1 2 1 1 3 1 1
110 0006108 2 35 3 3 16 0030 1 3 1 1 2 1 2 2 2 1 3 1 2 1 2 2 3 2 2 2
111 0004500 2 35 3 2 02 0023 1 3 1 4 4 1 2 2 3 2 3 2 2 1 3 2 1 2 1 3
112 0006600 2 35 3 2 08 0012 1 3 2 2 9 1 1 2 8 1 4 4 4 2 2 2 2 3 1 2
113 0016528 1 35 3 2 23 0020 1 3 2 2 2 1 1 2 5 2 4 2 3 1 3 8 8 8 2 2
114 0012825 1 35 3 1 20 0070 1 3 2 2 9 1 1 2 3 3 2 3 3 1 3 3 2 3 3 2
115 0038450 1 35 3 1 20 0035 1 3 3 2 9 8 1 3 3 2 2 2 3 1 3 1 2 2 2 2
116 0078000 1 37 4 2 14 0067 1 3 1 2 9 1 2 2 3 2 4 1 3 1 3 1 1 1 2 2
117 0030000 1 37 4 1 18 0042 1 3 1 2 9 1 1 2 3 2 2 1 3 1 3 2 2 3 2 2
118 0022000 2 38 1 2 14 0030 1 3 1 2 9 1 1 2 2 1 4 1 3 2 3 2 5 3 3 2
119 0011500 1 38 1 2 30 0013 1 3 2 1 2 3 1 2 3 2 2 3 3 1 2 2 3 3 2 2
120 0005166 1 38 1 4 03 0050 2 3 1 9 1 1 3 2 3 3 2 3 3 1 2 3 3 3 2 2
121 0042000 1 27 3 1 30 0300 1 3 2 2 8 9 1 3 8 8 8 2 8 1 5 5 5 5 3 2
122 0033500 1 26 4 1 17 0105 1 3 1 2 9 2 1 2 3 2 3 1 2 1 2 3 2 2 2 2
123 0019000 1 15 3 2 20 0023 1 5 2 2 9 2 1 3 3 2 2 2 3 1 3 1 3 3 4 2
124 0003200 1 15 3 2 17 0005 1 3 2 2 9 1 2 2 2 1 3 2 4 1 3 3 5 5 1 2
125 0005800 1 15 3 2 10 0006 1 3 2 2 9 1 2 2 2 1 4 2 3 1 3 2 2 2 2 2
126 0002300 1 15 3 1 15 0004 1 5 2 2 9 1 1 2 2 1 4 2 3 2 2 1 2 2 2 3
127 0016000 1 15 3 2 17 0030 1 4 1 2 9 2 1 3 2 1 2 2 3 2 3 1 2 3 3 1
128 0020600 1 15 3 1 20 0025 1 3 2 2 9 1 1 2 3 2 4 2 3 1 2 3 2 2 2 3
129 0006200 1 15 3 2 08 0005 1 3 2 1 2 2 1 2 3 3 2 1 2 1 2 3 1 2 2 1
130 0050000 1 15 3 2 29 0035 2 3 2 2 9 1 1 3 3 1 3 1 3 1 2 1 2 2 2 2
131 0053000 1 15 3 2 41 0045 1 2 1 2 9 1 1 2 3 2 2 2 3 2 3 2 2 3 1 3
132 0006200 1 16 3 2 11 0007 1 3 2 2 9 1 2 3 3 1 2 1 4 1 3 2 3 2 2 2
133 0003900 2 16 3 1 15 0004 1 3 2 2 9 1 2 1 3 2 2 1 4 1 4 4 1 3 1 2
134 0003400 2 16 3 1 30 0004 1 3 2 2 9 1 1 2 3 1 2 2 3 1 2 2 3 4 2 2
```

```
135 0005000 1 16 3 5 05 0005 1 3 1 2 9 1 1 2 3 2 2 2 3 2 3 2 2 2 2 3
136 0003200 1 16 3 2 06 0002 2 3 1 1 2 2 1 2 3 2 4 1 4 1 1 1 2 3 2 2
137 0040000 1 16 3 2 15 0024 2 3 2 2 9 1 3 3 2 2 2 1 2 1 2 2 2 4 2 2
138 0070000 1 38 1 1 25 0073 1 4 1 2 9 1 2 2 4 1 4 1 4 1 4 1 4 3 1 2
139 0012500 1 38 1 1 17 0010 2 5 3 2 9 1 2 2 2 2 4 1 3 1 1 2 1 2 2 2
140 0350000 1 37 4 2 30 0310 1 4 3 2 9 2 1 3 3 1 1 1 3 1 1 2 2 3 3 1
141 0018000 2 38 1 2 29 0016 1 2 2 2 9 1 2 3 3 2 2 9 9 9 9 9 9 9 9 9
142 0010500 2 49 3 5 09 0021 2 3 2 2 9 1 2 2 2 1 6 1 4 5 4 1 1 1 1 2
143 0028000 2 49 3 2 22 0250 1 3 1 2 9 1 2 3 1 1 4 1 4 2 2 1 1 1 2 1
144 0023000 1 49 3 4 12 0100 2 3 2 1 2 1 1 2 3 1 4 1 4 2 4 1 1 1 1 2 2
145 0005302 1 49 3 8 02 0020 1 3 2 2 9 1 1 3 2 1 4 2 4 2 3 1 1 2 2 3
146 0028000 1 49 3 1 28 9999 1 3 1 2 9 1 1 2 1 1 4 1 4 2 5 1 1 1 2 1
147 0263313 2 35 3 4 22 0225 1 3 2 2 9 8 2 3 3 2 1 3 2 1 3 2 2 3 1 2
148 0150194 2 35 3 1 27 0150 1 3 1 1 2 1 2 2 3 2 4 1 2 1 3 2 2 2 2 3
149 0010284 2 35 3 1 27 0012 1 3 2 2 9 1 2 1 2 1 4 2 3 1 3 2 3 3 1 3
150 0007487 1 35 3 2 11 0011 2 3 1 2 9 1 1 2 2 1 2 3 3 1 2 3 2 2 2 3
151 0198475 1 35 3 3 19 0180 1 3 2 2 1 2 2 2 3 2 6 1 3 1 2 2 2 2 1 2
152 0097500 1 51 1 2 40 0225 1 3 2 1 2 1 2 2 3 3 3 2 4 1 3 3 2 2 1 3
153 0038000 1 09 2 2 26 0052 2 5 1 2 2 1 1 2 3 1 4 1 1 1 2 1 3 3 2 2
154 0013500 1 21 1 2 11 0015 2 2 2 2 9 1 1 2 2 1 3 2 3 1 1 1 3 3 1 3
155 0014000 1 21 1 4 49 0009 1 1 2 2 9 1 2 2 3 2 4 1 3 1 2 3 2 1 1 2
156 0003650 1 43 2 5 00 0002 1 2 1 1 1 1 2 4 3 4 3 3 5 3 2 3 3 2 2
157 0004300 1 43 2 2 10 0005 1 3 2 2 9 1 4 2 5 5 1 4 3 2 3 2 3 3 3 2
158 0007560 1 43 2 2 25 0005 2 1 2 1 2 1 4 3 5 5 2 4 3 2 3 2 3 3 3 2
159 0023364 1 43 2 1 20 0006 2 1 2 1 2 1 4 2 5 5 1 4 3 2 3 2 3 3 3 2
160 0017000 2 10 2 2 17 0016 1 3 1 2 2 1 2 2 2 1 2 2 3 1 3 1 2 2 2 2
161 0008500 1 43 2 2 15 0005 1 2 1 1 1 1 2 4 3 4 3 3 5 3 2 3 3 3 2
162 0008300 1 43 2 2 25 0008 1 2 1 1 1 1 2 4 3 4 3 3 5 3 2 3 2 2 2
163 0008500 1 43 2 1 26 0009 1 3 2 2 9 1 1 3 2 1 4 1 3 1 1 1 1 1 1 2
164 0009500 2 43 2 1 25 0010 1 2 3 2 2 1 1 2 1 1 4 1 3 1 1 1 1 2 1 2
165 0012000 1 13 3 2 22 0019 1 3 2 2 2 1 2 2 2 1 4 2 4 2 3 3 2 3 2 3
166 0003400 1 36 2 2 30 0004 1 2 1 2 9 1 4 2 3 2 4 1 1 1 2 1 1 2 2 2
167 0015000 1 14 3 2 08 0019 2 3 2 2 2 1 1 3 3 2 4 4 4 4 2 4 4 4 2 2
168 0003000 1 36 2 2 02 0003 2 3 3 1 2 2 1 2 2 1 4 2 3 1 1 2 3 3 1 1
169 0003000 2 36 2 1 18 0003 1 3 2 2 9 1 2 2 3 3 1 2 3 1 4 3 3 3 2 3
170 0007184 1 36 2 1 04 0006 1 3 1 2 9 2 1 2 3 1 2 2 3 1 3 2 2 3 1 1
171 0005400 2 36 2 5 03 0003 1 3 1 2 9 2 1 2 3 2 2 3 4 1 3 2 2 3 2 1
172 0128311 2 36 2 4 25 0100 1 2 2 2 9 1 2 3 3 2 1 1 4 1 2 1 2 2 1 2
173 0006450 1 36 2 2 14 0005 1 3 2 2 9 1 1 3 2 1 2 2 4 1 2 1 2 2 2 2
174 0007410 1 13 3 1 07 0006 1 2 2 2 2 1 1 2 2 1 2 2 3 2 3 3 4 3 2 2
175 0005100 1 13 3 2 18 0004 1 3 2 1 2 2 1 2 2 2 3 1 2 1 3 2 2 1 2 3
176 0085000 1 09 2 2 16 0110 2 3 1 2 2 1 1 3 3 2 2 4 2 1 3 2 2 3 3 2
177 0017000 1 09 2 2 23 0016 2 2 2 2 2 1 2 2 3 3 3 2 4 1 2 4 2 4 2 2
178 0039000 1 13 3 2 25 0033 1 5 1 2 2 1 2 2 2 8 4 4 1 1 4 4 1 4 1 4
179 0052000 1 03 4 4 12 0070 2 3 1 4 9 3 2 2 3 2 4 2 3 1 2 8 2 3 2 3
```

```
180 0020500 1 03 4 1 28 0021 2 2 1 1 1 1 2 3 2 1 3 1 1 1 1 8 1 3 2 2
181 0015000 1 04 2 2 25 0024 1 3 2 2 9 1 1 2 3 1 3 2 4 2 3 2 2 2 2 2
182 0075000 1 03 4 1 24 0099 1 3 3 2 9 9 2 3 3 2 4 1 2 1 2 2 1 2 2 2
183 0010000 2 03 4 5 17 0010 1 3 2 2 9 1 2 2 3 2 2 2 4 2 3 3 3 3 2 2
184 0009500 2 04 2 2 13 0009 1 3 2 2 9 3 1 2 3 2 4 2 4 1 3 2 2 3 2 3
185 0005000 1 04 2 2 10 0005 1 3 2 2 9 1 1 2 2 2 6 2 3 2 2 2 2 2 2 2
186 0013000 2 01 2 2 25 0004 1 3 2 2 9 1 1 2 5 2 3 2 4 1 4 2 2 2 2 2
187 0009000 1 01 2 1 23 0016 1 2 2 2 9 2 1 2 3 2 3 1 3 1 2 5 2 3 1 2
188 0005000 1 15 3 2 12 0006 2 4 1 1 1 1 2 2 2 4 1 4 1 4 4 2 2 2 3
189 0059000 1 01 2 1 30 0083 1 3 1 1 1 2 1 2 2 2 2 1 2 1 2 2 1 3 1 2
190 0010500 1 23 3 1 20 0011 1 3 2 2 2 1 4 1 1 1 4 1 2 1 2 1 2 2 1 3
191 0024000 1 24 2 2 19 0025 1 3 1 1 2 1 1 1 2 2 2 2 4 3 3 1 4 4 5 1
192 0028000 1 24 2 4 20 0027 2 5 1 1 2 1 1 2 3 2 2 2 3 1 3 2 3 3 1 1
193 0005000 2 23 3 5 04 0035 1 3 2 2 2 1 1 3 3 3 1 3 2 2 2 3 3 3 2 2
194 0010000 1 23 3 1 14 0012 1 3 2 2 2 1 1 3 3 2 3 2 2 2 2 3 3 3 2 2
195 0015000 1 25 3 4 34 0020 1 3 2 2 2 1 1 3 4 2 2 2 4 2 4 2 2 4 1 3
196 0006000 1 25 3 4 10 0008 1 3 1 1 4 3 1 2 5 5 8 3 3 2 2 2 2 3 2 5
197 0039000 1 42 2 2 08 0043 1 4 1 2 9 1 1 3 3 2 4 1 3 1 2 8 2 8 2 2
198 0008000 2 14 3 2 20 0012 1 2 2 2 9 2 1 1 3 3 2 1 2 1 1 1 2 2 1 2
199 0004700 1 14 3 1 06 0003 1 3 1 2 9 1 2 2 3 1 4 2 3 1 3 2 3 3 1 2
200 0032000 1 05 4 1 25 0128 1 3 1 2 2 1 1 3 3 1 1 3 3 2 3 2 4 3 1 2
201 0008614 1 06 4 4 10 0067 2 2 1 1 2 1 1 2 3 5 2 3 4 3 4 3 4 4 1 1
202 0016000 1 05 4 3 33 0125 1 4 3 4 4 2 1 2 3 2 2 3 5 5 5 1 5 4 1 2
203 0430000 2 06 4 1 46 1500 1 1 2 1 2 1 4 2 5 2 2 2 3 1 3 1 5 3 1 3
204 0024500 1 06 4 4 21 0125 1 3 1 2 1 1 1 2 3 2 2 2 3 2 3 2 2 3 2 3
205 0003000 2 06 4 3 17 0030 1 3 2 2 2 2 1 2 3 2 2 2 4 2 4 2 3 3 1 2
206 0004500 1 06 4 1 12 0018 1 2 3 4 1 2 1 2 3 1 3 2 4 1 4 4 4 4 2 1
207 0030000 2 07 1 1 24 0200 1 4 2 1 1 1 1 2 2 4 1 3 1 1 1 2 2 1 2
208 0005300 1 06 4 1 30 0021 1 3 1 2 2 1 1 2 3 2 2 2 3 2 3 2 3 3 2 3
209 0012000 2 06 4 2 04 0045 1 3 1 2 2 1 2 2 2 2 4 2 3 1 2 1 1 2 1 3
210 0017000 2 06 4 2 19 0060 1 2 1 2 1 2 2 2 2 1 4 2 3 1 2 2 2 3 2 2
211 0035000 1 07 1 1 11 0198 1 3 1 1 1 1 2 2 2 1 4 2 3 1 2 2 3 3 1 2
212 0037500 1 07 1 2 14 0250 1 3 1 2 9 1 2 2 3 2 6 1 1 1 2 1 2 3 2 2
213 0008700 1 05 4 1 10 0045 1 3 3 2 9 1 1 3 3 2 3 1 2 5 2 2 1 1 1 1
214 0051000 1 13 3 4 15 0060 1 4 2 2 9 1 1 1 3 2 4 1 1 1 2 3 1 2 2 2
215 0006400 1 13 3 4 04 0006 1 3 1 2 9 2 1 4 3 2 1 1 4 1 3 1 4 4 5 2
216 0013100 2 10 2 4 05 0006 2 3 1 1 2 2 2 2 1 2 2 3 1 2 2 2 2 2 2
217 0110000 1 11 4 4 17 0090 2 5 1 2 9 1 1 3 2 2 4 1 3 1 2 5 2 2 2 2
218 0074500 1 10 2 2 11 0072 9 4 1 2 2 1 2 1 2 1 2 1 3 1 2 2 1 1 1 5
219 0025000 1 13 3 2 20 0038 1 3 1 1 2 1 4 2 2 1 2 2 4 1 4 2 3 2 2 2
220 0021000 1 10 2 2 16 0019 1 3 1 1 1 1 2 3 2 2 2 4 1 4 1 2 2 2 1
221 0040000 2 05 4 1 35 0040 1 3 1 2 2 1 2 2 2 1 2 1 4 1 4 3 3 3 1 2
222 0095000 1 05 4 2 09 0045 1 3 1 1 2 8 1 2 3 3 2 1 3 8 3 8 2 2 2 1
223 0011000 1 05 4 1 06 0010 1 2 1 1 1 1 2 2 2 2 4 2 2 1 2 3 2 3 2 2
224 0009000 1 05 4 1 15 0030 2 3 1 2 2 1 2 2 3 8 8 8 8 8 8 8 8 8 8
```

```
225 0010000 1 05 4 2 20 0010 1 3 2 2 2 1 1 2 3 2 2 1 3 1 2 3 2 4 2 2
226 0060000 2 05 4 2 44 0047 1 3 2 2 2 1 2 2 2 1 4 1 2 1 2 2 1 3 2 2
227 0135000 1 05 4 2 25 0140 2 3 1 2 2 1 2 3 8 2 4 2 3 3 3 2 2 3 3 2
228 0100000 1 05 4 2 22 0110 1 2 1 2 2 1 2 3 3 2 1 2 2 1 3 1 3 3 3 2
229 0044000 2 05 4 2 27 0200 2 3 1 2 2 1 1 2 2 2 2 3 1 3 1 3 3 2 3
230 0030000 1 05 4 1 21 0040 1 3 1 2 2 1 1 2 3 2 4 1 4 1 2 3 4 4 1 2
231 0090000 1 05 4 2 26 0100 2 5 1 2 2 1 1 3 2 2 1 1 1 1 1 1 1 2
232 0055000 1 05 4 2 20 0071 1 3 1 2 1 9 2 2 3 2 2 9 4 9 4 2 9 4 2 2
233 0037000 1 05 4 5 00 0050 1 5 1 4 1 1 2 2 2 1 4 1 3 1 1 1 1 2 1 2
234 0003700 2 07 1 1 40 0040 1 4 2 2 9 1 1 2 3 2 2 4 3 5 4 9 4 3 1 2
235 0032000 2 10 2 4 09 0015 1 3 1 1 2 3 1 2 2 1 2 2 3 1 2 2 2 3 2 2
236 0046000 2 13 3 2 19 0060 1 5 1 2 9 3 2 3 3 3 2 2 2 1 2 2 2 3 2 2
237 0014000 1 10 2 2 07 0014 1 3 2 1 1 1 3 3 3 2 1 2 1 2 3 2 2 1 3
238 0010000 2 12 4 1 15 0016 1 5 1 1 2 1 2 2 1 1 4 1 2 8 2 1 2 2 2 4
239 0020000 2 11 4 1 23 0025 1 2 1 2 9 1 2 2 3 2 3 2 3 1 2 4 2 4 2 2
240 0100000 2 05 4 2 10 0080 1 5 1 4 9 2 2 2 3 2 2 1 1 1 4 3 2 3 1 2
241 0004000 2 02 4 5 03 0011 9 5 1 2 1 2 3 3 2 1 4 2 3 2 2 2 3 3 2 3
242 0340000 1 05 4 2 28 0320 1 5 2 2 2 9 4 2 3 3 2 2 3 1 2 1 9 2 2 2
243 0009500 2 05 4 1 25 0020 1 2 1 2 2 9 2 9 3 2 3 9 3 1 2 2 9 3 3 3
244 0033900 1 05 4 1 24 0019 1 3 2 2 9 2 2 3 5 4 9 1 3 1 1 3 1 5 1 2
245 0004000 1 04 2 1 06 0017 1 5 2 2 9 1 2 1 3 2 2 2 4 1 4 2 2 2 1 2
246 0009500 1 04 2 1 24 0050 1 4 1 2 9 1 1 1 2 1 2 2 4 1 3 3 3 3 2 2
247 0040000 1 05 4 9 09 0060 1 3 1 4 9 1 2 3 5 2 2 1 5 1 1 5 2 1 2 2
248 0017000 1 05 4 1 15 0050 1 3 1 1 2 1 2 2 3 2 2 2 1 1 1 3 1 2 1 2
249 0022000 1 05 4 9 07 0012 1 3 2 2 2 1 2 2 3 2 3 2 3 5 4 2 2 3 2 3
250 0016000 1 04 2 1 10 0050 1 3 2 1 2 1 1 2 2 1 2 1 2 1 3 2 1 2 2 2
251 0018000 1 05 4 1 33 0140 1 2 1 1 2 1 1 2 2 1 9 2 4 1 5 2 2 2 1 2
252 0014000 1 05 4 1 20 0095 1 5 2 2 9 1 2 3 2 1 4 1 3 1 1 1 3 2 2 2
253 0190000 2 04 2 4 09 0250 1 5 1 1 2 2 1 2 2 2 1 2 1 2 1 2 1 1 2 1 1
254 0025000 2 33 2 3 10 0002 2 1 2 1 2 1 3 3 2 3 1 3 1 1 1 2 2 2 3 9
255 0008000 1 33 2 4 10 0100 2 2 1 1 2 1 2 1 2 1 3 1 3 1 1 1 1 1 2 3
256 0008000 2 33 2 4 05 0100 2 3 1 1 2 1 2 2 2 1 3 1 3 1 3 1 1 1 2 3
257 0010000 1 33 2 4 16 0250 1 3 2 1 2 1 2 3 2 1 4 1 3 1 5 2 2 2 2 3
258 0007000 1 33 2 4 08 0200 2 3 2 1 2 1 2 2 2 1 4 2 3 1 5 1 1 1 2 3
259 0025000 1 33 2 4 15 0500 1 3 1 1 2 2 8 8 2 1 4 1 3 1 5 1 1 2 2 3
260 0004000 1 33 2 4 05 0150 1 3 1 1 4 1 2 8 2 8 3 1 3 1 5 1 1 1 2 3
261 0010000 2 33 2 4 10 0300 1 3 1 1 2 1 2 8 2 1 4 1 3 1 5 1 1 1 2 3
262 0004500 1 43 2 5 48 0004 2 1 1 1 2 3 1 3 4 3 2 3 2 2 3 3 2 2 1 3
263 0008600 2 42 2 1 07 0008 9 3 1 1 2 2 1 2 3 2 2 2 3 2 3 3 3 2 2 2
264 0059000 1 01 2 4 18 0080 1 3 2 2 2 2 1 3 3 2 2 2 3 1 2 3 2 2 2 1
265 0016849 1 35 3 3 17 0018 1 2 1 8 8 2 8 3 3 3 1 2 3 1 4 2 2 4 2 2
266 0023489 1 43 2 1 16 0030 2 1 1 1 1 1 2 4 3 4 3 9 5 3 2 3 3 2 2
267 0030000 2 38 1 2 16 0100 1 4 2 9 9 1 1 2 2 1 2 1 3 2 2 2 1 2 1 3
268 0055000 2 21 1 2 19 0045 1 5 2 1 1 1 1 2 3 3 2 2 3 1 1 4 2 4 2 2
269 0015304 2 46 2 2 17 0021 1 2 4 4 4 1 1 1 1 2 3 1 4 1 1 1 1 1 1 1
```

```
270 0031881 1 47 4 2 15 0020 1 3 1 1 4 1 1 2 2 1 2 1 4 1 2 2 1 2 1 1
271 0051072 2 47 4 1 25 0017 1 4 4 8 8 1 4 2 2 2 1 1 4 1 3 2 1 3 2 2
272 0041161 2 46 2 2 18 9999 1 5 1 2 9 1 2 1 2 2 2 2 3 2 3 1 2 1 2 3
273 0030000 1 22 3 4 16 0041 1 3 2 9 9 1 2 2 2 1 2 2 3 2 4 1 1 1 1 3
274 0013000 1 22 3 2 10 0011 1 5 1 2 9 1 1 2 5 5 2 2 4 1 2 5 5 5 1 2
275 0040000 1 22 3 1 24 0037 1 3 1 2 9 1 2 2 3 1 2 1 4 1 4 2 2 2 1 2
276 0008000 1 23 3 2 15 0008 1 3 1 2 2 1 1 2 3 1 2 2 2 1 4 1 2 4 2 1
277 0031000 1 16 3 9 20 0105 1 3 2 2 9 1 1 3 2 2 2 2 3 1 2 3 3 3 2 2
278 0006000 2 16 3 5 02 0035 1 3 2 2 9 3 1 3 3 2 8 4 2 1 2 2 2 3 1 2
279 0045000 1 17 2 2 18 0045 1 3 1 2 1 1 2 3 3 2 2 2 3 1 2 1 2 3 2 2
280 0009800 1 17 2 1 10 0070 1 3 1 2 9 1 2 2 5 5 2 2 3 1 3 1 3 2 2 3
281 0015000 1 17 2 9 22 0140 1 3 1 2 9 1 1 2 2 2 2 4 4 1 4 4 4 4 2 2
282 0005000 1 18 2 2 05 0025 2 2 2 2 1 2 2 9 5 2 3 1 2 1 2 5 2 3 2 2
283 0007800 1 16 3 2 05 0050 9 4 2 2 9 1 1 3 3 2 3 2 4 1 3 4 2 4 2 2
end data.
```

recode   jobtitle (3 thru 4=5) (8=9)
                /circulat (0 thru 36772=1) (36773 thru 1325500=2)
                /yearsexp (0 thru 18=1) (19 thru 51=2) (88=99)
                /sex (8=9)
                /staff (0 thru 58=1) (59 thru 1500=2) (8888=9999)
                /educate (1=2) (4=5) (8=9)
                /code (4=9) (8=9)
                /policy to written (4=9) (8=9)
                /affairs (8=9)
                /personal (8=9)
                /compete (8=9)
                /married to family (8=9)
                /coverage (8=9)
                /health to psycho (8=9)
                /intimate (8=9)
                /credible (8=9).

missing value   jobtitle (9)
                /yearsexp (99)
                /sex (9)
                /staff (9999)
                /educate (9)
                /code (9)
                /policy to written (9)
                /affairs (9)
                /personal (9)
                /compete (9)
                /married to family (9)
                /coverage (9)
                /health to psycho (9)
                /intimate (9)

                    /credible (9).
variable labels ID "Questionnaire ID"
  /circulat "Newspaper circulation"
  /owners "Ownership"
  /state "State of newspaper location"
  /region "Region of newspaper location"
  /jobtitle "Job title of respondent"
  /yearsexp "Number of years as journalist"
  /staff "Number of newsroom employees"
  /sex "Gender of respondent"
  /educate "Highest level of education"
  /code "Does newspaper have code of ethics?"
  /policy "Formal privacy policy?"
  /written "Formal policy in writing?"
  /affairs "Coverage of extramarital affairs?"
  /personal "Attention to personal lives?"
  /compete "Response to competition..."
  /married "Discover candidate's affair..."
  /family "Family values candidate having affair..."
  /coverage "If candidate has affair, what do you do?"
  /health "Write about personal illness?"
  /cheater "Write about college cheating?"
  /crime "Write about crime record?"
  /sexual "Write about sexual harrassment?"
  /abortion "Write about abortion?"
  /drugs "Write about drugs treatment?"
  /psycho "Write about depression?"
  /intimate "Reader interest in intimate details..."
  /credible "Does this reporting hurt credibility?".
value labels / owners 1 "Group" 2 "Nongroup"
  /region 1 "East" 2 "South" 3 "Midwest" 4 "West"
  /jobtitle 1 "Editor, exec editor"
                2 "ME or AME"
                3 "Asst. to edit. or ME"
                4 "Section editor"
                5 "Other not list above"
                8 "Refused to answer"
                9 "Missing"
  /sex 1 "Male" 2 "Female"
  /educate 1 "High school or less"
                2 "Some college no deg"
                3 "College degree"
                4 "Some graduate school"
                5 "Graduate degree"
                8 "Refused to answer"

```
                    9 "Missing"
/code 1 "Yes"
                    2 "No"
                    3 "Uses another code"
                    4 "Don't know"
                    8 "Refused to answer"
                    9 "Missing"
/policy to written 1 "Yes"
                    2 "No"
                    4 "Don't know"
                    8 "Refused to answer"
                    9 "Missing"
/affairs 1 "Yes"
                    2 "No"
                    3 "Don't know"
                    8 "Refused to answer"
                    9 "Missing"
/personal 1 "Too much"
                    2 "Right amount"
                    3 "Too little"
                    4 "Not sure"
                    8 "Refused to answer"
                    9 "Missing"
/compete 1 "Consider it news"
                    2 "Check out charge"
                    3 "Ignore the charge"
                    4 "Don't know"
                    8 "Refused to answer"
                    9 "Missing"
/married to family
                    1 "Definitely disclose"
                    2 "Probably disclose it"
                    3 "Probably not disclose"
                    4 "Definite not disclose"
                    5 "Don't know"
                    8 "Refused to answer"
                    9 "Missing"
/coverage 1 "Nothing at all"
                    2 "Nothing, unless..."
                    3 "Ask candidate..."
                    4 "Seek rel. sources..."
                    5 "Hire Priv. Invest."
                    6 "Use surveillance"
                    8 "Refused to answer"
                    9 "Missing"
```

/health to psycho
                    1 "Very likely"
                    2 "Somewhat likely"
                    3 "Not very likely"
                    4 "Very unlikely"
                    5 "Don't know"
                    8 "Refused to answer"
                    9 "Missing"
/intimate 1 "Very interested"
                    2 "Somewhat interested"
                    3 "Not very interested"
                    4 "Very uninterested"
                    5 "Don't know"
                    8 "Refused to answer"
                    9 "Missing"
/credible 1 "Hurts very much"
                    2 "Hurts somewhat"
                    3 "Doesn't hurt vy much"
                    4 "Doesn't hurt at all"
                    5 "Don't know"
                    8 "Refused to answer"
                    9 "Missing".
frequencies jobtitle region
    /statistics all
    /histogram.
crosstabs circulat by affairs
    /cells count row column total
set printer off.

Appendix F: SPSS/PC+ Sample Output

The computer analysis output shown here was generated for the University of Miami ethics study by the Statistical Package for the Social Sciences (SPSS/PC+) Studentware for DOS. The job was set up by the file program contained in Appendix E.

```
SPSS/PC+ Studentware+ for IBM PC                        5/17/94
data list /ID 1-3
   circulat 5-11
   owners 13
   state 15-16
   region 18
   jobtitle 20
   yearsexp 22-23
   staff 25-28
   sex 30
   educate 32
   code 34
   policy 36
   written 38
   affairs 40
   personal 42
   compete 44
   married 46
   family 48
   coverage 50
   health 52
   cheater 54
   crime 56
   sexual 58
   abortion 60
   drugs 62
   psycho 64
   intimate 66
   credible 68.
begin data
end data.
   283 cases are written to the compressed active file.
```

```
This procedure was completed at 8:38:25
recode          jobtitle (3 thru 4=5) (8=9)
                /circulat (0 thru 36772=1) (36773 thru 1325500=2)
                /yearsexp (0 thru 18=1) (19 thru 51=2) (88=99)
                /sex (8=9)
                /staff (0 thru 58=1) (59 thru 1500=2) (8888=9999)
                /educate (1=2) (4=5) (8=9)
                /code (4=9) (8=9)
                /policy to written (4=9) (8=9)
                /affairs (8=9)
                /personal (8=9)
                /compete (8=9)
                /married to family (8=9)
                /coverage (8=9)
                /health to psycho (8=9)
                /intimate (8=9)
                /credible (8=9).
missing value   jobtitle (9)
                /yearsexp (99)
                /sex (9)
                /staff (9999)
                /educate (9)
                /code (9)
                /policy to written (9)
                /affairs (9)
                /personal (9)
                /compete (9)
                /married to family (9)
                /coverage (9)
                /health to psycho (9)
                /intimate (9)
                /credible (9).
variable labels ID "Questionnaire ID"
  /circulat "Newspaper circulation"
  /owners "Ownership"
  /state "State of newspaper location"
  /region "Region of newspaper location"
  /jobtitle "Job title of respondent"
  /yearsexp "Number of years as journalist"
  /staff "Number of newsroom employees"
  /sex "Gender of respondent"
  /educate "Highest level of education"
  /code "Does newspaper have code of ethics?"
  /policy "Formal privacy policy?"
  /written "Formal policy in writing?"
  /affairs "Coverage of extramarital affairs?"
  /personal "Attention to personal lives?"
  /compete "Response to competition..."
  /married "Discover candidate's affair..."
  /family "Family values candidate having affair..."
```

```
  /coverage "If candidate has affair, what do you do?"
  /health "Write about personal illness?"
  /cheater "Write about college cheating?"
  /crime "Write about crime record?"
  /sexual "Write about sexual harrassment?"
  /abortion "Write about abortion?"
  /drugs "Write about drugs treatment?"
  /psycho "Write about depression?"
  /intimate "Reader interest in intimate details..."
  /credible "Does this reporting hurt credibility?".
value labels / owners 1 "Group" 2 "Nongroup"
  /region 1 "East" 2 "South" 3 "Midwest" 4 "West"
  /jobtitle 1 "Editor, exec editor"
               2 "ME or AME"
               3 "Asst. to edit. or ME"
               4 "Section editor"
               5 "Other not list above"
               8 "Refused to answer"
               9 "Missing"
  /sex 1 "Male" 2 "Female"
  /educate 1 "High school or less"
               2 "Some college no deg"
               3 "College degree"
               4 "Some graduate school"
               5 "Graduate degree"
               8 "Refused to answer"
               9 "Missing"
  /code 1 "Yes"
               2 "No"
               3 "Uses another code"
               4 "Don't know"
               8 "Refused to answer"
               9 "Missing"
  /policy to written 1 "Yes"
               2 "No"
               4 "Don't know"
               8 "Refused to answer"
               9 "Missing"
  /affairs 1 "Yes"
               2 "No"
               3 "Don't know"
               8 "Refused to answer"
               9 "Missing"
  /personal 1 "Too much"
               2 "Right amount"
               3 "Too little"
               4 "Not sure"
               8 "Refused to answer"
               9 "Missing"
  /compete 1 "Consider it news"
```

```
              2 "Check out charge"
              3 "Ignore the charge"
              4 "Don't know"
              8 "Refused to answer"
              9 "Missing"
/married to family
              1 "Definitely disclose"
              2 "Probably disclose it"
              3 "Probably not disclose"
              4 "Definite not disclose"
              5 "Don't know"
              8 "Refused to answer"
              9 "Missing"
/coverage 1 "Nothing at all"
              2 "Nothing, unless..."
              3 "Ask candidate..."
              4 "Seek rel. sources..."
              5 "Hire Priv. Invest."
              6 "Use surveillance"
              8 "Refused to answer"
              9 "Missing"
/health to psycho
              1 "Very likely"
              2 "Somewhat likely"
              3 "Not very likely"
              4 "Very unlikely"
              5 "Don't know"
              8 "Refused to answer"
              9 "Missing"
/intimate 1 "Very interested"
              2 "Somewhat interested"
              3 "Not very interested"
              4 "Very uninterested"
              5 "Don't know"
              8 "Refused to answer"
              9 "Missing"
/credible 1 "Hurts very much"
              2 "Hurts somewhat"
              3 "Doesn't hurt vy much"
              4 "Doesn't hurt at all"
              5 "Don't know"
              8 "Refused to answer"
              9 "Missing".
frequencies jobtitle region
The raw data or transformation pass is proceeding
   283 cases are written to the compressed active file.
   /statistics all
   /histogram.
```

***** Memory allows a total of 11282 Values, accumulated across all Variables.

    There also may be up to   1410 Value Labels for each Variable.

Page   9   SPSS/PC+ Studentware+   5/17/94

JOBTITLE   Job title of respondent

Value Label	Value	Frequency	Percent	Valid Percent	Cum Percent
Editor, exec editor	1	102	36.0	37.1	37.1
ME or AME	2	117	41.3	42.5	79.6
Other not list above	5	56	19.8	20.4	100.0
Missing	9	8	2.8	Missing	
	Total	283	100.0	100.0	

Page 10   SPSS/PC+ Studentware+   5/17/94

JOBTITLE   Job title of respondent

```
    COUNT      VALUE

     102       1.00 ³**************************
     117       2.00 ³*****************************
       0       3.00 ³
       0       4.00 ³
      56       5.00 ³**************
               I.........I.........I.........I.........I.........I
               0        40        80       120       160       200
                          Histogram frequency
```

Page 11   SPSS/PC+ Studentware+   5/17/94

JOBTITLE   Job title of respondent

Mean	2.240	Std err	.088	Median	2.000
Mode	2.000	Std dev	1.468	Variance	2.154
Kurtosis	-.226	S E Kurt	.293	Skewness	1.141
S E Skew	.147	Range	4.000	Minimum	1.000
Maximum	5.000	Sum	616.000		

Valid cases   275   Missing cases   8

Page 12   SPSS/PC+ Studentware+   5/17/94

REGION   Region of newspaper location

			Valid	Cum
Value Label	Value	Frequency	Percent	Percent	Percent
East	1	45	15.9	15.9	15.9
South	2	97	34.3	34.3	50.2
Midwest	3	87	30.7	30.7	80.9
West	4	54	19.1	19.1	100.0
		-------	-------	-------	
	Total	283	100.0	100.0	

Page 13   SPSS/PC+ Studentware+   5/17/94

REGION   Region of newspaper location

COUNT	VALUE	
45	1.00	³***********************
97	2.00	³**
87	3.00	³**
54	4.00	³**************************

```
I.........I.........I.........I.........I.........I
```

```
0        20        40        60        80       100
```

Histogram frequency

Page 14   SPSS/PC+ Studentware+   5/17/94

REGION   Region of newspaper location

Mean	2.530	Std err	.058	Median	2.000
Mode	2.000	Std dev	.976	Variance	.952
Kurtosis	-.992	S E Kurt	.289	Skewness	.019
S E Skew	.145	Range	3.000	Minimum	1.000
Maximum	4.000	Sum	716.000		

Valid cases   283   Missing cases   0

Page 15   SPSS/PC+ Studentware+   5/17/94

This procedure was completed at 8:39:15

crosstabs circulat by affairs

    /cells count row column total.

Memory allows for 8,166 cells with 2 dimensions for general CROSSTABS.

Page 16   SPSS/PC+ Studentware+   5/17/94

CIRCULAT Newspaper circulation by AFFAIRS Coverage of extramarital affairs?

```
                  AFFAIRS              Page 1 of 1

         Count  ³

         Row Pct ³Yes     No      Don't kn

         Col Pct ³                ow      Row

         Tot Pct ³    1  ³    2  ³    3  ³ Total
```

CIRCULAT   --

         1 ³   159 ³   37 ³   20 ³   216

            ³ 73.6 ³ 17.1 ³   9.3 ³   79.1

            ³ 79.1 ³ 78.7 ³ 80.0 ³

            ³ 58.2 ³ 13.6 ³   7.3 ³

            ----

         2 ³   42 ³   10 ³   5 ³   57

            ³ 73.7 ³ 17.5 ³   8.8 ³   20.9

            ³ 20.9 ³ 21.3 ³ 20.0 ³

            ³ 15.4 ³   3.7 ³   1.8 ³

      Column   201   47   25   273

       Total   73.6   17.2   9.2   100.0

Number of Missing Observations: 10

Page 17   SPSS/PC+ Studentware+   5/17/94

Page 18   SPSS/PC+ Studentware+   5/17/94

This procedure was completed at 8:39:29

Page 19   SPSS/PC+ Studentware+   5/17/94

Glossary

9-Track—This is a system for storing data on a large reel of ½-inch magnetic tape commonly used to store data on mainframe computer systems. These tapes utilize a format of nine parallel tracks of data, which includes eight data bits and one parity bit.

Access numbers—Telephone numbers used by customers to connect to commercial online services.

Alphanumeric—Includes both numbers, letters, and certain control and spacing characters.

Analog—A continuously varying property of a device, within the ranges of that device.

ANSI—American National Standards Institute; most often used in reference to programming, interface, and device drivers.

Applications—Refers to computer programs written to complete a particular task such as word processing, database management, desktop publishing, or statistical analysis.

ASCII—American Standard Code for Information Interchange. This is the standard of 256 codes without software enhancements that is used by most computer systems. ASCII is most often used in reference to ASCII files. These are also often called "text files."

ASCII also refers to the character set. When referring to a database, an ASCII database has been stripped of any embedded codes such as formatting. ASCII databases are in a form that can be moved, or translated, from one database program to another. Most database programs offer utilities for importing and exporting ASCII database files.

AUTOEXEC.BAT—A batch file of instructions or commands used to start up a system when it is powered up. MS-DOS will read this file first. System users usually custom design this file to their own needs, such as the program in which the system first runs.

Backup—A second copy of a file for safety purposes or the process in which a data file is copied for protection against loss or damage. Often these files carry a *.BAK extension in the file name.

BASIC—Beginners All-purpose Symbolic Instruction Code. This is a programming language often used in personal computer systems.

Baud rate—In communications software, this is the unit of measurement for information transfer speed through modems. Typical baud rates are 1200, 2400, 4800, 9600, 14400, 28800, and 57600. The ratings measure the number of transmission events that occur per second.

378

BBS—Bulletin Board Service.

BIOS—Basic Input/Output System. This is a set of commands that a computer system uses to permit the systems elements to communicate with each other (e.g., the disk drives, the monitor, and the memory).

Boolean expressions—A set of algebraic logical values sometimes called conditional or logical expressions. These are commonly used in software programming, but also in database software or online services in setting up queries or searching for text. The three most frequently used Boolean operators are "and," "or," and "but not."

Browse—Searching or scanning a list of files or a database for a particular item.

Bug—An error that causes a malfunction in a software or hardware.

Cache—A memory subsystem in which data values that are often used are duplicated for quick access.

CAJ—see CAR.

CAR—Computer-Assisted Reporting. This is a form of reporting that utilizes computer software and hardware tools for information gathering and analysis. CAR includes online research. CAR is often called CAJ, or computer-assisted journalism.

CD-ROM—Compact Disc, Read-Only Memory. This is a system of storage of data characterized by its large capacity. CDs are capable of storing about 600 megabytes of information.

CPU—Central Processing Unit. This is the part of a computer that controls and processes information and interprets and carries out commands.

Communications software—A software package that enables a computer user to connect one system with another to exchange information or data.

Computer literacy—Knowledge about computers at a level that permits understanding of their uses and applications.

CONFIG.SYS—A system configuration file that contains instructions about operating behavior within MS-DOS. Commands include system resource limitations, access to added devices such as CD-ROM drives or mice, and so forth.

Copy protection—An electronic protection that is added to software to guard against unauthorized copying by users.

Data—Information. This is the plural form of *datum,* a Latin word.

Database—An aggregation of data, usually consisting of a format or structure. Common structures include records or cases (rows) and variables or fields (columns). A database can be a single file, a series of files, or a library of files. Databases are formed with alphabetic text, numbers, or graphics.

DBMS—Database Management System. This is a software application that is used for creation of a database, access to information in the database, and reports from the database.

DD—Double density, refers to the storage capacity of a disk. Double density 5.25-inch disks will store 360 KB of information. Early floppy diskettes had a density of 180 KB, so when the new disks were developed, they became known as DD. For microfloppy diskettes, or the 3.5-inch size, the capacity is 720 KB.

Device—Refers to computer components such as mice, printers, modems, CD-ROM readers, or disk drives.

Digital—Systems that represent information with digits.

Directory—An index of the contents of a storage disk that lists, among other things, the file name, the files location, file type, size of the file, and date the file was most recently updated.

Disc—Refers to nonmagnetic flat and circular optical or laser-based media used in CD-ROM systems.

Disk—Refers to other types of flat and circular magnetic media used for storage of information such as floppies, hard drives, microfloppies, and removable cartridges.

Document—A file that has been created by a word processing system or other application that usually has the file extension of *.DOC.

DOS—Disk Operating System. This is any system for operating a computer that is loaded into memory from a disk.

DOS prompt—An indication on the computers display that the processor is ready to execute its next command.

Downloading—This refers to transferring a file from another computer to the user's computer with a modem or other transfer system. In downloading, the user's computer receives information stored in another system, such as a bulletin board service or commercial service.

Driver—A program or hardware device that regulates a device such as a printer, mouse, or CD-ROM reader.

E-mail—see electronic mail.

Editor—A program that allows a computer user to create or modify text files. Usually these utilities are less powerful than word processors, but do offer some of the most basic features of word processors.

Electronic mail—Also known as E-mail, this is the transfer of memos, letters, or other message-type information through a communication network of computers.

Emulator—A computer program or device that has been written or designed to act like something else. For example, emulators are used in communications packages to make one keyboard configuration seem like another for easier communication between systems.

Error message—A statement from a computer program that tells the user that some sort of action is needed before the program can perform its function properly.

Escape—A keyboard key that permits a user to perform certain functions depending on the application. For most, however, it enables the user to stop a process and return to the last level of the process.

Field—In database creation and management, a field is a piece of information of a particular location that is part of a record. A field is also called a variable, a cell, or a column.

File—A collection of information used by a program or a set of commands to constitute a program itself, that is given a name for storage.

File size—The length of a file, usually listed in terms of byte size.

Filter—For computer applications, this is a program that reads input and converts it into a desired form such as a readable data file. A common use of filters is in word processing or database programs where data files generated by one program are read by another.

Flatfile system—A system of filing information in that there is no hierarchy and that no two files can have the same name.

Format—For database systems, format refers to the structure of the database. For diskettes and hard drives, format refers to the arrangement of data storage areas called tracks and sectors.

Formula—For certain applications, such as spreadsheets, this is a mathematical statement or procedure that winds up with some sort of calculation.

Freeware—Computer programs that are given away. This software is often found on bulletin board services or commercial online information services.

Function key—The 10 or 12 keys on most standard keyboards that are used by application programmers for specific functions. These functions will vary depending on the program being used.

GB—Gigabyte, or one billion bytes.

GIS—Geographic Information Systems. These software packages offer the ability to produce maps merged with database files.

GUI—Graphical User Interface (often called "gooey"). This is a form of screen display that uses graphical images that can be selected with a mouse or other device to choose commands (such as executing a program).

Handshake—An expression that refers to the electronic exchange of information when two modems initially communicate.

Hard disk—A magnetic mass storage device commonly called the "C" drive on most personal computer systems. Modern hard disk drives store from 20 megabytes to more than 2,000 megabytes of information.

Hardware—These are the components of a computer system such as the processor, monitor, printer, fax/modem, mouse, and other peripherals.

HD—High Density. This refers to the amount of information stored on a diskette. HD capacity is 1.2 KB of information for a 5.25-inch disk and 1.44 KB for a 3.5-inch disk.

High memory—A random access memory location used generally for controller hardware.

Hot key—A keyboard command involving one, two, or three keystrokes in combination to switch the computer to a second program, usually a memory-resident (TSR) program.

Hypercard—A Macintosh-designed program that provides information management using hypertext.

Hypertext—Refers to a presentation of linked text, graphic images, audio, and animation that permits the user to browse the database in any particular order.

Icon—For GUI systems, these are tiny graphic images representing a function or action performed by a program.

Input—Information entered by keyboard, or other means, into a computer application.

Install—The process of setting up a computer program or hardware device and preparing it for operation. Also called "set up."

Interface—The connection of two elements such as hardware devices or computer programs.

Internet—The massive global web of thousands of computer networks originally developed for U.S. government research and defense computer links. The Internet is an entry point to a network of thousands of databases on every subject imaginable, to electronic mail and communication, and to programs and powerful computing resources.

KB—Kilobyte, or 1,000 bytes.

LAN—Local Area Network. This is a group of computers linked together to share resources such as software and databases and to facilitate communication from computer to computer through such software as electronic mail services.

LCD—Liquid Crystal Display. This is a common form of display used in notebook and other small, portable computer systems.

Library—A collection of data files or databases commonly used by commercial online database services.

Logoff—This is the process of telling a computer system that the identified user is finished with a session. Also called "logout."

Logon—This is the process of telling a computer system a new user is beginning a session and the identity of the user. It is also called "login."

Low memory—Memory locations usually reserved for use by random access memory (RAM).

Mail merge—A process that combines a database of addresses and other personal information with a form letter or other document for mass mailing or distribution.

Mainframe—Large, sophisticated computer systems that offer the fastest speeds and largest storage capacities. These systems are most often used by major businesses or educational and/or research institutions that need to perform the most complicated computing

tasks. These systems are usually characterized by multiple user capacity.

MB—Megabyte, or one million bytes.

Memory-resident program—Also called a TSR (terminate-and-stay resident), this program remains in RAM until called on to be used. Because it is stored on a hard drive but loaded into RAM when the system starts up or when the user opens the program, it is quickly accessed and used. Until it is called with a hot key, it remains in background.

Microprocessor—A central processing unit (CPU) located on a single computer chip.

Minicomputers—An intermediate level computer, somewhere in between personal and mainframe computers. These are more powerful and faster than personal computers, but not as capable as mainframes.

Modem—A device used to connect two computer systems and enable them to communicate. Modem is a shortened version of modulation/demodulation, which is what the device does when the two systems are exchanging information. Modems range in speed, expressed as baud rate.

Monitor—The video display device that displays images from the video adapter.

Motherboard—This is the foundation of the computer, a piece of fiberglass, often green in color, which contains circuits and chips. This is also the location of the silicon chip known as the central processing unit.

Mouse—A display pointing device that moves the location of cursor within a graphical user interface platform.

MS-DOS—Microsoft Disk Operating System. This package of programs supervises other computer systems and permits users to carry out a variety of functions such as program execution and file maintenance.

Multimedia—Combination of graphics, animation, video display, and audio in a single computer system. These systems typically require minimal hardware capabilities such as hard drive size, CD-ROM, audio boards, and more. Personal computers using multimedia design are called MPCs.

Multitasking—Operation of a computer in such a manner that two or more applications are used at one time.

Network—A linkage of computers through telephone lines or cables for interchange of information and sharing of resources.

Number crunching—Statistical analysis of a database using one or more of several categories of software such as spreadsheets, relational database systems, or statistical packages.

OS—Operating System. This is the computer program package that dictates allocation and use of system resources.

Package—A set of computer programs designed to complete a particular type of task.

Password—An alphanumeric means for securing access to a computer program, a computer system, a user account, a database, or other software or hardware.

Path—When referring to file storage and location, the path is a command that instructs the computer how to find a files location.

PCMCIA—Personal Computer Memory Card International Associa-

tion. Refers to credit card-sized memory cards used for storage, fax/modem, and other functions.

PDA—Personal Digital Assistant. This is a portable computing device.

PIM—Personal Information Manager. This is a class of software applications that includes scheduling, calendars, address lists, task lists, and other similar information.

Platform—This is the hardware and software foundations upon which the computer system is built.

Printer driver—The computer program file that allows a single printer to interact with a number of different types of programs.

Program—Used interchangeably with software. This is a set of instructions that can be executed by a computer.

PROM—Programmable Read-Only Memory.

Prompt—See DOS prompt.

Proprietary software—This is a program owned by an individual and can be used only through buying the program or by obtaining permission to use it.

Protocol—This is a set of rules that are used by two computer systems in transferring information. There are numerous protocols in use, but the most popular ones include Xmodem, Zmodem, Kermit, and Ymodem.

Public domain software—A computer program placed in the public domain by the author for use by the public at no charge. There are no limitations on copying or distribution of these programs.

Query—A request within a database program to retrieve information from a given database. The request is usually a specific set of instructions that can be saved and used over and over. Queries can be made using structured query language (SQL) or query by example (QBE).

RAM—Random Access Memory.

README—Files that are usually text and contain instructions, software updates, and information not available in published users guides, online help files, or other documentation.

Record—Also called a row or a case, it is a collection of fields, columns, or variables in a database in a specified order.

Relational database packages—Database programs that permit creation of databases and storage of information in tables (columns and rows). These programs permit searching of the database using data in specific locations such as the fields or rows. Queries, or searches, can be conducted by combining several tables with at least one common or matching element.

ROM—Read-Only Memory. The information contained in ROM can be read by a computers operating system but it cannot be changed.

Root directory—In a disk data storage system, this is the most basic level of the index or directory of the information contained on that disk.

RS-232—The serial communications connection for personal computers. Typically, RS-232 ports are used for connecting a device to the PC.

Script file—A program that contains a set of instructions for an application.

Set up—See install.

Shareware—Software that is protected by copyright held by the author or another entity that is distributed free but contains a request for a payment of a usually minor amount of money if the user likes the program and plans to use it.

Software—Computer programs or instruction sets.

Spreadsheets—A category of computer application that follows the accounting spreadsheet style of data entry using columns and rows. These programs are most often used for financial tasks such as budgeting, for database development and analysis, and data graphing.

Structured query language—Called SQL, this is a sublanguage in many relational database management systems that permits the program user to prepare and execute queries of databases. SQL permits a variety of treatments of information contained within a database.

Support—Depending on usage, this term refers to two things. As a verb, it reflects the ability to work with another program or peripheral. As a noun, it means assistance given by a computer company to users of its product.

Surge—An unexpected and immediate jump in electrical voltage. Electricity surges, some not even detectable to the human eye, can damage hardware and software, depending on the length and intensity of the surge.

Syntax—A computer programming languages particular set of rules for content and order of commands.

SYSOP—System operator. This term is commonly used in reference to bulletin board services or networks.

Table—For relational database software, tables are the structures of the data in rows and columns containing information in a particular order. Tables are collections of records or cases (also called rows).

Tape drive—A device for storage of data on magnetic tape on a cassette, cartridge, or reel. Usually used for mass storage of large files, large numbers of files, or for data backup.

TSR—Terminate and stay resident. See also memory-resident program.

Upgrade—A newer or enhanced version of a computer program.

Uploading—This refers to transferring a file from your computer to another computer using a modem or other transfer system. In uploading, your computer sends information it has stored in a file to another system.

WAN—Wide Area Network. This is a network of computers connected over a large geographic area.

Window—In GUI systems, a portion of a screen that contains a document, message, or other instruction. Windows is the common name for Microsoft Windows, the popular GUI. Windows-type programs are characterized by use of icons, pull-down menus, file sharing, and other features.

Word processor—A computer program for writing, preparation of documents, and manipulation, such as editing, of text. Most word processors provide a wide range of features that go far beyond the preparation of a basic document.

WYSIWYG—What You See Is What You Get. This is a means for displaying as closely as possible on the computer screen the document as it will be printed.

Sources: JoAnne Woodcock (1991), *Computer Dictionary: The Comprehensive Standard for Business, School, Library, and Home.* Redmond, WA: Microsoft Press; and Elizabeth McGinnis (1993, May), Defining telecommunications terms, *Online Access, 8*(2), pp. 10–11.
For detailed definitions, see *The American National Dictionary for Information Processing,* American National Standards Institute, 1430 Broadway, New York, NY, 10018; and see *The ISO Vocabulary of Data Processing,* The International Organization for Standardization, 1 rue de Varemde, Case Postale 56, CH-1121, Geneva 20, Switzerland.

References

Adair, S. (1992, Fall). UK media librarians take a look at the future. *Library News, 15*(1), 1, 20.

American Association for Public Opinion Research. (1994). The blue book: *Agencies and organizations represented in AAPOR/WAPOR membership,* Ann Arbor, MI: Author.

Anderson, S. (1993, October 23). *MapInfo mapping overview.* Unpublished presentation at Computing: The News Frontier Conference, Investigative Reporters and Editors, Raleigh, NC.

Asher, H. (1992). *Polling and the public: What every citizen should know,* (2nd ed.), Washington, DC: Congressional Quarterly.

Auerbach, S., & Fisher, M. (1992, July 8). Summit notebook: Hefty menu of meetings and meat. *The Washington Post,* p. A35.

Aumente, J. (1989, April). Bauds, bytes and Brokaw: New PCs revolutionize the newsroom. *Washington Journalism Review, 11*(3), 39–42.

Aversa, J. (1994, March 28). *Software piracy.* Associated Press national wire, 2:17 p.m.

Balas, J. (1991, November). Bulletin board systems: Look how they've grown. *Small Computers in Libraries, 11*(10), p. 31.

Balboni, P. S. (1993, July/August). Memo to: All journalists re: The new information age. *Columbia Journalism Review, 32*(2), 49–50.

Bjorner, S. (1992). (Ed.). *Newspapers online.* Needham Heights, MA: Bibliodata.

Blankenhorn, D. (1991, February 25). Stations weigh benefits of online services. *Electronic Media, 10*(9), p. 18.

Blasko, L. (1988, March 25). Don't be snookered by high-priced software deals: With research you won't have to learn a hard lesson. *The Miami Herald,* p. 3B.

Booth, S. A. (1994, January). Batteries reborn. *Popular Mechanics, 171*(1), pp. 37–39.

Borland International. (1993). *Borland no-nonsense license statement and limited warranty.* Scotts Valley, CA: Author.

Bray, P. (1992, October). Accidents will happen. *Which Computer? 15*(10), p. S15.

Bray, P. (1993, May). Organiser [sic] software. *Which Computer? 16*(5), p. 79.

Briscoe, E. D., & Wall, C. (1992, February). Inexpensive news sources. *Database, 15*(1), pp. 28–35.

Brooks, B. S., & Yang, T. (1993, August). *Patterns of computer use in newspaper newsrooms: A national study of U.S. dailies.* Paper presented to the annual meeting of the Association for Education in Journalism and Mass Communication, Kansas City, MO.

Brown, J., Ricchiardi, S., Fisher L., & Schneider, A. (1990). *Lexis/Nexis spot news research project final report.* Indianapolis: National Institute for Advanced Reporting.

Buettner, R. (1993, October 21). *FoxPro versus Paradox: The good, the bad, and the ugly.* Unpublished presentation at Computing: The News Frontier Conference, Investigative Reporters and Editors, Raleigh, NC.

Bunch, W. (1992, June 1). Dems: They're all connected; Party plugged in to U.S. high-tech. *Newsday,* p. 5.

Bunker, M. D., Splichal, S., Chamberlin, B. F., & Perry, L. M. (1993, Winter). Access to government-held information in the computer age: Applying legal doctrine to emerging technology. *Florida State University Law Review, 20*(3), 543–598.

Burwell, H. (1992, Summer). Defending the good name of information brokers. *Online Access, 7*(2), pp. 6–7.

Business Software Alliance. (1994, January 11). Heads, it's real. Tails, it's fake. *PC Magazine, 13*(1), p. 269.

Bylinsky, G. (1991, December 30). Saving time with new technology. *Fortune, 124*(15), 98–104.

Caldwell, B., Gillooly, B., & Gillooly, C. (1994, December 19). Front end: Staying put. *Informationweek*, No. 906, p. 8.

Cantril, A. H. (1991). *The opinion connection: Polling, politics, and the press.* Washington, DC: Congressional Quarterly Press.

Casey, M. (1993, October 23). *Training the trainers: How to set up a CAR class.* Unpublished presentation at Computing: The News Frontier Conference, Investigative Reporters and Editors, Raleigh, NC.

Casey, W. (1993a, October 22). *Data analysis using spreadsheets.* Unpublished presentation at Computing: The News Frontier Conference, Investigative Reporters and Editors, Raleigh, NC.

Casey, W. (1993b, August 23). Newest Apple doesn't shine yet. *The Washington Post* online edition.

Casey, W. (1993c, October 11). Software solution: Keep it simple. *The Washington Post* online edition.

Castagna, R. (1994, February). Redefining the document. *Windows Sources, 2*(2), pp. 161–184.

Chamberlin, B. F., & Splichal, S. (1993). Protecting access to computerized government records. In B. P. Semonche (Ed.), *News media libraries: A management book* (pp. 339–345). Westport, CT: Greenwood Press.

Chichioco, T. (1989, September 2). Computer-assisted reporting: Newspapers are beginning to use it to their advantage. *Editor & Publisher, 122*(35), 20PC–21PC.

Cochran, W. (1993). *Nine steps of a CAR project.* Unpublished presentation at Computing: The News Frontier Conference, Investigative Reporters and Editors, Raleigh, NC.

Conroy, C. (1993, September). Tips on making your best research guess. *CompuServe Magazine, 12*(9), pp. 10–17.

Conroy, C. (1994, April). Away from the phone? Nope! *CompuServe Magazine, 13*(4), pp. 4–6.

Crossman, C. (1989, February 6). Phone hookup opens a new world. *The Miami Herald,* p. 37BM.

Crossman, C. (1993, August 31). Bevy of free software is yours for the asking. *The Miami Herald,* p. 27BM.

Crouse, T. (1973). *The boys on the bus.* New York: Ballantine.

Crowley, M. J. (1993). News library technology: State-of-the-art and future trends. In B. P. Semonche (Ed.), *News media libraries: A management book.* Westport, CT: Greenwood Press.

Currid, C. (1994, June). When it comes to upgrades, big companies are sooo slooow. [sic] *Windows Magazine, 5*(6), pp. 57–58.

Davis, D., & Marchak, B. (1993, October 21). *Government data: Online: 20+ sources you can't live without.* Unpublished presentation at Computing: The News Frontier Conference, Investigative Reporters and Editors, Raleigh, NC.

Davis, D., & Marchak, B. (1994, January/February). Government data on-line: Sources you shouldn't live without. *IRE Journal, 17*(1), 10–11.

Davis, D., & Wendling, T. (1993, February). A deadly cure: Analysis of nuclear regulatory data reveals realities of radiation treatment. *Uplink, 4*(2), pp. 1–2.

Davis, W. S. (1991). *Computing fundamentals: Concepts* (3rd ed.). Reading, MA: Addison-Wesley.

Davis, W. S., Byrkett, D. L., Schreiner, P. W., & Wood, C. A. (1993). *Mastering microcomputers: Core concepts and applications.* Redwood City, CA: Benjamin/Cummings.

DeCotis, M. (1994, January 19). *The* Florida Today *Newslink Forum system operator guidelines.* CompuServe.

DeFleur, M. H., & Davenport, L. (1993, Summer). Innovation lag: Computer-assisted classrooms vs. newsrooms. *Journalism Educator, 48*(2), 26–36.

DeFleur, M., & Ball-Rokeach, S. (1975). *Theories of mass communication.* New York: McKay.

Demers, D. P., & Nichols, S. (1987). *Precision journalism: A practical guide.* Newbury Park, CA: Sage.

Dennis, E. E. (1993). *Media, democracy, and the information highway.* New York: Freedom Forum Media Studies Center.

De Riemer, C. (1992, Winter). A survey of Vu/Text use in the newsroom. *Journalism Quarterly, 69*(4), 960–970.

Doig, S. (1992, December 20). Special report: What went wrong? *The Miami Herald,* pp. SR1–SR16.

Donoho, R. (1994, March). Terminal illness. *Successful Meetings, 43*(3), pp. 46–51.

Donovan, E. (1992, December). Journalism for the 21st Century: Online information, electronic databases, and the news: Book review. *Database, 15*(6), p. 90.

Donovan, S., & Schalit, N. (1989, July/August). Death of the morgue: A user-friendly institution yields to a profit center. *Washington Journalism Review, 11*(6), 36–38.

Drummond, R. (1994, April 1). Is X.500 your next directory? *Network Computing, 5*(4), pp. 66–72.

Eckhouse, J. (1993, March 15). Why nothing's secret anymore. *San Francisco Chronicle,* p. E1.

Editors choice: The database directory. (1993, September). *Online Access, 8*(5), pp. 61-77.

Elber, L. (1994, January 12). *Superhighway summit.* Associated Press features wire, 4:02 a.m.

Elinson, J. (1992). Methodology issues. In P. B. Sheatsley & W. J. Mitofsky (Eds.), *A meeting place: The history of the American Association for Public Opinion Research* (pp. 105–116). New York: American Association for Public Opinion Research.

Farnsworth, S. (1993, August 16). Give citizens access to government data bases. *The Houston Chronicle,* p. A-15.

Fasbinder, J. (1994, March 7). *Computer comment: Ami Pro: Is it or is it not a word processor?* United Press International national wire, 3:55 p.m.

Feola, C. J. (1993a, November). Small paper, big project. *American Journalism Review, 15*(9), 25–28.

Feola, C. J. (1993b, February 28). *Unpublished computer-assisted reporting database seminar.* Day 1, Journalism Forum, CompuServe.

Feola, C. J. (1993c, March 2). *Zen and the art of database design.* Unpublished CompuServe computer-assisted reporting seminar, Journalism Forum, CompuServe.

Fink, C. C. (1988). *Strategic newspaper management.* New York: Random House.

Fitzgerald, M. (1992, April 11). Wonked out? Journalists warned not to let their fascination with databases to get out of hand; advised to still use their traditional sources for news. *Editor & Publisher, 125*(11), pp. 15, 32.

Fitzgerald, M. (1993, May 15). Losing access to public records; Government trend to charge more and more for its electronic records is hampering the public's ability to acquire them. *Editor & Publisher, 126*(20), p. 9.

Fost, D. (1990, September). Inside the information industry: Newspapers enter the information age. *American Demographics, 12*(9), 14–17.

Foster, T. (1993, October). *Beat reporting: How computers can make you better.* Unpublished presentation at Computing: The News Frontier Conference, Investigative Reporters and Editors, Raleigh, NC.

Foxman, E. R., & Kilcoyne, P. (1993, Spring). Information technology, marketing practice, and consumer privacy: Ethical issues. *Journal of Public Policy & Marketing, 12,* 106+.

Frey, J. H. (1989). *Survey Research by Telephone* (2nd ed.). Newbury Park, CA: Sage.

Garrison, B. (1979). *The video display terminal and the copy editor: A case study of electronic editing at the* Milwaukee Journal. Unpublished doctoral dissertation, Southern Illinois University, Carbondale.

Garrison, B. (1992a). *Advanced reporting: Skills for the professional.* Hillsdale, NJ: Lawrence Erlbaum Associates.

Garrison, B. (1992b). *Professional news reporting.* Hillsdale, NJ: Lawrence Erlbaum Associates.

Garrison, B. (1994). *Professional feature writing* (2nd ed.). Hillsdale, NJ: Lawrence Erlbaum Associates.

Gates, J. K. (1994). *Guide to the use of libraries and information sources* (7th ed.). New York: McGraw-Hill.

Gaughan, T. (1993, October). Road scholar: A quick lesson in mapmaking, *Publish, 8*(10), pp. 50–57.

Gawiser, S. R., & Witt, G. E. (n.d.). *Twenty questions a journalist should ask about poll results.* New York: National Council on Public Polls.

Germain, J. (1993a, August). There's more than one way to join a computer network. *Online Access, 8*(4), pp. 16–20.

Germain, J. (1993b, August). 2 programs make it easy to run a BBS for home or office. *Online Access, 8*(4), pp. 30–32.

Gersh D., & Case, T. (1991, April 13). 75th annual Pulitzer Prize winners. *Editor & Publisher, 124*(15), pp. 7–9, 32–35, 44.

Giles, R. H. (1988). *Newsroom management: A guide to theory and practice.* Detroit: Media Management.

Giles, R. H. (1990). Hidden interests (special reprint). *The Detroit News,* pp. 1–16.

Gillmor, D. (1993, July 26). Improved gear, wide selection make shopping for a PC tricky. *The Miami Herald,* p. 25BM.

Glossbrenner, A. (1990). *The complete handbook of personal computer communications.* New York: St. Martins.

Goldberg, H. (1994, February 21). *Technology's victims—poll.* Associated Press features wire, 12:00 a.m.

Goldberg, R. (1994, January). PC marks the spot. *Popular Mechanics, 171*(1), pp. 44–45.

Goldstein, N. (Ed.). (1994). *Associated Press stylebook and libel manual.* New York: Associated Press.

Gordon, D. (1993, December). Information haves . . . and have nots. *Presstime, 15*(12), pp. 56–57.

Gordon, R. (1993a). Lesson one: Introduction to spreadsheets Lotus 1-2-3. In *IRE Raleigh Conference hands on training lessons* (pp. 143–152). Columbia, MO: Investigative Reporters and Editors.

Gordon, R. (1993b, October 22). *Spreadsheets vs. databases.* Unpublished presentation at Computing: The News Frontier Conference, Investigative Reporters and Editors, Raleigh, NC.

Government BBS list. (1993, August). *Online Access, 8*(4), pp. 11–15.

Grady, B. (1994, February 1). *Construction tie-ups on the information highway?* Reuter financial newswire, 4:46 p.m.

Grezlak, H. (1993, September 16). Computer program simplifies courthouses. *The Legal Intelligencer,* p. 1.

Griffith, C. (1994, January/February). Online legal resources. *Online Access, 9*(1), pp. 66–69.

Gross, D. (1991, November). Byting the hand that feeds them: Information vendors are robbing the government blind. *Washington Monthly, 23*(11), p. 37.

Guthrie, L. S. (1992, March). The role of the information professional over the next five years. *Specialist: The Newsletter of the Special Libraries Association, 15*(3), pp. 1, 6–7.

Hansen, K. A. (Ed.). (1993, September). National Credit Information Service. *The Database Files* [Special issue], *1,* 1–2.

Hansen, K. A., & Ward, J. (1991, Fall). Information technology changes in large newspaper libraries. *Special Libraries, 82*(4), pp. 267–273.

Hansen, K. A., Ward, J., & McLeod, D. M. (1987, Winter). Role of the newspaper library in the production of news. *Journalism Quarterly, 64*(4), 714–720.

Harnessing computers to cover news. (1993, September). *The Forum, 15*(7), pp. 4–7.

Harter, S. P. (1986). *Online information retrieval: Concepts, principles, and techniques.* Orlando, FL: Academic Press.

Hartman, J. K. (1994, March). *Newspaper 2003.* Paper presented to the Association for Education in Journalism and Mass Communication Southeast Colloquium, Charleston, SC.

Hartmann, E. (1994, April). Get a handle on database design. *Windows Magazine, 5*(4), pp. 174–180.

Hedlund, P. (1992, Fall). Computers, freedom & privacy. *Online Access, 7*(3), pp. 12–14.

Herz, J. C. (1993, September 23). Internet 101: A trip down the data highway. *The Miami Herald,* pp. 1G, 3G.

Hill, R. M. (1993, March). John Lehe: Computer sleuth. *Alaska Business Monthly, 9*(3), p. 24.

Homer, S. (1992, April 7). Computing: How to find the best travelling companion. *The Independent* (London), p. 25.

Houston, B. (1994, June 11). *Computer-assisted reporting.* Presentation to Florida Press Association and Florida Society of Newspaper Editors, St. Petersburg Beach, FL.

Howden, N., & Dillard, J. (1991, Fall). Technology used in online searching. *Special Libraries, 82*(4), pp. 288–293.

Hulden, G. (1993, October 23). *Training the trainers: How to set up a CAR class.* Unpublished presentation at Computing: The News Frontier Conference, Investigative Reporters and Editors, Raleigh, NC.

Hum, P. (1993, September 21). No secrets: Privacy under siege. *The Ottawa Citizen,* p. B3.

Hume, B. (1993, April 26). Lightweight notebook computer packs big punch. *The Washington Post,* p. F26.

Hunt, D. (1993, December 12). Computer inaccess: A barrier to open government; public has a right to know, but. . . .; Age of computer hampering access to government records. *The Houston Chronicle,* p. A1.

Hunt, D., & Silverman, D. (1993, December 14). Computer inaccess: First step may open some doors; Backlogs, lack of laws may still block public. *The Houston Chronicle,* p. A1.

Hunter, J. (1993). Polling research and news libraries: The *Columbus Dispatch* experience. In B. P. Semonche (Ed.), *News media libraries: A management book* (pp. 346–353). Westport, CT: Greenwood Press.

Hurteau, H. (1993). Legal guide, utilities, and glossary. *BBS Callers Digest, 4*(8), pp. 10–12.

Jacobson, T. L., & Ullman, J. (1989, Winter). Commercial databases and reporting: Opinions of newspaper journalists and librarians. *Newspaper Research Journal, 10*(2), 15–25.

Jacoby, M. (1993, September 20). The selling of Congress: How schrewd businesses are cashing in on repackaged public records. *Roll Call, 39*(20), p. B33.

Jaspin, E. G. (1991, December). Just do it! Or advice on how a totally computer-illiterate editor can manage computer-assisted reporting. *ASNE Bulletin, 739*, pp. 4–8.

Jaspin, E. G. (1994, January–February). Perspectives on how computers change journalism. *IRE Journal, 17*(1), 13–15.

Jennings, M. (1989, September). PCs help reporters track good stories through mazes of bureaucratic statistics. *ASNE Bulletin, 716*, pp. 13–17.

Johnson, J. T. (1992, June). The unconscious fraud of journalism education. *The Quill, 80*(5), pp. 31–34.

Johnson, J. T. (1993, June 16). *The digital revolution and its imperatives for journalism education.* Paper presented at the Poynter Institute Seminar on News Research, St. Petersburg, FL.

Johnson, J. T. (1994a, Fall). Journalism education in the information age. *Social Science Computer Review, 12*(3), pp. 405–414.

Johnson, J. T. (1994b, March). Tired of pushing pins into maps? Let GIS do it. *The Quill, 82*(2), p. 14.

Josar, D. (1993, September 12). How the story was done: The reporters perspective. Greensburg *Tribune-Review,* p. 5.

Kantor, A. (1994, March 15). Making on-line services work for you. *PC Magazine, 13*(5), pp. 110–158.

Kantrowitz, B. (1993, September 6). Live wires. *Newsweek, 122*(10), pp. 43–48.

Karaim, R., & Voboril, M. (1992, November 1). Life no longer a roving frat party for political reporters. *The Miami Herald,* p. 22A.

Keir, G., McCombs, M., & Shaw, D. L. (1991). *Advanced reporting: Beyond news events,* Prospect Heights, IL: Waveland Press.

Kerber, R. (1993, June 21). What cost public information? SEC's new data system prompts debate on commercial control of government records. *The Washington Post,* p. F5.

Kimbrough, T. (1991, April 26). *Reporter uses Vu / Text to link regional murders.* Unpublished press release from Vu/Text Information Services, Inc., Philadelphia.

Kirtz, B. (1991, May 13). Investigative reporting—A needed staple. *Publisher's Auxiliary, 127*(10), p. 12.

Koch, T. (1991). *Journalism for the 21st century: Online information, electronic databases, and the news.* New York: Praeger.

Krueger, B. (1993, October 21–24). *Beat reporting: How computers can make you better: A look at* The News & Observer's *computer-assisted reporting program.* Unpublished presentation at Computing: The News Frontier Conference, Investigative Reporters and Editors, Raleigh, NC.

Krumenaker, L. (1993, August). The practical government bulletin board. *Online Access, 8*(4), pp. 10–15.

Krumenaker, L. (1994, March). The electronic states of America. *Online Access, 9*(2), pp. 32–38.

Lacy, S., & Simon, T. (1993). *The economics and regulation of United States newspapers.* Norwood, NJ: Ablex.

LaFleur, J. (1993, October 23). *Mapping with Atlas * GIS.* Unpublished presentation at Computing: The News Frontier Conference, Investigative Reporters and Editors, Raleigh, NC.

LaFleur, J. (1994, May). Road shows launched. *Uplink, 6*(3), p. 1.

Langham, B. (1993, November). Using charts. *Successful Meetings, 42*(12), pp. 125–126.

Langstaff, M. (1993, September 13). The digital traveler. *Publisher's Weekly, 240*(37), pp. 46–54.

LaQuey, T., & Ryer, J. C. (1993). *Internet companion: A beginner's guide to global networking.* Reading, MA: Addison-Wesley.

Lauriston, R. (1994, April). Portable computing: A balancing act. *Windows Magazine, 5*(4), pp. 161–172.

Lavrakas, P. J. (1993). *Telephone survey methods* (2nd ed.). Newbury Park, CA: Sage.

Leonard, T. (1992, May). Databases in the newsroom: Computer-assisted reporting. *Online, 16*(3), pp. 62–65.

Levin, C. (1994, February 23). Don't pollute, telecommute. *PC Magazine, 13*(4), p. 32.

Loeb, P. (1993, October 23). *Training the trainers: How to set up a CAR class.* Unpublished presentation at Computing: The News Frontier Conference, Investigative Reporters and Editors, Raleigh, NC.

Long, K. (1993, December 19). Plugging in the public: Computers will soon bring computers home. *Seattle Times,* p. A1.

Loyd, B. H., & Gressard, C. P. (1986, Summer). Gender and amount of computer experience of teachers in staff development programs: Effects on computer attitudes and perceptions of the usefulness of computers. *AEDS Journal, 20*(4), 302–311.

Magazine joins CompuServe. (1993, October 12). United Press International, Mid Atlantic news wire, 11:55 a.m.

Magidson, S. (1994, February 15). PCMCIA: Finally standards bring compatible products. *Network Computing, 5*(2), pp. 124–127.

Makulowich, J. S. (1992, Summer). How to start your own BBS. *Online Access, 7*(2), pp. 32–34.

Makulowich, J. S. (1994). Electronic literacy. In *The Internet unleashed,* Indianapolis: SAMS.

MapInfo Corp. (1993). *Desktop mapping for state and local agencies.* Troy, NY: Author.

Marcaccio, K. Y. (1993a). (Ed.). *Gale directory of databases: Vol. 1: Online Databases.* Detroit: Gale.

Marcaccio, K. Y. (1993b). (Ed.). *Gale directory of databases: Vol. 2: CD-ROM, diskette, magnetic tape, handheld, and batch access database products.* Detroit: Gale.

Marchak, E. A. (1993, November 12). Software may not work on all computers. *Cleveland Plain Dealer,* p. 1C.

Markoff, J. (1994, January 30). Curtain's rising on a third generation of on-line services. *The New York Times,* p. 10F.

Marsh, J. D. (1992, December). Information broker: Mary Madden knew something about computers; Burton Goldstein knew something about lawyer's need for access to courthouse records; The result is Information America. *Georgia Trend, 8*(4), p. 50.

Marshall, P. (1992, December 7). PC mapping software matures. *Info World, 14*(49), pp. 82–98.

Martin, P. (1986, February 1). Overview: Computers and newspapers in the mid-80s. *Editor & Publisher, 119*(5), pp. 1C, 24C.

Matlack, C. (1991, January 12). Digging stories out of computer files. *National Journal, 23*(2), p. 88.

McCabe, K. (1993, December). Whats a BBS? *Online Access, 8*(8), p. 5.

McCargar, S. E. (1993). Starting a news library. In B. P. Semonche (Ed.), *News media libraries: A management book* (pp. 131–152). Westport, CT: Greenwood Press.

McCombs, M., Shaw, D. L., & Grey, D. (1976). *Handbook of reporting methods.* New York: Houghton Mifflin.

McGinnis, E. (1993a, May). BBS 101, *Online Access, 8*(2), pp. 6–9.

McGinnis, E. (1993b, May). Biggest boards, *Online Access, 8*(2), pp. 28–31.

McCombs, M., Shaw, D. L., & Grey, D. (1976). *Handbook of reporting methods.* New York: Houghton Mifflin.

McGinnis, E. (1993a, May). BBS 101, *Online Access, 8*(2), pp. 6–9.

McGinnis, E. (1993b, May). Biggest boards, *Online Access, 8*(2), pp. 28–31.

McGinnis, E. (1993c, May). Defining telecommunications terms, *Online Access, 8*(2), pp. 10–11.

McIntosh, S. (1993, October 21). *FoxPro versus Paradox: the good, the bad, and the ugly.* Unpublished presentation at Computing: The News Frontier Conference, Investigative Reporters and Editors, Raleigh, NC.

McLuhan, M. (1964). *Understanding media.* New York: Signet.

Mendelson, E. (1993, November 9). Documents take the center stage. *PC Magazine, 12*(19), pp. 108–182.

Metcalf, J. (1993). The electronic news library. In B. P. Semonche (Ed.), *News media libraries: A management book.* (pp. 220–231). Westport, CT: Greenwood Press.

Meyer, P. (1973). *Precision journalism.* Bloomington: Indiana University Press.

Meyer, P. (1979). *Precision journalism: A reporter's introduction to social science methods* (2nd ed.). Bloomington: Indiana University Press.

Meyer, P. (1991). *The new precision journalism.* Bloomington: Indiana University Press.

Middleton, T. (1993, July 8). The SEC's files are going online; cost of computer access is debated. *Newsday,* p. 39.

Miller, T. (1988, September/October). The data-base revolution. *Columbia Journalism Review, 27*(3), 35–38.

Mintz, A. P. (1991, Winter). Ethics and the news librarian. *Special Libraries, 82*(1), pp. 7–11.

Monmonier, M. (1989). *Maps with the news: The development of American journalistic cartography.* Chicago: University of Chicago Press.

Morgan, C. (1992, November 1). The electronic neighborhood. *The Miami Herald,* p. 1J.

Morokuma, S. (1993, September). Harnessing computers to cover the news. *The Forum, 15*(7), pp. 4–7.

Morrison, D. (1994, January 6). Guest commentary: Computers could open range of public access. *The Seattle Times,* p. 2.

Morrissey, D. H. (1993). *The electronic J-school: Teaching mass communication skills in the computer age.* Indianapolis, IN: National Institute for Advanced Reporting.

Morse, S. (1993, September). The national information infrastructure: No more reinventing the wheel. *Network Computing, 4*(9), pp. 24–25.

Murrie, M. (1987, September). Information at your fingertips. *RTNDA Communicator, 41*(9), pp. 36–40.

Nader, R., & Love, J. P. (1991, November 11). Public deserves access to federal databases. *Computerworld, 25*(45), p. 25.

National Technical Information Service. (1993). *Online catalog.* Washington, DC: FedWorld Online Service.

Naylor, R. (1991, April 29). *Credit reports.* The Associated Press national wire, 3:56 p.m.

Newton, E., & Thien, R. (1993). *No train, no gain: Continuing education in newspaper newsrooms.* Arlington, VA: The Freedom Forum.

Noack, D. (1993, November 27). A co-op of public information officers linked via Internet. *Editor & Publisher, 126*(48), pp. 14–15, 35.

Norusis, M. N. (1991). *SPSS/PC+ studentware plus.* Chicago, IL: SPSS.

No train, no gain. (1993, July). *The Forum, 15*(6), pp. 4–7.

O'Connor, R. J. (1991, August 5). The wave of the future is not that far away: Lines to blur between job, private life. *The Miami Herald,* p. 27BM.

Offley, E. (1994, January 22). Covering the military—The press needs to get its act together. *Editor & Publisher, 127*(4), p. 44.

Patch, K. (1993, November 8). Data starts to ride the information highway: Public access to federal government databases. *PC Week, 10*(44), p. 20.

Paul, N. (1991a, April). For the record: Information on individuals. *Database, 14*(2), pp. 15–23.

Paul, N. (1991b, February). *Researching the war.* Unpublished manuscript, *The Miami Herald* library.

Paul, N. (1993a, September). Database & bulletin board services: A guide to online resources. *The Quill, 81*(7), pp. 18–20.

Paul, N. (1993b, October 22). *People finding and online research.* Unpublished presentation at Computing: The News Frontier Conference, Investigative Reporters and Editors, Raleigh, NC.

Paul, N. (1993c). A primer for computer-assisted research. In B. P. Semonche (Ed.), *News media libraries: A management book* (pp. 317–338). Westport, CT: Greenwood Press.

Paul, N. (1994). *Computer assisted research: A guide to tapping online information* (2nd ed.). St. Petersburg, FL: The Poynter Institute.

Perenson, M. J. (1993, November 9). Digital computing takes flight. *PC Magazine, 12*(19), p. 31.

Piller, C. (1993, July 19). Privacy in peril; How computers are making private life a thing of the past. *The Recorder,* p. 6.

PM hotlines: Communicate with us. (1994, February). *Popular Mechanics, 171*(2), p. 12.

Port, B. (1993, June 17). *Computer-assisted reporting.* Unpublished presentation to Seminar on News Research, The Poynter Institute, St. Petersburg, FL.

Press, L. (1992, March). Dynabook revisited—Portable computers past, present and future. *Communications of the ACM (Association for Computing Machinery), 35*(3), p. 25.

Prosise, J. (1994, March 29). The magic of DDE. *PC Magazine, 13*(6), pp. 277–280.

Qindlen, T. H. (1992, May 25). Libraries search for new ways to link users. *Government Computer News, 11*(11), p. 79.

Quint, B. (1991a, May). Inside a searcher's mind: The seven stages of an online search— Part 1. *Online, 15*(3), pp. 13–18.

Quint, B. (1991b, July). Inside a searcher's mind: The seven stages of an online search— Part 2. *Online, 15*(4), pp. 28–35.

Rambo, C. D. (1987, March). Database searches. *Presstime, 9*(3), pp. 10–12.

Rathbone, A. (1993, November). How did the try-before-you-buy software become a big deal? By having faith in user's tastes. *CompuServe Magazine, 12*(11), pp. 11–17.

Rep. Major Owen introduces legislation to require federal agencies to make data public on 'cost' basis. (1991, November 8). *PACs & Lobbies,* Nexis online version.

Resnick, R. (1992, June). Strictly personal; personal information managers buyer's guide. *Compute! 14*(5), p. 76.

Resnick, R. (1993a). *Exploring the world of online services.* Alameda, CA: Sybex.

Resnick, R. (1993b, December 13). Hard at work in the comforts of home. *The Miami Herald,* pp. 24BM–26BM.

Resnick, R. (1993c, May 3). The information explosion. *The Miami Herald,* p. 20BM.

Resnick, R. (1994, February 12). Small newspapers going on line. *Editor & Publisher, 127*(7), pp. 34–35.

Rettig, H. (1994, May 17). Personal information managers: P is for personal. *PC Magazine, 13*(9), pp. 209–216.

Ricciardi, S. (1993, December 7). A solid foundation for your corporate applications. *PC Magazine, 12*(21), pp. 409–416.

Ricciardi, S. (1994a, January 25). Database design: Redundancy and normalization. *PC Magazine, 13*(2), pp. 285–287.

Ricciardi, S. (1994b, January 11). Introduction to logical database design. *PC Magazine, 13*(1), pp. 267–269.

Ricciardi, S. (1994a, January 25). Database design: Redundancy and normalization. *PC Magazine, 13*(2), pp. 285–287.

Ricciardi, S. (1994b, January 11). Introduction to logical database design. *PC Magazine, 13*(1), pp. 267–269.

Robinson, E. (1994, June). Use unmount to dump dblespace [sic]. *Windows Sources, 2*(6), pp. 233–234.

Rosenkrantz, H. G. (1991, April). Cast your vote: Dial 1-900-PROFITS. *Washington Journalism Review, 13*(3), 14.

Rosenthal, A. (1992, Summer). Editor's letter. *Online Access, 7*(2), p. 5.

Rosenthal, I., & Childs, T. (1992, October 9). *Software Publishers Association hails felonization bill.* Unpublished press release, Software Publishers Association, Washington, DC.

Ross, S. S. (1992, August 8). *Computer-assisted reporting: The future is now.* Unpublished presentation at the Association for Education in Journalism and Mass Communication convention, Montréal, Quebec.

Rothfeder, J. (1989). Is nothing private? Computers hold lots of data on you—and there are few limits on its use. *Business Week* (3122), pp. 74–82.

Rothfeder, J. (1992). *Privacy for sale: How computerization has made everyone's private life an open secret.* New York: Simon & Schuster.

Rowe, C. (1994, April 20). *Use and abuse of computerized morgues.* Unpublished message, Journet, Internet.

Rugge, S. (1993, May). Focus on information brokering. *Information Today, 10*(5), p. 15.

Russell, J. (1993, September). Never stop learning. *BBS, 4*(9), pp. 58–60.

Salwen, M. (1985, Summer). The reporting of public opinion polls during presidential years, 1968–1984. *Journalism Quarterly, 62*(2), 272–277.

Sanford, B. W., Hoberman, H. S., Lystad, R. D., & Marburger, D. L. (1993, April). *Society of Professional Journalists open records model law.* Greencastle, IN: Society of Professional Journalists.

Savetz, K. M. (1993, August). A brief history of Fido. *Online Access, 8*(4), p. 21.

Schonfeld, E. (1993, Autumn). Me and my modem. *Fortune: Information Technology Special Report, 128*(7), 127–138.

Scott, A. (1993a, October 21). *ABCs of databases.* Unpublished presentation at Computing: The News Frontier Conference, Investigative Reporters and Editors, Raleigh, NC.

Scott, A. (Ed.). (1993b). *Investigative reporters and editors 101 computer-assisted stories from the IRE morgue.* Columbia, MO: Investigative Reporters and Editors.

Scott, S. D. (1991, November 2). Statutory language needed: Access to computerized government records must be made easier. *Editor & Publisher, 124*(44), pp. 8PC–12PC.

Segal, S. (1993, October 23). *Graphics in computer-assisted reporting.* Unpublished presentation at Computing: The News Frontier Conference, Investigative Reporters and Editors, Raleigh, NC.

Seideman, T. (1994, March 7). Charting new directions into the bookstores. *Publishers Weekly, 241*(10), 24–26.

Semonche, B. P. (1993). Computer-assisted journalism: An overview. In B. P. Semonche (Ed.), *News media libraries: A management book* (pp. 265–316). Westport, CT: Greenwood Press.

Sharn, L. (1993, December 8). Missions not prime time, but viewers eating it up. *USA Today,* p. 11A.

Shaver, D. B., Hewison, N. S., & Wykoff, L. W. (1985, Fall). Ethics for online intermediaries. *Special Libraries, 76*(4), pp. 238–245.

Shea, B. (1992, April 5). Hotels bring office services to execs. *The Miami Herald,* p. 19F.

Sheatsley, P. B., & Mitofsky, W. J. (Eds.). (1992). *A meeting place: The history of the American Association for Public Opinion Research.* New York: American Association for Public Opinion Research.

Silverman, D. (1993, December 13). Computer inaccess: Computer-age irony: Data are harder to find. *The Houston Chronicle,* p. A1.

Sirkin, A. F. (1992, October). Librarians in the 21st century: Endangered species or future chief information officer? *Specialist: The Newsletter of the Special Libraries Association, 15*(10), 1, 3.

Snepp, F., & Kalbacker, W. (1993, April). No place to hide; Private investigator Al Schweitzer includes tips on protecting the privacy of personal information. *Playboy, 40*(4), p. 134.

Sohn, A., Ogan, C., & Polich, J. (1986). *Newspaper leadership.* Englewood Cliffs, NJ: Prentice-Hall.

Sparhawk, J. C. (1993, January 18). How does the fed data garden grow? By deeply sowing the seeds of TQM. *Government Computer News, 12*(2), p. 38.

Splichal, S. (1991, March). *Florida newspapers and access to computerized information: A study of how they are dealing with the new technology.* Paper presented to the Association for Education in Journalism and Mass Communication Southeast Colloquium, Orlando, FL.

Splichal, S. (1993). *The impact of computer privacy concerns on access to government information.* Unpublished doctoral dissertation, University of Florida, Gainesville.

The stay-at-home PC: Machines easy to use communication devices. (1993, August 26). *The Miami Herald,* p. 1C.

Stith, P. (1993, October 21). Unpublished databases presentation. Unpublished presentation at Computing: The News Frontier Conference, Investigative Reporters and Editors, Raleigh, NC.

Stone, M. D. (1994, January). Spreadsheets get smarter. *Windows Sources, 2*(1), pp. 196–228.

Strategic Mapping. (1993). *Unpublished 'company backgrounder' press release.* Santa Clara, CA: Author.

Strauss, J. (1994, February 18). *Computer piracy.* The Associated Press national wire.

Strazewski, L. (1993, September). Delphi gets competitive with Internet access and more. *Online Access, 8*(5), pp. 6–11.

Strom, D. (1993, August 23). Help me overcome my case of portable PC analysis paralysis. *InfoWorld, 15*(34), p. 60.

Sussman, V. (1993, December 6). Policing the digital world. *U.S. News & World Report, 115*(22), pp. 68, 70.

Tenopir, C. (1992, September 1). CD-ROM best sellers lists. *Library Journal, 152,* 155.

Tewlow, J. S. (1993, Spring). Electronic innovations liberate newsgatherers. *Newspaper Research Journal, 14*(2), 23–31.

Tillotson, J. (1993, September). Best selling Canadian reference CD-ROMs. *CD-ROM Professional, 6*(5), p. 129.

Trimble, K. L. (1993). News magazine libraries: *U.S. News & World Report.* In B. P. Semonche (Ed.), *News media libraries: A management book* (pp. 503–511). Westport, CT: Greenwood Press.

Ullman, J. (1993a, September 26–October 1). *Computer-assisted reporting sidebars.* Unpublished presentation to the American Press Institute seminar for Journalism Educators, Reston, VA.

Ullman, J. (1993b, March–April). Information America: This is the real deal when it comes to backgrounding individuals. *The Database Files, 1*(3), pp. 1–2.

Ullman, J., & Colbert, J. (Eds.). (1991). *The reporter's handbook: An investigator's guide to documents and techniques.* New York: St. Martin's.

Uttal, B. (1993, Autumn). When to be a beta site. *Fortune: Information Technology Special Report, 128*(7), 108–112.

Valauskas, E. J. (1993, October). Newspapers as databases: The *San Jose Mercury-News* and the Mercury Center. *Database, 16*(5), p. 88.

Van Asch, L. (1993, October 22). *On-line: Get me everything and get it now.* Unpublished presentation at Computing: The News Frontier Conference, Investigative Reporters and Editors, Raleigh, NC.

Vizard, F. (1994, January). Building the information superhighway. *Popular Mechanics, 171*(1), pp. 29–33.

Wall, C. (1991, April). Some 115 newspapers are on-line. *Presstime, 13*(4), p. 46.

Wall, C., & Williams, M. (1992, April). Transcripts online. *Database, 15*(2), p. 23.

Walter, R. (1993). *The secret guide to computers* (17th ed.). Somerville, MA: Russ Walter.

Ward, J., & Hansen, K. A. (1990, November 3). Newspapers and electronic technologies. *Editor & Publisher, 123*(44), 34–36.

Ward, J., & Hansen, K. A. (1991, Autumn). Journalist and librarian roles, information technologies and newsmaking. *Journalism Quarterly, 68*(3), 491–498.

Ward, J., & Hansen, K. A. (1993). *Search strategies in mass communication* (2nd ed.). New York: Longman.

Ward, J., Hansen, K. A., & McLeod, D. M. (1987, Winter). Role of the newspaper library in the production of news. *Journalism Quarterly, 64*(4), 714–720.

Ward, J., Hansen, K. A., & McLeod, D. M. (1988a, Winter). Effects of electronic library on news reporting protocols. *Journalism Quarterly, 65*(4), 845–852.

Ward, J., Hansen, K. A., & McLeod, D. M. (1988b, Spring). The news library's contribution to newsmaking. *Special Libraries, 79*(2), pp. 143–147.

Warden, S. P. (1992, June). *Structural barriers to computer-assisted journalism.* Unpublished paper presented to the American Association for Public Opinion Research, St. Petersburg, FL.

Webb, C. (1989, April). Government databases. *Presstime, 11*(4), pp. 18–20.

Webb, K. M. (1993, March). Personal services contain European news. *Link-Up, 10*(2), p. 10.

Weinberg, S. (1991, April). Don't believe everything you hear: Investigative reporting is alive, well and ready to grow stronger. *ASNE Bulletin, 731,* pp. 20–21.

Weintrob, G. (1993, May). Choosing BBS software. *Online Access, 8*(2), pp. 24–27.

Whisnant, E., & Skinner, M. A. (1992, September 5). The power inside: Creating and using in-house databases in the *Newsday* library. *Editor & Publisher, 125*(36), pp. 24–25.

Whiteside, M. A. C. (1991, November 2). Computers—just another reporting tool. *Editor & Publisher, 124*(44), pp. 1PC, 20PC.

Whitney, L. (1994, January). "Honey, did you download the mail?" *BBS, 5*(1), pp. 36–37.

Wilhoit, G. C., & Weaver, D. (1980). *Newsroom guide to polls and surveys.* Washington, DC: American Newspaper Publishers Association.

Williams, F., & Pavlik, J. V. (Eds.). (1994). *The people's right to know: Media, democracy, and the information highway.* Hillsdale, NJ: Lawrence Erlbaum Associates.

Williams, M. E. (1994). The state of databases today: 1994. In K. Y. Marcaccio (Ed.), *Gale directory of databases, Vol. 1: Online databases.* Detroit: Gale.

Willis, J. (1988). *Surviving in the newspaper business: Newspaper management in turbulent times.* New York: Praeger.

Wilson, K. (1993a, July). It's getting easier to know you (special reprint). *Newsday,* p. 27.

Wilson, K. (1993b, July). Your life as an open book (special reprint). *Newsday,* pp. 24–26.

Wilson, T. (1993, October 23). Learning to investigate in a paperless world: Reporters hone computer skills. *Raleigh News & Observer,* pp. 1B, 5B.

Wolfe, D. P. (1989a, October 20). *Online gatekeeping: New power for news librarians in the 1990s.* Paper presented to the Florida News Librarians Association, Orlando, FL.

Wilson, K. (1993b, July). Your life as an open book (special reprint). *Newsday,* pp. 24–26.

Wilson, T. (1993, October 23). Learning to investigate in a paperless world: Reporters hone computer skills. *Raleigh News & Observer,* pp. 1B, 5B.

Wolfe, D. P. (1989a, October 20). *Online gatekeeping: New power for news librarians in the 1990s.* Paper presented to the Florida News Librarians Association, Orlando, FL.

Wolfe, D. P. (1989b). *Newspaper use of computer databases and guidelines for access; A case study:* The St. Petersburg Times. Unpublished master's thesis, University of South Florida, Tampa.

Wolfe, D. P. (1990, Spring). Gatekeeping: New power for news librarians in the 1990s. *News Library News, 12*(3), pp. 4, 10.

Wolfe, D. P. (1993, June 17). *The news researcher.* Unpublished presentation, Seminar on News Research, The Poynter Institute, St. Petersburg, FL.

Woodcock, J. (1991). *Computer dictionary: The comprehensive standard for business, school, library, and home,* Redmond, WA: Microsoft Press.

Woods, D. (1993, March 6). *Five goals for your newsroom.* Unpublished presentation at the Region 3 conference, Society of Professional Journalists, Knoxville, TN.

Wooton, W. (1994, March 2). *The Rolling evidence: A case study of computer-assisted reporting techniques.* Unpublished manuscript.

Yakal, K. (1993, August). Contact management: Keeping in touch. *PC Magazine, 12*(14), pp. 271–327.

York, V., & Haight, A. J. (1992, November). Government information: CD-ROM roundup. *CD ROM World, 7*(10), p. 14.

Young, P. H. (1989). Library research in the future: A prognostication. *College & Research Library News, 50*(1), pp. 7–10.

Index